Essential SharePoint 2007

Other Microsoft Windows resources from O'Reilly

Related titles

Programming Excel with VBA and .NET

Programming WPF

SharePoint 2007: The Definitive Guide

SharePoint Office Pocket Guide

Windows Vista: The Definitive Guide

Windows Vista Administration: The Definitive Guide

Windows Vista in a Nutshell

Windows Books Resource Center

windows.oreilly.com is a complete catalog of O'Reilly's Windows and Office books, including sample chapters and code examples.

oreillynet.com is the essential portal for developers interested in open and emerging technologies, including new platforms, programming languages, and operating systems.

Conferences

O'Reilly brings diverse innovators together to nurture the ideas that spark revolutionary industries. We specialize in documenting the latest tools and systems, translating the innovator's knowledge into useful skills for those in the trenches. Visit *conferences.oreilly.com* for our upcoming events.

Safari Bookshelf (*safari.oreilly.com*) is the premier online reference library for programmers and IT professionals. Conduct searches across more than 1,000 books. Subscribers can zero in on answers to time-critical questions in a matter of seconds. Read the books on your Bookshelf from cover to cover or simply flip to the page you need. Try it today for free.

SECOND EDITION

Essential SharePoint 2007

Jeff Webb

O'REILLY®

Beijing · Cambridge · Farnham · Köln · Paris · Sebastopol · Taipei · Tokyo

Essential SharePoint 2007, Second Edition
by Jeff Webb

Published by O'Reilly Media, Inc., 1005 Gravenstein Highway North, Sebastopol, CA 95472.

O'Reilly books may be purchased for educational, business, or sales promotional use. Online editions are also available for most titles (*safari.oreilly.com*). For more information, contact our corporate/institutional sales department: (800) 998-9938 or *corporate@oreilly.com*.

Editor: John Osborn	**Indexer:** Angela Howard
Production Editor: Rachel Monaghan	**Cover Designer:** Karen Montgomery
Copyeditor: Nancy Reinhardt	**Interior Designer:** David Futato
Proofreader: Rachel Monaghan	**Illustrators:** Robert Romano and Jessamyn Read

Printing History:

May 2005:	First Edition.
September 2007:	Second Edition.

 This book uses RepKover™, a durable and flexible lay-flat binding.

ISBN-10: 0-596-51407-7
ISBN-13: 978-0-596-51407-5
[M]

Table of Contents

Preface

If your business needs to control its documents, structure its workflow, or share information over the Web, you need SharePoint. It's simply the quickest way to fill those needs using standard tools business users already know: Microsoft Office and Internet Explorer. Best of all, SharePoint is *free* (well, kind of); SharePoint Services are part of Windows Server 2003 so if you have Windows Server 2003 already, you can download the installation from Microsoft and install it fairly easily.

In this book, I cover the Microsoft Office SharePoint Server 2007 product editions as well as the underlying Windows SharePoint Services 3.0. I also cover how Share-Point integrates with Microsoft Office, SharePoint Designer, InfoPath, and Visual Studio.

Who This Book Is For

This book covers what SharePoint administrators, site owners, and SharePoint developers need to know. *SharePoint administrator* is an emerging job title that covers a wide range of experience. I've met administrative assistants, tech writers, programmers, and others who wear that hat. Basically, SharePoint administrators organize, customize, maintain, and support a SharePoint portal. *Site owners* are the people that create and maintain parts of the portal—usually there is one site owner for each department, and the site owner organizes the content and appearance of his department's site. *SharePoint developers* extend SharePoint and integrate it with other business systems. These developers need to know more than a programming language—they also need to understand what SharePoint provides out-of-the-box so they can extend it using the simplest approach.

I combine these audiences in one book because they have overlapping needs. First, they must understand what SharePoint can do for their businesses; next, they must know how it is used with the Microsoft Office applications; and finally, they need a framework for instructing others how to use what they have created.

A vast number of people may use your SharePoint portal, but they shouldn't really need to read a whole book on the subject. For those users, I've created the *Share-Point Office Pocket Guide* (O'Reilly). See *http://www.essentialsharepoint.com* for the pocket guide, samples, and bonus materials for this book. SharePoint also includes online Help, and I show you how to integrate that with your sites.

How This Book Is Organized

Chapters in this book are organized by task. I cover the most common tasks for each subject, and the tasks become more advanced as you read further. I believe in learning by doing, and the sequence of tasks is based on how I teach SharePoint: later chapters revisit and build on earlier tasks, and there are plenty of concepts and Best Practices along the way.

 I don't expect this book to be your only resource, and I don't duplicate information found in online Help. I provide links to Help and additional information whenever possible, and you can get a list of those references at *http://www.essentialsharepoint.com*.

Here is a brief overview of each chapter:

Chapter 1, *Using SharePoint*
> Provides a practical guide to using SharePoint in your business. It tells you what you need and what you can create, and includes tutorials that solve three common business problems in SharePoint.

Chapter 2, *Word, Excel, and Outlook*
> Shows how SharePoint integrates with Microsoft Office applications. This chapter includes important information on setting client security to avoid constant logon prompts, and provides a basis for training Office 2003 and 2007 users how to use SharePoint.

Chapter 3, *Creating Sites*
> Describes how to organize your portal by creating site collections and subsites, customize navigation web parts, summarize content, and control security. You'll also learn how to change the general appearance of sites by applying themes and style sheets.

Chapter 4, *Creating Lists*
> Teaches how to use SharePoint lists to solve business problems. It covers the built-in list templates, adding columns, creating views, using lookups, customizing the list forms, and saving and deploying list templates. This chapter includes a tutorial based on the built-in Issue Tracking list template.

Chapter 5, *Creating Libraries*

Extends the topics in Chapter 4 with the library-specific tasks including requiring document versioning and approval, adding content types, and organizing libraries. At the end of the chapter, I describe how to set up the four most common document library applications.

Chapter 6, *Building Pages*

Shows how to edit pages and customize web parts using SharePoint Designer. The tutorial walks you through creating connected summary and detail web parts, converting a List View to a Data View, and deploying the customized web part. The chapter also shows how to create client-side web parts, filter list views, and modify master pages.

Chapter 7, *Creating My Sites, Blogs, and Wikis*

Covers the personalization features of SharePoint. I discuss why these features are useful, how to use them in your workplace, and how to control them and monitor their use.

Chapter 8, *Enabling Email and Workflow*

Discusses how to use event-driven and time-driven alerts, allow incoming email to a library, and how to use workflows to manage approval and other document management processes.

Chapter 9, *RSS, Rollups, and Site Maps*

Shows how to summarize content from across sites in dashboard-type pages that allow drill-down. I also cover different approaches based on the edition of SharePoint you have installed.

Chapter 10, *Gathering Data with InfoPath*

Describes how to use Microsoft InfoPath with SharePoint to gather structured data. I show how to use Form Libraries to collect data, control forms through rules and actions, create data-bound controls, validate forms, enable editing through the browser, and program InfoPath forms in .NET.

Chapter 11, *Programming Web Parts*

Shows how to extend SharePoint by creating new, custom web parts through the SmartPart add-on and through the ASP.NET WebPart class. I cover how to set up your development environment, update 2003-version web parts, add child controls, create custom properties, add menus, create connectable properties, and deploy web parts. I *don't* provide a reference to the SharePoint libraries—those are available online through MSDN.

Chapter 12, *Consuming SharePoint Services*

Covers how to use SharePoint web services and other remote tools to create and change SharePoint content from client applications such as Excel and custom .NET applications. I provide an overview of the web services SharePoint provides, and include details on accessing lists and sites. I don't provide a reference to SharePoint web services.

Chapter 13, *Administering SharePoint*

Provides detailed instructions on installing and configuring SharePoint. It shows how to enable Internet access, use forms-based authentication, back up and restore portals, audit user activity, and enable non-Microsoft file types such as PDFs.

Appendix A, *Upgrading*

Discusses moving existing SharePoint portals to 2007. It covers the three upgrade scenarios: in-place, side-by-side, and database migration.

Appendix B, *Reference Tables*

Lists the compatibility differences between SharePoint and various Microsoft Office versions and includes reference tables for command-line utilities such as *stsadm.exe*.

What's New?

I don't think many people realized SharePoint's potential back in 2003. For the last four years, the SharePoint community has really taken the lead in stretching the limits of SharePoint and creating solutions. Microsoft has been watching: SharePoint 2007 incorporates the best ideas from the community and breaks new ground handling workflow. The following table lists the top-ten new features.

Request	How SharePoint 2007 solves this
Tabbed navigation	Tabs at the top of each page link to subsites.
Recycle Bin	Deleted items go to the Recycle Bin before they are completely removed. Those items can be easily restored if needed.
Customized QuickLaunch	You can easily add items to Quick Launch or use a hierarchical view of the site instead.
RSS feeds	Feeds allow you to collect content from any location and display it all on a single page.
Actions	Lists can record actions that users take, such as clicking on a link or sending email, and then change their status based on those actions.
Email improvements	Lists and libraries can receive email.
Workflow	Document approval and other structured tasks can be routed through workflows to track their progress and ensure completion.
Master lists	Lists can now be shared with subsites. For example, a top-level Departments list can be used as a look-up within all subsites.
Master pages	Master pages determine the initial layout and content for other pages that are based on them.
Performance	Pages that have been modified (unghosted) no longer incur a performance hit.

Conventions Used in This Book

Understanding the following font conventions up front makes it easier to use this book.

Italic is used for:

- Pathnames, filenames, program names, compilers, and options
- New terms where they are defined
- Internet addresses, such as domain names and URLs

`Constant width` is used for:

- Anything that appears literally in a page or a program, including keywords, data types, constants, method names, variables, parameters, commands, class names, and interface names
- Command lines and options that should be typed verbatim on the screen
- All code listings
- HTML and XML documents, tags, and attributes

`Constant width italic` is used for:

- General placeholders that indicate that an item is replaced by some actual value in your own program

`Constant width bold` is used for:

- Text that is typed in code examples by the user

> This icon designates a general tip or an important aside to the surrounding text.

> This icon designates a warning related to the surrounding text.

Using Code Examples

This book is here to help you get your job done. In general, you may use the code in this book in your programs and documentation. You don't need to contact us for permission unless you're reproducing a significant portion of the code. For example, writing a program that uses several chunks of code from this book does not require permission. Selling or distributing a CD-ROM of examples from O'Reilly books *does* require permission. Answering a question by citing this book and quoting example code does not require permission. Incorporating a significant amount of example code from this book into your product's documentation *does* require permission.

We appreciate, but do not require, attribution. An attribution usually includes the title, author, publisher, and ISBN. For example: "*Essential SharePoint 2007*, Second Edition, by Jeff Webb. Copyright 2007 Jeff Webb, 978-0-596-51407-5."

If you feel your use of code examples falls outside fair use or the permission given above, feel free to contact us at *permissions@oreilly.com*.

Samples, Comments, and Questions

The samples, *SharePoint Office Pocket Guide*, and bonus material for this book are available at *http://www.essentialsharepoint.com*. That site extends this book by providing current information and a forum to ask questions.

Please address other comments and questions concerning this book to the publisher:

O'Reilly Media, Inc.
1005 Gravenstein Highway North
Sebastopol, CA 95472
800-998-9938 (in the United States or Canada)
707-829-0515 (international or local)
707-829-0104 (fax)

We have a web page for this book, where we list errata and any additional information. You can access this page at:

http://www.oreilly.com/catalog/9780596514075

To comment or ask technical questions about this book, send email to:

bookquestions@oreilly.com

For more information about our books, conferences, Resource Centers, and the O'Reilly Network, see our web site at:

http://www.oreilly.com

Safari® Books Online

 When you see a Safari® Books Online icon on the cover of your favorite technology book, that means the book is available online through the O'Reilly Network Safari Bookshelf.

Safari offers a solution that's better than e-books. It's a virtual library that lets you easily search thousands of top tech books, cut and paste code samples, download chapters, and find quick answers when you need the most accurate, current information. Try it for free at *http://safari.oreilly.com*.

Acknowledgments

This book is based on my experience creating and deploying SharePoint solutions for my customers. I'm grateful to them for the business, for the questions they asked, and for the teamwork. In particular, I'd like to thank Michael Harclerode, Charlie Brasor, Michael Hurley, David Strum, and Scott Powers.

The excellent O'Reilly team also deserves credit for their input and support shepherding this book through review, production, and distribution. Thanks to my editor, John Osborn; reviewers, James Pyles and Robert McGovern; and the production staff.

Finally, my home team has been with me longer than anyone: Trish, Dorian, and Sophia are patient with my SharePoint stories, take me to the beach on weekends, and find me when I'm lost. I love them deeply.

CHAPTER 1

Using SharePoint

SharePoint delivers office applications over the Web. An office application can be something as simple as a way to store and manage a library of documents within a small office, or as complex as a project management system used across continents.

In this chapter, I'll tell you how SharePoint saves you time (and money), and I'll walk you through creating three SharePoint applications that almost all businesses can use right away.

How Does This Help Me Do My Job?

That was the question a clever woman asked me at one of the first training sessions I presented. I had to think a bit, but here's what I came up with—SharePoint helps you:

- Find the information you need quickly
- Link to that information to stay current
- Share the information you have with others
- Do all that through standard tools that folks already know

SharePoint does those things by creating a web site for your business that integrates with Microsoft Office applications: mainly, Word, Excel, and Outlook. From a user's perspective, it's just like using the Internet: click on links to go to a new page, search on a phrase to find something, and so on (see Figure 1-1). What's unique is the way that SharePoint integrates Office documents, task lists, calendars, email alerts, and other features in a way to simplify the flow of work through your business.

Instead of routing a document for approval via email, you post the document to SharePoint and collaborate with the reviewers interactively. Because the file is stored in a central location, everyone can see changes as they are made without resending the document each time it is changed; reviewers can discuss changes online, read one another's comments, and assign tasks and deadlines, and all changes are recorded in version history.

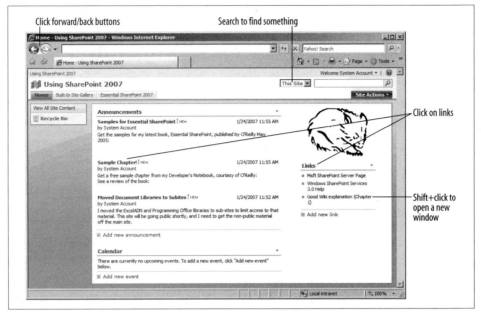

Figure 1-1. *Using SharePoint is just like using the Internet*

Document review is a simple but important example. Figures 1-2 and 1-3 illustrate the differences between SharePoint and email solutions to a document review workflow.

The biggest difference between Figures 1-2 and 1-3 is visibility. In the email workflow, reviewers don't see each other's comments or changes because those are stored away in each person's email. With SharePoint, comments and versions can be viewed by all reviewers. Additionally, you can include links to related topics, track tasks, and collect approvals in a structured way.

SharePoint is a big improvement over email solutions, but it comes with two conditions:

- SharePoint affects work processes, so you need to think about how you will use it before it can help. You need to be able to describe the steps in a work process and assign responsibilities to specific users.

- SharePoint is closely tied to Microsoft Office 2003 or 2007; you can use earlier Office versions or non-Microsoft applications, but you get the most benefit from the 2003 or 2007 Microsoft Office suites.

If you can live with those two conditions, then we can get started. Otherwise, you should probably consider other options.

 For a list of SharePoint features supported by all Microsoft Office versions, see Appendix B.

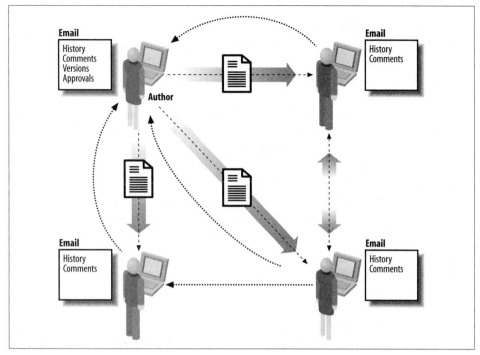

Figure 1-2. Document review through email (lots of copies)

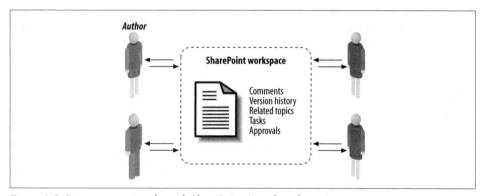

Figure 1-3. Document review through SharePoint (one shared copy)

What Types of Sites Can I Create?

SharePoint comes with a set of templates that you can use to create web sites right out of the box, and many more are available as downloads or from third-party vendors. Before we tackle those templates, however, it helps to sort them into a few main types:

Publishing sites

Present corporate communications (newsletters, press releases, events, holidays, announcements, and so on) through one or more web pages. This category also includes communication managed by employees through blogs and Wikis, which may or may not fit in your corporate culture.

Document control

Manages version and change control for standard forms such as NDAs, vacation requests, and so forth. This category also includes repositories for executed agreements that can be scanned in as PDFs.

Workflow applications

Encompass any multistep task that follows a defined process. A common workflow example is Issue Tracking, where a problem is reported, assigned to a team member, resolved, approved, and then published to a knowledge base for future reference.

Dashboards

Are a type of management application where related tasks and reports are centralized for easy access.

Extranet portals

Provide a contact point among your business, customers, and partners. You can use these to provide external access to your corporate information in a limited and secure way.

Combinations of these types are common; when we talk about an application type, we're really identifying its primary purpose, not its sole use. Table 1-1 organizes the built-in SharePoint templates by the type of site.

Table 1-1. Built-in site and list templates

Site type	Site templates	List templates
Publishing	• Wiki Site	• Web Pages
	• Blog	• Announcements
	• Meeting Workspace	• Wiki Page Library
	• Collaboration Portal[a]	• Discussion Board
	• Publishing Portal[a]	• Survey
	• News Site[a]	• Links
Document control	• Document Workspace	• Document Library
	• Document Center[a]	• Picture Library
	• Records Center[a]	• Translation Management Library[a]
	• Report Center[a]	• Slide Library
		• Languages and Translators[a]
Workflow	• Publishing Site with Workflow[a]	• Form Library
	• Decision Meeting Workspace	• Issue Tracking
		• Project Tasks

Table 1-1. Built-in site and list templates (continued)

Site type	Site templates	List templates
Dashboards	• Personalization Center[a] • My Site Host[a]	• Report Library[a] • Contacts • KPI List* • Data Connection Library[a]
Extranet portals	• Publishing Site[a] • Search Center[a]	
Navigation	• Search Center[a] • Search Center with Tabs[a] • Site Directory[a]	

[a] These templates are only available in Microsoft Office SharePoint Server (MOSS).

What Software Do I Need?

"SharePoint" means different things to different people. The blame for that confusion lies squarely with Microsoft—it labeled these products with long phrases that almost no one has the time to fully decipher. Table 1-2 is my attempt to inject some sense into the fray.

Table 1-2. What's in a name? "SharePoint" explained

Official name	Acronym	What it means
Microsoft SharePoint Team Services	STS	This is the first SharePoint. It's out-of-date but still in use in some places. STS is very different from later SharePoint versions, and I don't discuss it in this book.
Microsoft Windows SharePoint Services	WSS	The core services and templates used by SharePoint from 2003 on. WSS is part of Windows Server 2003 and is available as a free download. There are two versions of WSS in use: 2.0 and 3.0. In this book, I cover WSS 3.0.
Microsoft SharePoint Portal Server	SPS	The 2003 server product based on WSS 2.0. SPS includes additional templates and services and enables portal-wide searching. This product is sold through Microsoft Volume Licensing.
Microsoft Office SharePoint Server 2007	MOSS	The 2007 server product based on WSS 3.0. MOSS includes additional templates and services, enables portal-wide searching, and provides document control workflow templates. This product is sold through Microsoft Volume Licensing. MOSS is the server product I cover in this book.
Microsoft Office SharePoint Server 2007 for Search	MOSS/S	This is a limited version of MOSS that omits the enterprise templates and services. This product is sold through Microsoft Volume Licensing.

 If you are using WSS 2.0 and/or SPS, please see the previous edition of this book, *Essential SharePoint* (O'Reilly).

So what do you need? If you are starting fresh, it is really a choice between WSS version 3.0, MOSS, or MOSS/S:

- Install WSS 3.0 if you are cost-conscious. It provides a basic platform that can still do a lot. The major limitations of WSS are that it does not allow searching across multiple web sites and only includes a basic, three-state workflow template.

- Purchase MOSS if you are building an enterprise portal. In addition to search, full MOSS includes workflow templates for document control, action menus, records repository, personalized sites (My Sites), audiences (targeted content), listings (content expiration), and compliance policies. If you need those things, MOSS is well worth the cost.

- Purchase MOSS/S to add cross-site searching to a WSS server farm or to add a dedicated search server to a MOSS server farm.

There are Standard and Enterprise editions of MOSS. The Enterprise edition includes these additional services: InfoPath Forms Services, Excel Services, and Business Data Catalog. If you choose MOSS, you'll be talking to a salesperson anyway, so he or she should be able to help you choose based on your needs and budget. All of the MOSS editions include WSS 3.0.

If you are starting with an existing WSS 2.0 or SPS installation, you have some new choices. Some companies don't want personalization features like My Site. In those cases, upgrading to MOSS/S might make sense. Otherwise, the direct upgrade path is straightforward:

- Upgrade WSS 2.0 installations to WSS 3.0.
- Upgrade SPS installations to MOSS.

What Other Software Do I Need?

To run SharePoint, you must have the following software installed on a server:

- Windows Server 2003 (SP1 or higher). SharePoint runs only on this operating system, and the machine must be configured as an ASP.NET application server *without* FrontPage Server Extensions installed.

- .NET Framework version 3.0. Installing .NET 3.0 automatically installs .NET 2.0 if it is not already present; both versions are required.

- Microsoft SQL Server 2000 (SP4) or later, preferably installed on a dedicated server. SharePoint also supports the use of the free Windows Internal Database (WID), but that configuration should be considered only for limited applications such as small sites and staging servers since WID does not allow external connections or provide the database management tools that come with Microsoft SQL Server.

Users access SharePoint through their web browser—other than that, there are no real software requirements, but to get the most out of SharePoint, users should have *at least* Microsoft Office 2003 or later. Other software may also be needed based on what a user needs to do with SharePoint. Table 1-3 lists the applications that most users will need based on their role.

Table 1-3. Recommended client software by user role

User role	Client software	Details
Everyone	Internet Explorer version 6.0 or later	Non-Microsoft browsers work with SharePoint, but their capabilities are limited since Microsoft relies on ActiveX components for some advanced features.
	Adobe Reader version 6.0 or later	PDF documents are ubiquitous. Users may also need the print drivers to create PDFs.
	Microsoft Office 2003 or 2007 Professional Edition	Earlier versions of Microsoft Office do not fully integrate with SharePoint.
Data entry	Microsoft InfoPath 2007	Provides a way to create and display sophisticated data entry forms that validate entries, can be routed for approvals, and integrate with workflows.
Web designer	Microsoft SharePoint Designer 2007	Allows web designers to customize web pages, web parts, CSS, and workflows.
Developer	Microsoft Visual Studio 2005	Allows programmers to develop web parts, web services, site definitions, workflows, and other components using the SharePoint object model.
	Microsoft InfoPath 2007, Microsoft SharePoint Designer 2007	Developers may also need these tools depending on the tasks that they are assigned.

Try to make sure that users are all using the same version and edition of the products listed in Table 1-3. Mixed environments require more effort to support, particularly when different versions or editions of Office are installed. I strongly recommend Microsoft Office Professional Edition for use with SharePoint. The Standard and Small Business Editions do not include the component that enables the datasheet view used throughout SharePoint—you will get support calls about that, trust me!

Finally, you may want to consider the following optional server products:

- Microsoft Virtual Server 2005 R2 (or Microsoft Virtual PC 2004) for creating staging or test versions of SharePoint installations. This free tool is worth learning, especially when branding portals and programming web parts.
- Microsoft Forefront Security for SharePoint provides virus scanning on files uploaded to SharePoint.
- CorasWorks Workplace Suite and rPrograms from CorasWorks provide add-on components and templates.
- Other community or third-party web parts, such as Pentalogic SharePoint Reminder.

I don't get money from CorasWorks or Pentalogic, but I've used their products and they are worth a look.

Try It

It's a good idea to evaluate SharePoint versions before deciding what software you want to purchase. If you do not have a spare Windows 2003 server that can be dedicated to installing trial software, consider using a virtual server. The advantages of creating a virtual machine for evaluation are that you can more easily create multiple configurations to evaluate, and you can run the virtual machine on your desktop computer.

To install WSS for evaluation:

1. Set up a staging server or virtual machine running Windows 2003 by installing the required server software listed in the preceding section.

2. Download *SharePoint.exe* from *http://www.microsoft.com/downloads*.

3. Run *SharePoint.exe* and choose the Basic setup. That option creates a standalone SharePoint server using the Windows Internal Database (WID). It automatically configures the server and creates a default top-level site using the Team Site template (see Figure 1-4).

To install MOSS for evaluation:

1. Set up a staging server or virtual machine running Windows 2003 by installing the required server software listed in the preceding section.

2. Download *OfficeServer.exe* from *http://www.microsoft.com/downloads*.

3. Save the product keys displayed on the web page when the download is complete. You'll need the product keys any time you install MOSS, so keep them somewhere safe in case you need to reinstall later.

4. Run *OfficeServer.exe* and enter the product key for either the Standard or Enterprise edition and choose the Basic setup option. As with WSS, the Basic option creates a standalone SharePoint server using the WID. It automatically configures the server and creates a default top-level site using the Collaboration Portal site template (see Figure 1-5).

 When trying to locate downloads on the Microsoft web site, it is often easiest to search *www.microsoft.com* for the filename. Searching on the product name usually returns too many results.

The WSS download is included under your Windows 2003 Server license, but the MOSS download is a trial version that expires after 120 days. The MOSS download includes WSS, so you don't install that first unless you are upgrading an existing SPS installation. See Appendix A for details on upgrading.

Follow the instructions provided on screen by Setup. Doing one or more evaluation installations is a good idea before going live. See Chapter 13 for complete instructions on installing SharePoint and configuring it after installation. See Appendix A if you are upgrading from the previous version of SharePoint.

Parts of a Page

SharePoint setup creates a new, mostly empty web site with a default home page that looks like Figure 1-4 or 1-5, depending on which product you installed.

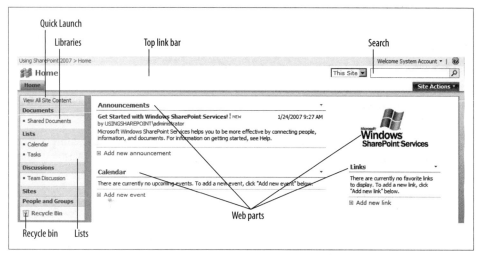

Figure 1-4. Default WSS home page

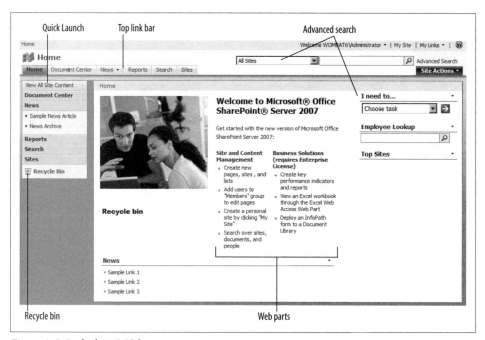

Figure 1-5. Default MOSS home page

The parts of a page labeled in Figures 1-4 and 1-5 are common throughout SharePoint:

Top link bar
Contains tabs that link to subsites within SharePoint. Use subsites to organize content and control who can see or change that content.

Quick Launch
Displays links to lists, libraries, and subsites.

Libraries
Collections of documents within a web site.

Lists
Are tables of data.

Recycle Bin
Allows you to restore content that was recently deleted—much the same as the Windows Recycle Bin.

Search
Is used to find information within a web site.

Advanced search
Finds information across web sites or by topic. This feature is only in MOSS.

Web parts
Display views of lists, libraries, or other content on a page.

Creating a Test Site

The Basic installations of WSS and MOSS create the default top-level sites shown in Figures 1-4 and 1-5. Those two sites are very different, and it's a good idea to keep those default sites intact for a while so you can use them as a reference as you learn. For those reasons, it's a good idea to create a test site at this point.

To create a test site in WSS:

1. Click Site Actions → Create in the upper-right corner of the page.
2. Click Sites and Workspaces under the Web Pages heading on the right side of the page.
3. Enter a Title and URL for the site, select the Team Site template, and click Create. SharePoint creates the site and displays its home page.

To create a test site in MOSS:

1. Click Site Actions → Create Site in the upper-right corner of the page.
2. Enter a Title and URL for the site, select the Team Site template, and click Create. SharePoint creates the site and displays its home page. SharePoint creates the site and displays its home page.

You can use this test site to try the procedures in this chapter and to experiment on your own. If you mess up and want to start over, simply delete the site and create a new one.

To delete the test site:

1. On the site's home page, click Site Actions → Site Settings.

2. Click "Delete this site" under the Site Administration heading.

3. Verify that you are deleting the correct site, and then click Delete. SharePoint deletes the site.

4. Click the Back button and then click one of the navigational links to return to the parent site.

The procedures in the rest of this section assume that you are working from a test site based on the Team Site template. Each site template creates different lists and libraries, so if you use a different site template, some of these procedures may not work exactly as stated.

Editing a Page

SharePoint pages are made up almost entirely of web parts. Some of those parts can be edited directly through the browser while others (like the link bar and Quick Launch) are controlled by site settings.

To edit a SharePoint page:

1. Click Site Actions → Edit Page in the upper-right corner of the page. SharePoint changes the page to Edit mode as shown in Figure 1-6.

2. Drag web parts between web part zones (marked Left and Right) to move them on the page, or click Edit on the web part's title bar to change the appearance of the web part.

3. Click Add a Web Part to include new content from a list or library on the page.

4. When you're done, click Exit Edit Mode in the upper-right corner of the page.

Changing the Top Link Bar and Quick Launch

The top link bar and Quick Launch are static web parts—they are controlled by site settings rather than by the page editor. The procedure for changing these links varies a bit between WSS and MOSS, so I include both approaches here.

To change the links on the top link bar in WSS:

1. Click Site Actions → Site Settings in the upper-right corner of the page.

2. Click Top link bar under the Look and Feel heading in the middle of the Site Settings page.

3. Click New Link on the toolbar of the Top Link Bar page to add a new tab, or click "Use Links from Parent" to import the tabs that appear on the web site that contains the current site.

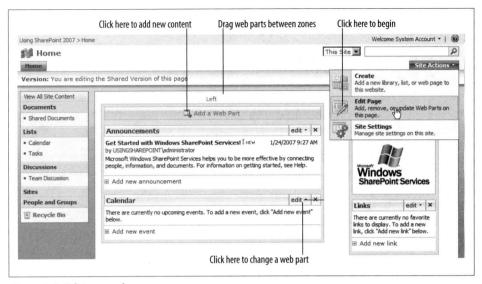

Figure 1-6. Editing a web part page

To change the links on Quick Launch in WSS:

1. Click Site Actions → Site Settings in the upper-right corner of the page.
2. Click Quick Launch under the Look and Feel heading in the middle of the Site Settings page.
3. Click New Link on the toolbar of the Quick Launch page to add a new tab, or click New Heading to add a new section on Quick Launch.

To change the links on either the top link bar or Quick Launch in MOSS:

1. Click Site Actions → Site Settings in the upper-right corner of the page.
2. Click Navigation under the Look and Feel heading on the Site Settings page.
3. In the Global Navigation section, select "Display the navigation items below the current site." That setting causes the site to have a unique top link bar, rather than inheriting the link bar from its parent site.
4. In the Navigation Editing and Sorting section, select Global Navigation and click Add Link to add a new tab to the top link bar.
5. Select Current Navigation in the Navigation Editing and Sorting section and click Add Link to add a new item to the Quick Launch.
6. Click OK to apply the changes.

MOSS refers to the top link bar as *Global Navigation*, and it calls the Quick Launch *Current Navigation*. You can also use the Site Navigation Settings page in MOSS to group and reorder the links that appear on the top link bar and Quick Launch.

Adding Content

SharePoint stores the content you want to share in lists and libraries. To add a new link to the Links list:

1. Return to your test site's home page.
2. Click the "Add new link" at the bottom of the Links web part on the right side of the page. SharePoint displays a web form for you to fill out for the new list item.
3. Fill out the fields and click OK to save the item. SharePoint adds the link to the list and displays it in the Links web part on the home page.

To add a new document to a library:

1. On your test site's home page, click "Add new document" at the bottom of the Shared Documents web part in the middle of the page. SharePoint displays the Upload Document page.
2. Click Browse and select a Word or Excel document from your computer to upload.
3. Click OK to upload the document. SharePoint copies the file from your computer to SharePoint and displays the new file in the Shared Documents web part.

List items and documents uploaded to a site are available to anyone who has access to the site. For example, you can open the document you just uploaded by clicking on it in the Shared Documents web part. SharePoint keeps track of user's permissions so only authorized users can see or change items.

Lists and libraries are stored in folders within each site. What you see on the home page is just a view of the list or library displayed as a web part. Every list and library has a web part associated with it that you can use to display different views on the site's home page and elsewhere.

To view the actual list or library:

- Click on the title of the web part.

Or:

- Click on the link to the list or library in the Quick Launch area.

Or:

- Click View All Site Content, and then click on the list or library shown on that page.

The View All Site Content link lets you get at lists and libraries not shown on the site's home page. You choose what to put on the home page based on what is most important for others to see. For instance, you might want to feature the Task list on the home page instead of Announcements. To make that change:

1. Navigate to the home page of your test site.

2. Click Site Actions → Edit Page in the upper-right corner of the page. SharePoint changes the page to Edit mode.

3. On the Announcements web part, click Edit → Delete and click OK. SharePoint removes the Announcements web part, but does not delete the Announcements list (it becomes hidden).

4. Click Add a Web Part. SharePoint displays the Add Web Parts web page dialog box.

5. Select Tasks and click Add. SharePoint adds the Tasks list web part to the page.

6. Drag the web parts to change their order on the page.

7. Click Exit Edit Mode in the upper-right corner of the page when you are done. The completed page should appear as shown in Figure 1-7.

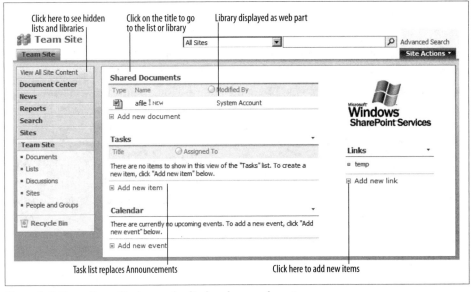

Figure 1-7. Every list or library can be displayed as a web part

Uploading Large Groups of Files

SharePoint libraries are very similar to file folders in Windows. In fact, you can view them in the Windows Explorer! To do that:

1. From the test web site home page, click on the title of the Shared Documents web part. SharePoint displays the Shared Documents library.

2. On the library toolbar, click Actions → Open with Windows Explorer. Share-Point opens the library folder as shown in Figure 1-8.

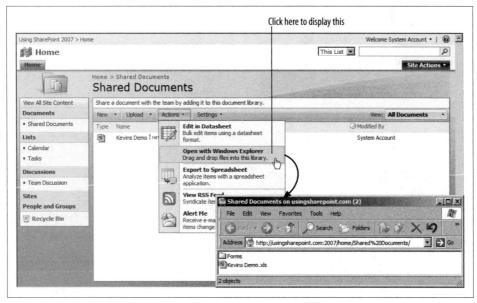

Figure 1-8. Opening a library in Windows Explorer

Using the Windows Explorer, you can create new folders, cut and paste files between the library and your desktop, or move whole folders from your desktop to Share-Point. This is the quickest way to upload a large number of files into SharePoint and preserve their organization.

There are a few restrictions on what you can upload:

- File and folder names can't include the following characters: &, ?, %, or .. (two periods together). Those characters have special meaning on the Web.
- Executable file types are blocked by default to avoid the spread of malicious code. To share executables, DLLs, and other file types, ZIP them before uploading.
- Files over 50 MB are blocked by default.

The blocked file types and maximum upload sizes can be changed through the SharePoint Central Administration settings. However, it's a good idea to stick with the defaults initially.

 Since SharePoint lists and libraries are shown as web pages, you may need to Refresh (F5) the page in your browser to see newly created items. That's always true if others are uploading items—you'll need to refresh to see their changes.

Creating Sites

Sites group related lists and libraries. In practice, most sites are organized by function or by department. For example, you might have a Legal Helpdesk site for questions and contract requests, and a Legal Department site for contract templates, executed contracts, and other things used internally by the Legal department.

Use sites to control access. The main reason to create two separate sites in the preceding example is access: all employees should be able to ask legal questions, but only the Legal department should draft new contracts.

To create a new site:

1. Click Site Actions → Create in the upper-right corner of a page.
2. Click on Sites and Workspaces under the Web Pages heading on the right side of the Create page. SharePoint displays the New SharePoint Site page (see Figure 1-9).
3. Fill out the web page and select a template for the site. *Templates* determine what lists and libraries are included automatically in the new site. There are instructions on the page for the other items you must complete.
4. Click Create when done. SharePoint creates the site and displays its home page.

 On some pages in MOSS, click Site Actions → Create Site instead in step 1 and go directly to step 3.

Controlling Access to a Site

Sites can inherit permissions from their parent site, or they can use unique permissions. It is usually a good idea to create new sites with inherited permissions, and then to change that setting once the site is created. That copies in the users from the parent site; you can then delete unneeded users, which is easier than adding users from scratch.

To change from inherited permissions to unique permissions:

1. Click Site Actions → Site Settings in the upper-right corner of a page.
2. Click Advanced permission under the Users and Permissions heading on the left side of the Site Settings page. SharePoint displays the Permissions page.
3. Click Actions → Edit Permissions on the toolbar. SharePoint warns you before creating unique permissions. Click OK to confirm.

Once a site has unique permissions, the users and groups that have access to the site appear with checkboxes next to them as shown in Figure 1-10.

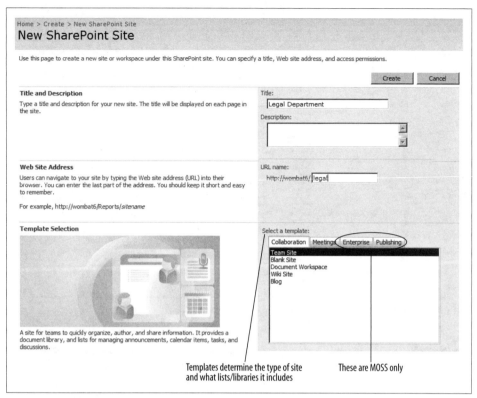

Figure 1-9. Creating a new site

Removing Users and Editing Permissions

To remove users:

1. Click the checkbox next to the user or group name as shown in Figure 1-10.
2. Click Actions → Remove User Permissions. SharePoint removes the user from the group.

Once a user is removed, she can no longer view the site. If you only want to restrict a user's access, Click Actions → Edit User Permissions, and select the permissions as shown in Figure 1-11.

Grouping Users

Groups control access based on the user's role. If you add a user to a group, then he will have permissions that are appropriate for that role. For example, all employees in one department might be members of their department site, meaning they can upload documents and add list items, but not design pages or create new lists or libraries.

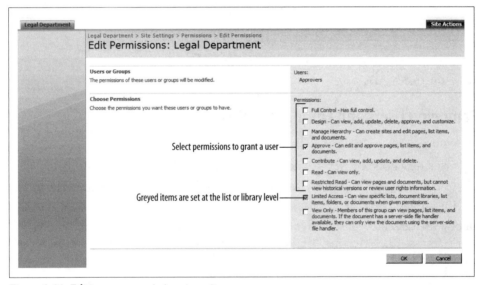

Figure 1-10. Use the Permissions page to control access to a site

Figure 1-11. Editing user permissions in a site

Rather than assigning permissions to each user, you can simply assign permissions to the group and then move users into and out of the group as required.

SharePoint groups may map to Active Directory security groups in your company. For example, you could add the Legal security group to the Members group in the Legal Department site. Then, all members of that security group can contribute to that site.

If your company uses Active Directory, it is a good idea to use security groups wherever possible in SharePoint, rather than adding users individually. Then when employees are hired or fired, those changes are automatically reflected in SharePoint because of the change in Active Directory.

To add an Active Directory security group to a SharePoint group:

1. Click Site Actions → Site Settings in the upper-right corner of a page.
2. Click People and groups under the Users and Permissions heading on the right side of the Site Settings Page.
3. Click New → Add Users on the toolbar of the People and Groups page. SharePoint displays the Add Users page.
4. Type the Active Directory security group name in the Users/Groups text box, and choose the SharePoint group that corresponds to the role those users will play within the site as shown in Figure 1-12.
5. Click OK when done.

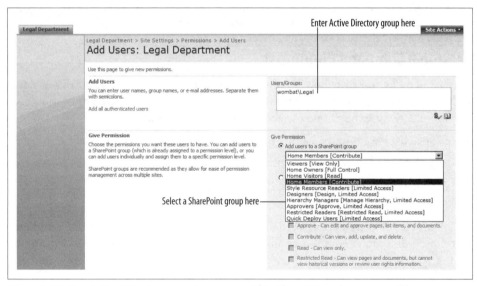

Figure 1-12. Use Active Directory security groups within SharePoint wherever possible

Putting SharePoint to Work

If you followed along carefully this far, you should now know how to:

- Customize pages by adding or changing web parts
- Add content to lists and libraries
- Create sites
- Control who can see and use a site

Congratulations! That's about 90 percent of what most folks need to know about using SharePoint. Of course you are more than just a user, so I'll go on for a few more chapters. Right now, I'd like to put what you've learned to work by walking you through "the big three" applications for SharePoint. Specifically, I want to show you how to:

- Create a company-wide phone list
- Replace shared drives
- Control document revisions

The following tutorial sections walk you through creating those applications. Please follow along using SharePoint as the tutorials teach you the core skills you will use when creating many different types of applications.

 You will be prompted for your username and password at various times in the following procedures. In each case, enter the user name and password you use to sign on to your network (usually you can substitute your full email name and password). In Chapter 2, I'll show you how to use your network credentials automatically.

Creating a Company Phone List

Many companies still distribute printed employee phone lists. Those go out-of-date quickly and are a pain to keep up-to-date—this is a perfect first application for SharePoint! Creating the phone list involves these major tasks:

- Create a list based on the Contacts template.
- Customize the list to add a Departments column.
- Create a new view to simplify data entry.
- Place the list on the home page as a web part.

SharePoint comes with a set of predefined list templates, and the Contacts template most closely fits the needs of a company phone list. By basing our new list on an existing template, we save the effort of creating columns for name, phone number, and so on.

To create the phone list:

1. Navigate to the top-level web site in SharePoint.
2. In WSS, click Site Actions → Create in the upper-right corner of a page. In MOSS, click Site Actions → View All Site Content → Create.
3. Click Contacts under the Communications heading on the left of the Create page. SharePoint displays the New page.
4. Name the list "Phone List" and click Create. SharePoint creates a new phone list based on the Contacts list template.

The Contacts template doesn't include a Department column, which is useful for grouping employees. So, we'll need to add that column next.

To add a Department column to the list:

1. Click Settings → Create Column on the Phone List toolbar.
2. Fill out the Create Column page as shown in Figure 1-13 and click OK to create the column.
3. Click OK to add the Department column to the list.

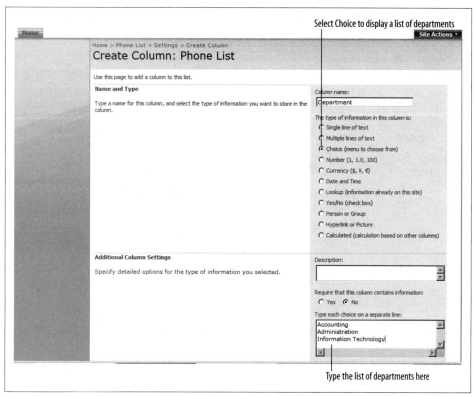

Figure 1-13. Adding a column to a list

The Contacts template includes a lot of columns we don't really need. We could delete them, but it doesn't really hurt to leave them there—it just makes data entry more complicated. To simplify that data entry, create a new datasheet view for entering records in bulk.

> The datasheet view is only available if you have Office Professional Edition (or higher) installed.

To create a datasheet view for the list:

1. Click Settings → Create View on the Phone List toolbar.

2. Click Datasheet View under the "Choose a view format" header on the left of the Create View page.

3. Name the view Edit Data and select the following columns in the Columns section of the Create Datasheet View page: Last Name, First Name, Business Phone, Department, and Mobile Phone.

4. Deselect all other columns.

5. Change the "Position from Left" number for the Department column from 8 to 1.

6. Click OK when done. SharePoint displays the new view of the list as shown in Figure 1-14.

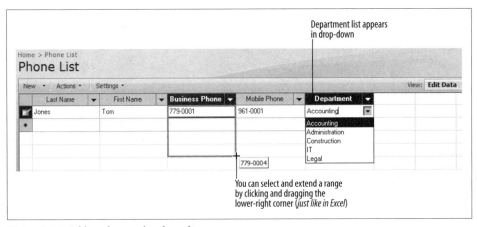

Figure 1-14. Adding data to the phone list

Add some names and numbers to the phone list. If you have an existing phone list in an Excel workbook, you can actually cut/paste columns of data from that workbook into the list. Be sure to add numbers for a few different departments, since we'll use this list in the next task.

Phone lists should be easy to find, so I usually put them on the home page. To do that, create a web part for the phone list on the home page and customize the web part to display phone numbers by department.

To add the phone list web part:

1. Navigate to the home page and click Site Actions → Edit Page. SharePoint displays the home page in Edit mode.

2. Click "Add a Web Part in the Right web part zone" on the right side of the page. SharePoint displays the Add Web Parts to Right page.

3. Select the Phone List web part in the Lists and Libraries section of the page and click Add. SharePoint adds the phone list to the page as a web part.

4. Click Edit → Modify Shared Web Part on the Phone List toolbar. SharePoint displays the web part properties page on the right.

5. Click "Edit the current view" under the Selected View heading. SharePoint displays the Edit View: Phone List page as shown in Figure 1-15.

6. Deselect the E-mail Address column, scroll to the end of the page, expand the Group By section, and select "First group by the column: Department."

7. Click OK. SharePoint displays the phone list as shown in Figure 1-16.

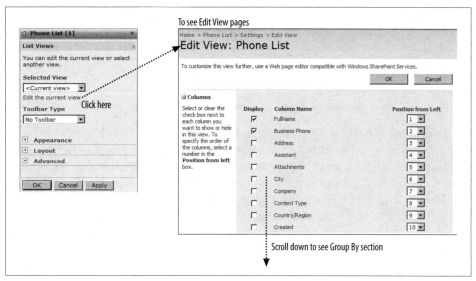

Figure 1-15. Editing the web part view

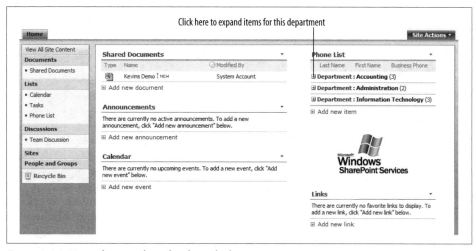

Figure 1-16. Using the new phone list from the home page

Replacing Network Drives with Libraries

Most companies store shared files on network drives. These are usually mapped to drive letters on employee desktops—for example, P: for personal files, R: for released files, and so on. Learning those drive letters and their folder structures is often one of the first things a new employee needs to know.

By replacing those network drives and their folder structures with SharePoint libraries, you get some big benefits very quickly:

- Files are discoverable. SharePoint uses a web page interface, which is easier to navigate than network drives.
- The contents of documents stored in SharePoint are searchable.
- Libraries support version control for files.
- You can filter, sort, and format views of the library in useful ways, such as only showing recently changed files.
- Employees can get to their files securely from home or while on the road without using a Virtual Private Network (VPN).

The hardest part of migrating from network drives to SharePoint libraries is determining how you want to organize the files you move over—it is best to flatten deep folder structures. For example, a path like R:\Departments\Legal\Templates\Contracts might map to the Contract Templates library in the Legal Department site. Also, since libraries can keep version history, you might want to change naming conventions that incorporate version information into the filename. Those aspects of the migration generally require some discussion and planning. The actual migration is much simpler and involves these major tasks:

- Create department sites.
- Create libraries for the department.
- Upload files to the libraries.

To create a department site, follow the instructions in the section "Creating Sites," earlier in this chapter. Use the title "Legal Department" and the address "Legal" as shown earlier in Figure 1-13.

To create a library in the Legal Department site:

1. Click Site Actions → Create in the upper-right corner of a page.
2. Click Document Library under the Libraries heading on the left of the Create page.
3. Name the library "Contract Templates" and select Yes under "Create a version" at the bottom of the page as shown in Figure 1-17; then click OK. SharePoint creates a new, empty library with version control.

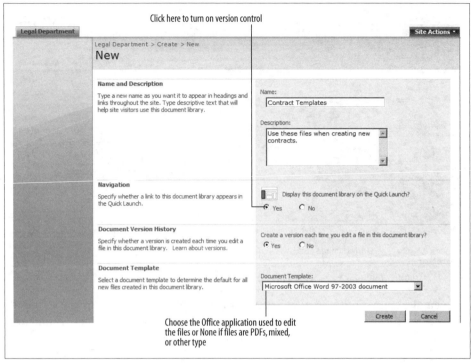

Figure 1-17. Creating a new library with version control

To upload documents to the library:

1. On the Contract Templates toolbar, click Actions → Open with Windows Explorer. SharePoint opens the library in Windows Explorer.

2. Open the network drive folder that you want to move files from, select the files to move, and drag them onto the library's Windows Explorer window as shown in Figure 1-18.

The address in the library's Windows Explorer window (for example, *wombat6*\ *legal\Contract Templates*) is the Windows notation for the address of the library. You can drag the folder icon to your desktop as a shortcut to the library, map a drive letter to the address, or use it in command scripts.

Using Document Version Control

Now that you've migrated your network drives to SharePoint (grin), employees can manage revisions to documents through shared workspaces. *Shared workspaces* are special sites that allow team members to work together privately on revisions and then publish those revisions once approved. SharePoint can also track version history and control access to documents through a check-out/check-in procedure.

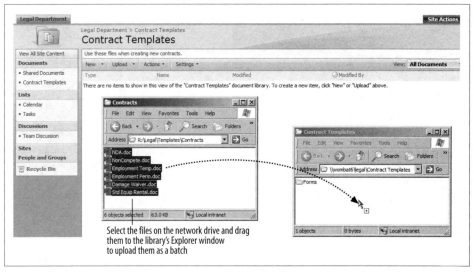

Figure 1-18. *Uploading files from a network drive to a SharePoint library*

For example, suppose the Legal Department needs to make changes to the standard non-disclosure agreement (NDA) that was uploaded to the Contract Templates library in the preceding section. The author performs these major tasks:

1. Checks out the document.

2. Creates a workspace for the revision.

3. Revises the document and collects feedback from the reviewers.

4. Publishes the approved document back to the library.

5. Checks in the final document.

Checking a document out prevents others from making changes and indicates to others that the document is under revision. To check out the document:

• Navigate to the Contract Templates library and click Check Out from the NDA document's Edit menu. SharePoint adds a little icon to indicate that the document is checked out.

You handle revisions through a shared workspace rather than through email so that comments are shared among reviewers and can be stored for future reference. To create the shared workspace:

1. Click Send To → Create Document Workspace from the NDA document's Edit menu as shown in Figure 1-19. SharePoint displays the Create Document Workspace page.

2. Click OK to create the workspace. SharePoint creates a workspace and copies the NDA document into the Shared Documents library.

3. Click "Add new user" in the Members section on the right side of the page. SharePoint displays the Add Users page.

4. Type the reviewers' email addresses and select Contribute in the list of permissions, and then click OK. SharePoint adds the user to the Members list for the workspace.

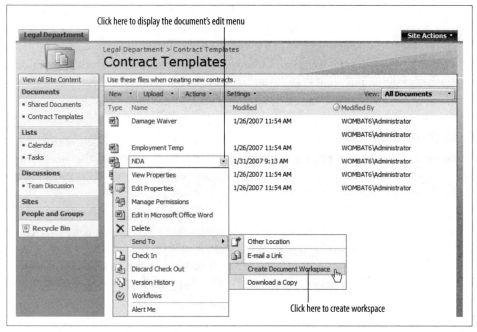

Figure 1-19. Creating a shared workspace

Only the members of this shared workspace can view the page in Figure 1-19, and it is not automatically added to site navigation. The author must notify reviewers that the workspace exists and send them a link to it asking for their feedback. To make changes to the document and send it for review:

1. Return to the workspace home page.

2. Click Edit in Microsoft Office Word from the NDA document's Edit menu. SharePoint prompts you for your user name and password and then opens the document with Word in Edit mode.

3. Turn on change tracking and edit the document in Word as you would normally. Click Save when done and close Word.

4. Click Send To → E-mail a Link from the document's Edit menu. SharePoint creates an Outlook email message containing a link to the document.

5. Fill out the email's To, CC, and Subject fields; compose a message instructing the reviewers to use the Team Discussion to submit their comments; and click Send.

Once all the comments are in, it's time to publish the document back to the library so others can start using it. To publish the approved document:

1. Click Edit in Microsoft Office Word from the NDA document's Edit menu, accept all changes to the document, and then save and close.

2. Click Send To → Publish to Source Location from the document's Edit menu. SharePoint displays the Publish to Source Location page.

3. Click OK to confirm that you want to publish the document. SharePoint copies the completed document back to the Contract Templates library.

4. Return to the Contract Templates library and click Check In from the NDA document's Edit menu. SharePoint displays the Check In page.

5. Enter a comment in the Check In page and click OK to make the changes visible to others.

The shared workspace does not go away after the document is published. The author may choose to keep it in place for a period of time or request that the SharePoint administrator archive it. It's a good idea to have some policy in place for how that is handled.

The preceding review process requires a lot of management on the author's part. If reviewers don't respond, the process can stall, and multiple reviewers might have conflicting changes. MOSS addresses those problems with workflows. *Workflows* are a set of tasks that must be completed in a particular order within a specified time frame. That topic is beyond the scope of this chapter; see Chapter 8 for more information.

Best Practices

By now, you should have a good idea of what SharePoint can do for you and should be in the process of evaluating which edition to acquire. The following practices should guide you as you move forward:

- Set up a staging server or virtual machine for evaluation. This is a valuable way to try out different configurations before installing in production, and the evaluation environment can be used for web part development later.

- Think about your existing work processes and how using SharePoint may change them. SharePoint can replace email as a workflow tool. Some subtle things, like document-naming conventions, may also change since SharePoint includes version control.

- If you are considering MOSS, verify that management wants the personalization features. If the idea of employee My Sites and blogs gives them the willies, plan on disabling My Sites. Read Chapter 7 for more information on personalization features, why they are useful, and how to control them.

- Try to build instructions into your SharePoint sites. SharePoint is easy to use, but the applications you create with it may need explaining, especially where they replace existing procedures. The SharePoint setup procedure uses a task list to tell you the steps you need to perform after installation—it's a good example of a self-documenting approach.

- Plan to deliver high-value, low-effort projects first. SharePoint is uniquely suited for Agile development: you can get applications in users' hands quickly and adjust as needs evolve.

- Add users to web sites through Active Directory security groups wherever possible. That way, you won't need to edit SharePoint security settings as new employees start, leave, or transfer.

- Open libraries in Window Explorer to upload groups of files quickly.

- Use the datasheet view to add or edit list items in bulk.

CHAPTER 2

Word, Excel, and Outlook

SharePoint works closely with Microsoft Word, Excel, and Outlook. In this chapter, I show you how to use SharePoint through those client applications. Both you and your users need to know these things, so you might consider using this chapter as a starting point for your internal user training.

SharePoint works best with Office 2003 and 2007, so I feature those product versions here. There is a big difference between the 2003 and 2007 Office versions: Office 2007 replaces the menus that most of us know with the Ribbon. The Office Ribbon is a tabbed set of toolbars with commands displayed as icons and text.

You can use SharePoint 2007 with Office 2003 if your organization isn't ready for Office 2007. Office 2007 offers some improved integration with SharePoint, but it is not a requirement. In this chapter, I note where features are specific to Office 2007.

Setting Client Security

Before you can fully use SharePoint with Office, you must change the security settings on your computer so that the SharePoint domain is trusted. If your computer is part of a domain, you'll probably also want to enable automatic logon so that Share-Point will automatically use your network credentials rather than prompting you for your user name and password. To make those changes:

1. Start Internet Explorer and choose Tools → Internet Options → Security → Trusted Sites → Sites. Internet Explorer displays a list of the trusted sites for your computer.

2. Type the address of your SharePoint site and click Add → OK. Use an asterisk to include subdomains. For example *.somecompany.com* includes *intranet.somecompany.com*, *extranet.somecompany.com*, *www.somecompany.com*, and so on.

3. Click Custom Level, scroll to the bottom of the page, and select "Automatic logon with current user name and password." Click OK → OK to close the dialog box.

Figure 2-1 illustrates the security settings. Step 3 prevents SharePoint from prompting you for your user name and password. Instead, SharePoint uses your network identity. These changes can be made for all users through the group policy settings in Active Directory by your system administrator.

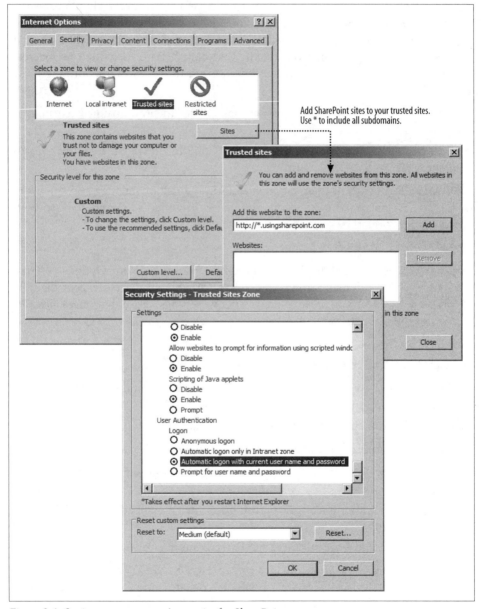

Figure 2-1. Setting your computer's security for SharePoint

Your system administrator may have made these changes for you already, but you need to be aware of these settings if you plan to access SharePoint from home. You won't be able to create workspaces, and you will be repeatedly prompted for your user name and password unless you make the preceding changes.

Whenever you open an Office document from SharePoint, Internet Explorer warns you that "Some files can harm your computer. If the file looks suspicious or you do not fully trust the source, do not open the file." That warning is intended to prevent you from accidentally opening documents that contain viruses written as macros. Most folks learn to ignore the warning, but you can turn it off by performing these tasks:

- Verify that Office macro security settings are set to prevent untrusted macros from running.
- Change the Explorer options to disable "Confirm download for Office document types" to turn off the warning.

You must perform both of these tasks or you run the risk of catching and spreading viruses. Setting macro security is done differently in Office 2003 and 2007 so both procedures are covered below.

To verify Office 2007 macro security settings:

1. From Microsoft Word 2007, click the Office button → Word Options → Trust Center → Trust Center Settings and select "Disable all macros except digitally signed macros" or any of the more restrictive settings above that one. Click OK to close the dialog boxes.
2. Repeat for Excel and PowerPoint if you use them.

To verify Office 2003 macro security settings:

1. From Microsoft Word, click Tools → Macros → Security and select High or Very High on the Security Level tab.
2. Repeat for Excel and PowerPoint if you use them.

To turn off the warning when opening Office documents:

1. From Windows Explorer, click Tools → Folder Options → File Types and select the DOC file type.
2. Click Advanced and deselect "Confirm open after download"; then click OK as shown in Figure 2-2.
3. Repeat steps 1 and 2 for the Excel and PowerPoint document types.

The new Office 2007 default document formats (DOCX, XLSX, etc.) omit macros, so you can more safely trust those file types. If you are seriously concerned about macro-borne viruses, consider turning off warnings for only DOCX and XSLX file types, and establish a company policy that discourages use of the older file types.

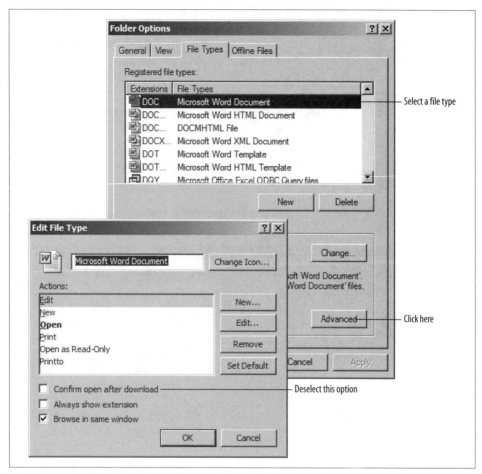

Figure 2-2. Turning off warnings when opening Office documents

Editing, Saving, and Sharing Documents

To open a Microsoft Office document from SharePoint in read-only mode, click on the file. To open an Office document in Edit mode, click Edit in the document's Edit menu. The *Edit menu* is the drop-down list shown in Figure 2-3 that appears when you click the triangle to the right of the filename.

Saving an open document saves your changes back to SharePoint. To see how that works, click Save As and save a copy of the document to SharePoint with a new name as shown in Figure 2-4.

While you have a document open for editing, no one else can edit it. If someone tries, Office displays a dialog box giving three choices as shown in Figure 2-5.

The last option in Figure 2-5 is the most useful one: it opens the file in read-only mode and then lets you switch to Edit mode when the other user closes the file.

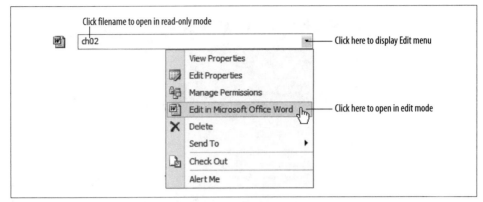

Figure 2-3. Using the SharePoint Edit menu to open documents

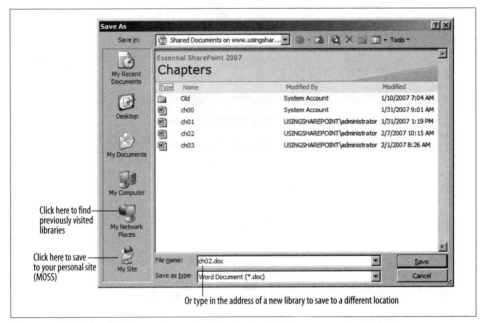

Figure 2-4. Office applications can save to libraries as if they were regular file folders

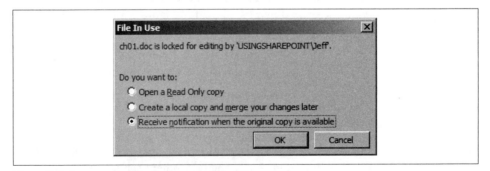

Figure 2-5. Someone else has the file open for editing

Using the Task Pane

When working with documents from SharePoint, Office enables the Document Management task pane (see Figure 2-6), which lists information about the documents in the library and provides quick access to alerts, document versions, and other features.

To display the Document Management task pane in Office 2007:

- Open an Office document from SharePoint and click the Office button → Server → Document Management Information.

> To display the equivalent task pane in Office 2003, click Tools → Shared Workspace. (The task pane is named "Shared Workspace" in Office 2003.)

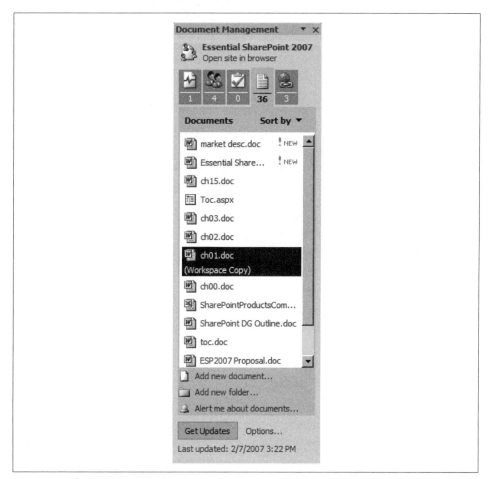

Figure 2-6. The Document Management task pane

Each of the icons at the top of the task pane maps to an equivalent task that you can perform from the SharePoint library. Table 2-1 describes the icons and lists the tasks you can perform with them.

Table 2-1. Task pane buttons

Office 2007	Office 2003	Name	Use to
		Status	Check whether or not the open document is up-to-date.
		Members	View or add team members to the SharePoint site that contains the document.
		Tasks	View or assign tasks for members of the SharePoint site that contains the document.
		Documents	Add documents to the library, open other documents from the library, or save a local copy of the file linked to the Share-Point site.
		Links	Add or view links to related information.
N/A		Document Information	View the document's revision history. In Office 2007, click the Office button → Server → View Version History.

The Document Management task pane is pretty handy when working with documents from SharePoint, but it does not appear automatically in Office 2007 the way it does in Office 2003. To change that:

1. On the Document Management task pane, click Options at the bottom of the Status tab on the task pane.

2. Under the Document Management heading, select the option to show the task pane at startup when the document is part of a workspace (that's the first option on the page), and click OK.

Working Offline in Office 2007

One of the problems of a connected environment is that sometimes you need to disconnect, like when you're flying coast-to-coast and you want to get some work done. SharePoint solves that problem by letting you check out the file before your trip. Checking out creates an updatable copy of the file on your computer and prevents others from changing the document until you check in your changes.

The following procedure works only in Office 2007.

To check out a document for offline changes:

1. From SharePoint, click Check Out from the document's Edit menu. SharePoint displays a dialog box confirming that you want to check out.

2. Click OK. SharePoint checks the document out to you and creates an updatable copy on your computer in your *My Documents\SharePoint Drafts* folder.

To edit the file offline:

1. Open the document from your *My Documents\SharePoint Drafts* folder. Office displays a dialog box asking if you want to get updates. Since you are offline, click Don't Update.

2. Make your changes and save the file.

Once you are back in the office, you can connect to the network and check in your changes. To do that:

1. In SharePoint, display the document's Edit menu and click Check In. That uploads your changes from the *SharePoint Drafts* folder on your computer and allows others to edit the document.

2. Verify that SharePoint deleted the document from your *SharePoint Drafts* folder. With some library types, SharePoint does not automatically delete this file, which can cause conflicting updates later.

Working Offline in Office 2003

Office 2003 does not create an updatable copy of a document when you check out, so working offline is a little different. To work offline in Office 2003, follow these steps:

1. From SharePoint, click Check Out from the document's Edit menu. SharePoint checks the file out to you, which prevents others from changing it.

2. From the Edit menu, click Send To → Download a Copy and save the file to your computer. SharePoint creates a copy of the file that is *not* linked to SharePoint.

3. Open and edit the copy of the document as needed.

Once you are back online, upload your changes to SharePoint and check the file back in. To do that:

1. From the SharePoint library, click Upload and select the document downloaded in step 2 above. SharePoint displays the Check In page.

2. Click Check In. SharePoint uploads your changes and checks in the document.

3. Delete the copy of the document from your computer.

Resolving Conflicting Updates

The difference between the preceding two sections is that Office 2007 makes it easy to store updatable copies of SharePoint documents on your computer. In Office 2007, you can actually create updatable copies without checking the file out, but that's a bad idea because offline changes can very easily overwrite changes made by others.

For example, if you make a copy of a document while it was checked out, you can edit that copy later even though the original file has been checked back in. When you close the file, Office attempts to send your changes to SharePoint; if someone else has edited the file since you opened your copy, Office displays the Document Updates task pane (see Figure 2-7).

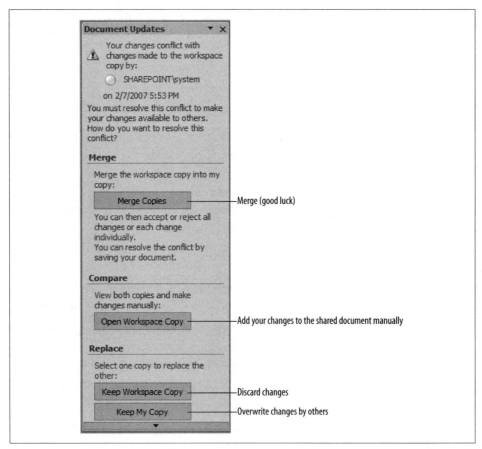

Figure 2-7. Using the Document Updates task pane

At that point you can merge the two files, re-enter your changes, discard your changes, or overwrite the other user's changes. Merging sounds like a good idea, but it rarely turns out well. You usually have to manually compare the documents and re-enter your changes in the SharePoint copy.

Requiring Check Out to Avoid Conflicts

You can avoid conflicting updates by requiring that documents be checked out before they are edited. To do that:

1. From the SharePoint library, click Settings → Document Library Settings. SharePoint displays the Customize page.

2. Click Versioning Settings under the General Settings heading on the left side of the page and select Yes for the Require Check Out section at the bottom of the page as shown in Figure 2-8. Click OK to close the page.

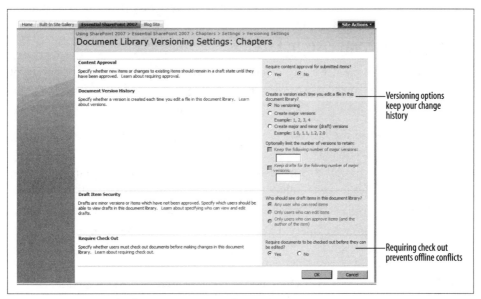

Figure 2-8. Requiring check out to prevents conflicts

Why isn't this setting the default? I think the answer is flexibility: not all libraries have multiple authors, so requiring check out might seem burdensome. Also, anyone who can edit a file can always overwrite someone else's changes intentionally; requiring check out just makes accidental overwriting unlikely.

Editing Lists in Excel

The preceding sections apply equally to Word, Excel, and PowerPoint. Each of those applications includes the Document Management task pane, and supports check out and working offline. The rest of this chapter is devoted to the unique SharePoint features offered by individual Office applications. The first, and most important, is the lists feature offered in Excel.

In Excel, *lists* are ranges of cells that can easily be sorted, filtered, or shared. Lists have these advantages over regular ranges of cells:

- Lists automatically add column headers to the range.
- XML data can be imported directly into a list.
- Excel can automatically check the data type of list entries as they are made.
- Lists can be shared and synchronized with SharePoint.

That last item is the key advantage: lists are a way to share tables of data. Those tables can be edited and viewed by multiple people at the same time, much the way that a database works; but unlike a database, lists are very easy to create and change.

Viewing SharePoint Lists in Excel

There are a lot of different ways to create lists in SharePoint. In fact, since SharePoint uses lists everywhere, most tasks involve either creating lists or adding new items to lists.

To view a list in Excel:

1. Display the list in the browser. For example, navigate to the Phone List sample you created in Chapter 1.
2. Click Actions → Export to Spreadsheet on the list toolbar as shown in Figure 2-9. SharePoint creates an Excel query and displays the File Download dialog box.
3. Click Open to display the query results in Excel. Excel displays a security warning.
4. Click Enable to run the query. Excel creates a new workbook and inserts the list as shown in Figure 2-10.

In Excel 2003, click Open instead of Enable in step 4. The appearance of the resulting list is also somewhat different.

Why view a list in Excel? SharePoint lets you sort and filter lists, but it won't let you analyze data, chart, or print the way that Excel can. You can also use Excel to bring data together from a number of sources: SharePoint, databases, web pages, host systems, and so on. You can also use Excel to move data from a source into SharePoint.

Editing Lists Offline and Resolving Conflicts

The list in Figure 2-10 is linked to the Phone List in SharePoint. You can add phone numbers in Excel and then synchronize those changes with SharePoint. That's like working with documents offline, but only the cells with changes are sent to SharePoint. That lets Excel resolve conflicts with changes from other users on a cell-by-cell basis—when working with lists, merging your changes with others actually works!

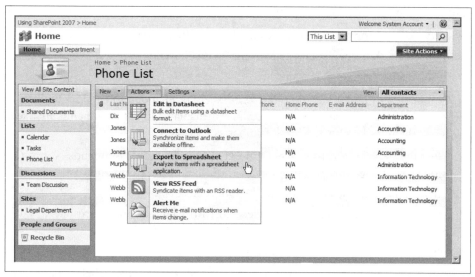

Figure 2-9. *Exporting the Phone List to Excel*

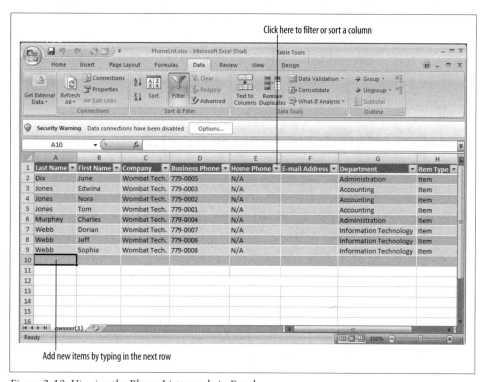

Figure 2-10. *Viewing the Phone List sample in Excel*

Editing lists offline involves these tasks:

- Add the synchronize commands to the Excel 2007 toolbar.
- Make changes to the list and synchronize with SharePoint.
- Resolve any conflicts that occur.

The commands to update SharePoint from Excel are included in the List toolbar in Excel 2003, but are hidden in Excel 2007. To display the list commands in Excel 2007, add them to the Quick Access Toolbar as follows:

1. Click the Office button → Excel Options → Customize → Commands Not in the Ribbon, and select Synchronize List near the end of the commands list.
2. Click Add to add the command to the Quick Access toolbar.
3. Scroll up in the commands list, select Discard Changes and Refresh, and click Add.
4. Click OK to close the Customize page.

Figure 2-11 shows the list commands in both versions of Excel. Click Synchronize List to update both the worksheet and the SharePoint. Click Refresh to discard your changes and update the worksheet with data from the SharePoint.

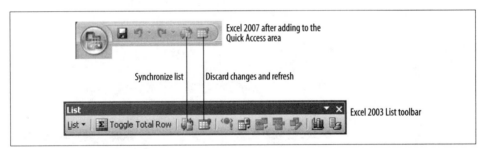

Figure 2-11. Synchronizing a SharePoint list in Excel

If your changes conflict with changes made by someone else, Excel displays Figure 2-12 to resolve the conflicts.

To replace the other member's changes with yours, choose Retry All My Changes.

Importing Data into SharePoint from Excel

One of the most common tasks in the IT world is moving data from one system to another. It's not exciting or creative, but it is a terribly useful skill. The easiest way to import data into SharePoint is through Excel. That's because Excel can read data from almost any source (CSV files, databases, spreadsheets, web queries, etc.), and then import that data into a SharePoint list.

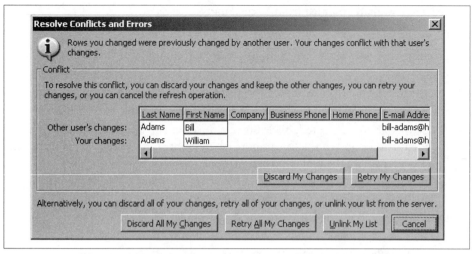

Figure 2-12. Reconciling conflicting edits in a shared list

Why import data into SharePoint lists? So information can be shared more widely or in a more useful format. For example, a company has an application that tracks the progress and costs of construction projects; the company wants managers to be able to see and analyze the data, but doesn't want to reprogram the application to produce those reports. To tackle this through SharePoint, complete these tasks:

- Create a database query to import the data into Excel and save the resulting workbook.
- Create a new list in SharePoint by importing the data from the workbook.
- Create views in the SharePoint list to group and total the data as needed.
- Make sure the managers are members of the site where the list is shared and email them the list address.
- Gather feedback and create new views as needed (there are always feature requests).

This approach is best suited for a one-time import or for infrequent updates. To see live data in SharePoint, use SQL Reporting Services.

When importing data into Excel for use in a list, make sure that the columns have headings, that the data is in a consistent format, and that the rows are contiguous. Gaps in rows and inconsistent columns, subheadings, and column totals cause problems when importing into SharePoint. You may have to manually clean up a worksheet before you can import the data into SharePoint.

To create a new SharePoint list from Excel data:

1. Close the workbook if it is open in Excel.

2. From SharePoint, click Site Actions → Create. SharePoint displays the Create page.

3. Click Import Spreadsheet under the Custom Lists heading in the middle-right side of the page. SharePoint displays the New page.

4. Name the list to be created, click Browse to select the Excel workbook containing the list to import, and click Import. SharePoint starts Excel, opens the workbook, and displays the dialog box shown in Figure 2-13.

5. Select "Range of Cells" from the Range Type drop-down list and select the range to import into SharePoint; then click Import. SharePoint creates the list based on the columns in the range, imports the data from Excel, and closes the workbook.

Figure 2-13. Importing Excel data into SharePoint

The Range Type drop-down in Figure 2-13 lets you import from Excel data lists and named ranges. Use the named range type when importing from an Excel database query—Excel automatically creates named ranges for any query it creates.

Once SharePoint creates the list, you'll want to customize it to add views and control access to the data. Chapter 4 describes how to do those things.

Viewing SharePoint Calendars from Outlook

A *SharePoint calendar* is a special type of list that displays events in a calendar view as shown in Figure 2-14. SharePoint calendars can be viewed from Outlook much like Exchange shared calendars. Also, you can export individual events from a SharePoint calendar into your personal Outlook calendar so you can get reminders and plan your time while offline.

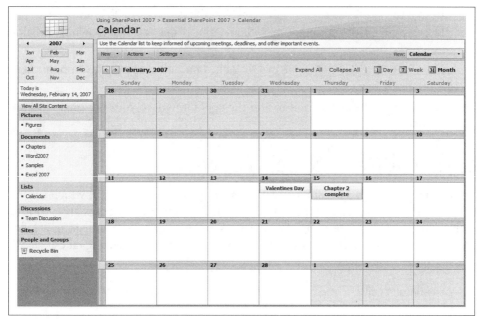

Figure 2-14. Use SharePoint calendars to view events

The Team Sites and Document Workspace site templates include calendars, but other site templates do not. To add a calendar to a site:

1. From SharePoint, click Site Actions → Create, and click the Calendar link under the Tracking heading in the middle of the page. SharePoint displays the New page.

2. Name the list and click Create. SharePoint creates a new calendar within the site.

To view a SharePoint calendar in Outlook:

1. Display the calendar in SharePoint and click Actions → Connect to Outlook on the list toolbar. Outlook displays a warning that SharePoint Services is adding a folder to Outlook.

2. Click Yes to allow SharePoint to add the folder. Outlook adds the SharePoint calendar under the Other Calendars heading in the Navigation Pane.

SharePoint calendars are read-only in Outlook, so you can't add events from there. To add an event to the calendar:

1. Display the calendar in SharePoint and click New on the list toolbar.

2. SharePoint displays the new item page. Fill out the fields and click OK. SharePoint adds the event to the calendar.

If you want to receive a reminder for an event, export the event from a SharePoint into your personal Outlook calendar. To do that:

1. Click on the event in the SharePoint calendar to view the event details.

2. Click Export Event on the toolbar. SharePoint displays a File Download dialog box.

3. Click Open to open the event in Outlook. Outlook displays the Appointment details dialog box.

4. Select Reminder and click OK to add the appointment to your personal Outlook calendar.

Organizing Meetings from Outlook

SharePoint provides a special type of site called a *meeting workspace*, which can be created from meeting requests sent from Outlook. Meeting workspaces are meant to prepare attendees by publishing the objectives and agenda before a meeting is held, and they help record decisions and related documents after the meeting takes place.

Workspaces are used to organize the meeting process like this:

1. Attendees receive a meeting request in Outlook that links to the SharePoint workspace.

2. Attendees can click on the link to see details about the meeting and add items as needed.

3. Optionally, someone can open the workspace and make notes during the meeting.

4. Later, the person who called the meeting can go to the workspace to record conclusions, assign follow-up tasks, or add key documents.

Meeting workspaces aren't online meeting places, but they can be used in conjunction with Microsoft Live Meeting or other online meeting services.

The following sections show you how to create SharePoint meeting workspaces from Outlook.

Creating a Meeting Workspace

To create a meeting workspace from Outlook:

1. Select the Calendar in the Navigation pane to choose a date and time for the meeting.

2. Choose Action → New Meeting Request. Outlook displays the Meeting Request dialog box.

3. Complete the fields on the dialog box and click Meeting Workspace. Outlook displays a workspace task pane in the dialog box as shown in Figure 2-15.

4. Click Create. Outlook creates a Meeting Workspace for the meeting and adds a link to the workspace in the dialog box.

5. Click the link and add objectives and agenda items to the workspace as shown in Figure 2-16.

6. Return to Outlook and click Send to close the dialog box and send the meeting request. The request includes a link to the meeting workspace so attendees can review the objectives, agenda, and add documents before attending.

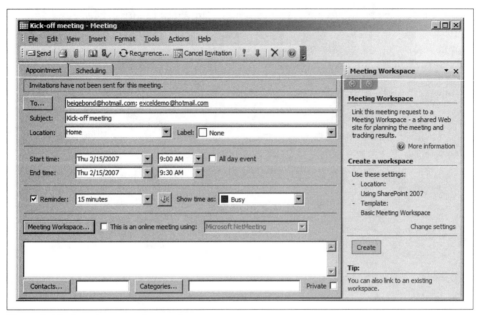

Figure 2-15. Creating a meeting workspace

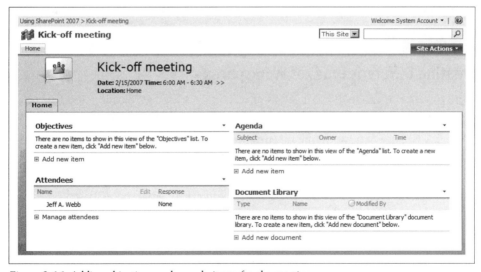

Figure 2-16. Adding objectives and agenda items for the meeting

The workspace in Figure 2-16 is for a meeting that happens once. Recurring meetings create a different type of workspace called a *meeting series*. To create a meeting series from Outlook:

- Choose Action → New Recurring Meeting instead of Action → New Meeting Request in step 2 of the preceding procedure.

Meeting series list recurring meetings by date as shown in Figure 2-17.

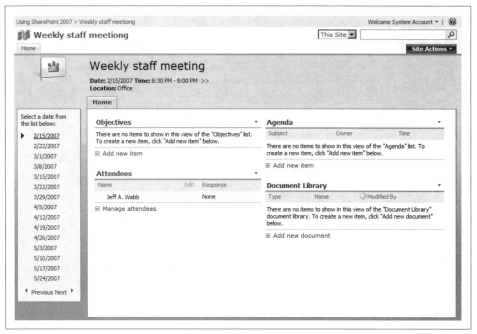

Figure 2-17. Using a meeting series for recurring meetings

Creating Different Types of Workspaces

Outlook lets you create different types of meeting workspaces or link a meeting to an existing workspace. To see the different options before creating a meeting workspace:

- Click Change Settings in the meeting workspace task pane (refer to Figure 2-15). Outlook displays the options shown in Figure 2-18.

By default, Outlook creates a Basic Meeting workspace that includes Objectives, Attendees, and Agenda lists. Figure 2-18 lets you create workspaces based on different templates as described in Table 2-2.

Figure 2-18. Choosing other workspace options

Table 2-2. Other meeting workspace templates

Template	Use to
Blank Meeting	Start from scratch, adding your own lists and content.
Decision Meeting	Include Tasks and Decisions lists in addition to the basic lists.
Social Meeting	Include Directions, Things to Bring, Pictures, and Discussions lists.
Multipage Meeting	Include the basic lists and add two blank pages for additional information.
Custom	Create a custom meeting workspace from a custom template installed on your site.

Linking to an Existing Workspace

Sometimes, you or someone else may have already created the workspace before you send the meeting request from Outlook. In that case, you can use Figure 2-18 to link the request to the existing workspace. To do that:

1. Select the team site that contains the meeting workspace in step 1 on Figure 2-18.

2. Select "Link to an existing workspace" in step 2.

3. Select the workspace from the "Select the workspace" drop-down list and click OK.

Sharing Contacts with Outlook

Outlook provides a set of tools for viewing and maintaining the list of contacts in your address book. If your company uses Exchange Server, you may already use a public list of contacts from Outlook to contact someone in your organization. SharePoint provides another way to share contacts from your address book with others. Rather than providing a single, public list containing everyone's information, SharePoint is focused more on team-based or project-based lists of contacts.

For example, a Team Site might include everyone on the team in the contact list. Later, as new members join and lines of communication are established across groups, the contact list grows. In this case, the contact list is a way to share the collected knowledge of who the key people are and how to get in touch with them.

For a project site or a document workspace, the contact list obviously includes everyone with responsibilities on the project. Outside resources, such as sales people or customers, would be added as they become available.

Of course, you can also use SharePoint to share a general, company-wide list of contacts. One advantage of that approach is that SharePoint contacts are easily shared over the Internet.

Finally, there's nothing stopping you from using all these approaches to help organize contacts by company, team, and project.

It's not a great idea to add the same contact to multiple lists. If the contact's information changes, it then has to be changed in all the lists. Instead, it's a good idea to follow rules about where you store contacts and how you use them. Here are some suggestions:

- Decide whether you are going to use SharePoint or Exchange Server to share company-wide contacts.
- If using SharePoint for company-wide contacts, organize those contacts into one or more lists at the top-level site.
- Restrict who can add or change contacts in the top-level SharePoint lists.
- Use project or workspace contact lists as temporary resources that have a limited lifetime.

A company might provide Employee, Customer, and Vendor contact lists in its top-level site that can't be edited by most members, but then allow team members to create their own ad hoc contact lists in team sites and workspaces. Although the ad hoc lists might become out-of-date, they allow members to organize the contacts that the team needs and perhaps include contacts that don't belong in the company-wide lists.

The following sections show how to work with SharePoint contact lists in Outlook.

Creating Contact Lists

SharePoint team sites and document workspaces include a list of contacts by default. That list is simply named "Contacts," and it appears on the Quick Launch bar of the site's home page. You can rename that list or create new contact lists for different types of contacts.

To rename the default contact list:

1. Display the list in the browser.
2. Select Modify settings and columns → Change general settings.
3. Type the new name in the Name field and click OK.

Changing the name of a list changes the name displayed on the list page and on the Quick Launch bar. It also determines the name of the list displayed in the Outlook Navigation pane if you link the list to Outlook.

You may want to create more than one contact list for a site. For example, you might want to organize employees, customers, and vendors into separate lists so you can better control who has access to the different lists. To create additional contact lists:

1. Select Create from the Navigation bar, then choose Contacts from the lists section of the Create page.
2. Enter a name for the new contact list, select whether or not a link to the list should appear on the home page Quick Launch bar, and click Create.

This creates a new list based on the contacts template. Lists based on the contacts template can be linked to Outlook as shared lists.

To control access to a list:

1. Display the list in the browser.
2. Select Modify settings and columns → Change permissions for this list.
3. Select a group and click Remove Selected Users to prevent members of that group from viewing the list; or select a group and click Edit Permissions of Selected Users to change the access privileges of those members.

Exporting Contacts from Outlook to SharePoint

You can export one or more contacts from Outlook to a SharePoint web site by following these steps:

1. Display the SharePoint site in your browser and click Contacts on the site's home page. You'll see the contact list for the site.
2. Click Import Contacts. You'll see a list of the contacts from your local address book.

3. You can import some or all of your contacts. To import some of the contacts, hold down the Ctrl key while clicking on the contacts to import. To import all of the contacts, click the first contact, scroll to the end of the list, hold down the Shift key, and click the last contact. Figure 2-19 illustrates importing all of the contacts.

4. Click OK to import the selected contacts. You'll see a security warning that SharePoint is trying to access your address book (see Figure 2-20). Select "Allow access for 1 minute" and click Yes to allow the import to continue.

5. When complete, the new contacts appear in the Contact list.

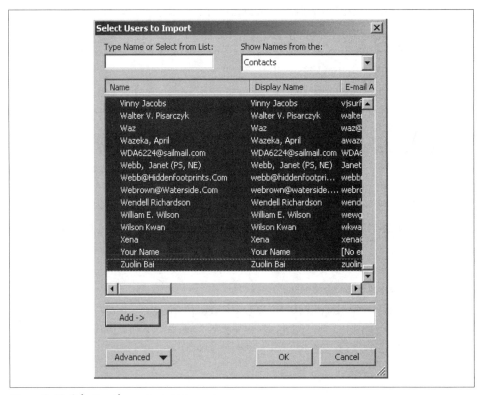

Figure 2-19. Selecting the contacts to import

Linking SharePoint Contacts to Outlook

To link shared contacts back to Outlook:

1. Display the contact list in the browser and click Link to Outlook.

2. Outlook displays a security warning. Click Yes to import the SharePoint contact list into Outlook. When finished, Outlook shows the shared list in the Other Contacts section of the Contacts Navigation pane as shown in Figure 2-21.

Figure 2-20. Allowing access to the address book

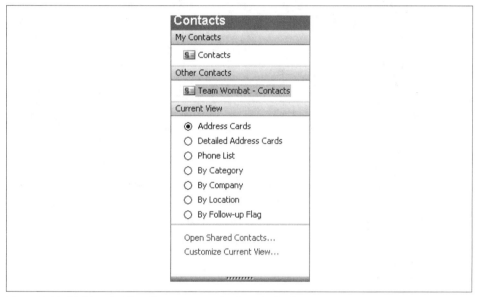

Figure 2-21. Linking the SharePoint contacts back to Outlook

Editing Shared Contacts from Outlook

The SharePoint contact list is stored on the SharePoint server so it can be used by all members of the site. That means you can't edit those contacts directly from Outlook. Instead, you must follow these steps:

1. Open the contact to change in Outlook. Outlook displays the detailed contact information as Read Only, shown in Figure 2-22.

2. Click the link in the Edit area. Outlook opens the SharePoint Edit page for the contact.

3. Make your changes and click Save and Close to complete the change.

4. Return to Outlook and close the Contact dialog box.

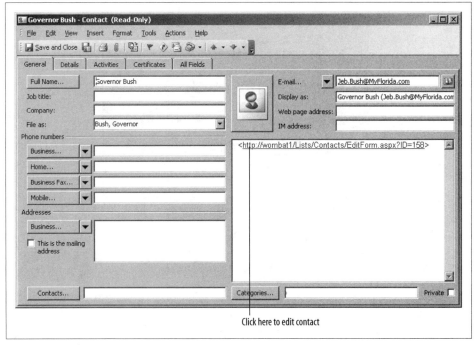

Figure 2-22. Changing shared contacts from Outlook

If you view the contact in Outlook right away, you won't see the changes you just made. Outlook updates its shared lists when the Outlook application starts and once every 20 minutes after that. To refresh the list immediately:

1. Right-click the shared contact list in the Navigation pane (refer to Figure 2-21).
2. Select Refresh from the context menu.

Best Practices

You should now be comfortable opening and editing documents from SharePoint with Office 2003 or Office 2007. You should understand how to check files in and out, work offline, and edit lists in Excel. The following practices should guide you as you move forward:

- Choose between Office 2003 and 2007. Trying to support both versions within a company is difficult.
- When transitioning between Office versions, set a timeline for the change and convert one department at a time.
- Ask your system administrator to add SharePoint domains to the list of trusted sites and enable automatic logon for all users through a group policy setting.

- The default library versioning settings apply very loose control such as those you might use on a small team project. For more complete document control, change the library's settings to require check out and keep version history.
- Use Excel to quickly import data into SharePoint lists from other systems.
- Use SharePoint calendars to track events for a team or project. Export an event to your personal Outlook calendar to receive a reminder for that event.

CHAPTER 3
Creating Sites

SharePoint sites organize and control access to information. You create a new site when access needs are unique or when the purpose of the site is unique. For example:

- Create sites for each department in your organization so department members can add and edit documents, but others can't (unique access).

- Create a general Helpdesk site where employees can ask questions of any department (unique purpose).

In Chapter 1, I showed you how to create a simple document control site for a Legal department. In this chapter, I'll tell you how to organize your sites, control access, customize their appearance, and create custom site templates.

Choosing a Location and Template

Sites are organized hierarchically within SharePoint sort of like the folders in a conventional filesystem, only instead of drives, folders, and subfolders, SharePoint uses web applications, site collections, and subsites:

Web application
   A web site that has been extended using the SharePoint administration tools. Each web application has a unique address—usually a subdomain of your organization's web address such as *http://intranet.something.com*.

Site collection
   A group of sites that all exist under a top-level site. Web applications usually have several top-level sites: one at the root and others under the */sites* and */personal* paths.

Subsite
   A site beneath the top-level site in a site collection.

Figure 3-1 illustrates a typical configuration with public, internal, and partner web applications.

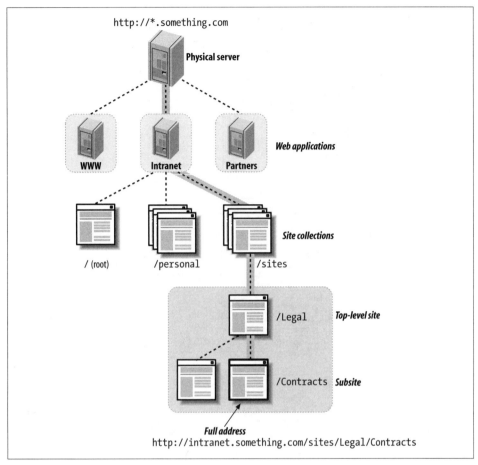

Figure 3-1. How SharePoint organizes sites

The */root* and */sites* paths are the default locations for site collections when you install SharePoint; the */personal* path is for employee sites (My Sites), which is a feature that comes with MOSS.

When choosing a location for a site, consider these factors:

- Who needs access? Top-level sites have the widest audience; subsites are typically more restricted.
- How will users find the site? It's easiest to create navigation links that follow the physical structure, so put the most widely used sites just under the root.
- Is it a department site? It's generally best to create a site collection for each department under the */sites* path.

For example, Figure 3-2 illustrates how you might organize a company intranet.

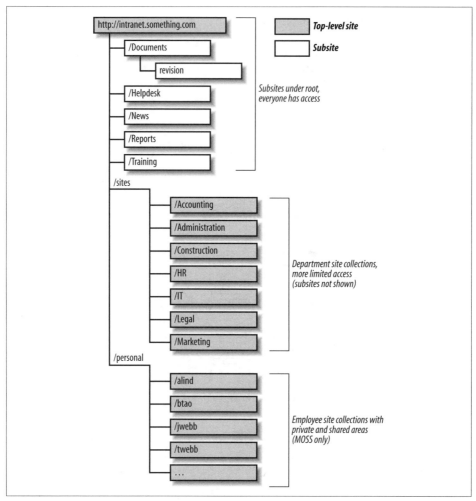

Figure 3-2. Organizing subsites and site collections

In Figure 3-2, the subsites under *http://intranet.something.com* are available to everyone in the organization. Each department has its own site collection with subsites as needed, and each employee has his or her own site collection.

 The */sites* and */personal* paths are used to organize site collections; they aren't sites themselves. If you navigate to *http://intranet.something.com/sites*, you'll get a Not Found error.

Creating Site Collections

Create a site collection if you expect there to be a lot of subsites or a lot of content beneath a level. In Figure 3-2, I show departments as their own site collections because each department may have many subsites and may include a large amount of content. Using site collections there allows me to move a department to its own database in the future if needed. It also allows me to assign ownership to someone within the department.

Users may or may not be allowed to create new site collections, depending on how SharePoint is configured. That feature is called *self-service site creation*; see Chapter 13 for instructions on enabling or disabling self-service site creation.

To create a new site collection with self-service site creation enabled:

1. Navigate to the site collection creation page in the */_layouts* folder (for example, *http://intranet.something.com/_layouts/scsignup.aspx*). There may be a link to this page in the Announcements list or on the Site Directory page.

2. Choose the folder to create the site collection in and complete the page as shown in Figure 3-3, and then click Create. SharePoint creates a new site collection and displays the Set Up Groups page (see Figure 3-4).

3. Add visitors (read-only access), contributors (read/write access), and owners (full control) to the site collection and click OK. SharePoint displays the new top-level site for the site collection.

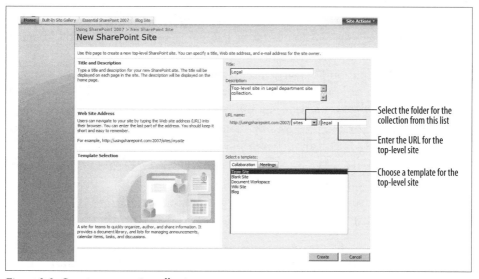

Figure 3-3. Creating a new site collection

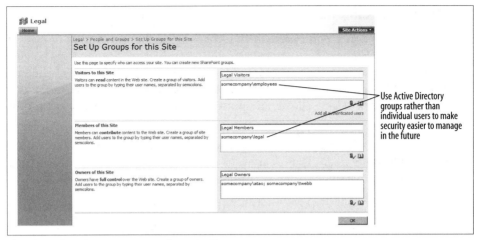

Figure 3-4. Configuring access to the site collection

Site collection owners have full control over all the sites in the site collection. They may also receive email from the site collection when someone requests access to the site, or when a site exceeds its size limit or is no longer actively used. For those reasons, they need special SharePoint training and perhaps a copy of this book.

If self-service site creation is not enabled, only SharePoint Administrators can create new site collections. To create a new site collection using the SharePoint Central Administration pages:

1. Navigate to the SharePoint Central Administration site. From the server, select Start → All Programs → Administrative Tools → SharePoint 3.0 Central Administration. SharePoint displays the Central Administration page.

2. Click the Application Management tab and click "Create site collection" under the SharePoint Site Management heading on the righthand side of the page. SharePoint displays the Create Site Collection page.

3. Choose the folder to create the site collection in and complete the page; then click OK. SharePoint creates a new top-level site for the site collection.

4. Navigate to the site and click Site Actions → Site Settings → "People and groups" to configure access to the site.

Creating Subsites

To group related content, create a subsite within a site collection. Any site can contain many different lists and libraries, so subsites are really a tool for organizing those lists and libraries. For example, you might create a subsite for each project within the Construction department. Each project subsite might contain a library for designs, a task list, a discussion board, and a calendar. Using subsites allows you to keep the names of those lists and libraries the same for each project and lets you create a custom site template to make site creation easier.

To create a subsite within a site collection:

1. Navigate to the top-level site in the collection.
2. In WSS, click Site Actions → Sites and Workspaces, and complete the New SharePoint Site page. In MOSS, click Site Actions → Create Site, and complete the page.

Choosing a Template

SharePoint comes with a set of built-in site templates. I described those templates briefly in Chapter 1, and you can see them listed on the New SharePoint Site page (refer to Figure 3-3) any time you create a new site. The site template defines what lists, libraries, and pages are included in the new site as well as what theme is assigned to the site. Tables 3-1 and 3-2 list the specific items included in each of the built-in templates.

Table 3-1. Built-in site template contents

Template	Lists	Libraries	Use to
Team Site	• Announcements • Calendar • Links • Tasks • Team Discussion	• Shared Documents	Organize a project within a department.
Blank Site	• None	• None	Create a site from scratch.
Document Workspace	• Announcements • Calendar • Links • Tasks • Team Discussion	• Shared Documents	Collaborate on a document.
Wiki Site	• None	• Wiki Pages	Collaborate on web content through a Wiki.
Blog	• Categories • Comments • Links • Other Blogs • Posts	• Photos	Share your thoughts with others.
Basic Meeting Workspace	• Agenda • Attendees • Objectives	• Document Library	Organize a meeting.
Blank Meeting Workspace	• Attendees	• None	Create a meeting site from scratch.
Decision Meeting Workspace	• Agenda • Attendees • Objectives	• Document Library	Organize a meeting to make a decision.

Table 3-1. Built-in site template contents (continued)

Template	Lists	Libraries	Use to
Social Meeting Workspace	• Attendees • Directions • Discussion Board • Things to Bring	• Picture Library	Organize a party.
Multipage Meeting Workspace	• Agenda • Attendees • Objectives	• None	Organize a meeting with tabbed pages.

Table 3-2. Additional built-in site templates included with MOSS

Template	Lists	Libraries	Use to
Document Center	• Announcements • Tasks	• Documents	Centrally manage company-wide documents and templates.
Records Center	• Holds • Links • Record Routing • Records Center • Submitted E-mail Records • Tasks	• Hold Reports • Missing Properties • Unclassified Records • Records Pending Submission	Store records in a central repository and prevent changes to records after they are stored.
Personalization Site	• Workflow Tasks	• Documents • Images • Pages	Target content to user's My Sites.
Site Directory	• Sites • Tabs • Workflow Tasks	• Documents • Images • Pages	List and categorize sites.
Report Center	• Announcements • Report Calendar • Sample Dashboard KPI Definitions • Sample KPIs • Workflow Tasks	• Data Connections • Documents • Images • Pages • Reference Library • Reports Library	Create, manage, and deliver reports.
Search Center with Tabs	• Tabs in Search Pages • Tabs in Search Results • Workflow Tasks	• Documents • Images • Pages	Create a tabbed-page search tool.
Search Center	• None	• None	Create a single-page search tool.
Publishing Site	• Workflow Tasks	• Documents • Images • Pages	Publish web pages.

Table 3-2. Additional built-in site templates included with MOSS (continued)

Template	Lists	Libraries	Use to
Publishing Site with Workflow	• Workflow Tasks	• Documents • Images • Pages	Publish web pages using an approval process.
News Site	• Workflow Tasks	• Documents • Images • This Week in Pictures • Pages	Publish articles, links, and RSS feeds.

One of the best ways to learn about the various templates is to create a gallery containing subsites that use each of the built-in templates. Then, as you create custom templates or buy add-on ones, you can add samples of those to the gallery . That helps site collection owners choose templates, and makes custom templates self-descriptive.

Customizing Site Navigation

There are three navigation web parts on the home page (see Figure 3-5) that you can customize:

- The link bar web part displays tabs at the top of the page that link to other sites.
- The Quick Launch web part displays links to lists and libraries within the current site on the left side of the page.
- The Tree View web part provides a hierarchical alternative to the Quick Launch.

The following sections tell you how to change to those web parts to make it easier to find key information.

Changing Link Bar Tabs in WSS

The tabs that appear in the top link bar on the home page usually correspond to the top-level web sites within a site collection. Those tabs are inherited from the parent site by default. To change the tabs on the link bar:

1. Navigate to the home page and click Site Actions → Site Settings, and then click "Top link bar" under the Look and Feel heading. SharePoint displays the Top Link Bar page.
2. Click Stop Inheriting Links on the toolbar. SharePoint changes the toolbar as shown in Figure 3-6.
3. Click New Link to add a new tab, or click the Edit icon to change an existing link.

To restore the inherited tabs, click "Use Links from Parent."

Figure 3-5. The navigation web parts on the home page

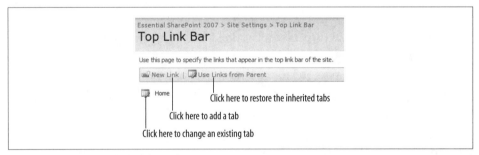

Figure 3-6. Changing the link bar tabs

Adding Links to Quick Launch in WSS

The Quick Launch web part displays links to the lists and libraries in a site on the left side of the home page. When you create a new list or library, you can choose whether or not it should appear in Quick Launch. To change those links:

1. Navigate to the home page and click Site Actions → Site Settings, and then click Quick Launch under the Look and Feel heading. SharePoint displays the Quick Launch page (see Figure 3-7).

2. Use the toolbar to create new links or headings or click on the Edit icon to change or delete an existing link.

Figure 3-7. Changing the Quick Launch links

Changing the Link Bar and Quick Launch in MOSS

MOSS manages the link bar and Quick Launch tabs using a single Site Navigation Settings page (see Figure 3-8) rather than the Top Link Bar and Quick Launch pages found in WSS.

MOSS refers to top link bar tabs as *Global Navigation*, and Quick Launch links as *Current Navigation*. To manually change the link bar tabs and Quick Launch links:

1. Navigate to the home page and click Site Actions → Site Settings and then click Navigation under the Look and Feel heading. SharePoint displays the Site Navigation Settings page.

2. In the Subsites and Pages section, deselect "Show subsites" to remove subsites from the link bar and Quick Launch. This allows you to selectively add subsites in step 5.

3. In the Global Navigation section, select "Display only the navigation items below the current site" to stop inheriting link bar tabs from the parent site.

4. In the Current Navigation section, select "Display only the navigation items below the current site" to stop inheriting Quick Launch links from the parent site.

5. In the Navigation Editing and Sorting section, use the toolbar to change the tabs that appear in the link bar and Quick Launch. Add items to the Global Navigation folder to have them appear in the link bar; add items to the Current Navigation folder to have them appear in the Quick Launch.

6. Click OK when done.

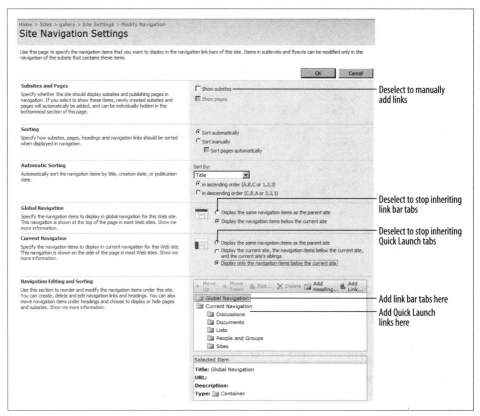

Figure 3-8. MOSS combines the link bar and Quick Launch settings into one Navigation Settings page

Adding a Help Tab

SharePoint includes a Help system for users, but strangely does not feature it in any of the built-in site templates. In fact, Help is kind of hidden in SharePoint, so I generally add a Help tab to any new site collection I set up.

To add a tab for SharePoint Help in WSS:

1. Follow the steps in "Changing the Link Bar in WSS" to add a tab to the link bar.
2. Use the following URL for the link address (be sure to omit *http://*):

    javascript:HelpWindowKey("NavBarHelpHome")

You can't add that URL to the top link bar in MOSS, so to add a Help tab in MOSS:

1. Follow the steps in "Changing the Link Bar and QuickLaunch in MOSS" to add a tab to the link bar.
2. In the Navigation Link web page dialog box, use the following URL:

    /_layouts/help.aspx?Key=NavBarHelpHome

3. Select "Open link in new window" and click OK.

The SharePoint Help system provides instructions on how to create and use lists, libraries, sites, and create formulas. It is a good alternative to the books that simply march through SharePoint features without explaining why they exist or when to use them, and (even better) it is free.

Adding Tree View Navigation

The Quick Launch web part allows you to organize links however you like. Microsoft refers to that as *logical navigation*. The Tree View web part displays links to subsites, lists, and libraries in a hierarchical fashion. Microsoft refers to that as *physical navigation*. There are benefits to either approach:

- Use the Quick Launch web part for content-oriented sites such as Document Centers where you want to feature some libraries and hide others.
- Use the Tree View web part for dashboard-type or top-level sites where the subsites are already organized logically (such as by project) and where there are many subsites. The Tree View web part doesn't require as much maintenance as the Quick Launch web part.

To replace the Quick Launch web part with a tree view:

1. Navigate to the home page and click Site Actions → Site Settings, and then click "Tree view" under the Look and Feel heading. SharePoint displays the Tree view page (see Figure 3-9).
2. Select Enable Tree View to add the Tree View web part to the home page.
3. Optionally, deselect Enable Quick Launch to remove the Quick Launch web part.
4. Click OK to make the change.

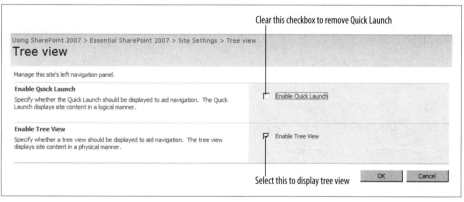

Figure 3-9. Replacing Quick Launch with a tree view

Summarizing Content with Web Parts

The home page is the first page users see, and it's often the only page they need if you design it correctly. Even though a site may include many lists and libraries representing hundreds or even thousands of documents, you can effectively summarize that content by displaying web parts that show only the most relevant content on the site's home page.

In Chapter 1, I showed you how every list and library can be displayed as a web part. You can use that technique to summarize recent changes on the home page of any site. For example, to feature the 10 newest documents on a home page, complete these tasks:

- Add the library as a web part to the home page.
- Modify the view displayed in the web part to sort documents by the Created column.
- Limit the number of items to display in the view to 10.

To add the library as a web part:

1. Navigate to the home page and click Site Actions → Edit Page. SharePoint changes the page to Edit mode.
2. Click Add a Web Part on the page in the location where you want to add the new library summary. SharePoint displays the Add Web Parts page.
3. Select the library to display and click Add. SharePoint adds the library as a web part and displays the web part properties in the task pane on the right.

To modify the view displayed in the web part:

1. Click "Edit the current view" in the web part properties. SharePoint displays the Edit View page.
2. Scroll halfway down the page to the Sort section and choose "First sort by the column Created (descending order)."

To limit the number of items displayed in the view:

1. Scroll to the end of the page, expand the Item Limit section, and change the Number of items to display to 10.
2. Select "Display items in batches of the specified size" and click OK.

Now, the home page will include a list of the 10 most recent documents. You can use this technique to feature key information from any list or library by changing the view displayed in the web part. For more information on creating custom views, see Chapter 4.

Adding Other Pages

In practice, I find that many users have a hard time navigating among lists and libraries—once they leave the home page, they are easily lost. You can make life easier for those folks by creating additional pages that appear as tabs on the home page, and then add web parts to those pages that summarize key lists and libraries.

The Multipage Meeting Workspace is a simple example of this design: it includes a home page, plus three other pages that appear as tabs next to the Home tab as shown in Figure 3-10. All of the built-in meeting site templates include this feature, though only the multipage template includes sample pages.

Figure 3-10. Meeting site templates include tabbed pages

To use this tabbed approach:

1. Create a new site based on any of the meeting templates. I'll use the Blank Meeting Workspace site template in this example, and I'll name the site "Construction Project."

2. Create the lists and libraries that your site will use. In this example, I've created a Drawings library, a Tasks list, and a Calendar.

3. On the home page, click Site Actions → Add Pages. SharePoint displays the Add Page task pane.

4. Name the first page "Drawings" and click OK. SharePoint displays the new page in Edit mode.

5. Drag the Drawings library web part from the task pane onto the Left web part zone. SharePoint adds the library as a web part on the page.

6. Repeat steps 4 and 5, naming the page "Tasks" and dragging the Tasks web part onto the page.

7. Repeat steps 4 and 5, naming the page "Calendar" and dragging the Calendar web part onto the page.

8. Click Exit Edit Mode in the upper-right corner of the page to view the result (shown in Figure 3-11).

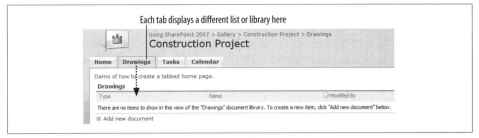

Figure 3-11. Using tabbed pages to display lists and libraries to create a Construction Project site

To delete a page:

1. On the home page, click Site Actions → Manage Pages. SharePoint displays the Pages task pane.

2. Click Order → Delete at the top of the task pane. SharePoint changes the task pane to Delete mode.

3. Select the page to delete and click Delete. SharePoint deletes the page.

Setting Security (Controlling Access)

As you saw earlier in "Creating Site Collections," you can determine who has access when you create a top-level site. For subsites, I recommend inheriting permissions from the parent site and then changing them as needed. The benefit of inheriting permissions is that all the members of the parent site are automatically copied into the subsite. You can then remove members or restrict permissions in the subsite.

To change from inherited permissions to unique permissions:

1. Navigate to the home page and click Site Actions → Site Settings, and then click Advanced Permissions under the Users and Permissions heading. SharePoint displays the Permissions page.

2. On the toolbar, click Actions → Edit Permissions. SharePoint displays a warning that you are about to create unique permissions.

3. Click OK. SharePoint displays the permissions in Edit mode.

To add new users to the site:

1. On the Permissions page toolbar, click New. SharePoint displays the Add Users page (see Figure 3-12).

2. Type the name of the Active Directory (AD) security group or user in the Users/ Groups text box, select "Give users permissions directly," select the permission, deselect "Send welcome e-mail to the new users," and click OK. SharePoint adds the security group or user.

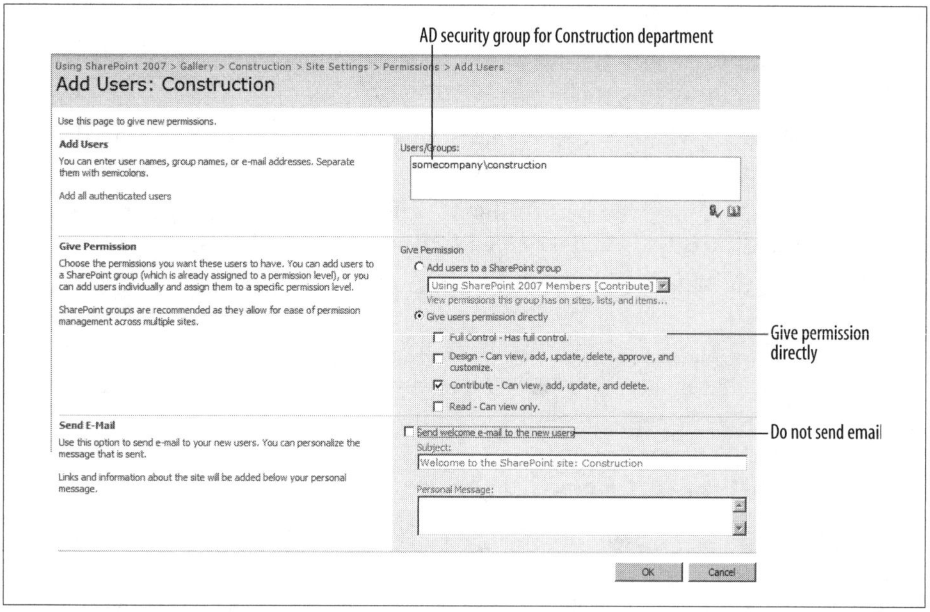

Figure 3-12. Adding an AD security group to the Construction site

Why do I choose not to send an automatic email when adding users? Because the email that SharePoint generates tends to confuse people, especially when I'm setting up a new site. I tend to get the site through the approval process and then send out my own email announcing it and telling folks how to use it.

To remove a user or group from a site (restrict permissions):

1. On the Permissions page, select the user or group to remove.
2. Click Actions → Remove User Permissions. SharePoint deletes the user or group.

Using the Site Users Web Part

The Site Users web part (see Figure 3-13) provides an easy way to view the users and groups that have access to a site. If a site has unique permissions, it also includes a link that allows you to add new users without going through the Site Settings pages.

Figure 3-13. Using the Site Users web part to view and add users

To add the Site Users web part to a page:

1. Navigate to the page to modify and click Site Actions → Edit Page. SharePoint displays the page in Edit mode.

2. Click the Add a Web Part link in one of the web part zones. SharePoint displays the Add Web Parts page.

3. Select the Site Users web part in the Miscellaneous section near the bottom of the page and click Add. SharePoint adds the web part to the page.

4. Click Exit Edit Mode in the top right corner of the page when done.

 I usually add an Admin page to web sites with a Site Users web part and other administration links on it to make it easy for site owners to administer their own sites.

Using Active Directory Security Groups

At the risk of repeating myself, I encourage you to use Active Directory (AD) security groups rather than individual identities wherever possible. That makes it much easier to administer security in SharePoint, because members can be added or removed through Active Directory rather than by visiting individual sites and changing security.

You may need to sit down with your security administrator to map out what security groups your company uses. Most companies have security groups for departments, but management, administrative, and other role-oriented groups may be less clearly defined.

It's OK to use individual identities for site owners, as those roles tend to be filled by one or two people—it doesn't really make sense to create an AD security group in those cases.

Working with SharePoint Groups

SharePoint has its own type of security group that determines permissions across one or more site collections. Use SharePoint groups when users have a specific role across sites, such as approving documents or designing web pages. The built-in SharePoint groups are listed in Table 3-3 for WSS, and Table 3-4 for MOSS.

Table 3-3. SharePoint groups

SharePoint Group	Permissions	Specific permissions
Members	Contribute	View, add, update, and delete list items and documents
Owner	Full Control	Administer the site, lists, and libraries
Visitors	Read	View lists and libraries

Table 3-4. Additional SharePoint groups in MOSS

SharePoint Group	Permission	Specific permissions
Approvers	Approve	Edit and approve pages, list items, and documents
		View lists and libraries when given access
Designers	Design	View, add, update, delete, and customize design
		View lists and libraries when given access
Hierarchy Managers	Manage Hierarchy	Create sites, edit pages, lists, and documents
		View lists, libraries when given access
Quick Deploy Users	Limited Access	View lists, libraries when given access
Records Center Web Service Submitters	Limited Access	View lists, libraries when given access
Restricted Readers	Restricted Read	View pages and documents, but not version history or user rights
		View lists, libraries when given access
Style Resource Readers	Limited Access	View lists, libraries when given access

Earlier versions of SharePoint called these *cross-site groups* because you could add users to one of these groups, and then add that group to a number of different sites. SharePoint groups are useful for management roles where you want to grant read or approval access across all site collections.

To add users to a SharePoint group:

1. On the Permissions page toolbar, click New. SharePoint displays the Add Users page.
2. Type the name of the AD security group or user in the Users/Groups text box, select "Add users to a SharePoint group," select the group, and click OK. Share-Point adds the user to the SharePoint group.

To create a new SharePoint group:

1. Navigate to a site with unique permissions. Top-level sites in each site collection have unique permissions, as do subsites that are explicitly set to have unique permissions; see "Setting Security (Controlling Access)," earlier in this chapter.
2. On the Permissions page toolbar, click New → New Group. SharePoint displays the New Group page.
3. Complete the page and select the permissions to assign the group in the last section of the page, and then click Create.

Members of a SharePoint group have permissions on every site that includes that group. For example, members of the Visitors group of the top-level site can view all of the subsites that inherited permissions.

To restrict general access to a site, remove the SharePoint groups from that site:

1. Navigate to the home page of the subsite and click Site Actions → Site Settings, and then click Advanced Permissions under the Users and Permissions heading. SharePoint displays the Permissions page.

2. On the toolbar, click Actions → Edit Permissions. SharePoint displays a warning that you are about to create unique permissions.

3. Click OK. SharePoint displays the permissions in Edit mode.

4. Select the SharePoint groups to remove and click Actions → Remover User Permissions on the toolbar. SharePoint removes the groups from the permissions list.

Permission inheritance, AD security groups, and SharePoint groups can be confusing at first. I recommend starting slowly with simple permissions at the top-level site, inherited by subsites, and restricted where necessary. Use SharePoint groups sparingly in the beginning. Once access needs are clearer, you can use SharePoint groups to simplify granting access to users who need privileges across sites.

Changing the General Appearance

To change the title, description, and icon displayed on a site:

1. Navigate to the home page of the site and click Site Actions → Site Settings, and then click "Title, description, and icon" under the Look and Feel heading.

2. Change the settings on the page, and click OK to make the changes.

The color, fonts, and backgrounds used by a site are controlled by the site theme. The default theme is blue and orange with a white background. To change the theme of a site:

1. Navigate to the home page of the site and click Site Actions → Site Settings, and then click "Site theme" under the Look and Feel heading. SharePoint displays the Site Theme page.

2. Select a theme in the list box on the right side of the page. SharePoint shows a preview of the theme.

3. Click Apply to change the site's theme.

In MOSS, you can also apply an alternate cascading style sheet (CSS) to redefine the styles used throughout a site. Creating CSS files is a task for web design experts, but once you have the CSS file, you can apply it to your site by following these steps:

1. Upload the CSS file to a library within the site. Copy the address of the uploaded file; you'll need it for step 3.

2. Navigate to the home page of the site and click Site Actions → Site Settings, and then click "Master page" under the Look and Feel heading.

3. Scroll to the bottom of the page and select "Specify a CSS file" under the Alternate CSS URL heading. Paste the address of the CSS file in the text box and click OK.

To override the styles in WSS, modify or replace the CSS files used by SharePoint on the server; see "Applying Stylesheets," later in this chapter.

Creating Custom Themes

The themes that appear on the Apply Theme page are at this location on the server:

C:\Program Files\Common Files\Microsoft Shared\web server extensions\12\ TEMPLATE\THEMES

To change an existing theme:

1. Edit *THEME.CSS*, *.gif*, and other files in the theme's folder.
2. Restart SharePoint by running *iisreset.exe*.

Changes to a theme automatically appear in sites based on the theme after Share-Point restarts.

To create a new, custom theme based on an existing theme:

1. Copy and rename a theme's folder in *\TEMPLATE\THEMES*.
2. Edit the files in the new theme folder.
3. Rename and edit the *theme.inf* file in the theme folder to match the theme's name.
4. Edit the file *SPTHEMES.xml* in the *\TEMPLATE\LAYOUTS\1033* folder. This file loads the theme definitions in SharePoint.

The theme's *.inf* file contains the theme's title and localized name displayed for different languages, as shown here:

```
[info]
title=NewTheme
codepage=65001
version=3.00
format=3.00
readonly=true
refcount=0

[titles]
1031=NewTheme
...
```

The *SPTHEMES.xml* file tells SharePoint where to find the theme definitions. For example, the following snippet adds NewTheme to the list of available themes:

```
<?xml version="1.0" encoding="utf-8" ?>
<SPThemes xmlns="http://tempuri.org/SPThemes.xsd">
    ...
    <Templates>
        <TemplateID>newtheme</TemplateID>
        <DisplayName>New Theme</DisplayName>
```

```
        <Description>Demo theme</Description>
        <Thumbnail>../images/thice.png</Thumbnail>
        <Preview>../images/thice.gif</Preview>
    </Templates>
</SPThemes>
```

You don't have to restart SharePoint for the new theme to be available.

Applying Stylesheets

SharePoint uses CSS to control the fonts, background, and foreground colors used by the sites on the SharePoint server. The default stylesheet is *CORE.CSS*, which is found at this location on the server:

```
C:\Program Files\Common Files\Microsoft Shared\web server extensions\12\TEMPLATE\
LAYOUTS\1033\STYLES
```

Changes to *CORE.CSS* affect all of the SharePoint sites on the server. For example, making the following change:

```
body {
    font-family: verdana, arial, helvetica, sans-serif;
    background: white;
    color: red;
}
```

turns all of the body text on the server red! Be careful when editing this file.

Sites using themes are also affected by *THEME.CSS* found in the */TEMPLATE/ THEMES/** folders. You can edit *THEME.CSS* to change the styles applied by a specific theme. For example, the following change to *THEME.CSS* in the NewTheme folder changes the page title font color for the theme created in the preceding section:

```
.ms-pagetitle{
color:black;
font-family:Verdana,Arial,Helvetica,sans-serif;
font-weight:bold;
}
```

Changing styles in a theme doesn't immediately change existing sites based on that theme, because stylesheets are cached on the client. If you don't see the changes you've made, force a full refresh of the page by pressing Ctrl+F5 in the browser. The full refresh reloads any cached stylesheets—just clicking the Refresh button won't do that.

Identifying the class name of styles that SharePoint uses on a page is difficult. Appendix B includes instructions on how to use a custom web part provided with this book's samples to view and edit styles on any web part page.

You can also find a full reference to the style names used by SharePoint at *http:// www.heathersolomon.com/content/sp07cssreference.htm*. Ms. Solomon includes a wealth of information about rebranding SharePoint through "CSS Trickery," and her site is by far the best source on the subject.

Creating and Using Site Templates

One of the biggest advantages of SharePoint over other web tools is how easy it is to duplicate your work using site templates. Once you get a project or department site set up the way you want it, you can simply save the site as a template and then create other similar sites based on that template.

There are two types of site templates in SharePoint:

- Built-in templates are stored on the server as *site definitions*. These come with SharePoint and are sometimes provided by add-on vendors.
- Custom templates are stored in the database as template files (*.stp*). You create these from existing sites.

Site definitions are collections of XML and ASPX files stored in folders at this location on the server:

> *C:\Program Files\Common Files\Microsoft Shared\web server extensions\12\ TEMPLATE\Site Templates*

Site definitions are complex, difficult to create, and almost impossible to debug. In contrast, custom templates are simple, easy to create, and don't need debugging. So why worry about site definitions? For the most part you shouldn't, but it helps to understand three things:

- Custom templates are based on site definitions. In order for a custom template to work, the underlying site definition must be installed on the server.
- Changes to site definitions propagate to all the sites that are based on them. In practice, changing a site definition in a live environment risks breaking sites, but minor changes can be OK.
- Changes to custom templates don't change the sites that are based on them. You can't reapply a new custom template after a site is created, so changes must be made manually in each site.

How to Develop Custom Templates

Because you can't change a site's template once the site is created, it is best to follow these steps when developing custom templates:

1. Create a prototype site with live data.
2. Gather feedback on the site from actual users.
3. Make their changes and get confirmation that the site is working as needed.
4. Create a custom template based on the approved prototype and use it to create subsequent sites.

These steps are familiar to most programmers and they fit well with the Agile development process. It is easy to prototype sites with SharePoint, so it is better to do that and get early feedback than to spend a lot of time in meetings planning exactly how the site should work.

If needs change after you deploy a custom template, you can modify individual sites manually or work on a time-forward basis with a new version of the custom template. (New sites get the new features; older sites will be upgraded as needed.)

Saving a Site As a Custom Template

The Construction Project site shown earlier in Figure 3-11 was based on the Blank Meeting Workspace template. I added a Drawings library, Tasks list, Calendar list, and three tabbed pages to the site. To save that site as a custom template:

1. Navigate to the site home page and click Site Actions → Site Settings and then click "Save Site as template" under the Look and Feel heading. SharePoint displays the Save Site Template Page.

2. Complete the page as shown in Figure 3-14 and click OK. SharePoint saves the site as a template and displays a link to the Site Template Gallery.

3. Click on the link to display the Site Template Gallery, as shown in Figure 3-15.

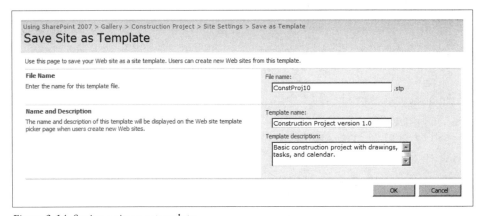

Figure 3-14. Saving a site as a template

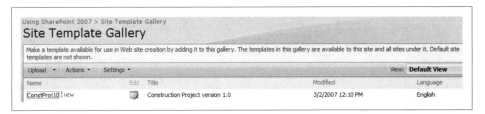

Figure 3-15. The Site Template Gallery

Be sure to include a version number in the template's file name and title when creating custom templates. It helps you keep track of changes later.

When creating templates, you can choose whether or not to include content from the site in the template in step 2 in the preceding list. Choose Include Content if your site contains lists that provide values to other lists (look-up lists); if you include a list of tasks that must be completed after a new site is created (an instructions list); or if the site includes a Help library or other documents that should always be copied into new sites based on the template.

Using and Deploying Custom Templates

Custom templates appear on the Custom tab of the template list when you create a new site within the current site collection, as shown in Figure 3-16. To use the template, simply select it when you create a new site. The new site will contain the same lists, libraries, and pages as the source site.

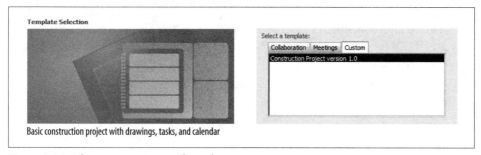

Figure 3-16. Selecting a custom template when creating a new site

The custom template is not visible from other site collections, however. To use it outside the current site collection, you must deploy the template.

To deploy the custom template to another site collection:

1. Navigate to the top-level site in the source site collection.
2. In WSS, click Site Actions → Site Settings and then click "Site templates" under the Galleries heading. In MOSS, click Site Actions → Site Settings → Modify All Site Settings, and then click "Site templates" under the Galleries heading. SharePoint displays the Site Template Gallery as shown earlier in Figure 3-15.
3. Click on the template name. SharePoint displays the File Download dialog box.
4. Click Save and save the file to a *Templates* folder on your computer.

5. Display the Site Template Gallery of the destination site collection. As a shortcut, you can edit the URL of the source gallery (*./_catalogs/wt/Forms/Common.aspx*) in the address bar to go there.

6. Click Upload on the toolbar and upload the *.stp* file you saved in step 3. SharePoint adds the template to the list of custom site templates for the site collection.

To deploy the custom template to all site collections:

1. Follow steps 1 to 3 above, then copy the *.stp* file to a *Templates* folder on the server.

2. On the server, run the command prompt and enter the following commands to install the custom template on all site collections:

```
path=C:\Program Files\Common Files\Microsoft Shared\web server extensions\12\
BIN;%path%
stsadm -o addtemplate -filename constproj10.stp -title "Construction Project
version 1.0" -description "Basic construction project template with drawings,
tasks, and calendar."
iisreset -noforce
```

The *stsadm.exe* utility provides a command-line interface to administrative functions in SharePoint. Some of those functions are also available through the SharePoint Central Administration site. See Appendix B for a full list of the *stsadm.exe* commands.

Templates deployed using *stsadm.exe* don't appear in the Site Template Gallery, but they are available when you create new sites. To remove a template deployed using *stsadm.exe*, use the following command:

```
stsadm -o deletetemplate -filename constproj10.stp -title "Construction Project
version 1.0"
```

 Create a Templates folder on the server and on your development computer to help keep track of the templates you have created and deployed.

Viewing and Editing Template Files

The custom template file (*.stp*) is actually a compressed cabinet file containing an XML template description. To see the contents of the template file:

1. Download the template file as described in the preceding section.

2. Rename the downloaded file to have the *.cab* file extension.

3. Open the file using Extract, WinZip, or another file compression utility and extract the file *manifest.xml*.

4. Open *manifest.xml* using FrontPage, WordPad, or an XML editor (not Notepad—*manifest.xml* doesn't include whitespace and you won't be able to decipher it).

 The elements in *manifest.xml*, like all XML elements, are case-sensitive. Errors in the element names or nesting will prevent the template from working.

To make changes to a custom template directly:

1. Edit *manifest.xml*. You can find reference information about the elements in the WSS SDK Help file (*WSS3SDK.chm*) under Reference → General Reference → Collaborative Markup Language Core Schemas.

2. Package the changed file using *CabArc.exe*. For example, the following command packages changes as *TeamWithPics2.stp*:

   ```
   CabArc n TeamWithPics2.stp manifest.xml
   ```

3. Upload the packaged file to the Site Template Gallery. SharePoint adds the new template and displays its description in the Site Template Gallery.

 CabArc is available at *http://msdn.microsoft.com/library/en-us/ dncabsdk/html/cabdl.asp*. The WSS SDK can be found by searching *http://www.microsoft.com* for *WSS3SDK.chm*.

Replacing a Built-in Template

Microsoft recommends that you avoid modifying the built-in site definitions, because upgrading to a new release of SharePoint would overwrite your changes and possibly break sites based on those templates.

It's simpler and safer to create a new, custom template with the same name, then hide the built-in template—in effect replacing the built-in template with your own. To replace a built-in template with a custom template:

1. Create a new custom site template based on the built-in template you are replacing.

2. Deploy the custom site template to all site collections on the server.

3. On the SharePoint server, edit the *WebTemp.xml* configuration file to hide the old site definition and list the new one.

4. Stop and restart IIS to refresh SharePoint's template list. To stop and restart IIS, run *iisreset.exe* on the SharePoint server.

The *WebTemp.xml* file is found in the *C:\Program Files\Common Files\Microsoft Shared\web server extensions\12\TEMPLATE\1033\XML* folder of the SharePoint server. To hide a template, change the Hidden attribute to TRUE, as shown here in bold:

```
<Templates xmlns:ows="Microsoft SharePoint">
 <Template Name="STS"     ID="1">
    <Configuration ID="0" Title="Team Site" Hidden="TRUE" ImageUrl="/_layouts/images/
stsprev.png" Description="A site for teams to quickly organize, author, and share
information. It provides a document library and lists for managing announcements,
calendar items, tasks, and discussions." DisplayCategory="Collaboration" >
    </Configuration>
    ...
 </Template>
 ...
</Templates>
```

After you restart IIS, your new custom site template appears in the template list and the old definition doesn't. Sites that were based on the old site definition will still work, but new sites can't be created easily based on that old definition.

Best Practices

You should now understand how to organize sites using web applications, site collections, and subsites. You should be able to customize the navigation and appearance of a site, add tabbed pages, apply themes, and create custom site templates. Use the following practices as you move forward:

- Add a Help tab to the top-level link bar of your site collections. The built-in SharePoint Help system provides the basic instructions most users need, but it is not featured in the default site navigation.
- Check existing sites before creating a new one. Often new site requests will fit into an existing site.
- Broad sites are more usable than deep hierarchies.
- Create a site collection for any set of related sites that might need separate storage or administration in the future.
- Build a site gallery containing demonstration sites for each built-in or custom site template. That makes it easier for site collection owners to choose the template that fits their needs.
- Add the Site Users web part to an Admin page so site owners can easily view existing users and add new ones.
- Prototype sites and get agreement from users before creating custom templates based on the site. SharePoint is ideally suited for Agile development.
- Include a version number in custom template filenames and titles.
- Save the custom templates you create to a *Templates* folder, and add a *Templates* folder to the server for all custom templates you deploy using the *stsadm.exe* utility.

CHAPTER 4
Creating Lists

SharePoint lists are tables of data, much like Excel spreadsheets. In Chapter 2, I showed you how to create lists from spreadsheets. But lists can do a lot more than just store columns and rows of data—in fact, lists are like mini-applications in SharePoint.

I've organized this chapter to follow the steps I use when creating new list-based applications for my clients:

1. Create a list using one of the built-in templates.
2. Add columns to collect additional data and calculate values as required.
3. Create supporting lists for lookups and master lists.
4. Add views to display required reports.
5. Enable email, versioning, and item approval as required.
6. Optionally customize the data entry forms.
7. Save the final list as a template and deploy it to other site collections.

That's similar to the process I showed for creating sites: start with what's provided, customize, get approval, and deploy. Don't skimp on the approval part of that process—it's a lot harder to change lists once they are deployed. Get agreement that the prototype you've created meets the stated needs *before* you save it as a template and deploy it across multiple sites.

This chapter builds on the Phone List sample we created together in Chapter 1. If you skipped that, you'll want to go back and do it now. I also introduce the Problem Reports application, which is based on the Issue Tracking list template.

Using Built-in List Templates

SharePoint provides a set of built-in list templates that you can start from and customize as needed. Tables 4-1 and 4-2 describe the list templates that come with SharePoint.

Table 4-1. Built-in list templates

Category	List	Use to
Communications	Announcements	Share news, status, and other time-sensitive information.
	Contacts	Collect and store phone numbers, email addresses, and other information about employees or external contacts. Contact lists can be shared with Outlook.
	Discussion Board	Create threaded discussions among team members. Discussion boards are similar to newsgroups.
Custom Lists	Custom List	Create a new list starting with basic columns and a standard view.
	Custom List in Datasheet view	Create a new list starting with basic columns and a datasheet view.
	Import Spreadsheet	Create a new list with columns and data from a spreadsheet. Includes a datasheet view.
Tracking	Links	List web pages and other resources related to a task or project.
	Calendar	Track events, milestones, and deadlines that can be displayed graphically as a calendar page. Calendar lists can be shared with Outlook.
	Tasks	Track work items.
	Project Tasks	Track work items that can be displayed graphically in a Gantt Chart.
	Issue Tracking	Assign issues or problems to individuals and then track the progress of the resolution.
	Survey	Poll individuals using a series of questions and display the results graphically.

Table 4-2. Additional list templates provided by MOSS

Category	List	Use to
Custom Lists	Languages and Translators	Add languages and translators used by the Translation Management workflow.
	KPI List	Track and display progress toward a set of goals graphically.

As with site templates, it's a good idea to create one sample of each type of list in a gallery that site owners can browse. Then, as you create new custom lists, you can add them to the gallery. It really helps users to see the available list types before creating their own.

When you create a new site, some lists are created automatically by the site template. Figure 4-1 shows a site created from the Team Site template, which automatically includes Announcements, Calendar, Links, Tasks, and Discussion lists. See Chapter 3 for tables of what lists and libraries each site template includes.

These new lists are empty to start with: list templates define the columns that the list will contain and the views of the list items that are displayed. The list items are provided by the users. Figure 4-2 shows the parts of a Links list.

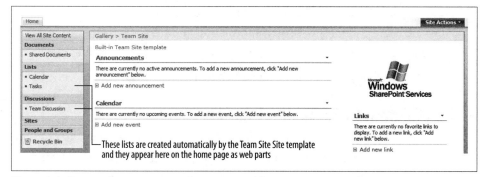

Figure 4-1. *Site templates automatically create some lists*

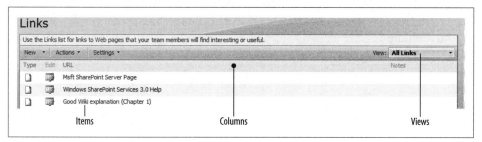

Figure 4-2. *The parts of a list*

Items

Items are the rows of data in a list. Users add new items or change existing ones.

Columns

Columns define the types of data that a list contains. The Links list contains columns for a URL and Notes as well as a set of predefined columns that SharePoint uses such as ID, Created, Created By, and so on. Those predefined columns are usually not displayed. Columns are also called *fields* in the Microsoft documentation.

Views

Views control what columns are displayed, how they appear, and what filters or grouping are applied to the rows. Views are similar to reports.

Adding Columns

The built-in list templates give you most of what you *need*, but you'll quickly find that you have to make some changes to get what you *want*. I gave a quick example of how to create and customize a list in the Phone List example in Chapter 1, so I won't repeat that information here, but I will go into more detail about the types of changes you can make and why you make them:

- Add columns to gather additional information.
- Add calculated columns to display information in different ways.
- Add choice or look-up columns to provide new ways to group or filter items.

The following sections describe those tasks in detail.

Adding Columns to Gather Information

You can extend any list by adding new columns to it. Let's look at the Phone List sample again to show how that works. To add an Assistant column to the Phone List:

1. Navigate to the Phone List sample list created in Chapter 1. Tip: you can navigate to a list by clicking on the title bar of the web part that displays a list.

2. On the list toolbar, click Settings → Create Column. SharePoint displays the Create Column page.

3. Complete the page as shown in Figure 4-3 and click OK. SharePoint adds a new text column to the list.

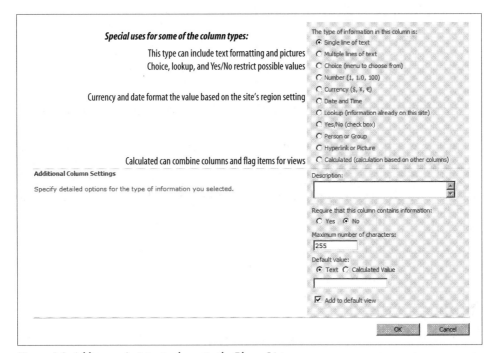

Figure 4-3. Adding an Assistant column to the Phone List

Once you add an Assistant column, it's up to you to add data for each row in the list. Because you selected Add to default view in Figure 4-3, Assistant automatically shows up in the main view of the list, so you can just click Actions → Edit in Datasheet to fill in the new column. But don't do that yet! I'll change and expand this example shortly.

Assistant is a simple text column. Figure 4-3 lists the special uses for some of the other column types. Most of them are obvious, but I'll explain the Calculated and Lookup columns in detail in the following sections.

Adding Calculated Columns

Use calculated columns to bring together values from other columns. For example, the Phone List contains a Full Name column that is a single line of text. Since the list already has First Name and Last Name in it, it makes more sense to create Full Name out of those two columns. To do that:

1. On the Phone List toolbar, click Settings → Create Column. SharePoint displays the Create Column page.

2. Complete the page as shown in Figure 4-4 and click OK. The formula shown in Figure 4-4 is =[First Name] & " " & [Last Name]. SharePoint adds a new calculated FullName column to the list.

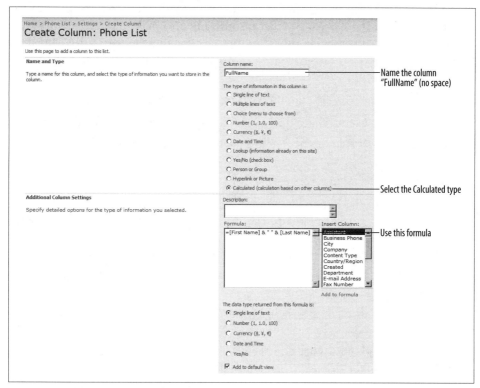

Figure 4-4. Adding a calculated column to a list

To get help using formulas, display the SharePoint Help and click "Formulas and functions." To display SharePoint Help, use the following link: *./_layouts/help.aspx?Key=NavBarHelpHome*.

Notice that I told you to name the column "FullName." The Phone List already has a "Full Name" column, and you can't have two columns with the same name! We're not using the Full Name column, so let's delete it. To delete a column:

1. On the list toolbar, click Settings → List Settings. SharePoint displays the Customize page.

2. Scroll down and click Full Name in the Columns list. SharePoint displays the Change Column page.

3. Scroll to the end of the page and click Delete. SharePoint warns you that data for this column will be deleted. Click OK to delete the column.

Adding a Choice, Lookup, and Yes/No Columns

Use the Choice, Lookup, and Yes/No column types to structure the information entered in the column. In Chapter 1, I added a Department Choice column to the Phone List. I used the Choice type because I wanted to make sure the entries were consistent—users can only choose from the selections in the list of departments I provided. That prevents misspelled or incorrect department names and allows the Phone List to be grouped by department.

Choice, Lookup, and Yes/No column types have these advantages:

- Values are consistent, so grouping and filtering on these columns is effective.
- It's easier to enter values, since choices are provided as drop-down lists or multiple-choice selections.
- Choices can be shared across lists and sites.

Let's continue with the Phone List sample a bit more and change the Assistant column from a text column to a lookup. You can't change the type of a column once it's created, so we'll have to delete the Assistant column and re-create it with the new type. (Remember, I told you not to enter data in it!) To change the Assistant column:

1. On the Phone list toolbar, click Settings → List Settings. SharePoint displays the Customize page.

2. Scroll down and click Assistant in the Columns list. SharePoint displays the Change Column page.

3. Scroll to the end of the page and click Delete. SharePoint warns you that data for this column will be deleted. Click OK to delete the column.

4. On the Change Column page, click Create Column. SharePoint displays the Create Column page.

5. Complete the page as shown in Figure 4-5 and click OK to create the new Assistant column.

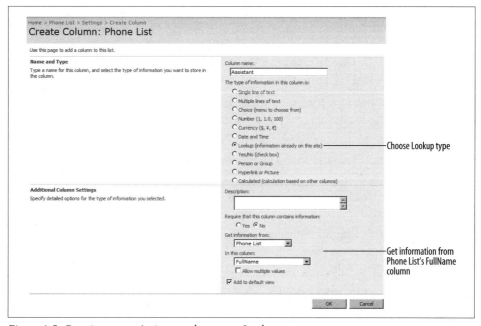

Figure 4-5. Creating a new Assistant column as a Lookup type

Now, you can fill out the Assistants in the phone list. To do that:

1. On the Phone list toolbar, click Actions → Edit in Datasheet.

2. Click the Assistant column and then click the down arrow on the right side of the column to drop-down the list of choices.

3. Click the choice to select the assistant as shown in Figure 4-6.

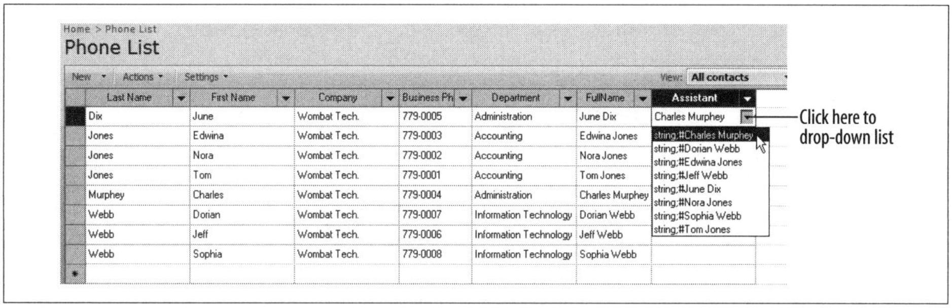

Figure 4-6. Using the Lookup column

The Assistant column is a circular lookup. That is, you can choose any name provided that the person is already entered in the Phone List. You can use a lookup to pull data from another list in the site by selecting a different source list and column name.

Why Use a Lookup?

Lookup and Choice column types serve similar purposes. Both provide choices from a list of values. With Choice columns, the values are entered directly in the column settings. With Lookup columns, the values come from another list.

Why go to the trouble of setting up a whole list just for a lookup? Because changes to the lookup list appear automatically in the Lookup column. To see how that works:

1. Select Charles Murphey as an assistant in the first row of the Phone List as shown in Figure 4-6, and then change his first name to Charley in the fifth row of the Phone List.

2. Click Actions → Show in Standard View, and "Charley Murphey" now appears in the first row.

3. Finally, click on Charley Murphey in the first, and you'll see his contact details. Lookups link lists together!

In this case, you've got to enter assistants before you enter managers (otherwise, you won't be able to find their assistant). That's always true of lookups: the source list must contain the values you want to look up before you can fill out the destination list.

Lookups can be used across any list or library in the current site. For example, you might add a Lookup column to a Task List that gets its values from a library containing Contracts. Each task then links to the contract that spells out the exact terms of the task as shown in Figure 4-7.

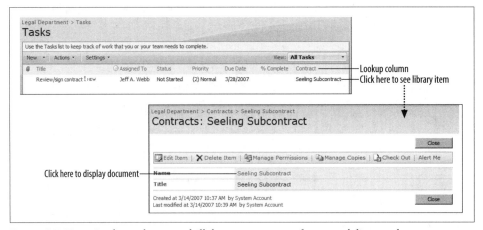

Figure 4-7. Using Lookup columns to drill down to a contract from a task list to a document

Adding Site Columns

One thing you'll notice when working with lookups is that you can't look up values from a list in another site. Lookups can only get values from lists in the current site. To get values from another site, you need to create a site column.

SharePoint provides quite a few built-in site columns for general types of lookups. To add one of the built-in site columns to a list:

1. On the list toolbar, click Settings → List Settings, and scroll to the end of the Columns list.

2. Click Add from existing site columns (it's the second link after the end of the columns list). SharePoint displays the Add Columns from Site Columns page.

3. To add a site column to a list, select the column from the list on the left and click Add; then click OK. Figure 4-8 shows adding a Gender column to the Phone List.

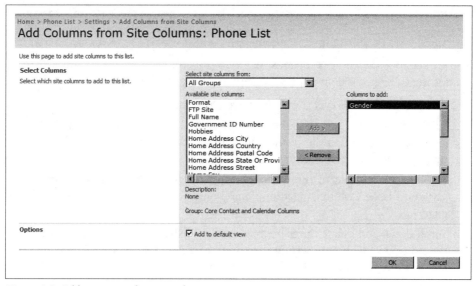

Figure 4-8. Adding a site column to a list

The Gender site column is a simple choice column containing Male/Female options. The advantages of using a site column in this case are:

- You don't have to create your own Gender column each time you want to provide this choice.

- The choice is consistent across sites: it's always Male/Female, not M/F, or Yes/No (just kidding).

Customizing Site Columns

Most of the built-in site columns are simple text or date columns that include the name and description of the column. Exceptions to that rule are listed in Table 4-3.

Table 4-3. Special built-in site columns

Site column	Values
Append Only Comments	Multiline text: can only add text, not change or delete
Assigned To	Lookup from site users
Gender	Choice: Male/Female
Issue Status	Choice: Active/Resolved/Closed
Language	Choice from list of spoken languages
Priority	Choice: (1) High/(2) Normal/(3) Low
Related Issue	Lookup from Issues list
Status	Choice: Not Started/Draft/Reviewed/Scheduled/Published/Final/Expired
Task Status	Choice: Not Started/In Progress/Completed/Deferred/Waiting on someone else
UDC Purpose	Choice: Read Only/Write Only/Read Write

You can change the choices for most of these site columns—interestingly, you *can't* change the Gender site column. For example, to simplify the Status choices:

1. Navigate to the top-level site in the site collection.
2. Click Site Actions → Site Settings, and then click Site Columns under the Galleries heading in the middle of the page. (In MOSS, click Site Actions → Site Settings → Modify All Site Settings.)
3. Scroll to the bottom of the page and click the Status link just above the Core Task and Issue Columns heading. SharePoint displays the Change Site Column page.
4. Scroll down and delete the Scheduled and Published choices from the list under the Additional Columns Settings heading; then click OK. SharePoint changes the list of choices for all lists that use the column.

 Removing choices from a site column doesn't change the data in lists, it just changes the choices displayed when a user adds a new item to a list or edits an existing item.

Creating New Site Columns

Site columns share values across all of the sites within a site collection. They are set at the top-level site in the site collection, and those changes aren't shared with other site collections.

You create new site columns to share values across all sites in a collection. A Department Lookup column makes a good example, since it's best to have a single place to maintain the list of departments in case of a reorg. To create a Department site column complete these tasks:

1. Create a Departments list in the top-level site and add items to the list.

2. Delete the built-in Department site column. That column is a text column, so we'll be replacing it with a Lookup column.

3. Create a new Department site column that looks up its values from the Departments list.

4. Add a new custom Department site column to the Phone List sample.

To create a top-level Departments list:

1. Navigate to the top-level site in the site collection.

2. Click Site Actions → Create, and click Custom List under the Custom Lists heading. (In MOSS, click Site Actions → View All Site Content → Create.) SharePoint displays the Site Column Gallery page.

3. Name the list "Departments," select No for "Display this list on the Quick Launch," and click Create. SharePoint displays the new list.

4. Click Actions → Edit in Datasheet and enter a list of your company's departments.

To delete the built-in Department site column:

1. Click Site Actions → Site Settings, and then click Site Columns under the Core Contact and Calendar Columns heading. (In MOSS, click Site Actions → Site Settings → Modify All Site Settings.) SharePoint displays the Change Site Column page.

2. Scroll to the bottom of the page and click Delete. SharePoint displays a warning. Click OK to delete the column.

To add the new custom Department column:

1. On the Site Column Gallery page, click Create. SharePoint displays the New Site Column page.

2. Complete the page as shown in Figure 4-9 and click OK. Name the column "Dept" as shown; we'll change that next.

3. Click on the Dept column in the Site Column Gallery and change the name from Dept to Department; then click OK.

 You can't name the new column Department directly—that name is reserved by SharePoint. That's why you have to name it Dept; then change that name to Department in step 3. That create-and-rename trick solves similar problems in other places, so please remember it!

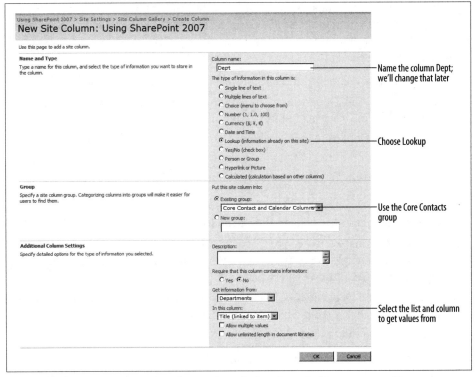

Figure 4-9. Creating a custom site column using a lookup from the Departments table

To use the new Departments site column in the Phone List sample:

1. On the Phone List toolbar, click Settings → List Settings, and click the Department column in the columns list.

2. Rename the Department column "Department Old" and click OK.

3. Scroll to the end of the Columns list and click "Add from existing site columns."

4. Select the Department site column, click Add, and then click OK.

5. Display the Phone List and click Actions → Edit in Datasheet.

6. Select the values in the Department Old column and drag them to the Department column. SharePoint moves the values from one column to the other.

After you move the values, you can delete the Department Old column from the Phone List and update the view used by the web part on the home page.

Creating Master Lists

Figure 4-10 shows the updated Phone List web part that uses the new Department Lookup column to group the phone numbers. To see why I used a lookup site column in this sample rather than a choice site column, follow these steps:

1. Click on the Information Technology department link on the Phone List web part. SharePoint displays the item in the Departments list.
2. Click Edit Item and change the name to "IT," then click OK.
3. Go back to the Phone List web part and refresh the page. The Information Technology department is now shown as IT.

Not only that, but the name is updated throughout the site collection! In this case, the Department list functions as a *master list* for the site collection.

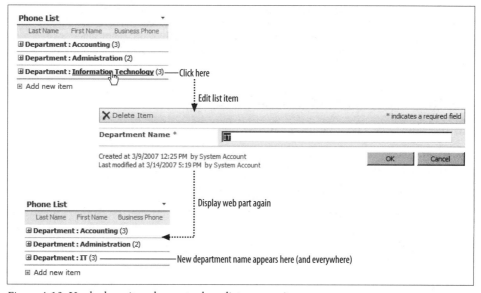

Figure 4-10. Use lookup site columns to share lists across sites

Lookups link lists together. Site columns span site boundaries. You combine them to create master lists. Master lists have these characteristics:

- Exist at the top-level site in a site collection
- Have a lookup site column
- Hold values that need to be reused throughout the site collection

SharePoint does not have a way to create global master lists—lists can't span site collections. To reuse the master list in other site collections, you must copy the list to the other site collection and create a new site column in that collection.

Creating Views

So far we've created a simplified view for entering items in the Phone List, we've seen the datasheet view, and we've created a view for the Phone List web part. That's a pretty good survey of the basic uses of views. We use views to:

- Simplify data entry.
- Summarize information in a web part.
- Group or filter information for a specific purpose or audience.

Earlier, I said views are like reports. Actually, they are a lot better: reports are static, but views are updated every time you refresh the web page. In this section, I'll focus on how to create views that help monitor the status of items in an Issue Tracking list.

 The Issue Tracking list is one of the most useful templates included in SharePoint. It helps manage problems (a friend calls those opportunities) and their resolutions. It can automatically send email when an issue is assigned, and it keeps a history of the issue as changes are made.

Creating Report Views for Issue Tracking

To create the Issue Tracking list for this sample:

1. Click Site Actions → Create, and click the Issue Tracking link under the Tracking heading in the middle of the page.
2. Name the list "Problem Reports" and click Create.

The Issue Tracking template includes views that display All Issues, Active Issues, and My Issues (issues assigned to you). Management wants to see issues that have not yet been assigned and issues that are either overdue or are taking a long time to resolve. In this sample, I'll create two new views to address those needs:

- The Unassigned view will show only items that have not yet been assigned to anyone.
- The Alert view will display items that are past their due date or more than two weeks old.

The Unassigned view is the easiest, so I'll create that first. To create a view of unassigned items:

1. Drop-down the View list and click Create View as shown in Figure 4-11. SharePoint displays the Create View page.
2. Click Standard View. SharePoint displays the Create View page.
3. Name the view "Unassigned," select "Make this the default view," and scroll down to the Filter section.

4. Click And, and select "Assigned To is equal to" as shown in Figure 4-12. (Leave the last field blank.)

5. Scroll to the end of the page and click OK. SharePoint creates the view and makes it the new default view for the list.

6. Click New; add a test item to verify that the view displays only unassigned items.

Figure 4-11. Creating a new view for the Problem Reports list

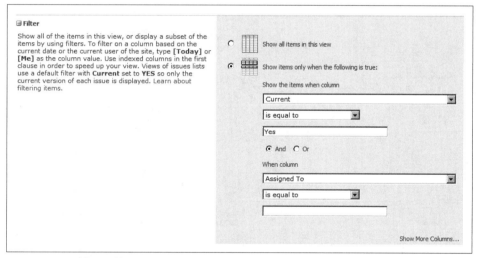

Figure 4-12. Adding a filter to display only unassigned items

The Current column filter in Figure 4-12 ensures that the most recent item appears in the view. If you remove that filter, the item history is also displayed.

 Use the And filter operator to *narrow* the list of items displayed in a view. Use the Or filter operator to *broaden* the list of displayed items.

Creating the Alert view is more complex because there are two different criteria:

- Management wants to see items that aren't resolved by their due date.
- It also wants to include items that are more than 14 days old.

To satisfy that last requirement, we need to add a calculated column based on the Created date. Then, we can create a view that uses a filter to combine the criteria. To add the calculated column:

1. On the list toolbar, click Settings → Create Column. SharePoint displays the Create Column page.

2. Complete the page as shown in Figure 4-13 and click OK. SharePoint adds a new calculated Alert column to the list.

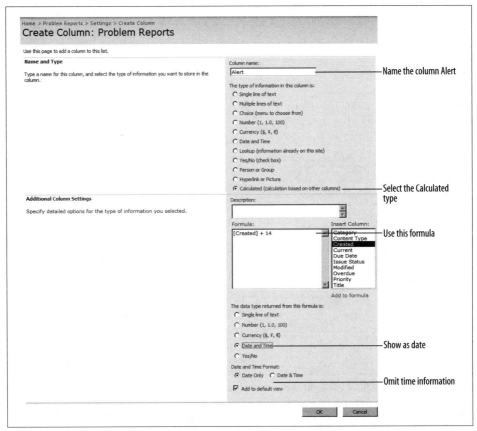

Figure 4-13. Create an Alert column that calculates the date two weeks after the problem is reported

To create the Alert view:

1. Drop-down the View list and click Create View. SharePoint displays the Create View page.

2. Click Standard View. SharePoint displays the Create View page.

3. Name the view "Alert" and scroll down to the Filter section.

4. Complete the filter as shown in Figure 4-14.

5. Scroll to the end of the page and click OK. SharePoint creates the view and makes it the new default view for the list.

6. Change the Due Date of the test item to verify that the view displays only overdue items.

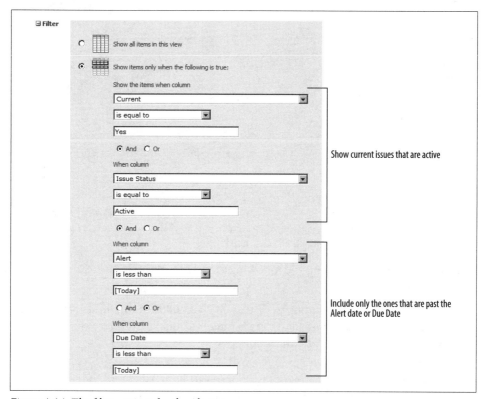

Figure 4-14. The filter settings for the Alert view

The trick of adding a calculated column to help create a view is a good one to know, especially when working with dates. That technique is required because SharePoint doesn't let you perform calculations within filters. Try entering the filter "Due Date is less than [Today] – 7"—it won't work!

Formatting Views

In addition to the filter settings, views have a number of other settings that let you format their appearance on the Create View and Edit View pages (see Figure 4-15).

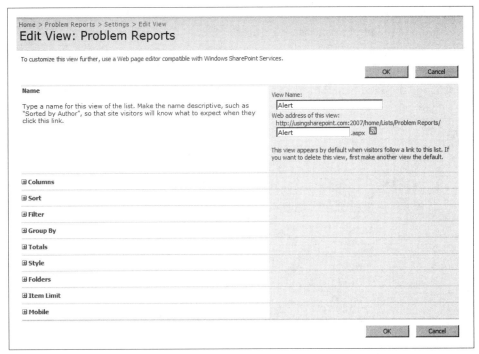

Figure 4-15. View settings are organized into sections

View settings are organized into the following sections:

Columns section

Lets you select which columns to display. It's a good idea to limit the number of columns to what fits horizontally on a standard display. Otherwise, users will have to scroll sideways to get the whole view.

Sort section

Specifies the columns to sort on. Use sorting to help users find the information they want. Usually that means sorting by Title in ascending order or by Create (creation date) in descending order (most recent first).

Group By section

Use this section to create tree-views of list items. Group By sections also sort items and take precedence over the Sort section. The Phone List web part uses Group By to organize phone numbers by department.

Total section

Use this section to provide a count or sum of items. Totals combine with Group By to give running totals for each category.

Style section

This section applies formatting to the view. I like to use the Shaded view for most lists since it makes rows easier to read. (Shaded applies shading to alternate rows.)

Folders section

This section applies to document libraries, so I'll discuss that in Chapter 5.

Item Limit section

This section sets the size of the batch of items displayed on a page. If you want to display all of the items in a list, set the number very high. Otherwise, large lists are broken into multiple pages.

Mobile section

The Mobile lets you create a view for mobile devices, which have much smaller screens.

The best way to learn about formatting views is to experiment with the settings yourself. It's a good idea to create a style guide when you find a combination of settings that you like. I've found these general design rules work best:

- Limit the number of columns to what will appear on a screen that is 1,024 pixels wide. 800 pixels generally won't fit enough information, and most displays now support 1,024.

- Use the Shaded style. I've noticed folks have less trouble reading that style, and it looks nice.

- Avoid Totals in standard views. They look better and make more sense in datasheet views.

- Set the item limit so that views page *or* scroll—don't do both. I've found users often miss the paging links at the bottom of the page, but they understand how to scroll. I reserve paging for lists with more than 1,000 items, and then I try to fit each page on a single screen (Number of items to display: 20, display items in batches of specified size).

Feel free to use those suggestions as a starting point for your own style guide, or come up with one that's completely your own. If you include pictures and print it out, folks will be more likely to follow the guide (and you'll be surprised by how welcome it is).

Renaming a List and Changing Other Settings

To rename a list after it is created:

- On the list toolbar, click Settings → List Settings and then click "Title, description, and navigation" under the General Settings heading on the left side of the page (see Figure 4-16).

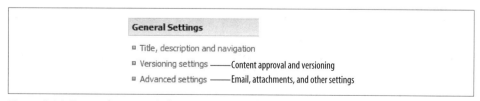

Figure 4-16. Types of settings on the List Settings page

Changing Email and Attachment Settings

The Problem Reports list can send email notifying employees when an item is assigned to them. To enable that feature:

- Click Advanced Settings on the list Settings page and select Yes under the E-Mail Notification section.

If the E-Mail Notification section is disabled, SharePoint's email features are not configured or are disabled. Figure 4-17 shows the other advanced settings.

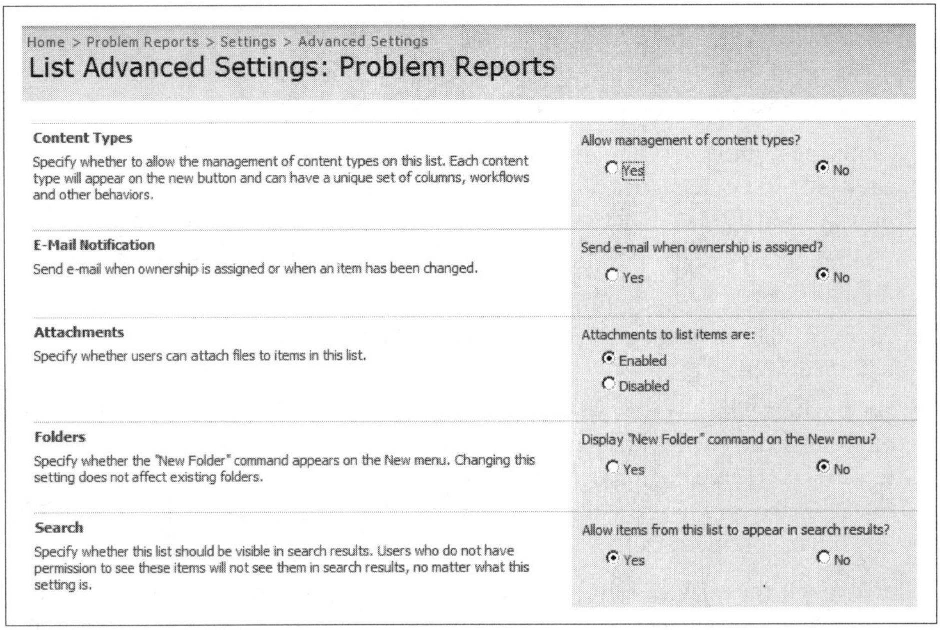

Figure 4-17. Use the Advanced Settings page to send email when an issue is assigned

Advanced Settings can also enable or disable file attachments to list items. Attachments allow users to upload files (such as a screenshot of an error) when they create a new item. In the case of the Problem Reports list, attachments are very useful, but for other list types they may not be needed.

Approval and Change History

The Problem Reports list tracks the change history of each item—that's one of the main features of the Issue Tracking template—so versioning is On by default. To enable change history for other list types:

- Click "Versioning settings" on the list Settings page and select Yes under the Item Version History section (see Figure 4-18).

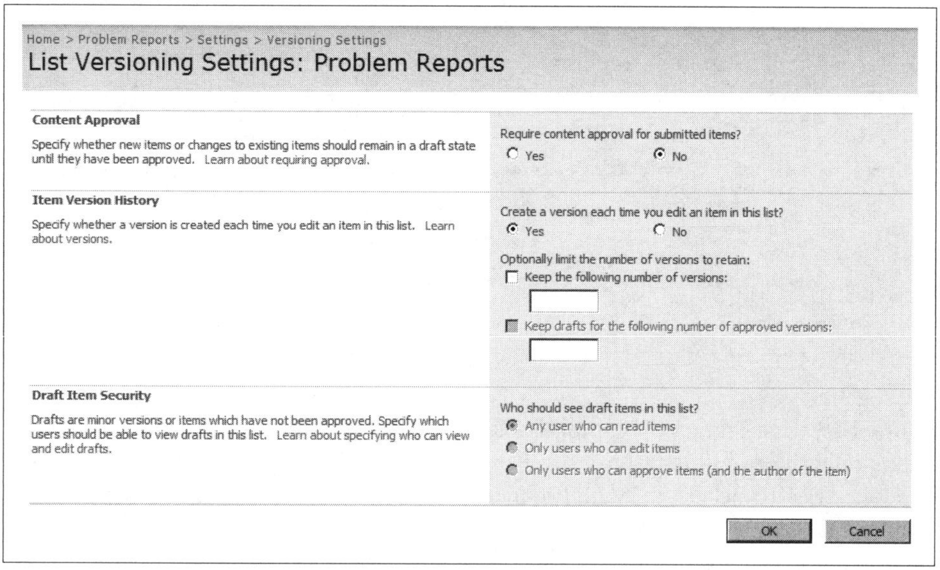

Figure 4-18. Use the Versioning settings to enable change history and to require content approval

Use the Content Approval option when you want to control what items appear in a list. I use that setting in Discussion Board lists that are open to the public—I want to review all posts before they appear on my web site.

Enabling Content Approval adds a view to the list that lets the site owner approve, reject, or delete items submitted to the list. It's a good idea to set an alert on lists that require content approval so you know when something is pending your approval. See Chapter 8 for instructions on setting alerts.

Controlling Access to Lists

Lists inherit permissions from their parent site. You can restrict access to an entire list or to items within a list.

To restrict who has access to a list:

1. On the list toolbar, click Settings → List Settings, and click "Permissions for this list" under the Permissions and Management heading in the middle of the page. SharePoint displays the Permissions page.

2. Click Actions → Edit Permissions. SharePoint displays a warning that you are creating unique permissions.

3. Click OK to proceed. SharePoint changes the display of the Permissions page so that you can edit the permissions.

4. Select a user or group and click Actions → Remove User Permissions to remove access to the list for those users as shown in Figure 4-19.

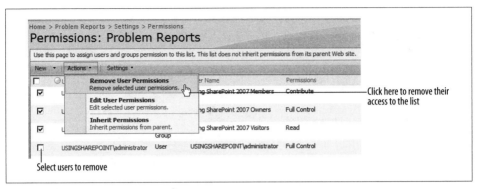

Figure 4-19. Restricting access to a list

Figure 4-19 shows removing permissions for all users except the Administrator. That means only the Administrator can see the list; it is hidden from everyone else and if someone tries to access it, SharePoint displays an Error: Access Denied page (see Figure 4-20). Those two points confuse some folks:

- In SharePoint, you generally can't see what you can't access. That means some lists, libraries, and sites may not appear on the Quick Launch or link bar for some users. That makes instructing users interesting sometimes!

- The Access Denied page lets you sign in as a different user. Most folks have only one account, so that makes little sense to them. But when you're helping someone, it's handy to sign in as yourself, grant that person access, and then sign out by closing the browser (be sure to do that so the user doesn't proceed with your credentials).

Figure 4-20. What the user sees if he/she doesn't have permissions to access something

You can also restrict access to individual items in a list. To do that:

1. Click Manage Permissions on the list item's Edit menu, as shown in Figure 4-21.

2. Follow the same steps as for restricting access to a list.

Notice that I've only talked about restricting access. Actually, you can increase permissions as well, but that's a much less common practice. In general, permissions are more restricted the deeper you go into a site hierarchy.

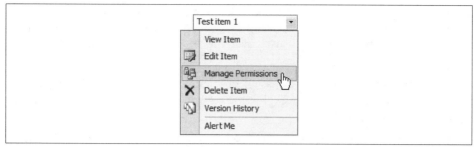

Figure 4-21. Use the edit menu to restrict access to individual items

Part of the reason for that is simplicity—it's way too hard to remember how permissions are set if they don't follow the physical structure. The other reason is visibility: as I mentioned above, SharePoint hides restricted items, so if a user has read access to a list within a site that she can't see…it's very hard for her to find that list.

Editing List Pages

SharePoint lists use these web pages to add, edit, and view items:

NewForm.aspx
> Creates a new item and adds it to the list.

EditForm.aspx
> Edits an item from the list.

DispForm.aspx
> Displays an item in read-only mode.

AllItems.aspx, MyItems.aspx, and so on
> Display a view of the list; views are stored as *.aspx* files alongside the add/edit/display pages.

These files are stored in the list's folder within the site. For example, the Problem Reports new item page is stored at *./Lists/Problem%20%Reports/NewForm.aspx*.

Why is that important? Because you can edit those pages to hide fields, add web parts, or change them in any other way. To edit pages directly, you'll need Share-Point Designer. SharePoint Designer is "new" for 2007, but really it is just an updated and renamed version of Microsoft FrontPage.

There are a number of reasons why you might want to edit one of these standard pages:

- To restrict what information is entered in new items
- To display additional information on the page
- To create a page that combines tasks

In the following sample, I'll use SharePoint Designer to create a custom page to submit problem reports. I won't go into detail on how to use SharePoint Designer (that's a subject for another book); I'll just cover the basics required to complete these application requirements:

- Managers don't want users to assign problems, set their priority, change their status, or categorize problems. Those tasks will be performed once the item is reviewed by a technician.

- Users need a single place to go to submit items—they don't want to navigate deep into a site or lose their place once they've submitted an item.

- Users want to see the items they've submitted so they can tell if the issues have been resolved.

The following sections address each of those needs in turn.

Simplifying the New Item Form

The first task is to remove the unwanted fields from the *NewForm.aspx* page. To do that:

1. Open the web site in SharePoint Designer.

2. Open the *NewForm.aspx* page from the *./Lists/Problem%20%Reports/* folder.

3. Click on the Problem Reports list web part and change the IsIncluded element to false in the code pane as shown here:

        <IsIncluded>false</IsIncluded>

4. Click Insert → SharePoint Controls → Custom List Form. SharePoint Designer displays the List or Document Library Form.

5. Select the Problem Reports list and the New item form, and clear the Show standard toolbar checkbox as shown in Figure 4-22. SharePoint Designer adds a list form web part that can be edited.

6. Select the Assigned To, Issue Status, Priority, Category, and Related Issues table rows and press Ctrl+X to remove those rows.

7. Save the page and review the changes in SharePoint by clicking New on the list toolbar. It should look like Figure 4-23.

The Assigned To and Due Date fields are blank for new problem reports. You can set default values for those fields from the list settings page. You might want to set the default Due Date to [Today] + 14, and the default Assigned To person to the department manager. Since the Due Date appears on the *NewForm.aspx* page, it can be changed by the user; but since Assigned To doesn't, new items are always assigned to that default person.

If this were a real application, you'd go back to your customer at this point and ask what default values he wants—that information was left out of the spec!

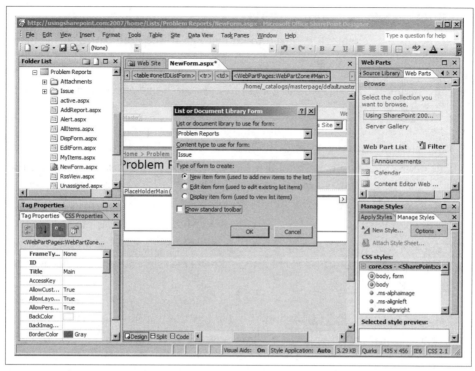

Figure 4-22. Replacing the form web part with a custom list form in SharePoint Designer

Figure 4-23. The vastly simplified form for entering Problem Reports

Making It Easier to Submit Items

Under the current scheme, users need to know to go to the Problem Report list and click on New to submit a report. Once the report is submitted, they are returned to the Problem Reports list. That's more clicking than they should really need to do. We can simplify their task by adding a tab to the site's home page for the *NewForm. aspx* page. To do that in WSS:

1. Click Site Actions → Site Settings, and then click Top link bar tab under the Look and Feel heading. SharePoint displays the Top Link Bar page.

2. Click New Link and enter the full address of the *NewForm.aspx* page; enter the label for the tab in the description field, and then click OK. SharePoint adds a tab to the top link bar for submitting problem reports.

To add a top link bar tab for the new item form in MOSS:

1. Click Site Actions → Site Settings → Modify All Site Settings, and then click Navigation under the Look and Feel heading. SharePoint displays the Site Navigation Settings page.

2. In the Global Navigation section, select "Display only the navigation items below the current site" to stop inheriting link bar tabs from the parent site.

3. In the Navigation Editing and Sorting section, select Global Navigation, click Add Link, and enter the full address of the *NewForm.aspx* page. Enter the label for the tab in the description field; then click OK. SharePoint adds a tab to the top link bar for submitting problem reports.

Providing Feedback After Submitting

When a user completes the new item form and clicks OK, SharePoint automatically displays the default view of the list. That's not great feedback and it leaves the user with a few questions: Was the new item accepted? Which one is it? What do I do next?

To solve those problems, modify the default view of the list to display the new item clearly and to let the user know what to do next. To create the new view, follow the steps in "Creating Views," earlier in this chapter, to create a new standard view for the Problem Reports list with the settings shown in Table 4-4.

Table 4-4. Create View page settings for the Submitted view

Section	Field: Setting
Name	View Name: Submitted
	Make this the default view: Checked
	Create a Public View: Selected
Columns	Select: Attachments, Issue ID, Type, Title, Assigned To, Due Date

Table 4-4. Create View page settings for the Submitted view (continued)

Section	Field: Setting
Sort	Modified, descending order
Filter	Current is equal to Yes
	And
	Created By is equal to [ME]
Group By	Issue Status, ascending order
	By default, show groups: Expanded
Style	Shaded
Item Limit	20, display items in batches

The new view displays only the items the current user has submitted, and new items appear at the top of the list under the Active group with a green New! icon beside them. That's clearer feedback, but the user still won't know what to do next. To fix that, edit the view page to add a web part containing instructions:

1. Display the Submitted view.
2. Click Site Actions → Edit Page. SharePoint displays the view in Edit mode.
3. Click Add a Web Part in the middle of the page, select the Content Editor Web Page, and click Add. SharePoint adds the new web part to the page.
4. Click the "Open the tool pane" link on the web part, click the Source Editor button, and enter the following code:

```
<script type="text/javascript">
if(document.referrer.indexOf("NewForm")>=0)
  document.write("<h3>Thank you for your report</h3>
    <a href='./NewForm.aspx'>Click here</a> to submit
    another report or <a href='../..'>click here</a>
    to go Home.");
</script>
```

5. Click Save and then click OK to close the property pane of the web part.

The preceding example shows how to create a web part that runs client-side code. I call those *client-side web parts,* and they are powerful tools for customizing Share-Point. In this case, the web part displays a thank you message if the user has just submitted an item. That message is not displayed if the user just clicked on a link to the list.

When complete, the changes to *NewForm.aspx* and *Submitted.aspx* establish the simple Problem Reports workflow shown in Figure 4-24.

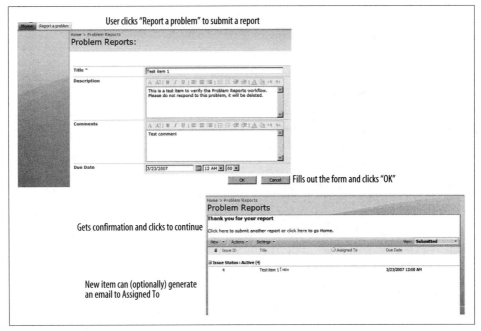

Figure 4-24. The completed Problem Reports application

Resetting the List Forms

SharePoint Designer sometimes breaks the link between the pages used to view, edit, and create list items. If the list starts showing Page Not Found errors, you'll need to reset the form files for the list. To do that:

1. Open the web site in SharePoint Designer.
2. Expand the *Lists* folder in the Folder List pane on the left side of the screen.
3. Right-click on the list in the Folder List pane and select Properties. SharePoint displays the list properties.
4. Click the Supporting Files tab and select the correct new item form as shown in Figure 4-25.

Saving the List As a Template

Part of the beauty of SharePoint is that you can easily reuse your work. In the case of the Problem Reports list, this means you can save the list as a template, and then use that template to create new lists that include your unassigned and alert views, and any other customizations. Saving a list as a template is very similar to saving a site as a template.

Figure 4-25. Resetting the form pages used by the list

To see how this works:

1. On the list toolbar click Settings → List Settings, and then click "Save list as template" under the Permissions and Management heading. SharePoint displays the Save as Template page.

2. Enter the settings in Table 4-5 and click OK. SharePoint saves the list as a template and adds it to the site collection's list template gallery.

3. Click Site Actions → Create, and then click Problem Report Sample 1.0 beneath the Tracking heading to create a test list based on the template.

4. Add items to the list to verify that it works.

Table 4-5. List template settings

Option	Setting
File name	ProblemReport10
Template title	Problem Report Sample 1.0
Template description	Sample list for tracking/assigning opportunities
Include content	Clear

Deploying List Templates

List templates are saved at site collection level. That means the *ProblemReport10* template is available to all sites in the site collection. Deploying a list template is very similar to deploying a site template. To deploy the template to another site collection:

1. Navigate to the top-level site in the source site collection.
2. Click Site Actions → Site Settings, and click "List templates" under the Galleries heading. (In MOSS, click Actions → Site Settings → Modify All Site Settings.) SharePoint displays the List Template Gallery.
3. Click the *ProblemReport10* link in the gallery. SharePoint asks if you want to save the file.
4. Click Save to download the template. Be sure to store it in your *Templates* folder on your computer to stay organized.
5. Navigate to the site collection where you want to install the template and repeat step 1 to display the List Template Gallery for that site collection.
6. Click Upload on the gallery toolbar and upload the file you created in step 3. SharePoint copies the file into the List Template Gallery.

Lists that include Lookup columns will have problems when used in other site collections since the source list for the lookup won't exist in the new location. Avoid Lookup columns when creating lists for reuse as list templates. The exceptions to that rule are when the list template is reused within the current site or when the lookup is a site column and the template is reused within the current site collection.

Best Practices

- Create a gallery containing sample lists created from the built-in list templates and any general-purpose custom list templates you create.
- Use Lookup columns to link lists together and to provide drill-down.
- Lookups link lists together. Site columns span site boundaries. You combine them to create master lists that cross site boundaries.
- Use calculated columns to create alert dates within lists. You can then filter on those dates to create views that highlight items *before* they are overdue.
- Create a style guide for creating list views. This will help views have a more consistent appearance across sites and save users a lot of time trying out different settings.
- Avoid Lookup columns when creating lists for reuse as list templates.
- Restrict permissions as you go deeper into the site hierarchy. Permissions should follow the physical structure.
- Create a custom default view to display feedback to users after they submit new items.
- Use a client-side web part to display a conditional message confirming new items.

CHAPTER 5

Creating Libraries

Libraries organize content within a site. Technically, libraries are a special type of list that provides these key features:

- Templates for creating new documents
- An optional approval status field that indicates whether the document is pending, approved, or rejected
- Storage for previous versions of documents
- The ability to reserve documents by checking them in and out
- Synchronization between list columns and properties stored in the document
- Integration with Microsoft Office products like Word, Excel, and PowerPoint

Just about anything you can do with a list, you can do with a document library, so the topics covered in Chapter 4 apply equally to libraries. I won't repeat those here. Instead, I will talk about the features that are unique to libraries and explore their use. At the end of the chapter, I'll apply what you've learned and show you how to use document libraries for project, task, document control, and archive applications.

 If you need help adding columns, lookups, or views to a library, see Chapter 4. If you need help working with libraries from Microsoft Office, see Chapter 2.

Using the Built-in Library Templates

SharePoint provides a set of built-in library templates that you can use as a starting point. Tables 5-1 and 5-2 describe the library templates that come with SharePoint.

Table 5-1. Built-in library templates

Category	Library	Use to
Libraries	Document Library	Collect and share Office documents and other files.
	Form Library	Publish InfoPath forms for collecting structured data such as timesheets, purchase order requests, and other business forms.
	Wiki Page Library	Share web pages that can be edited by multiple authors.
	Picture Library	Collect and share image files.
Web Pages	Basic Page	Store HTML-format web pages.
	Web Part Page	Store SharePoint web part pages.

Table 5-2. Additional library templates provided in MOSS

Category	Library	Use to
Libraries	Translation Management Library	Create documents in multiple languages and manage their translation.
	Report Library	Publish Excel report spreadsheets.
	Data Connection Library	Publish Office Data Connection (ODC) and Universal Data Connection (UDC) files.
	Slide Library	Publish slides from PowerPoint 2007 presentations.

Choosing a Document Template

The web page libraries shown in Table 5-1 are actually subtypes of the Document Library template. To see all of the library subtypes:

1. Click Site Actions → Create, and then click Document Library under the Libraries heading. SharePoint displays the New library page.

2. Click the Document Template drop-down list. SharePoint displays the available templates as shown in Figure 5-1.

Selecting a template in Figure 5-1 creates a new, blank template file in the library's Forms folder and associates the library with that document type. For example, choosing the Microsoft Office Excel spreadsheet template creates a *template.xlsx* file in the Forms folder and associates the library with Excel 2007 as shown by the Edit menu (see Figure 5-2).

Removing Unneeded Document Templates

Having both Office 97 through 2003 and Office 2007 document types in Figure 5-1 can cause confusion. If your company has transitioned to Office 2007, it is a good idea to remove the previous Office versions from the list of choices. Conversely, if you are standardized on Office 2003, you should remove the 2007 types until you make the transition.

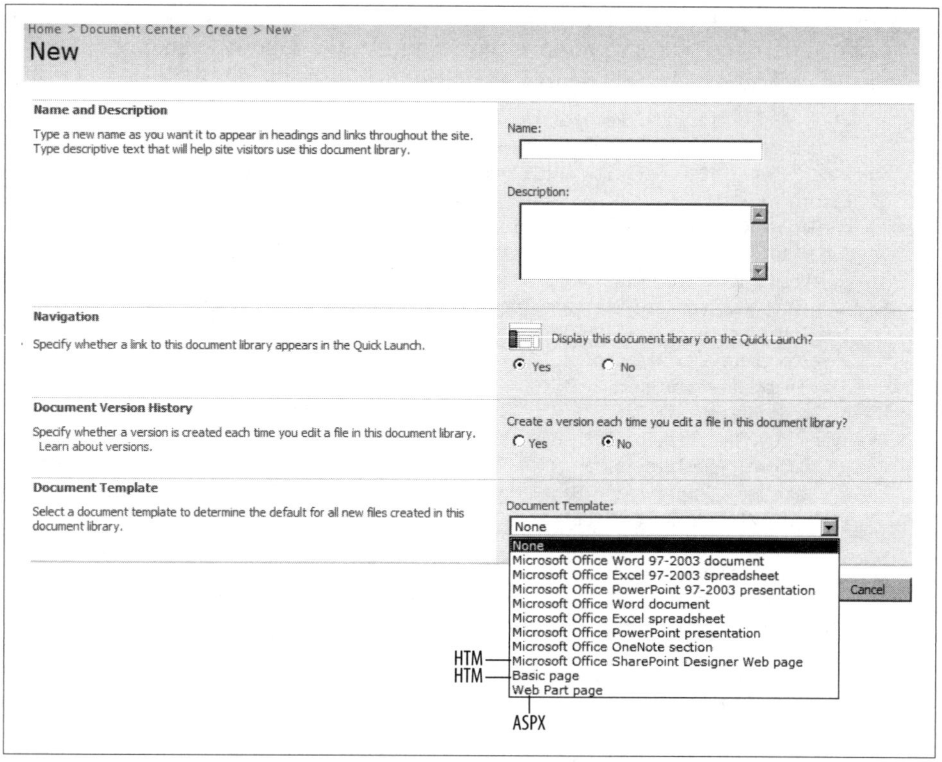

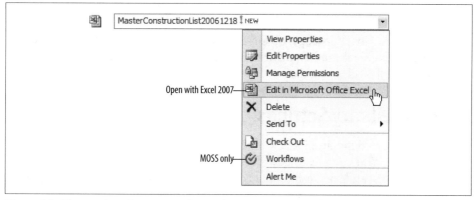

Figure 5-1. Choosing a document template determines the subtype of the library

Figure 5-2. The template determines what application appears on the Edit menu

To remove file types from the document templates list:

1. Make a backup copy of the following file on the SharePoint server:

   *C:\Program Files\Common Files\Microsoft Shared\web server extensions\12\
   TEMPLATE\SiteTemplates\sts\xml\ONET.xml*

2. Open *ONET.xml* for editing and comment out the <DocumentTemplate> elements for document templates to remove. For example, the following changes remove the Office 97 through 2003 template choices:

```
<!-- JAW, 03/19/2007: Removed the Office 97-2003 file types.
    <DocumentTemplate Path="STS" Name="" DisplayName="$Resources:core,doctemp_
None;" Type="100" Default="FALSE" Description="$Resources:core,doctemp_None_
Desc;" />
    <DocumentTemplate Path="STS" DisplayName="$Resources:core,doctemp_Word97;"
Type="101" Default="TRUE" Description="$Resources:core,doctemp_Word97_Desc;">
      <DocumentTemplateFiles>
        <DocumentTemplateFile Name="doctemp\word\wdtmpl.doc" TargetName="Forms/
template.doc" Default="TRUE" />
      </DocumentTemplateFiles>
    </DocumentTemplate>
    <DocumentTemplate Path="STS" DisplayName="$Resources:core,doctemp_Excel97;"
Type="103" Description="$Resources:core,doctemp_Excel97_Desc;">
      <DocumentTemplateFiles>
        <DocumentTemplateFile Name="doctemp\xl\xltmpl.xls" TargetName="Forms/
template.xls" Default="TRUE" />
      </DocumentTemplateFiles>
    </DocumentTemplate>
    <DocumentTemplate Path="STS" DisplayName="$Resources:core,doctemp_
Powerpoint97;" Type="104" Description="$Resources:core,doctemp_Powerpoint97_
Desc;">
      <DocumentTemplateFiles>
        <DocumentTemplateFile Name="doctemp\ppt\pptmpl.pot" TargetName="Forms/
template.pot" Default="TRUE" />
      </DocumentTemplateFiles>
    </DocumentTemplate>
-->
```

3. Run *iisreset.exe* to restart SharePoint and load the changes.

Be sure to make a backup copy of *ONET.xml* and to comment your changes as shown here. If you break something or if you need to deploy your changes to another installation, you'll be glad you did!

Changing Library Settings

Most of the built-in templates include a new, empty Shared Documents library when they are created. You can create new documents, upload existing ones, create folders, check out files, and sort or filter the contents of the library using the toolbar and Edit menu, as shown in Figure 5-3.

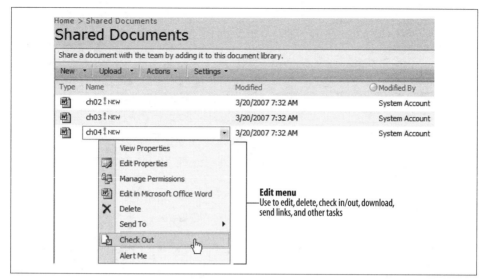

Figure 5-3. Using the library toolbar and Edit menus

The Shared Documents library is very generic, and you often need to make these common adjustments to it:

- Turn on versioning and/or document approval.
- Modify the template used when creating new documents.

The following sections show you how to work with those settings.

Turning On Versioning and Approval

The standard Shared Documents library doesn't include approval status or version history by default. To enable these features:

1. Click Settings → Document Library Settings, and then click "Versioning settings" under the General Settings heading on the left side of the page. SharePoint displays the Document Library Versioning Settings page.

2. Change the settings as shown in Figure 5-4 and click OK.

Versioning is not turned on by default when you create a new document library because it requires additional storage space and because the versioned libraries are slightly harder to use: the versioning process can hide minor revisions and may require files to be checked out before changes can be made. Be sure to explain your versioning process to those who will be editing documents in these libraries.

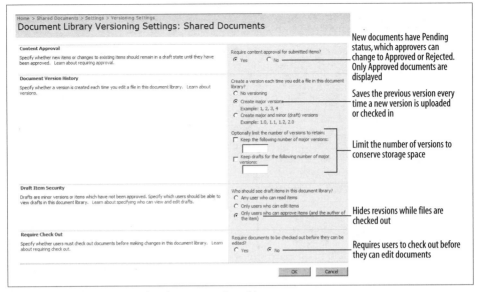

Figure 5-4. Enabling approval and versioning for a library

Approving Documents

If you select Yes in Content Approval in Figure 5-4, new documents must be approved before they appear to a general audience. Members of Approvers, Owners, and Administrative groups have the honor of approving or rejecting documents.

To approve or reject pending documents:

1. Navigate to the library and select "Approve/Reject" items from the toolbar's View menu. SharePoint displays a view that groups documents by their approval status.

2. Select Approve/Reject from the document's Edit menu. SharePoint displays the Approve/Reject page (see Figure 5-5).

3. Select an approval status, enter a comment, and click OK.

When you enable approval status, SharePoint adds views for changing the status and for checking documents that were submitted. The My Submissions view lets contributors check the status of their pending documents.

Approvers can see the pending documents awaiting their approval by checking the Approve/Reject Items view or by setting an alert on the document library.

To set an alert:

1. Click Actions → Alert Me on the library toolbar. SharePoint displays the New Alert page.

2. In the Change Type section, select "New items are added." In When to Send Alerts, select "Send a daily summary" and then click OK. SharePoint will now send you a daily email if documents are added to the library.

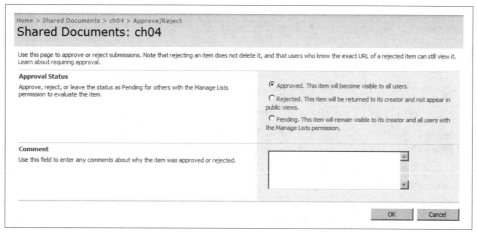

Figure 5-5. Approving/rejecting documents

I recommend getting daily summaries rather than immediate alerts because it is more efficient to group your work in batches. If you set a lot of alerts, it is easy to get bombed by email and it's more likely you will miss something.

Granting Approve Permission

MOSS includes an Approvers group specifically for users who can approve and reject documents but do not have other special permissions. In WSS, the Owners and Administrators groups can Approve/Reject, but they also have considerably more power. If you are using WSS, you may want to create a separate permissions level for approvers.

To create an Approve permission level in WSS:

1. At the top-level web site, click Site Actions → Site Settings, and click "Advanced permissions" under the Users and Permissions heading. SharePoint displays the Permissions page.

2. On the toolbar, click Settings → "Permission levels," and then click Add a Permission Level. SharePoint displays the Add a Permission Level page.

3. Name the permission "Approve," select Approve Items in List Permissions, and click Create at the bottom of the page. SharePoint creates the new permission level.

The Approve permission level now appears in the list of permissions that can be assigned to users or groups.

Changing the Document Template

The document template in Shared Documents (*template.doc*) is really just a place-holder for your own template. SharePoint uses *.doc* files rather than *.dot* files for templates because it doesn't actually tell Word to create a new file when you click New

Document, it just downloads the template as a starting point. When the user saves the document, Word saves the file to the document library.

You change the document library template when you want to use that library for a specific type of document, such as an NDA agreement or other standard contract.

To edit the template used by a library:

1. Click Settings → Document Library Settings, and then click Advanced Settings under the General Settings heading on the left side of the page. SharePoint displays the Document Library Advanced Settings page (see Figure 5-6).

2. Click the Edit Template link in the Document Template section. SharePoint opens the document template for editing.

3. Make your changes or cut and paste content from an existing template. Save and close the document when you're done.

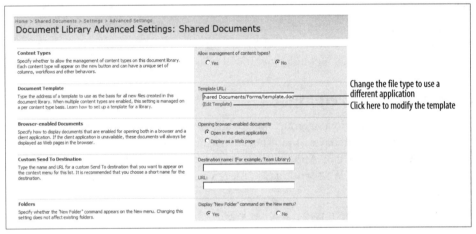

Figure 5-6. Changing the library's document template

Now when you choose New Document from the library, SharePoint uses your new template document. SharePoint uses the file type of the document template to determine which application to use when creating new documents.

To change the application from Word to Excel:

1. Create an Excel file on your desktop to use as the template. SharePoint calls these templates, but they are really just documents (not *.xlt* files). For consistency, name the file *template.xls*.

2. In the document library, click Actions → Open with Windows Explorer. SharePoint opens the library in an Explorer window.

3. Open the Forms folder and drag and drop *template.xls* from your desktop to the Forms folder.

4. On the Document Library Advanced Settings page for the library, change the template file name from *template.doc* to *template.xls*.

5. Click OK to make the change.

Document library templates are limited to the file types that SharePoint knows how to open for editing: Word (*.doc/.docx/.docm*), Excel (*.xls/.xlsx/.xlsm*), or PowerPoint (*.ppt/.pptx/.pptm*). SharePoint also provides specific library templates for some other file types, such as SharePoint Designer pages (*.htm*), Web Part Pages (*.aspx*), Picture Libraries (image types), and InfoPath Form Libraries (*.xml*).

Adding Content Types

Most libraries are associated with one document template, which determines the default application used to create new files. You add templates by creating new content types for the site, and then adding them to the library. This creates a mixed-type library, which displays more than one application on the New menu, as shown in Figure 5-7.

You may want a mixed-type library if your document-creation process requires multiple types of documents for a specific project. For example, your project management team might need a Statement of Work (*.doc*), Project Plan (*.mpp*), Deliverables List (*.xls*), and executive briefing (*.ppt*) for each project. By putting the templates for all of the document types in the same library, you can then group the documents by Project using a custom view.

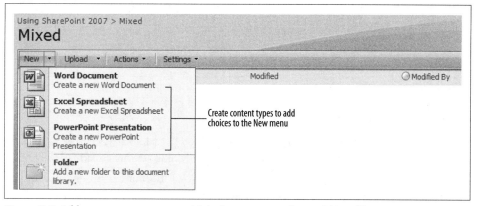

Figure 5-7. Add content types to use multiple document templates within a library

To create a new content type:

1. Create the documents to use as templates (*template.xls*, *template.doc*, etc.) for each Office application you wish to use from the library. Save them in a *Templates* folder on your desktop.

2. Navigate to the top-level site and click Site Actions → Site Settings, and then click "Site content types" under the Galleries heading in the middle of the page. SharePoint displays the Site Content Type Gallery page.

3. Click Create on the toolbar. SharePoint displays the New Site Content Type page.

4. Name the content type and click OK. The name you set here will appear in the New menu. SharePoint creates the type and displays the property page for the type.

5. Click Advanced settings in the middle of the page, complete the page as shown in Figure 5-8, and click OK. SharePoint uploads the template for the content type.

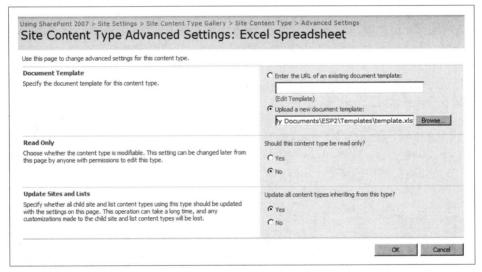

Figure 5-8. Creating a new content type

To add the content type to a library:

1. Navigate to the library and click Settings → Document Library Settings, and click "Advanced settings" under the General Settings heading on the left side of the page.

2. In the Content Types section, select Yes and click OK. SharePoint enables multiple content types for the library and adds a Content Types section to the Settings page (see Figure 5-9).

3. Click "Add from existing content types," select the content types you created in the preceding procedure, and click "Add from existing site content types." SharePoint adds the content types to the library.

Content Types

This document library is configured to allow multiple content types. Use content types to specify the information you want to display about an item, in addition to its policies, workflows, or other behavior. The following content types are currently available in this library:

Content Type	Visible on New Button	Default Content Type
Word Document	✔	✔
Excel Spreadsheet	✔	
PowerPoint Presentation	✔	

▫ Add from existing site content types
▫ Change new button order and default content type

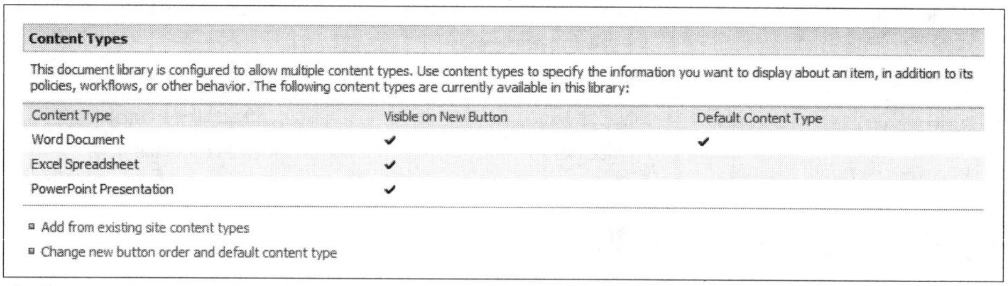

Figure 5-9. Adding content types to the library

Content types not only define the template used for new documents, they also define the properties that a document supports. For example, you could create a Specification content type for a Word document template that includes Revision, Product, and Module properties, then use that content type across multiple libraries.

In other words, content types let you structure the information you store with a document based on the type of document you are creating, regardless of where you store it. They can also be used with lists, though they are much more common in libraries.

Organizing Libraries

Libraries are a way to organize documents within a site. There are a couple of factors to help you decide when to create a new library and where to put it:

- WSS limits searches to the site level. If you're not using MOSS or MOSS/S, include all of the libraries you want members to be able to search in top-level sites rather than subsites.

- There is no hard limit to the number of files you can have in a document library, but fewer than 4,000 files per folder provides the best performance. Also, it makes sense to organize libraries in such a way that users can find documents without too much scrolling or paging.

- You can have a very large number of libraries in a single site. Again, it makes sense to organize libraries in such a way that users can find them without too much scrolling or paging.

You organize the documents within a library using folders or views. Each approach has advantages and disadvantages, as shown in Table 5-3.

Table 5-3. Organizing documents with folders or views

Organize using	Advantage	Disadvantage
Folders (Physical structure)	• Easy to create • Easy to migrate from network drives • Work well with batch uploads	• Deep structures are hard to navigate • Documents can be misfiled
Views (Logical structure)	• Flexible, most customizable • Visually appealing • Easy to hide files	• You have to enter properties for files • More difficult to create/maintain • Not all users understand views

Organizing Documents with Folders

Organize documents into folders when migrating from network drives or when working with a large number of files. When migrating network drives to SharePoint, you can just drag and drop folders from the drive into the library, as shown in Figure 5-10.

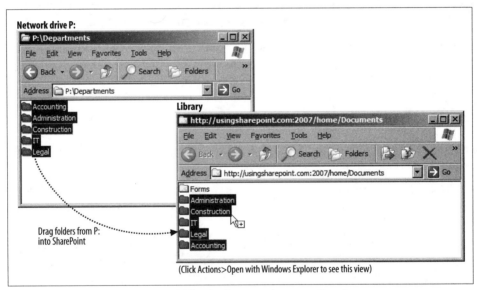

Figure 5-10. You can upload whole folders by dragging them into SharePoint

The advantage of this approach is that users are often already familiar with the folder structure. There's no point in changing it!

Drag-and-drop can have some problems, however. Uploads fail if a filename or folder name contains any of these characters: &, ?, %, or .. (two periods together). If a name like that occurs anywhere in the batch of files you are uploading, you'll get an error message stating "An error occurred copying some or all of the selected files." You need to rename the file and then retry uploading.

Organizing Documents with Views

Organize documents using views to create more sophisticated displays such as the collapsible tree view shown in Figure 5-11.

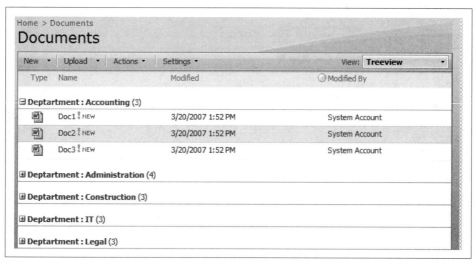

Figure 5-11. *Views can group and filter documents to create logical organizations*

To group files by department as shown in Figure 5-11, you have to enter a department for each file. That's more work than just putting the file in a folder, but it means that if you want to just display the files for one department, you can do it through a simple view.

To group files by department, complete these tasks:

1. Add a Choice or Lookup column to the library named Department. See Chapter 4 for instructions on how to add a column to a list. The steps are the same for libraries.

2. Create a view that groups the documents by department. Again, the steps are the same for libraries as for lists.

3. Set the Department property for each document.

When you add a new column to a library, that column becomes a property that can be set from Word or Excel. Those applications prompt you for the property setting when you save the document to the library, as shown in Figure 5-12.

In Office 2007, the properties appear in a window at the top of the screen. You are also prompted for those properties when you upload a single file to a library. You *are not* prompted when you upload documents in bulk—in those cases, the properties are set to the default column value.

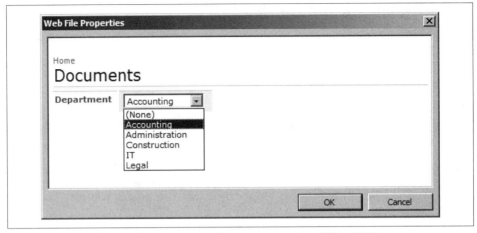

Figure 5-12. New library columns appear as document properties (Office 2003)

Libraries automatically use the built-in Title property from the document to fill in the Title column; all other custom columns are filled in using the Web File Properties page. Required columns show up as required properties; choice and lookup columns display drop-down choices; and so on.

Document properties are sometimes referred to as *metadata*, because they describe the contents of the document. Metadata forms the basis for organizing documents logically through views, but it can be hard to gather especially when there is a large number of existing files. You need to balance the effort involved in collecting metadata against the benefits of the views you can create from it.

Combining Approaches

Of course you can combine folders and views to get the best of both worlds. One solution during migration is to upload files in folders and then set the properties of those files in bulk using the datasheet view. Once those changes have been made, you can hide the folders by selecting "Show all items without folders" in the view's Folders section as shown in Figure 5-13.

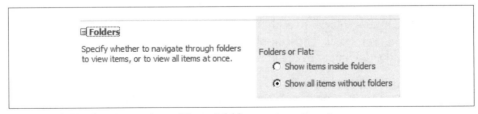

Figure 5-13. Use this view setting to "flatten" folder structures in a view

Saving a Library As a Template

As with lists and sites, you can save customized libraries as templates and then reuse them to create similar libraries elsewhere. When you save a library as a template, the columns, views, and document template are included, but settings such as versioning and document approval are not. You'll need to reestablish those settings for each new library you create.

To save a library as a template:

1. On the library toolbar, click Settings → Document Library Settings, and then click "Save document library as template" under the Permissions and Management heading. SharePoint displays the Save as Template page.
2. Complete the page and choose OK. SharePoint saves the library as a template and adds it to the site collection's List Template Gallery.

Library templates are saved at site collection level. To deploy the template to another site collection:

1. Navigate to the top-level site.
2. Click Site Actions → Site Settings, and click "List templates" under the Galleries heading. SharePoint displays the List Template Gallery. (In MOSS, click Site Actions → Site Settings → Modify All Site Settings.)
3. Click on the library to move. SharePoint asks if you want to save the file.
4. Click Save to download the template. Be sure to store it in your Templates folder on your computer to stay organized.
5. Navigate to the site collection where you want to install the template and repeat step 1 to display the List Template Gallery for that site collection.
6. Click Upload on the gallery toolbar and upload the file you created in step 3. SharePoint copies the file into the list template gallery.

Libraries that include Lookup columns will have problems when used in other site collections since the source list for the lookup won't exist in the new location. Avoid Lookup columns when creating libraries for reuse across site collections.

Creating Library Applications

So far, this chapter has talked about *how* you do things with libraries but has said very little about *what* you can do with them. One reason for that is kind of obvious: libraries are for storing documents. But the real reason is because libraries are usually closely associated with the sites that contain them. It's hard to talk about a library application without using examples based on site templates.

So, let's forget that this is Chapter 5 for a moment and look at some of the site templates that create library applications. The four main types of library applications are listed in Table 5-4.

Table 5-4. Library application types

Application type	Site template	Core needs
Project	Team Site	• Organized by project • Keep version history • Multiple authors, editors, reviewers • Only team members have access
Task	Custom	• Organized by type (template) • Grouped by client or case • Multiple authors, editors, reviewers • Department has access
Document control	Document Center (MOSS)	• Single location • Track versions • Formal process (workflow) • Approve/reject submissions • Single (or few) authors • Revisions occur offline • Everyone can read
Archive	Records Center (MOSS)	• Central location for final documents • Once stored, can't be changed • Track status of submissions • Controlled access

The application types listed in Table 5-4 are the types I see over and over again with clients. Really, I've just sorted common client needs into four groups and picked the site template that most closely matches those needs.

Project Applications

Projects are the simplest library application. They organize the documents and tasks used to complete a single project, such as this book or a piece or software or a strategic plan or…well, you get the idea. The main things that define a project are:

- It has a defined scope and lifespan.
- Team membership can cross department boundaries (matrix-style).
- Documents are a central focus either as the end product (e.g., a book) or in support of the project (e.g., design specs).

Figure 5-14 illustrates a project site for a book—this one, actually.

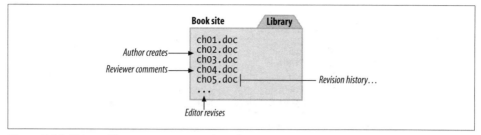

Figure 5-14. Using a library to organize project documents

To create the Book project application, complete these tasks:

1. Create a new site named "Book" using the Team site template.
2. Click on People and Groups on the left side of the home page and add the team members who will review and edit the book to the Contributors group.
3. Turn on versioning for the Shared Documents library.
4. Create or upload chapter files for the book.
5. Click on a chapter's Edit menu and select Send to → E-mail a Link, and send a message to the reviewers letting them know the chapter is ready for review.
6. Have reviewers open the chapter for editing from the library, turn on revision tracking, and make their corrections and comments.

You don't really need to write any of my chapters; I include those steps to illustrate the process and to make the points that project applications usually:

- Use an informal process
- Involve a limited number of people
- Focus on collaboration

Task Applications

Task applications are a variation on a project application and are often used within department sites. They store and organize the documents used to complete a task for one or more clients. The main things that define a task application are:

- It continues to grow over time.
- Team membership is usually contained within a department (hierarchical).
- The type or category of the document is the central focus.
- There are multiple categories of documents.

Figure 5-15 illustrates a task application for a Legal department.

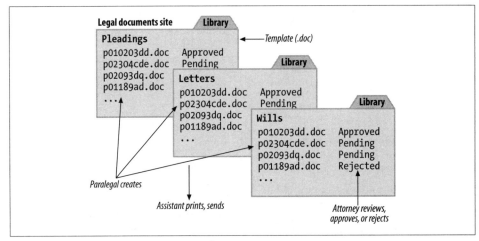

Figure 5-15. Using libraries to organize tasks

To create a Legal Document task application, complete these tasks:

1. Navigate to the Legal Department site and create a new site named "Legal Documents" using the Blank site template.

2. Click on People and Groups on the left side of the home page and add paralegals to the Contributors group, assistants to the Visitors group, and attorneys to the Owners group.

3. Create libraries for each of the document categories: pleadings, letters, and wills.

4. Turn on approval for each of the libraries.

5. Edit the document template for each of the libraries to match the standard form the Legal department uses.

6. Have the attorney set an alert to receive notification when new documents are created in each of the libraries.

7. Walk the legal team through the process of creating, approving, and printing the documents.

Again, this is an exercise to show how to apply the skills from this chapter and present a different type of use for libraries. The task application is unique from the project application because:

- The process is more formal.
- Team members have distinct roles.
- There is a library for each document type that makes use of a document template.

Document Control Applications

Document control applications are created to comply with a document control process that defines exactly how drafts are created, reviewed, revised, approved, and stored. The main things that define a document control application are:

- It follows a formal process (workflow).
- It has an open lifespan, but limited scope (only controlled documents).
- Only one or two employees can change documents.
- All employees may be able to read documents.
- Documents are generally stored in a single library and categorized by department.
- Documents usually define business processes, such as forms, work instructions, policies, and procedures.

Figure 5-16 illustrates a company-wide document control application.

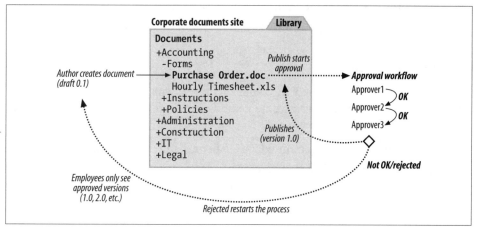

Figure 5-16. Using a library for document control

To create the document control application, complete these tasks:

1. Navigate to the top-level portal site in MOSS and create a new site named "Corporate Documents" using the Document Center site template on the Enterprise tab.

2. Navigate to the site's Documents library and add required columns for Department and Document Type. For Document Type, specify the choices: Form, Instruction, and Policy.

3. Create a view to group documents by Department and Document Type.

4. In the library's versioning settings, specify that only users who can edit items can see drafts.

5. In the library's workflow settings, add an Approval workflow and select the Start Option: "Start this workflow to approve publishing a major version of an item."

6. Specify who will approve documents and how approval is handled (parallel or serial).

7. Create a new document in the Documents library and check in the draft. That creates version 0.1 of the document.

8. Click Publish on the document's Edit menu to begin the approval workflow.

9. Once approved, the document is published as a major revision (version 1.0) and appears to all users.

Those tasks are abbreviated because we haven't really talked about document workflows yet. In reality, you might define separate review and approval workflows based on your document control policy, but that would make Figure 5-16 way too complicated. The main features of the Document Control application are:

- Uses a well-defined process
- Limits who can make changes and how they are approved
- Only approved versions are available to a general audience
- Tracks revision history using minor versions (draft) and major versions (final)

Archive Applications

Archive applications are created to comply with a document retention policy that defines where and how long records are kept. The main features of an archive application are:

- Allows documents to be submitted via email or scanned to a location
- Prohibits changes to submitted items
- Routes records to specific libraries based on the type of document
- Allows holds to be placed on records to suspend disposition

Figure 5-17 illustrates a company-wide archive application.

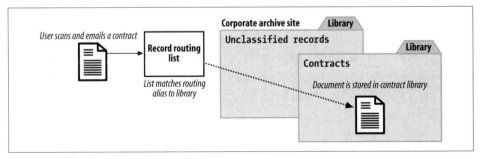

Figure 5-17. Using a library as an archive

To create the archive application, complete these tasks:

1. Navigate to the top-level portal site in MOSS and create a new site named "Corporate Archive" using the Records Center site template on the Enterprise tab.

2. Click on People and Groups on the left side of the home page and add the employees who can submit records as Contributors. You may want to allow all employees to submit records, or you can restrict it to the accounts used by the scanners.

3. Create a Contracts library.

4. Click on the Records Routing link and add aliases to route documents to the Contracts libraries.

5. Email documents to the Contracts alias to test the settings.

Scanners/copiers/printers now often include scan-to-email features that fit well with Archive applications. The key features of the Archive application are:

- The Record Routing list directs incoming documents to the appropriate library. This lets you change libraries without changing the alias, so you can keep separate libraries for each year if you like.

- The Unclassified Records library collects documents that don't have a matching type in the Record Routing list.

- The Holds list lets you place holds on certain records because of pending litigation or other needs.

- Records can also be submitted via a web service, so archives can integrate with other applications.

Best Practices

- For libraries that contain a mix of document types, organize the documents by how they are used.

- For libraries that contain only one type of document, include a template for creating new documents, and create separate libraries for each template you use.

- WSS limits searches to the site level. If you're not using MOSS or MOSS/S, include all of the libraries you want members to be able to search in top-level sites rather than subsites.

- Use folders (physical organization) when migrating files from network drives to SharePoint. Folders provide the easiest migration path.

- Use views (logical organization) when your library serves a wide audience with varying needs. Views give you the greatest flexibility.

- Before uploading large groups of files, check for these characters in file or folder names: &, ?, %, or .. (two periods together). SharePoint can't accept files or folders with those characters in their names.

- Use default column values to populate document properties when uploading files in bulk.

- Use the datasheet view to quickly change property settings after uploading files in bulk.

- When creating libraries that use versioning, be sure to explain your revision process to users who will be working with those libraries. Depending on how the library is set up, they may need to know how to check files in and out, how minor and major revisions work, and that documents may require approval.

CHAPTER 6

Building Pages

Most SharePoint pages are made up of web parts. In Chapters 1 and 3, I showed you how to add web parts to a page and how to set the properties of those parts to change their appearance. In this chapter, I'll show you how to:

- Customize list web parts by converting them to data views.
- Connect web parts to create summary/detail views.
- Copy customized web parts to other pages and deploy them to other sites.
- Develop client-side web parts using JavaScript and other techniques.
- Apply filters to web parts on a page.
- Customize page layout and navigation with master pages.

These are the advanced techniques that you need to design and build effective SharePoint pages. These skills don't require a lot of programming knowledge, but some knowledge of HTML, JavaScript, and XML/XSL will come in handy.

 You will need SharePoint Designer to complete some of the tasks in this chapter.

Using the Built-in Web Parts

SharePoint includes a set of built-in web parts that you can add to any page. Tables 6-1, 6-2, and 6-3 list the web parts that come with SharePoint.

Table 6-1. Built-in web parts

Category	Web part	Use to
Lists and Libraries	List View	Display a view of a list or library on a page.
	Data View	Create highly customized views of lists and libraries using SharePoint Designer.

Table 6-1. Built-in web parts (continued)

Category	Web part	Use to
Miscellaneous	Content Editor	Include HTML and JavaScript on a page.
	Form	Connect form controls to other web parts.
	Image	Display an image from a URL.
	Page Viewer	Display another page as an IFrame on the current page.
	Relevant Documents	Display documents targeted at the current user.
	Site Users	Display a list of the users and groups who have permissions within a site.
	User Tasks	Display tasks assigned to the current user.
	XML Web Part	Display XSL transformations on XML input.
Navigation	Quick Launch	Display links to site lists and libraries on the left side of the home page.
	Link Bar	Displays links as tabs across the top of a page.
	Tree View	Display a hierarchical list of links on the left side of the home page.
	Title Bar	Display a title and logo for a page.

The navigation web parts don't appear in the Add Web Parts list. They are controlled by site settings and can't be edited directly. See Chapter 3 for information on controlling those web parts.

Table 6-2. Additional web parts included with MOSS Standard Edition

Category	Web part	Use to
Content Rollup	Site Aggregator	Create a toolbar that displays documents from other sites.
Default	Content Query	Roll up content from the entire site collection or a subset of sites.
	I need to...	Display items from a task list as a drop-down list of choices.
	RSS Viewer	Display RSS feeds.
	Summary Link	Display a list of links that can be formatted and support drag-and-drop.
	Table of Contents	Display site navigation.
	This Week in Pictures	Display a picture from an Image library that links to a slide show of the entire library.
Miscellaneous	Contact Details	Display contact information for the portal area (portal sites only).

Table 6-2. Additional web parts included with MOSS Standard Edition (continued)

Category	Web part	Use to
Outlook Web Access	My Calendar	Display the user's Outlook calendar on a page.
	My Contacts	Display the user's Outlook contacts list.
	My Inbox	Display the user's Outlook Inbox.
	My Mail Folder	Display the user's Outlook mail folders.
	My Tasks	Display the user's Outlook task list.
Search	Advanced Search Box	Display the Advanced Search options.
	People Search Box	Display the People Search options.
	People Search Core Results	Display the results from a people search.
	Search Action Links	Display optional search view options and links.
	Search Best Bets	Display the search Best Bets results.
	Search Core Results	Display search results.
	Search High Confidence Results	Display keyword, best bets, and high confidence results.
	Search Paging	Display paging links for more results.
	Search Statistics	Display the number of results and the time that the search required.
	Search Summary	Display the "Did you mean" search feature.
Site Directory	Categories	List categories from the portal Site Directory.
	Sites in Category	List sites from the portal Site Directory.
	Top Sites	List top sites from the portal Site Directory.

Table 6-3. Additional web parts included with MOSS Enterprise Edition

Category	Web part	Use to
Business Data	Business Data Actions	Perform actions on a Business Data Catalog.
	Business Data Item	Display an item from a Business Data List.
	Business Data Item Builder	Create a Business Data Item.
	Business Data List	Display a list of items from a Business Data Catalog.
	Business Data Related List	Display a list of related items from a Business Data Catalog.
	Excel Web Access	Work with an Excel spreadsheet as a web page.
	IView	Display IViews from SAP portal servers.
	WSRP Consumer	Display services provided by other web sites using Web Services for Remote Portlets (WSRP).
Dashboard	Key Performance Indicators	Graphically display the status of important measures.
	KPI Details	Display details for a single status indicator.

Category	Web part	Use to
Filters	Business Data Catalog Filter	Filter the contents of a list or library web part using values from the Business Data Catalog.
	Choice Filter	Filter the contents of a list or library web part by selecting from a list of choices.
	Current User Filter	Filter contents based on the current user.
	Filter Actions	Refresh the filter results and allow filter settings to be saved.
	Page Field Filter	Filter contents of web parts using information about the current page.
	Query String (URL) Filter	Use a query string sent to the page through the URL to filter web parts.
	SharePoint List Filter	Filter web parts using values from a list.
	SQL Server 2005 Analysis Services Filter	Filter web parts using values from an SQL Server 2005 Analysis Services data cube.
	Text Filter	Filter web parts using a value entered in a text box.

MOSS adds a lot of web parts! Some of those are variations of similar web parts, such as the Outlook, Search, and Site Directory categories. All of the MOSS web parts rely on services that are only available in MOSS; you can't move MOSS web parts to servers running only WSS.

Customizing List View Web Parts

Whenever you add web parts to a page, the lists and libraries in the current web site show up at the top of the list of available web parts. Each of those is actually a List View web part. The *List View* is a special type of web part created automatically for each list or library in a site.

I showed you how to add lists as web parts way back in Chapter 1, so I won't repeat that here. Instead, I'll show you how to use advanced techniques to:

- Connect one List View to another to show summary/detail views.
- Convert a List View to a Data View to fully customize the web part using SharePoint Designer.
- Move web parts from one page to another.
- Export, Import, and Deploy customized web parts for use on other pages and sites.

The following sections cover each of those tasks in turn using the Phone List sample from Chapters 1 and 4. These tasks apply to all types of List Views and are fundamental to working with web parts.

Connecting Summary/Detail Views

In this sample, we'll add a detail view of the employees that appear in the Phone List web part. When the user selects an employee on the Phone List, the employee's details will appear in a box below. To complete this sample, perform the following tasks:

1. Add a detail view of the Phone List to the home page.
2. Connect the detail view to the Phone List web part (the summary view).
3. Test the connection to see how the summary/detail web parts work.

To add the detail view:

1. Navigate to the home page where the Phone List web part appears, and click Site Actions → Edit Page. SharePoint displays the page in Edit mode.
2. Click Add a Web Part, and add another Phone List web part to the Right web part zone.
3. On the new web part toolbar, click Edit → Modify Shared Web Part. SharePoint displays the web part properties task pane on the right side of the page.
4. Change the web part properties as shown in this table and click Apply.

Section	Property	Set to
Top	Selected View	All contacts
	Toolbar Type	No Toolbar
Appearance	Title	Summary
	Chrome Type	Title Only
Layout	Zone Index	2
	Description	Click on Last Name to edit item.

5. Click the "Edit the current view" link in the top section of the properties pane and make the changes shown in this table. Click OK when done.

Section	Property	Set to
Style	View Style	Boxed, no labels
Item Limit	Number of items to display	1
	Limit the total number of items returned to the specified amount	Selected

Next, connect the Phone List web part to the Summary web part. To do that:

1. Click Site Actions → Edit page. SharePoint displays the page in Edit mode.
2. Click the Edit menu on the Details web part toolbar and select Connections → Get Sort/Filter From → Phone List as shown in Figure 6-1. SharePoint displays the Configure Connection dialog box.

3. Click Next, select the Column Last Name, and click Finish. SharePoint connects the Last Name columns on both web parts.

4. Click Exit Edit Mode at the top-right corner of the screen.

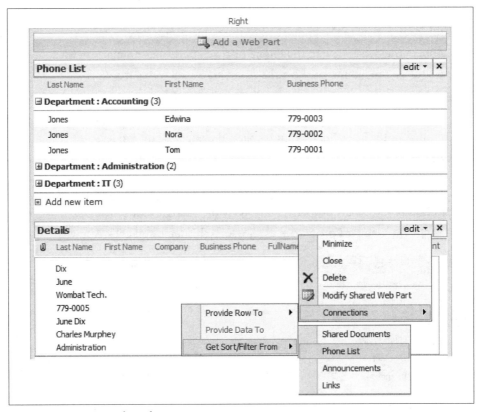

Figure 6-1. Connecting the web parts

Selecting a name in the Phone List now displays that person in the Details web part, as shown in Figure 6-2.

Converting a List View to a Data View

Figure 6-2 works OK, but the Details web part is way too wide. That's because SharePoint includes the column headings even though they aren't needed. You can try changing the web part's Width property, but it won't do anything—SharePoint still claims the space to display those column headings!

To change the width, perform these tasks:

- Convert the Details web part to a Data View and customize its appearance.
- Reconnect the web parts and test whether they still work.

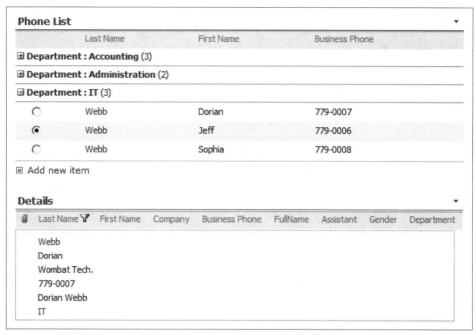

Figure 6-2. The summary/detail views in action

To convert the Details web part to a Data View:

1. Open page in SharePoint Designer.

2. Right-click the web part in the Design pane and select Convert to XLST Data View. SharePoint Designer displays a warning that the connections to other web parts will be lost. Click OK to continue.

3. Select the column headings row and press Ctrl+X to cut.

4. Save the page and then preview it in the browser. It should appear much narrower with no column headings.

The Details web part looks a lot better, but we broke the connection. To reconnect the web parts:

1. Display the page in the browser and click Site Actions → Edit Page. SharePoint displays the page in Edit mode.

2. Click the Edit menu on the Details web part and select Connections → Get Sort/ Filter From → "Phone list" as shown earlier in Figure 6-1. SharePoint displays the Configure Connection dialog box.

3. Select the column name to connect First Name, Last Name, and Business Phone. Click Finish when done. SharePoint connects the web parts.

4. Click Exit Edit Mode at the top-right corner of the screen. When you're done, the two web parts should appear as shown in Figure 6-3.

You had to select more columns when connecting the web parts because the Summary web part is now a Data View, not a List View. There are other differences between Data Views and List Views that we'll get to in a minute.

Figure 6-3. Convert the Details web part to a Data View to remove column headings

When working with web pages in SharePoint Designer, there are a few tips you should know:

- Get your List View as close as possible to the way you want it to appear before converting it to a Data View. That's the easiest approach.

- Save the page and view it separately in the browser to review the changes.

- You can undo your changes in SharePoint Designer by pressing Ctrl+Z even after you save. If you break a web part, you can sometimes step backward and fix it.

- You can convert a Data View back to a list view by right-clicking on the view in the Design pane and selecting "Revert to SharePoint list view." Remember this if Undo doesn't work.

Moving Web Parts to Other Pages

The preceding sample modified the web parts on the "live" home page. That's fine for this example, but if you're working on the home page of your company's portal, you might get some complaints because of the sudden changes.

In that situation, you should do your development in a separate Pages library, then move your web parts onto the home page when they are final. This approach lets you get review comments on the parts before you deploy them, which is a very good idea. To develop web parts in this way, complete these tasks:

1. Create a Pages document library within the site using the Web Part page document template.
2. Create a new test page within the Pages library on which to do your development.
3. Create your web parts on the test page.
4. Send links to the test pages via email to gather feedback.
5. Make the required changes.
6. Move the approved web parts to their final destination.

Use SharePoint Designer to move the List View web part to other pages in a site. To do that:

1. Open the source page in SharePoint Designer.
2. Select the List View web part in the Design pane.
3. Press Ctrl+C to copy the web part.
4. Open the destination page, select the target web part zone, and then press Ctrl+V to insert the web part.
5. Save the destination page and preview it in the browser.

That's the only way to move a List View web part; however, other types of web parts can be exported and then loaded on pages or into a site's web part gallery, which is similar to the site and list template galleries. You'll see that next.

Converting a List View to a Drop-Down List

I didn't convert the Phone List web part to a Data View in the preceding samples because it is difficult to connect the two web parts once they are both converted. For now, I'd rather focus on something more interesting: how to convert the Phone List into an exportable web part. To do that, complete these tasks:

- Move the Phone List to a new test page using SharePoint Designer.
- Customize the web part using the browser.
- Reopen the test page in SharePoint Designer.
- Convert the web part to a Data View.

To move the Phone List web part to a test page:

1. Create a new Pages library in the site.
2. Add a test page to the Pages library named *page1.aspx*.
3. Open the home page in SharePoint Designer and copy the Phone List web part.

4. Open the test page in SharePoint Designer and paste the Phone List web part on to a web part zone.

5. Save the page and preview the result in the browser.

I've got a goal in mind for the Phone List—I want to display the phone numbers as a drop-down list. That will be better than the current view, but it means I've got to put all of the information I want to display into one column. To do that, complete two major tasks:

1. Add a calculated column to the list that combines the name and phone number.

2. Modify the view used in the web part to display only that column.

To add a calculated column that combines name and phone information:

1. In the browser, click the Phone List link on the title bar of the web part. Share-Point displays the full Phone List. (That's a shortcut to the list.)

2. On the list toolbar, click Settings → Create Column. SharePoint displays the New Column page.

3. Create a column using the settings shown in this table. Click OK when you're done.

Section	Property	Set to
Name and Type	Column Name	Web Part
	Column Type	Calculated
Additional Column Settings	Formula	=[First Name] & " " & [Last Name] & " " & [Business Phone]
	Add to default view	Cleared

To modify the view used by the web part:

1. Return to the test page (*page1.aspx*).

2. Click the Edit menu on the Phone List web part and select Modify Shared Web Part. SharePoint displays the web part properties task pane on the right side of the page.

3. Click "Edit the current view." SharePoint displays the Edit View page.

4. Deselect all of the columns, select the new Web Part column, remove the Group By settings, and click OK. SharePoint displays the modified web part.

5. Click the Edit menu on the Phone List web part and select Modify Shared Web Part again.

6. Select Toolbar Type: No Toolbar and click OK. SharePoint removes the toolbar that was erroneously added by the preceding step (that's an annoyance in SharePoint).

When complete, the First Name, Last Name, and Business Phone columns are now all combined in a single column named Web Part. Next, we'll convert the web part to a Data View to display the information as a drop-down list:

1. Open the test page in SharePoint Designer. If you had it open from earlier steps, close the page and reopen it so you get the changes that we just made.

2. Right-click on the Phone List web part in the Design pane and select Convert to XSLT Data View. SharePoint Designer converts the List View to a Data View web part.

3. Click Data View → Data View Properties and click the Layout tab. The Layout tab displays the built-in styles you can apply to the Data View.

4. Scroll to the end of the list of view and select the drop-down menu style. It's next-to-last in the list. Click OK to make the change.

5. Save the page and preview the change in the browser.

That was a lot of work, but now the phone numbers appear in a handy drop-down menu, as shown in Figure 6-4.

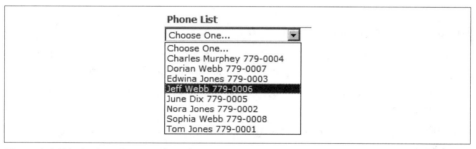

Figure 6-4. Displaying a list as a drop-down menu

Exporting Web Parts

You can't export List View web parts; you can only copy List Views from one page to another using SharePoint Designer. To be able to export a customized List View, you must first convert the List View web part to a Data View.

To export a web part:

1. Create a WebParts folder on your computer.

2. Click on the web part's Edit menu and select Export as shown in Figure 6-5. SharePoint displays the File Download dialog box.

3. Click Save and save the file to your WebParts folder. Be sure to include a version number in the filename! SharePoint saves the file using the *.dwp* or *.webpart* file extension.

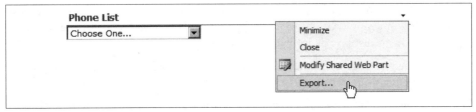

Figure 6-5. Exporting a web part so it can be reused

Exported web part files are XML descriptions of the web part's property settings. In the case of a Data View web part, the properties include the general web part properties, the source list ID, and the XSL transformation used to format the web part.

You can edit the XML description directly, or you can make changes directly in the web part from the web part properties pane.

These changes are for XML/XSL pros.

To edit the XSL for a Data View web part:

1. Click on the web part's Edit menu and select Modify Shared Web Part. SharePoint displays the web part properties pane on the right of the screen.

2. Click the XSL editor button. SharePoint displays the web part's XSL in a text entry page.

3. The text is unformatted, so copy the contents of the text box and paste it into an XML editor to make changes.

4. Paste your changes back into the text box and click Save.

5. Click Apply to test your changes.

6. Once your changes are complete, export the web part again—don't forget to version the file!

Be careful with your edits. XSL is case- and tag-sensitive. If you make a single mistake, your web part won't load and you'll see an error instead of your expected list.

Importing and Deploying Web Parts

Once you've exported a web part to a file, you can import it to a page or deploy it to the site gallery:

- Import web parts to a page when you only want to reuse them once or twice. Web parts imported this way don't show up to other folks creating pages.

- Deploy web parts to the site gallery when you want to allow others to add the web part to pages throughout a site collection.

You need to consider visibility when deploying web parts to the server gallery. Data View web parts depend on lists within the current site. Those lists aren't visible outside of the current site, so you can't use the web part there.

To import a web part to a page:

1. Display the page in the browser and click Site Actions → Edit Page. SharePoint displays the page in Edit mode.

2. Click the Add a Web Part link in the zone where you want to put the web part.

3. Click the Advanced Web Part gallery and options link at the bottom of the page. SharePoint displays the Add Web Parts task pane on the right side of the page.

4. Click Browse → Import as shown in Figure 6-6. SharePoint displays the Import task pane.

5. Click Browse, select the file to import from your WebParts folder, and click Open.

6. Click Upload to load the web part.

7. Drag the web part from the task pane onto the web part zone. SharePoint adds the web part to the page. Click Exit Edit Mode when done.

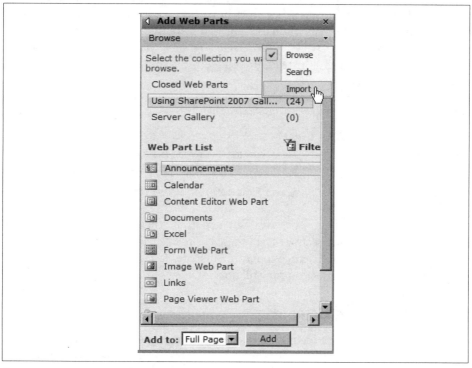

Figure 6-6. Importing a web part to a page

To deploy a web part to the site collection web part gallery:

1. Navigate to the top-level site and click Site Actions → Site Settings, and then click Web Parts under the Galleries heading in the middle of the page. (In MOSS, click Site Actions → Site Settings → Modify All Site Settings.)

2. Click Upload to upload the web part from your WebParts folder. SharePoint displays the edit item page for the new web part.

3. Complete the page and click OK. SharePoint adds the web part to the site gallery.

Web parts in the site gallery show up in the Add Web Parts page when a user clicks on the Add a Web Part link.

 It's not a good idea to deploy custom Data View web parts to the site gallery, since they can't be used outside of their source site; use import instead. You'll learn how to create custom web parts that are useful across the site collection in the next section.

Creating Client-Side Web Parts

You can do a lot with SharePoint Designer, and you might be tempted to use it to add formatted text, tables, and other types of content to SharePoint pages. *Don't do it.* One of the biggest benefits of SharePoint is the ability to edit pages through the web browser, and editing pages in a designer ignores that benefit, harms performance, and can break pages. Instead, use one of the web parts listed in Table 6-4 to include custom content.

Table 6-4. Web parts used for including custom content

Web part	Use to
Content Editor	Add formatted text, HTML controls, JavaScript, Flash animations, etc.
Page Viewer	Display a page, file, or folder from another location in an IFrame.
XML Web Part	Render XML output using an XSL transformation.

Once you create your web part, you can export it, then deploy it for reuse as described in the preceding section. I call these *client-side web parts* because any code they include runs on the client—you can't include ASP.NET code or access the SharePoint object model, but you can still do a lot.

Including Repeated Elements

Use the Content Editor to include an element on multiple pages. You can import HTML files using the Content Editor, so you can store your element one place and use it throughout a site collection. To see how that works:

1. Navigate to the top-level site and create a library named "Includes." Use these settings: Display this document library on the Quick Launch? No; Document Template, None.

2. Check the library's Permissions settings to verify that all users of the site collection have Read permission.

3. Create an HTML file named *main_nav.htm* on your desktop and upload it to the library. (The code for *main_nav.htm* is shown later.)

4. Add the Content Editor web part to a test page using the following property settings.

Section	Property	Set to
Top	Content Link	*http://www.somecompany.com/includes/main_nav.htm*
Appearance	Title	Main_Nav
	Chrome Type	None

Use your site's URL in the Content Link property. Here is the code for *main_nav.htm*:

```
<!-- main_nav.htm -->
<script type="text/javascript">
var root = document.domain;
var src = "<a href='http://root/'>home</a> | <a href='http://root/pages/
info.aspx'>info</a> | <a href='http://root/pages/faq.aspx'>faq</a>
 | <a href='mailto:contact@somecompany.com?Subject=More information'>
contact</a>"
document.write(src.replace(/root/g, root));
</script>
```

The Replace method in the JavaScript code ensures that the links on the page work wherever the web part is used. Hardcoding the domain would be a little simpler, but SharePoint servers sometimes have multiple domain aliases. Figure 6-7 shows the web part in action.

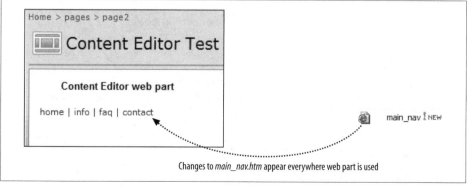

Figure 6-7. The Main_Nav web part gets its content from the Includes library

Because Main_Nav is linked to a file, any changes to that file automatically appear anywhere that the web part is used. To reuse the web part:

1. Export the Main_Nav web part from the test page.
2. Upload the exported file to the web part gallery.
3. Add the web part to the other page.

Including Images and Flash Animations

The Content Editor web part also makes it easy to include images that link to an address. For example, to add a logo to the Main_Nav web part:

1. Upload a logo to the Includes library that you created in "Including Repeated Elements" earlier.
2. Add an Img element to *main_nav.htm* as shown here:

```
<!-- main_nav.htm -->
<script type="text/javascript">
var root = document.domain;
var src = "<a href='http://root/'><img src='http://root/includes/logo_small.bmp'
style='border:0' alt='Home'><br>home</a> | <a href='http://root/pages/
info.aspx'>info</a> | <a href='http://root/pages/faq.aspx'>faq</a>
 | <a href='mailto:contact@somecompany.com?Subject=More information'>
contact</a>"
document.write(src.replace(/root/g, root));
</script>
```

Adobe Flash animations can also be included using the same technique:

1. Upload the animation file to the Includes library.
2. Upload an HTML file that has the necessary JavaScript and Object elements to run the animation.
3. Create a Content Editor web part that references the HTML file from step 2.
4. Export the web part and reuse it as needed.

Here's an example of the HTML tags for a Flash animation:

```
<!-- flash.htm -->
<script type="text/javascript">
var root = document.domain;
var src = "<object classid='clsid:D27CDB6E-AE6D-11cf-96B8-444553540000'
codebase='http://download.macromedia.com/pub/shockwave/cabs/flash/swflash.
cab#version=7,0,19,0' width='424' height='179' title='Do your part'><param
name='movie' value='http://root/Flash/scientist1.swf' /><param name='quality'
value='high' /><embed src='http://root/Flash/scientist1.swf' quality='high'
pluginspage='http://www.macromedia.com/go/getflashplayer' type='application/x-
shockwave-flash' width='424' height='179'></embed></object>"
document.write(src.replace(/root/g, root));
</script>
```

Displaying Pages in Frames

The Page Viewer web part creates an IFrame on the page that can display a web page from any valid address. When the user clicks on links within a Page Viewer web part, the destination page is displayed within the same IFrame. In other words, use the Page Viewer to display a page without navigating away from the surrounding page.

The Page Viewer is useful when working with external tools, such as Google. To create the Google search sample:

1. Create a search page named *gsearch.htm* on your desktop.
2. Upload the sample to the Includes library you created earlier in "Including Repeated Elements."
3. Create a Page Viewer web part on a test page with the following property settings.

Section	Property	Set to
Top	Link	*http://www.somecompany.com/includes/gsearch.htm*
Appearance	Title	Google Search
	Height	2024 Pixels
	Chrome Type	None

I set Height very large so that the Page Viewer does not display a scroll bar when the results are returned from the search. Otherwise, you wind up with two scroll bars on the right: one for the page and one for the web part. Very confusing!

Here is HTML for *gsearch.htm*:

```
<!-- GSearch.htm -->
<form method="get" action="http://www.google.com/custom" target="_self">
  <table border="0" bgcolor="#ffffff">
    <tr>
      <td nowrap="nowrap" valign="top" align="left" height="32">
      <a href="http://www.google.com/" target="google_window">
      <img src="http://www.google.com/logos/Logo_25wht.gif" border="0" alt="Google"
      align="middle"></a>
      </td>
      <td nowrap="nowrap">
      <input type="hidden" name="domains"
      value="www.usingsharepoint.com;msdn.microsoft.com">
      <input type="text" name="q" size="50" maxlength="255" value="">
      <input type="submit" name="sa" value="Search"> </td>
    </tr>
    <tr>
      <td> </td>
      <td nowrap="nowrap">
      <table>
        <tr>
          <td><input type="radio" name="sitesearch" value="">
          <font size="-1" color="#000000">WWW</font> </td>
```

```
<td>
<input type="radio" name="sitesearch" value="www.usingsharepoint.com"
checked="checked"></input>
<font size="-1" color="#000000">This site</font> </td>
<td>
<input type="radio" name="sitesearch"
value="msdn.microsoft.com/library"></input>
<font size="-1" color="#000000">MSDN</font> </td>
<td></td>
    </tr>
  </table>
  <input type="hidden" name="client" value="pub-6777259683278720">
  </td>
 </tr>
</table>
</form>
```

 You can't include *gsearch.htm* in a Content Editor web part; the Content Editor doesn't allow Form elements!

Figure 6-8 shows the Google search sample in action.

Figure 6-8. The Page Viewer displays the results on the containing page

One of the annoyances of working with IFrames is that they tend to "drill down" visually. If you click on the Amazon link in Figure 6-8, you'll get the Amazon navigation bar displayed in the frame; and if you keep clicking around, the usable space gets smaller and smaller. You solve that in two ways:

- Display the results in a new window.
- Provide navigation that resets the IFrame.

To open a new window from an IFrame, change the target of the embedded Form element. For example:

```
<!-- GSearch.htm -->
<form method="get" action="http://www.google.com/custom" target="_GoogleWindow">
```

To control the navigation within the IFrame, add a Content Editor web part to the page with the following HTML:

```
<a href="#" onclick="window.history.back()"><<</a> 
<a href="http://www.somecompany.com/includes/gsearch.htm"
target="MSOPageViewerWebPart_WebPartWPQ2">Restart</a> 
<a href="#" onclick="window.history.forward()">>></a>
```

The middle link targets the Page Viewer's IFrame on the page. SharePoint creates the IDs for all of the elements on a page, but you can find their IDs by selecting View Source and searching for the IFrame. That ID may change if you add web parts to the page, so be sure to recheck it after any changes.

 Using IFrames on a web part page is not for everyone. If you use this approach, don't allow others to change the page. Any web parts they add will usually change the ID of the Page Viewer web part and break the link between the IFrame and its source.

Performing XSL Transformations

Use the XML Web Part to render XML data as a table on a web page. You can work with any XML data source, so if you are an XSL wizard, this is a powerful tool. You can combine this web part with the *stsadm.exe* utility to produce customized administration pages for SharePoint site collections. To create the Intranet Administration sample:

1. Run the following command line on the server to create an XML file containing information about all of the site collections:

   ```
   stsadm -o enumsites -url http://www.somecompany.com/ > intranet.xml
   ```

2. Upload the resulting *intranet.xml* to the Includes library you created earlier in "Including Repeated Elements."

3. Create *intranet.xsl* (shown later) and upload it to the Includes library.

4. Create an XML Web Part on a test page with the property settings listed in the following table.

Section	Property	Set to
Top	XML Link	*http://www.somecompany.com/includes/intranet.xml*
Top	XML Link	*http://www.somecompany.com/includes/intranet.xsl*
Appearance	Title	Intranet Administration
	Chrome Type	Title Only

The Intranet Administration sample builds a table out of the enumsites output that includes links to set permissions, monitor usage, and apply themes to sites, as shown in Figure 6-9.

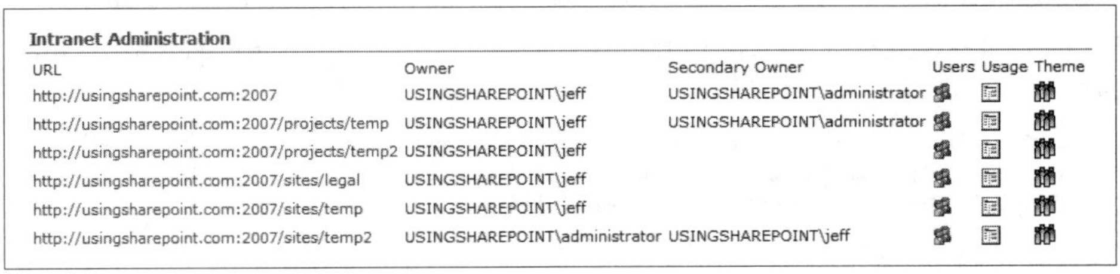

Figure 6-9. The Intranet Administration XML sample in action

The transform is performed by the following XSL.

```
<!-- intranet.xsl -->
<xsl:stylesheet version="1.0" xmlns:xsl="http://www.w3.org/1999/XSL/Transform">
<xsl:template match="/">
    <html>
  <body>
  <table cellspacing="5" cellpadding="0">
    <tr>
      <td>URL</td>
      <td>Owner</td>
      <td>Secondary Owner</td>
      <td>Users</td>
      <td>Usage</td>
      <td>Theme</td>
    </tr>
        <xsl:for-each  select="Sites/Site" >
        <xsl:sort select="@Url" />
          <tr>
      <td>
            <xsl:element name="a">
              <xsl:attribute name="href">
                <xsl:value-of select ="@Url" />
              </xsl:attribute>
              <xsl:value-of select ="@Url" />
            </xsl:element>
            </td>
      <td>
            <xsl:value-of select ="@Owner" />
            </td>
      <td>
            <xsl:value-of select ="@SecondaryOwner" />
            </td>
      <td>
            <xsl:element name="a">
              <xsl:attribute name="href">
                <xsl:value-of select ="@Url" />
```

```
              <xsl:text>/_layouts/1033/user.aspx</xsl:text>
            </xsl:attribute>
            <img src="@Url/_layouts/images/allusr.gif" border="none" />
          </xsl:element>
          </td>
      <td>
            <xsl:element name="a">
              <xsl:attribute name="href">
                <xsl:value-of select ="@Url" />
                <xsl:text>/_layouts/1033/UsageDetails.aspx</xsl:text>
              </xsl:attribute>
              <img src="_layouts/images/icaspx.gif" border="none" />
            </xsl:element>
            </td>
      <td>
            <xsl:element name="a">
              <xsl:attribute name="href">
                <xsl:value-of select ="@Url" />
                <xsl:text>/_layouts/1033/themeweb.aspx</xsl:text>
              </xsl:attribute>
              <img src="_layouts/images/sts_site16.gif" border="none" />
            </xsl:element>
            </td>
    </tr>
        </xsl:for-each>
      </table>
  </body>
</html>
  </xsl:template>
</xsl:stylesheet>
```

To automate updates to the data, add the stsadm command as a scheduled task on the server.

Filtering Lists and Libraries in MOSS

The filter web parts included in MOSS limit what is shown on a page. You can use them in three main ways:

- Show personalized results based on the current user.
- Allow users to limit what is shown by entering their own filter criteria.
- Automate what is shown based on a passed-in query string.

The following sections demonstrate each of these techniques using the filter web parts. These web parts are available only in MOSS.

Filtering Based on the Current User

The Current User Filter web part is similar to using [Me] to filter a view of a list. The web part filter can apply to multiple items on a page, however, which is easier than creating individual views.

To see how that works:

1. Navigate to a sample site containing a document library and a task list.
2. Create a test page, and add the document library and task list to it as web parts.
3. Add the Current User Filter web part to the page.
4. On the web part toolbar, click edit → Connections → Send Filter Values To → Tasks. SharePoint displays the Configure Connections dialog box.
5. Select the Consumer Field Name Assigned To and click Finish. SharePoint applies the filter to the Tasks list.
6. Repeat step 4 for the document library.
7. Select Consumer Field Name: Modified By in the Configure Connections dialog box and click Finish. SharePoint applies the filter to the document library web part.

Figure 6-10 shows the Current User Filter web part in action.

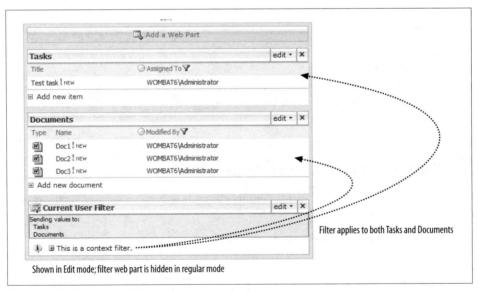

Figure 6-10. Filtering multiple web parts on a page by current user

The filter applies only to columns that are visible in the web part. That's why only the Type and Modified By columns showed up in the Consumer Field Name drop-down for the document library. If you want to filter on Created By or some other column, you have to add that column to the view displayed in the Documents web part.

Creating Custom Filters

The Choice, SharePoint List, and Text Filter web parts accept filter values selected by the user. Use these web parts in conjunction with the Filter Actions web part to create pages that the user can filter however he pleases.

To see how that works:

1. Navigate to the same sample site used in the preceding section and create a new test page.

2. Add the Task list, document library, and Text Filter web parts to the page.

3. On the Text Filter web part toolbar, click Open on the tool pane and name the filter Sample Text Filter. Click OK to close the tool pane.

4. Connect the Text Filter to the Documents and Tasks web parts as described in the preceding section. Click Exit Edit Mode when done.

5. The text filter lets the user type in a name to see tasks and documents that relate to that user, as shown in Figure 6-11.

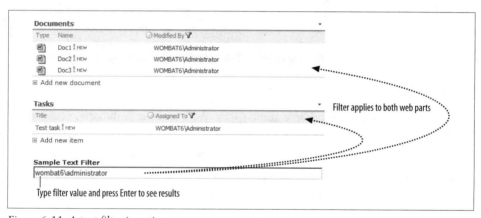

Figure 6-11. A text filter in action

The text filter is not case-sensitive, but it must otherwise exactly match. There are no wild-card characters or partial matches. A better way to create the sample in Figure 6-11 is to use the SharePoint List Filter web part, which looks up its filter values from a list. To make that change:

1. Delete the Sample Text Filter web part and add a SharePoint List Filter to the page.

2. Use the following property settings for the new SharePoint List Filter web part.

Section	Property	Set to
Top	Filter Name	Sample List Filter
	List	Documents
	View	All Documents

Section	Property	Set to
	Value Field	Modified By
	Description Field	Modified By

3. Connect the filter web part to the Documents and Tasks web parts.

4. Click Exit Edit Mode when done. The Sample List Filter now displays a list of filter choices when you click the filter button, as shown in Figure 6-12.

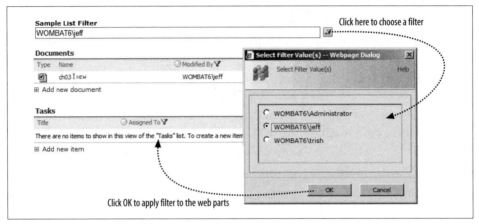

Figure 6-12. A SharePoint list filter in action

The other filter web parts work in a similar way. With all filter web parts, you should remember the following limitations:

- You must name the filter before you can connect it to other web parts.
- Once connected, you can't change certain filter properties. To change those properties, disconnect the filter, change the properties, and then reconnect.
- Web parts can only connect to one filter at a time.

Saving Filter Options

The preceding sample looks up the filter choices from the Modified By column of the Documents library to display only the documents and tasks for a specific user. If you navigate away from the page and then return to it, the selection is cleared and all of the documents and tasks are displayed. To allow the filter to be saved:

- Add a Filter Actions web part to the page.

The Filter Actions web part displays a button that allows the user to apply the filter and a checkbox that enables the user to save the filter as the default when she returns to the page later, as shown in Figure 6-13.

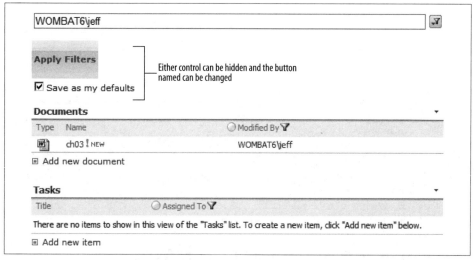

Figure 6-13. Saving a filter using the Filter Actions web part

The Filter Actions web part applies all of the filters on the page, so it's a way to perform multiple filter operations with one click.

Using Passed-in Filters

The Query String Filter web part reads its filter value from a parameter passed to the page as a query string. Use it to automatically filter a page based on a link or value from another page. To see how it works:

1. Create a new test page and add Task, Documents, and Query String Filter web parts.

2. Use the property settings defined in the following table for the Query String Filter web part.

Section	Property	Set to
Top	Filter Name	Sample QueryString
	Query String Parameter Name	Filter

3. Connect the Query String Web part to the Task and Documents web parts and then click Exit Edit Mode.

4. Change the URL in the address bar to apply a filter, as shown in Figure 6-14.

In Figure 6-14, the URL is *http://wombat6/samples/page3.aspx?filter=wombat6\jeff*.

So, the filter only displays the documents and tasks for the user *wombat6\jeff*. By generating different query strings, you can have the same page display different results depending on how you link to it.

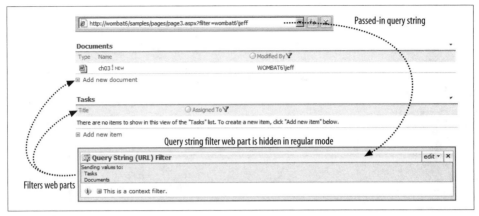

Figure 6-14. The Query String Filter web part in action

Connecting to Data with WSRP in MOSS

The MOSS WSRP web part displays results from web services that implement the Web Services for Remote Portlets (WSRP) standard. WSRP generates HTML markup fragments rather than the unformatted XML that most web services provide. The HTML markup is easier to display on a web page.

To use WSRP from SharePoint:

1. Add a *TrustedWSRPProducers.config* file (shown later) to this location on the SharePoint server:

    C:\Program Files\Microsoft Office Server\12.0\Config

2. Run *iisreset.exe* on the server.

3. Add the WSRP web part to a page and select the service to use.

This sample configures the NetUnity WSRP producer demo for use on the server:

```
<!-- TrustedWSRPProducre.config -->
<Configuration xmlns="http://schemas.microsoft.com/office/sps/2005/WSRP/
Configuration" ProxyAddress="http://wombat6:80">
<Producer Name="NetUnity" AllowScripts="true">
<ServiceDescriptionURL>http://wsrp.netunitysoftware.com:80/WSRPTestService/
WSRPTestService.asmx</ServiceDescriptionURL>
<RegistrationURL>http://wsrp.netunitysoftware.com:80/WSRPTestService/WSRPTestService.
asmx</RegistrationURL>
<MarkupURL>http://wsrp.netunitysoftware.com:80/WSRPTestService/WSRPTestService.asmx</
MarkupURL>
<PortletManagementURL>http://wsrp.netunitysoftware.com:80/WSRPTestService/
WSRPTestService.asmx</PortletManagementURL>
<!--SsoApplication Name="NetunityWSRP"/-->
</Producer>
</Configuration>
```

Modifying Master Pages

SharePoint defines the layout, web zones, navigational web parts, and styles used on pages through the site's *master page*. Modify a site's master page to change:

- The appearance of a site
- The navigational web parts used throughout the site

How you make those changes depends on whether you have MOSS or WSS. In MOSS, you can select from a list to swap the default master page to one of the other designs. In WSS, you must edit the default master page to make changes. The following sections cover each of those approaches.

Swapping the Master Page in MOSS

In MOSS, you can swap the master page of a site to quickly change its appearance. These changes are similar to applying a theme to the site, but they go deeper because they change the page layout and the navigational web parts as well as the styles and fonts.

To change the appearance of the top-level portal site:

1. Navigate to the top-level site and click Site Actions → Site Settings → Modify All Site Settings, and then click "Master page" under the Look and Feel heading. SharePoint displays the Master Page Settings page.
2. In the Site Master Page section, select "OrangeSingleLevel.master" as shown in Figure 6-15.
3. Scroll to the System Master Page section, select "OrangeSingleLevel.master," and click OK. SharePoint changes the layout and styles used on the pages in the site.

I chose the OrangeSingleLevel master page because it is the most radical departure from the default layout. There's no overlooking the difference! The *Site Master Page* setting controls the appearance of the publishing pages, whereas the *System Master Page* setting controls the appearance of list and library pages.

In the top-level portal site, the publishing pages are stored in the Pages folder. The main home page (*default.aspx*) is a publishing page. The list and library pages include the views, new item form, edit form, and so on. The master page settings do not change the appearance of the settings pages.

Please use a consistent look and feel throughout your entire portal. It's best to pick a single master page and set it as your Site Master Page and System Master Page at the top-level site, and then inherit that setting in all the subsites.

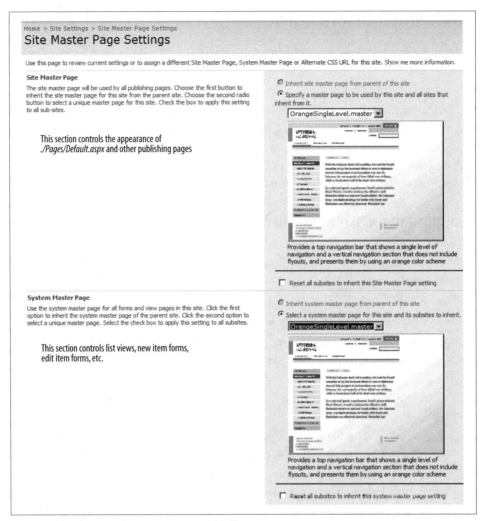

Figure 6-15. Changing the master page in MOSS

Editing the Master Page

WSS doesn't provide a way to quickly swap master pages. Each site has one master page, and the only way to change it is to edit that page. There are two ways to edit SharePoint master pages:

- Download the page from the master page gallery, make your changes in a text editor, and then upload the file. This approach gives you the most control and doesn't require special tools.

- Open the master page directly from the gallery using SharePoint Designer. This approach is a little simpler but requires SharePoint Designer.

SharePoint master pages are similar to ASP.NET 2.0 master pages, but you can't edit them using your development tools—Visual Studio 2005 doesn't support opening SharePoint web sites!

Whenever you edit master pages, it's a good idea to first create a test site in which to make your changes. Once the edits are final, you can deploy the new master page to the target site's gallery.

To edit a master page using the download approach:

1. Create a *MasterPages* folder on your computer.
2. Create a test site using the same site template as the target site. The target site is the site where you will deploy your final master page when you are done with the edits.
3. Click Site Actions → Site Settings, and click "Master pages" under the Galleries heading in the middle of the page. SharePoint displays the Master Pages Gallery.
4. Click the *default.master* page's Edit menu and select Send To → Download a Copy, and download the file to the *MasterPages* folder.
5. Open the file in Notepad and make your changes.
6. Upload the changed file to the Master Pages Gallery.

Uploading creates a new version of the master page in the gallery. If the changes you made broke anything, you can revert to the previous version by following these steps:

1. Navigate to the Master Page Gallery, click the page's Edit menu, and select Version History.
2. Click on the version to restore and then click "Restore this version" on the toolbar.

To edit a master page using SharePoint Designer:

1. Navigate to the Master Pages Gallery, click the page's Edit menu, and select Edit in Microsoft Office SharePoint Designer. SharePoint opens the file in SharePoint Designer.
2. Make your change and save the file. SharePoint Designer saves a new version of it.

What kind of changes can you make? It's best to start small and work your way up. The following change (shown in bold) displays lists and libraries as cascading menus in the Quick Launch:

```
<SharePoint:AspMenu
id="QuickLaunchMenu"
DataSourceId="QuickLaunchSiteMap"
runat="server"
Orientation="Vertical"
StaticDisplayLevels="1" <!-- was 2 -->
ItemWrap="true"
MaximumDynamicDisplayLevels="1" <!-- was 0 -->
StaticSubMenuIndent="0"
SkipLinkText="">
```

Figure 6-16 shows the change in action.

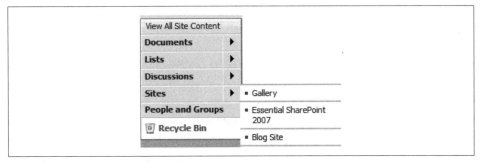

Figure 6-16. Changing default.master to display cascading menus on Quick Launch

Deploying Master Pages

Once the edits to the master page are final, you can deploy the master page to individual sites or to the entire server.

To deploy a master page to an individual site:

1. Download the file to your *MasterPages* folder.
2. Upload the file to the target site's Master Pages Gallery.

To deploy a master page to the server:

1. Download the file to your *MasterPages* folder.
2. Copy the file to this location on the server:

    *C:\Program Files\Common Files\Microsoft Shared\web server extensions\12\
    TEMPLATE\GLOBAL*

3. Refresh one of the affected pages in your browser to see the change; you don't need to run *iisreset.exe* on the server.

The preceding location is for the master pages provided by WSS. The additional master pages provided by MOSS are stored at:

*C:\Program Files\Common Files\Microsoft Shared\web server extensions\12\
TEMPLATE\FEATURES\PublishingLayouts\MasterPages*

SharePoint includes two main master pages in the GLOBAL folder:

- *default.master* is used by most site templates (Team Site, Blank Site, etc.).
- *mwsdefault.master* is used by the meeting workspace site templates.

The *mwsdefault.master* page includes a set of page tabs at the top that are tied to the meeting workspace site template. You can't use that master page from other types of sites, and if you swap the master page of a meeting workspace to one of the MOSS master pages, you'll lose that tab feature.

MOSS includes the following additional master pages in the *MasterPages* folder.

Master page	Color scheme	Quick Launch	Link bar
BlackBand.master	Black	Yes	Yes
BlackSingleLevel.master	Black background	Yes	Yes
BlackVertical.master	Black	Yes	No
BlueBand.master	Blue	Yes	Yes
BlueGlassBand.master	Blue Glass	Yes	Yes
BlueTabs.master	Blue	Yes	Yes (as tabs)
BlueVertical.master	Blue	Yes	No
OrangeSingleLevel.master	Orange	Yes	Yes

Best Practices

- Convert List Views to Data Views in SharePoint Designer to fully customize their appearance.

- List Views can't be exported as web parts; Data Views can and are therefore easier to reuse throughout a site.

- Use the Content Editor web part to include HTML snippets on multiple pages.

- Use the Page Viewer web part to display HTML that includes Form elements.

- Use master pages to customize the appearance of your portal. Sometimes this is referred to as *rebranding*. The two other techniques for rebranding (site theme and cascading style sheets) are covered in Chapter 3.

- From a design standpoint, it's best to pick a single master page and set it as your Site Master Page and System Master Page at the top-level site, and then inherit that setting in all of the subsites.

CHAPTER 7

Creating My Sites, Blogs, and Wikis

My Sites, blogs, and Wikis fall into an area called *personalization features*—features tied to a user's identity, which help maintain the user's presence on the Web. Managers often ask why SharePoint includes these features, and then they ask me to disable them: the last thing they want is for an employee to start a blog. I understand that point of view, but I feel the benefits of these sites outweigh the risks. Specifically:

- My Sites can replace personal storage on network drives and provide communication across teams and projects.
- Blogs allow subject experts to share their knowledge.
- Wikis are a way to easily create online Help, reference, and employee resources.

SharePoint is all about leveraging the community to get work done and share the results. In this chapter, I'll cover applications for these site types and describe how to control their use.

 My Sites are only available in MOSS.

Creating My Sites in MOSS

My Sites define your identity on the intranet. They are a place to share information that doesn't fit neatly into a project or department site. They are also a great place to prototype lists and experiment with SharePoint. Many companies provide network drives for files that users need to share, and My Sites are a great way to replace those.

As employees become proficient at using SharePoint, they can extend their use of My Sites to fill these advanced needs:

- Create their own portal for accessing internal and external resources.
- Find subject area experts within the company.
- Locate the correct person to talk to in other departments or locations.

To create your My Site:

1. Click the My Site link at the upper-right corner of any page. SharePoint creates the site if it does not already exist.

2. Once the site is created, SharePoint takes you to the site and displays a dialog box asking if you want to link your Office applications to the site. Figure 7-1 illustrates the process.

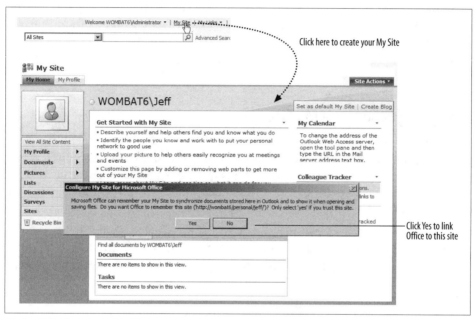

Figure 7-1. Creating a My Site

Clicking Yes in the dialog box in Figure 7-1 adds the site to the default list of save locations in Office applications.

Using My Sites for Training

The next steps for setting up the site are described on the home page under the heading "Get Started with My Site." Just click on the links and complete the tasks. When I train folks, I walk them through setting up their My Sites in class, and I've learned to:

- Bring a camera. I take head shots of everyone at the break and upload the pictures myself. It's a way to control what pictures are put up and to keep track of who I've trained.

- Have the class fill out their Profiles in class. It's a good exercise and they enjoy it.

- Show how to upload public files to the Shared Documents library, and demonstrate how others can see it. Then I show the Personal Documents library for private information.

- Stress the public nature of My Sites: don't post anything you don't want others to see.

- Hand out diplomas at the end of training.

My Sites are a good place to teach SharePoint because each individual is the Administrator of his My Site. He can create new lists, libraries, and subsites; control access; add web parts; and delete things.

Anything you can do with other SharePoint sites, you can do with My Sites. I won't repeat all those things here—the built-in instructions are pretty good. Instead, I'll use the rest of this section to focus on controlling My Sites once they are in use. For all of these remaining My Site tasks, you will have to be signed on as the SharePoint Administrator.

Controlling Who Has a My Site

By default, all authenticated users can create a My Site. Of course, not everyone needs one, and it's a good idea to provide training before turning on the feature. When rolling out SharePoint, I usually turn on My Sites for each department right before I train it. That lets me use My Sites in class and helps prevent problems with inappropriate material being posted in the meantime.

Another advantage of a department-by-department rollout is that it helps build a base of users who can support one another. Try to find one or two potential power users within each department and then channel books and other special training to those users.

To authorize My Sites on a department-by-department basis:

1. Sign on to the server as the SharePoint administrator.

2. Navigate to the SharePoint Central Administration web site and click Shared Services Administration → Shared Services on the left side of the page. SharePoint displays the Shared Services Administration page (see Figure 7-2).

3. Click "Personalization services permissions" under the "User Profiles and My Sites" heading. SharePoint displays the Manage Permissions page (see Figure 7-3).

4. Select the Authenticated Users group and click Remove Selected Users. SharePoint removes the My Site feature for that general audience.

5. Click Add User/Groups and add the department Active Directory (AD) security group to authorize. Select the "Create personal site" and "User personal features" permissions as shown in Figure 7-4, and then click Save. SharePoint authorizes My Sites for members of the AD security group.

I authorized the IT department to have personal sites first in Figure 7-4. It's not a bad idea to train IT first so it can provide support as the other departments roll out.

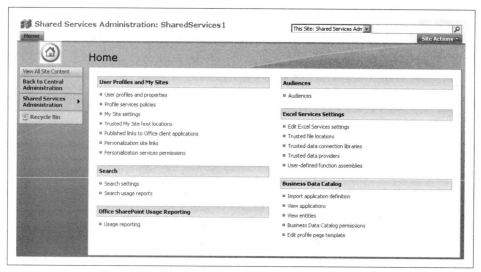

Figure 7-2. Use the Shared Services Administration to control personalization features

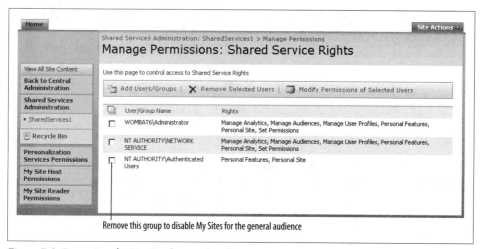

Remove this group to disable My Sites for the general audience

Figure 7-3. Removing the My Site feature for all users

The "Create personal site" right in Figure 7-4 authorizes the user to have a My Site. The "Use personal features" right displays My Site | My Links in the upper-right corner of pages. If users create a My Site and their permission is later removed, the site continues to exist, but they do not have access to it.

Setting the Site Quota

My Sites have a storage quota of 100 MB by default. Once a user's My Site site collection reaches 80 MB, she starts getting SharePoint emails alerting her that she's near her limit. Once she reaches 100 MB, she can no longer upload data or create new subsites.

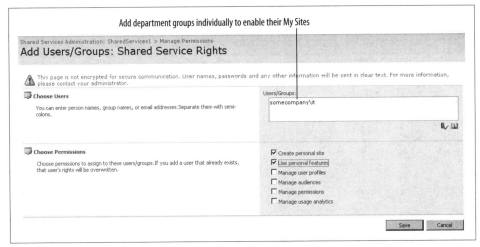

Figure 7-4. *Authorizing a department to have My Sites*

To change the quota:

1. Navigate to the SharePoint Central Administration web site and click Application Management, and then click "Quota templates" under the SharePoint Site Management heading. SharePoint displays the Quota Templates page (see Figure 7-5).

2. Change the settings in the Storage Limit Values section and click OK. SharePoint changes the quota.

You can also use this page to create new quotas, and then apply those quotas to sites individually. To apply a quota to a site:

1. Return to the Application Management tab in SharePoint Central Administration and click "Site collection quotas and locks" just underneath the "Quota templates" link. SharePoint displays the Site Collection Quotas and Locks page.

2. Select the address of a site collection to change and then select the quota template as shown in Figure 7-6. Click OK when done.

The My Sites are stored in the Personal folder by default in SharePoint. Each My Site is a site collection, and its URL matches the user's AD account name. You can change that location and naming convention by clicking the "My Site settings" link on the Shared Services Administration page shown earlier in Figure 7-2.

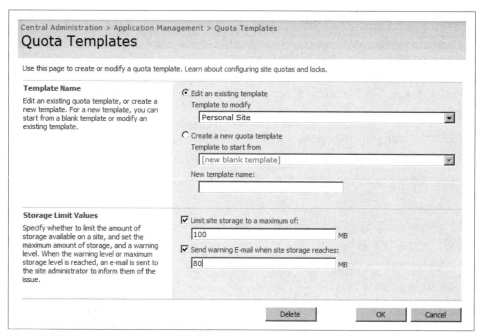

Figure 7-5. Changing the storage quota for My Sites

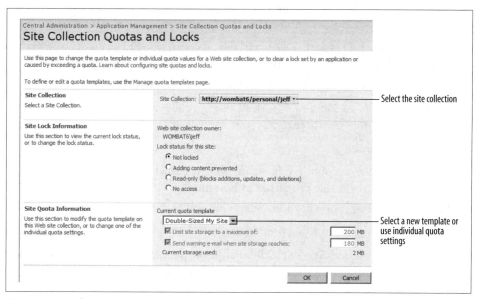

Figure 7-6. Applying a new quota template to a site collection

Managing Users' My Sites

The objections I hear from management about My Sites relate to control: managers are afraid users will post objectionable material, or waste their time writing personal blogs. Those issues are nontechnical, really, but technology can certainly make the problem more noticeable. If a problem occurs, you can take several actions:

- Lock the user's site to prevent access to it.
- Edit the user's site to remove the objectionable material.
- Edit the user's profile to remove objectionable settings in profile fields.
- Lock profile fields to prevent user edits.

To lock a site:

1. Navigate to the Site Collection Quotas and Locks page shown earlier in Figure 7-6.
2. Select "No access" in the Site Lock Information section and click OK. SharePoint prevents access to the site for all users except Administrators.

To edit the user's My Site:

1. Navigate to the Shared Services Administration page (refer to Figure 7-2) and click "User profiles and properties" under the "User Profiles and My Sites" heading. SharePoint displays the User Profiles and Properties page (see Figure 7-7).
2. Click View User Profiles. SharePoint displays a list of the profiles imported from Active Directory.
3. Choose Manage Personal Site from the account's Edit menu as shown in Figure 7-8. SharePoint displays the user's My Site Site Settings page.
4. Use the Site Settings page to make the required changes to the site.

Use the search fields in Figure 7-8 to find user profiles in large organizations. My demonstration site only has three users; your list will certainly be longer.

To edit a user's profile:

1. Click Edit on the account's Edit menu shown earlier in Figure 7-8. SharePoint displays the user's profile properties in Edit mode.
2. Make your changes and click OK. SharePoint saves the changes.

To prevent user changes to profile properties:

1. Return to the Shared Services Administration page and click "Profile services policies" under the "User Profiles and My Sites" heading. SharePoint displays the Manage Policy page.
2. Click the items to change and select Edit Policy from the Edit menu as shown in Figure 7-9.
3. Deselect the "User can override" checkbox and click OK. SharePoint changes the profile property to read-only for all users.

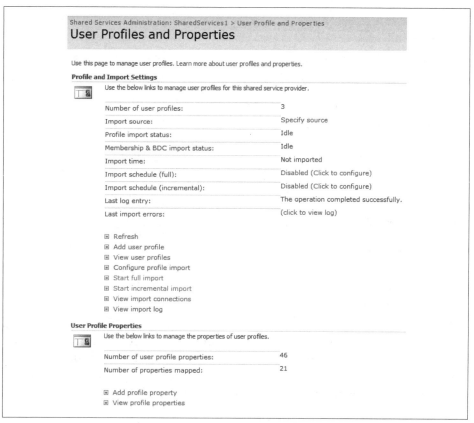

Figure 7-7. Use this page to manage the import of profiles from Active Directory and to control profile properties

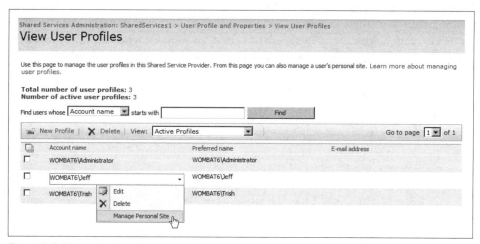

Figure 7-8. Managing users' My Sites

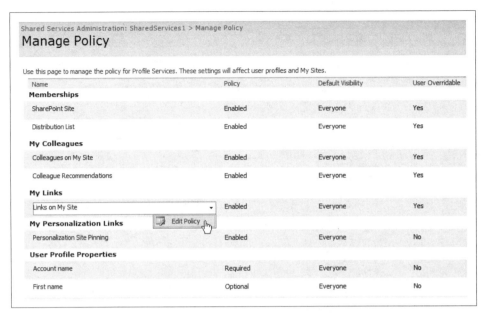

Shared Services Administration: SharedServices1 > Manage Policy
Manage Policy

Use this page to manage the policy for Profile Services. These settings will affect user profiles and My Sites.

Name	Policy	Default Visibility	User Overridable
Memberships			
SharePoint Site	Enabled	Everyone	Yes
Distribution List	Enabled	Everyone	Yes
My Colleagues			
Colleagues on My Site	Enabled	Everyone	Yes
Colleague Recommendations	Enabled	Everyone	Yes
My Links			
Links on My Site ▾	Enabled	Everyone	Yes
My Personalization Links [Edit Policy]			
Personalization Site Pinning	Enabled	Everyone	No
User Profile Properties			
Account name	Required	Everyone	No
First name	Optional	Everyone	No

Figure 7-9. Preventing user changes to profile properties

SharePoint imports user profiles from Active Directory, LDAP, or Business Data Catalog. You can control how that import is performed from the User Profile and Properties page shown earlier in Figure 7-7. Changes to the user's profile in SharePoint aren't exported back to those sources—provided imports are read-only.

Creating Blogs

A *blog* is a personal journal with comments from the audience. Entries are organized chronologically, so the site owner doesn't have to put a lot of thought into organizing or maintaining the site. Blogs are best suited for topic experts who want to teach others—for example, Microsoft makes extensive use of blogs within MSDN.

 If you want to learn about business applications for blogs, check out Andy Wibbel's *Blogwild!: A Guide for Small Business Blogging* (Portfolio Hardcover) or *Naked Conversations: How Blogs are Changing the Way Businesses Talk with Customers* by Robert Scoble and Shel Israel (Wiley).

Each My Site comes with a link in the top-right corner that allows the user to create a blog (see Figure 7-10). These blogs are usually only visible to other employees within the company.

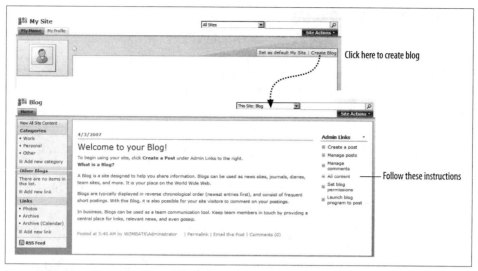

Figure 7-10. Creating a blog from a My Site

After you create a blog, it appears on the public view of your My Site. You can see the public view of your My Site by clicking on the My Profile tab as shown in Figure 7-11.

Figure 7-11. Others see your blog through the public view of your My Site

 Word 2007 actually links to this blog so you can create posts directly from that Office application.

Creating Blogs Without My Sites

If you are not using MOSS or if your organization blocks My Sites, you can still create blogs. In this case, it is a good idea to create a site collection for the blogs and then place all of them in that location. Appoint someone to administer the site collection—that person will be responsible for creating new blogs.

To set up a collection for blog sites:

1. Create a site collection named "Blogs" using the Blank Site template and add all authenticated users to the Visitors group and the administrator to the Owners group.

2. Customize the home page of the site collection to display a list of the blogs and to make it easy for users to request them.

3. Replace the Quick Launch on the left side of the page with a tree view, so users can easily find blogs.

Figure 7-12 shows a sample site collection for blog sites with a customized home page. A template for this site is included in the online samples for this book.

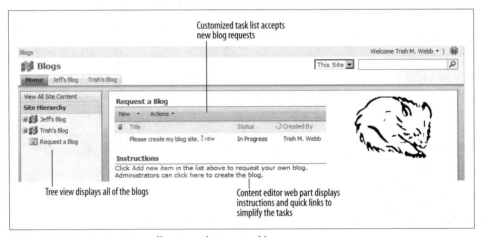

Figure 7-12. Setting up a site collection to house user blogs

The blog site administrator (blogistrator?) follows these steps when he receives a new site request:

1. Confirms that the user is allowed to have a blog.

2. Clicks on the link in the instructions to display the New SharePoint Site page.

3. Creates a new site using the Blog Site template.

4. Add the requestor as the site owner. That page sends email notifying the user that she is now the site owner.

5. Return to the blog home page and change the status of the request to Completed.

I include these procedures to show how you might control blog site creation. You may want to create your own procedure for approval and auditing of blog sites, depending on how comfortable management is with the concept.

Requiring Approval for Comments

In public forums, it is a good idea to require approval for comments before they appear on the blog. To do that:

1. Navigate to the blog site.
2. Click View All Site Content on the left side of the page.
3. Click Comments. SharePoint displays the list that holds the replies to the author's blog.
4. On the list toolbar, click Settings → List Settings, and then click Versioning Settings under the General Settings heading.
5. Select Yes in the Content Approval section and click OK.
6. Return to the Comments list, click Actions → Alert Me, and create an alert to notify the site owner when new comments are posted so she can approve or reject them.

Blocking Blogs

The approach described in "Creating Blogs Without My Sites" is one way to control who can have a blog and who cannot. If you want to prohibit blogging altogether, there are a couple of approaches:

- Hide the Blog Site template to prevent new blogs from being created.
- Remove the Blog Site template to prevent new blogs and stop existing blog sites.

To hide the template:

1. Open the *WEBTEMP.XML* file from this location on the server:

   C:\Program Files\Common Files\Microsoft Shared\web server extensions\12\ TEMPLATE\1033\XML

2. Change the `Hidden` property to `TRUE` as shown below (in bold).

   ```
   <Template Name="BLOG" ID="9">
       <Configuration ID="0" Title="Blog" Hidden="TRUE"
       ImageUrl="/_layouts/images/blogprev.png" Description="A site for a person or
       team to post ideas, observations, and expertise that site visitors can
   comment
       on." DisplayCategory="Collaboration" >    </Configuration>
       </Template>
   ```

3. Save the file and run *iisreset.exe* to load the changes.

Hiding a template in *WEBTEMP.XML* removes it from the list of available site templates displayed when someone creates a new site.

To remove the blog template, comment out the `Template` element in *WEBTEMP.XML*, as shown here:

```
<!-- JAW, 04/03/07: Removed Blog template.
<Template Name="BLOG" ID="9">
    <Configuration ID="0" Title="Blog" Hidden="TRUE"
    ImageUrl="/_layouts/images/blogprev.png" Description="A site for a person or
    team to post ideas, observations, and expertise that site visitors can comment
    on." DisplayCategory="Collaboration" >    </Configuration>
</Template>
-->
```

Commenting out the template breaks any existing blog sites—users will get an error if they try to navigate to a blog, so you should delete those sites when time allows.

Creating Wikis

Wikis are web sites that everyone can edit. Well, not everyone—just Contributors, actually. Wikis are best used to collect content where there's not just one expert. Wikipedia is the largest and most successful example of a Wiki.

Wikis have several practical applications:

- Provide Help for custom applications.
- Create and publish HR assets such as employee handbooks and policies.
- Define terms and acronyms that are unique to your organization.
- Gather history and feedback on projects.

Wikis are suited for any situation where you have multiple authors for documents organized by topic. Most people think of Wikipedia, where everyone is a contributor, as the model for Wikis, but the Contributors list can be one or two authors if you like.

To create a Wiki:

1. Navigate to the site collection where you want the site to reside. If the Wiki is for a project, navigate to the project site.
2. Click Site Actions → Create, and then click Sites and Workspaces under the Web Pages heading on the right.
3. Complete the New SharePoint Site page, select the Wiki Site template, and click Create. SharePoint creates the Wiki site.
4. Click Site Actions → Site Settings, and then click People and Groups under the Users and Permissions heading.
5. Add users who will contribute to the Wiki to the Members group. Add users who will read the Wiki but not contribute to the Visitors group.

When you create a new Wiki site, SharePoint automatically includes a home page and a "How to use this site" page. Edit the home page to provide links to other pages in the Wiki—it is the best place to organize the information in the Wiki. It's a good idea to link to the "How to use this page" on the home page so new users can get help.

To make these changes:

1. On the Wiki home page, click Edit in the upper-right corner of the page. SharePoint switches the page to Edit mode.

2. Make the changes shown in Figure 7-13 (or similar changes), and click OK to save them.

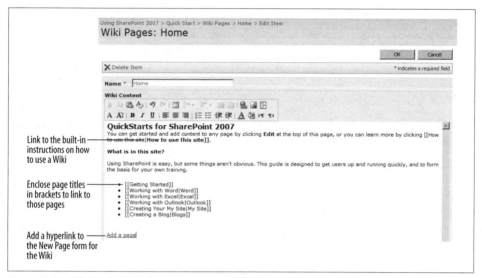

Figure 7-13. Editing the Wiki home page to provide navigation

There are very good instructions on how to link to other pages, add hyperlinks, and make other edits on the "How to use this Wiki" Site page that comes with every new Wiki, so I won't repeat those here.

Organizing a Wiki

A Wiki site contains one Wiki Page library. The home page for that library is displayed when you navigate to the site. To see the whole library, click View All Pages on the left side of the page. Figure 7-14 shows the whole Wiki Page library.

This simple one-to-one organization is good for subjects with a flat organization, such as definitions or reference topics. It's less well-suited for subjects that require a hierarchical or sequential organization.

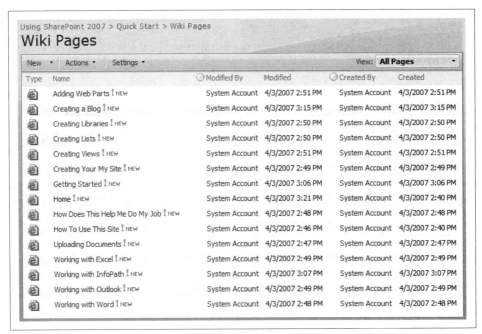

Wiki Pages

New ▾	Actions ▾	Settings ▾			View: **All Pages** ▾

Type	Name	Modified By	Modified	Created By	Created
📄	Adding Web Parts ! NEW	System Account	4/3/2007 2:51 PM	System Account	4/3/2007 2:51 PM
📄	Creating a Blog ! NEW	System Account	4/3/2007 3:15 PM	System Account	4/3/2007 3:15 PM
📄	Creating Libraries ! NEW	System Account	4/3/2007 2:50 PM	System Account	4/3/2007 2:50 PM
📄	Creating Lists ! NEW	System Account	4/3/2007 2:50 PM	System Account	4/3/2007 2:50 PM
📄	Creating Views ! NEW	System Account	4/3/2007 2:51 PM	System Account	4/3/2007 2:51 PM
📄	Creating Your My Site ! NEW	System Account	4/3/2007 2:49 PM	System Account	4/3/2007 2:49 PM
📄	Getting Started ! NEW	System Account	4/3/2007 3:06 PM	System Account	4/3/2007 3:06 PM
📄	Home ! NEW	System Account	4/3/2007 3:21 PM	System Account	4/3/2007 2:40 PM
📄	How Does This Help Me Do My Job ! NEW	System Account	4/3/2007 2:48 PM	System Account	4/3/2007 2:48 PM
📄	How To Use This Site ! NEW	System Account	4/3/2007 2:46 PM	System Account	4/3/2007 2:40 PM
📄	Uploading Documents ! NEW	System Account	4/3/2007 2:47 PM	System Account	4/3/2007 2:47 PM
📄	Working with Excel ! NEW	System Account	4/3/2007 2:49 PM	System Account	4/3/2007 2:49 PM
📄	Working with InfoPath ! NEW	System Account	4/3/2007 3:07 PM	System Account	4/3/2007 3:07 PM
📄	Working with Outlook ! NEW	System Account	4/3/2007 2:49 PM	System Account	4/3/2007 2:49 PM
📄	Working with Word ! NEW	System Account	4/3/2007 2:48 PM	System Account	4/3/2007 2:48 PM

Figure 7-14. A Wiki site contains a single Wiki Page library

There are several solutions to that problem:

- Add links to the Quick Launch to organize the pages.
- Create navigational pages for each top-level topic and then link to those pages on the home page.
- Add columns and create views for the library to organize the pages.

The following sections explore each of those approaches in turn.

Adding Links to Quick Launch

The Quick Launch area of a new Wiki site includes links to the home page and "How to use this site" page by default. To add links to other pages:

1. Open the Wiki in two browser windows. You'll use one window to get the address of pages and the other window to enter the information in the Quick Launch.

2. In the first window, navigate to the page you want to add to Quick Launch, select the URL in the address bar, and press Ctrl+C to copy the address.

3. In the second window, click Site Actions → Site Settings, and then click Quick Launch under the Look and Feel heading.

4. Click New Link and paste the page address into the web address field. Enter a title for the page in the description field and click OK.

Quick Launch allows two levels of organization: New Heading creates a new section on the web part, and New Link adds an item beneath a heading (see Figure 7-15).

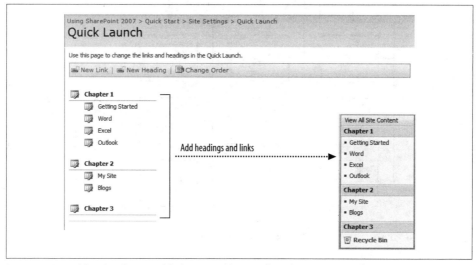

Figure 7-15. Adding headings and links to Quick Launch

There are several disadvantages to this approach:

- The space on the Quick Launch is limited.
- You only have two levels of organization.
- The links are static, so they can become out of date.

Creating Navigational Pages

Earlier I recommended you use the home page of the Wiki to provide links to other pages. You can create additional navigational pages by repeating that procedure for each top-level topic as needed (see Figure 7-16).

The advantages of this approach are:

- You can create as many levels as needed.
- You can create and maintain the links fairly easily (broken links are underlined).

The disadvantage is that it's hard to get an overview of all of the information unless you manually create a table of contents.

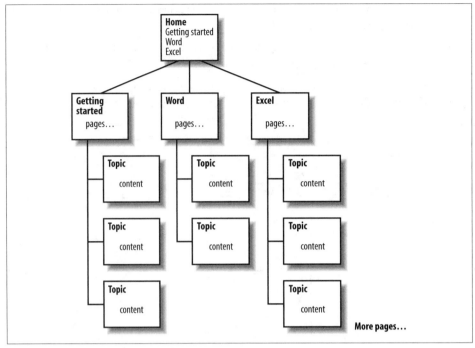

Figure 7-16. Organizing Wikis by creating navigational pages

Using Views to Organize Wiki Libraries

Since Wikis are libraries, you can add columns and create views to group the pages however you want to organize them. Figure 7-17 shows topics grouped by chapter in a Contents view.

The advantages of this approach are:

- You can see the organization clearly.
- You can create, maintain, or change the view easily.

The disadvantage is that you have to enter the metadata for each page—in this case, its chapter number. The more metadata, the more options for organization, and the greater the difficulty in creating new pages.

Creating Wiki Libraries

The default Wiki site comes with one library, but you can create as many additional libraries as you like. For example, you might create separate libraries for Reference and How To topics in a Help site.

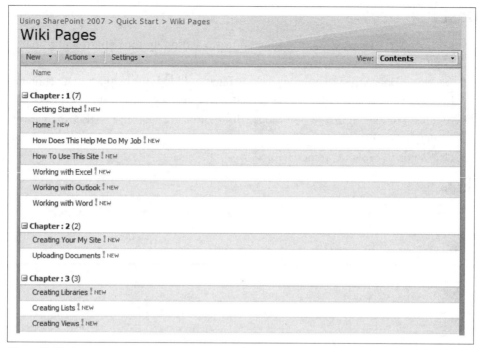

Figure 7-17. Create a custom view to organize Wiki pages

To create a new Wiki Page Library:

1. Click Site Actions → Create, and then click Wiki Page Library under the Libraries heading on the left.

2. Complete the "New library" page and click Create. SharePoint creates the new Wiki Page Library within the current site.

You can add a Wiki Page Library to any type of site—it is a great way to create a Help system for a SharePoint application.

Controlling Access

Many of the same concepts that apply to blogs also apply to Wikis:

- You should designate a site owner who is responsible for the Wiki.
- In public forums, you may want to require approval for edits and send notification to the site owner when changes are made.
- You can block Wikis by hiding or removing the template in *WEBTEMP.XML*.

See the earlier section "Creating Blogs" for information on how to perform those tasks.

Best Practices

- Activate My Sites by department just prior to setting up the department's Share-Point site and providing training.
- Develop a policy to audit employees' My Sites and blogs for inappropriate content. Be sure to clearly communicate what your organization considers inappropriate.
- Require content approval for blogs, discussion groups, and Wikis that allow anonymous posts.
- Use Wikis to provide online Help.

CHAPTER 8

Enabling Email and Workflow

I think people rely on email because it is immediate, centralized, and stores work history. But because email is private, finding the status of an item means sending more email. As the number of work items grows and the need for updates increases, email quickly overflows.

SharePoint addresses these problems by creating Team Sites. Team members can communicate through that site so that all their comments and actions are stored in a central, searchable location. However, that approach is passive. To be effective, Team Sites often need to actively notify members when tasks are assigned, new items are posted, or when other events occur. SharePoint handles those notifications through email alerts and workflows.

Alerts have these advantages over unstructured email:

- Alerts link to items so changes to their status or history can be viewed by others.
- Users can turn most alerts on or off and choose how frequently alerts are sent.
- Site owners can schedule alerts for overdue tasks or cyclical events.
- Libraries can also receive email to help gather history in a central location.

Workflows are a way of assigning tasks and sending alerts to users in a step-by-step fashion that follows a business process. They go beyond email notifications by:

- Assigning actionable tasks for a work item.
- Tracking the progress of a work item through a process.
- Recording the history of the process, including how long it took.

In this chapter, you will learn how to integrate email with your SharePoint applications and how to create workflows that manage the approval process and help automate document control.

Receiving Alerts

SharePoint *alerts* send email when an item in a list or library changes. To create an alert:

1. Click Alert Me from the list Actions menu or from the item's Edit menu, as shown in Figure 8-1. SharePoint displays the New Alert page.

2. Complete the New Alert page as shown in Figure 8-2 and click OK. SharePoint sends an email confirming that your alert was created.

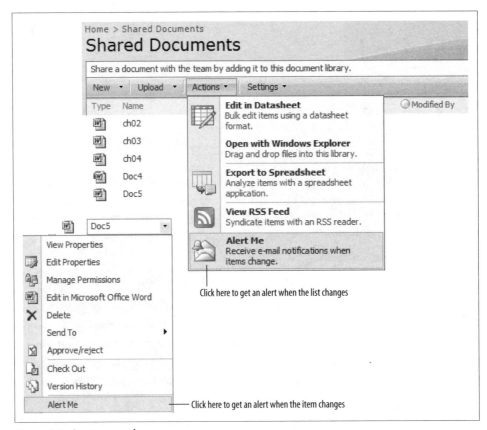

Figure 8-1. Creating an alert

I tell people to ask for daily summaries rather than immediate alerts, because it is easy to get overwhelmed by alerts. A daily summary organizes the changes in a single message. If you need more frequent notification, create two daily summary alerts: one in the morning and one after lunch.

You can set alerts on a single item or on an entire list. SharePoint checks for changes every five minutes using the SharePoint Timer service.

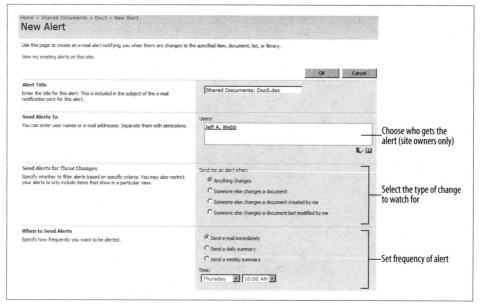

Figure 8-2. Choosing alert settings

Creating Alerts for Others

The New Alert page lets site owners create alerts for others. Contributors and visitors won't see the Send Alerts To section in Figure 8-2; they can only create their own alerts.

Managing Alerts

To change your alerts:

1. Click My Settings on the Welcome Edit menu in the upper-right corner of the page, as shown in Figure 8-3. SharePoint displays your user information.
2. Click My Alerts on the toolbar. SharePoint displays a list of your alerts.
3. To change an alert, click on the alert link, as shown in Figure 8-4.

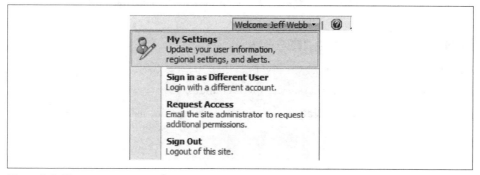

Figure 8-3. Viewing your user information

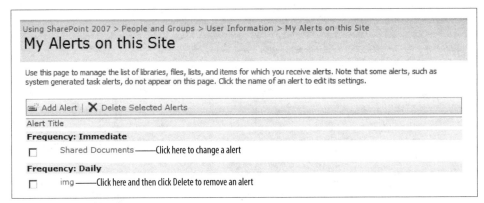

Figure 8-4. *Managing your alerts*

To manage the alerts of others:

1. Click Site Actions → Site Settings, and then click "User alerts" under the Site Administration heading. SharePoint displays the User Alerts page.

2. Select the user to display, and click Update, as shown in Figure 8-5.

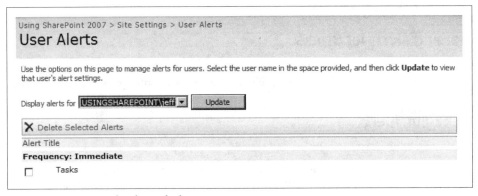

Figure 8-5. *Managing the alerts of others*

You can only delete alerts from this page, so if you need to change an alert for someone else, delete the previous alert and create a new one as described earlier.

Emailing Task Assignments

Tasks, Project Tasks, and Issue Tracking lists can send email when an item is assigned to a person or when an assignment changes.

To turn on assignment notification for one of these types of lists:

1. Navigate to the list, click Actions → List Settings, and then click "Advanced settings" under the General Settings heading.

2. Select Yes in the E-Mail Notification section and click OK.

As with other alerts, task assignment changes are sent every five minutes using the SharePoint Timer service. Once assignment notification is enabled, the Assigned To person receives email when the item is first assigned to him and whenever the item changes, as shown in Figure 8-6.

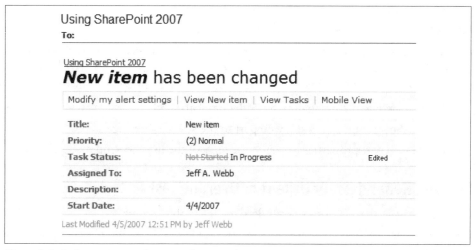

Figure 8-6. A change was made to a task assigned to me

The user will receive also receive an email when the item is assigned away from him to someone else. Users can't turn off or change this type of notification, but they can block the email or divert it to a folder by creating a rule in Outlook. Some internal spam filters block these types of alerts, particularly if a task list is active.

Changing the From Address

Alerts and task assignment notifications all use the From address set for the SharePoint web application. To change that address:

1. Navigate to the SharePoint Central Administration web site and click the Application Management tab.

2. Click "Web application outgoing email settings" under the SharePoint Web Application Management heading.

3. Set the From address and Reply-to address and click OK.

If you need to send alerts from more than one email account, you have to create a separate web application and then create the list on that web application.

Time-Driven Alerts

SharePoint alerts are event-driven; they only occur in response to an item being added, changed, or deleted. If you want to send an alert when a deadline approaches, you need to install a third-party web part such as SharePoint Reminder from Pentalogic.

To get SharePoint Reminder:

1. Download the web part from *http://www.pentalogic.net/SharePointReminder*.
2. Install the web part on the server.
3. Run *iisreset.exe* to load the changes.

SharePoint Reminder includes free licenses for five web part instances, with five more provided when you register the product. You can purchase additional licenses as needed. Once installed, you enable time-based alerts on a list by completing these tasks:

- Create a view of the list that displays the items to send.
- Add the SharePoint Reminder web part to the site's home page.
- Set the web part properties to watch the view of the list and send mail as needed.

Sending Reminders for Urgent or Overdue Tasks

Use time-driven alerts to send reminders for tasks that are urgent or overdue. For example, to send reminders two days prior to a Due Date in a task list:

1. Add a calculated column to the task list with the following settings.

Section	Property	Setting
Name and type	Column name	Alert1
	Type	Calculated
Additional Column Settings	Formula	[Due Date] – 2
	The data type returned	Date and Time
	Date and Time Format	Date Only

2. Create a new standard view for the list with the following settings.

Section	Property	Setting
Name	View Name	Urgent
Filter	Show the items when column	Alert1
		is less than or equal to
		[Today]
		And
	When column	Task Status
		is not equal to
		Completed

3. Add a SharePoint Reminder web part to the site's home page with the following property settings.

Section	Property	Setting
Appearance	Title	Task Reminder
Layout	Hidden	Selected
Reminder Configuration	Watch List	Tasks - Urgent
	Show all columns	Selected
	Email To	Assigned To
	Subject	Urgent task reminder: [Title]
	Message	The following task is assigned to you and is due in two days or less. You will continue to receive these reminders until the task is marked Completed or is assigned to someone else.
	Send Email	Always
	Check List	At 6:00
		Daily

In this example, the Alert1 column provides a value for the view to use, the Urgent view collects all of the tasks that are not completed and are due in two day or less, and the Reminder web part checks the view every morning to find the tasks that need reminders.

To include values in the Subject and Message text, enclose the column name in brackets (e.g., [Title]). The web part automatically includes a link to the list item after the message text, as shown in Figure 8-7.

Create additional reminder web parts and views to create a sequence of reminders as needed: Urgent, Overdue, Final warning, Clean out your desk, and so on.

Sending Scheduled Announcements

Another application for time-driven alerts is scheduled announcements, such as holiday announcements and timesheet reminders. Because company-wide messages usually come from a specially authorized email alias, you may need to create a separate web application just for this purpose (see "Changing the From Address," earlier in this chapter).

To create a web application for sending scheduled announcements:

1. Create a new web application using the Central Administration pages.

2. Set the From address for the web application to Corporate Communications, and clear the "Reply to" address.

3. Create an Announcements list and add the following columns: To Address and Send Date.

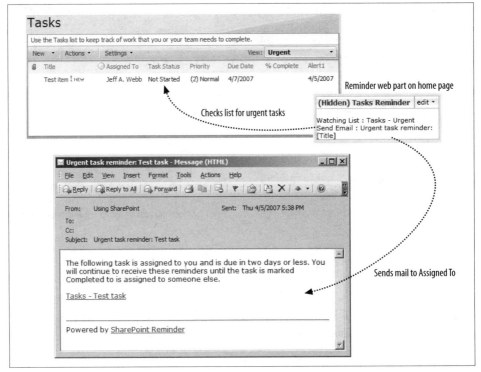

Figure 8-7. The SharePoint Reminder in action

4. Create a Today's Announcements view to show the items to send today (filter: Send Date is equal to [Today]).

5. Add a SharePoint Reminder web part to watch the Today's Announcements view of the list.

You should restrict who has access to the site or require content approval for the list to avoid spamming the company. Once complete, you can schedule announcements far in advance—for example, you might add the holiday announcements for an entire year.

Emailing from Libraries

Avoid sending documents through email; emailing documents creates multiple copies that are difficult to keep in sync. Instead, send links to documents.

To send a link from SharePoint:

• On the document's Edit menu, click Send To → E-mail a Link, as shown in Figure 8-8.

When SharePoint inserts a link in an email message, it encodes the URL in this way:

http://usingsharepoint%2Ecom/home/Shared%20Documents/ch02.doc

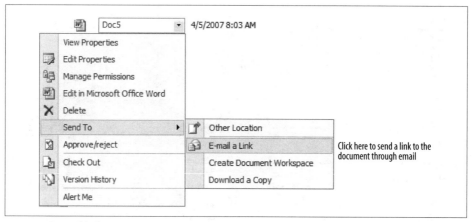

Figure 8-8. Send links, not copies!

That link only works if the recipient receives mail in HTML format. If the recipient uses plain text, edit the link to use periods in the domain name before sending:

http://usingsharepoint.com/home/Shared%20Documents/ch02.doc

If you don't want to go through that hassle, use this procedure instead:

1. Right-click on the document in SharePoint and click Copy Shortcut.

2. Create a new email and paste the shortcut into the message. This technique creates a link that works in all email formats.

Emailing to Libraries

SharePoint libraries can be configured to receive email. Once configured, users can simply email attachments to an alias set up for the library. SharePoint checks for new messages every five minutes or so using the SharePoint Timer service; if it finds a message, it loads the attached document into the library and optionally loads the message as well. Figure 8-9 illustrates the process.

To use this feature, you or a system administrator need to complete the following tasks:

- Configure the mail exchange (MX) record in DNS to relay email to the Share-Point server.

- Install the SMTP service on the SharePoint server to receive the relayed mail.

- Create an Active Directory (AD) organizational unit (OU) to contain the contacts for the SharePoint libraries. Delegate control of that OU to the AD account used by the SharePoint application pool so SharePoint can create and delete items in that OU.

- Configure SharePoint to allow libraries to receive mail.

- Enable email for the library.

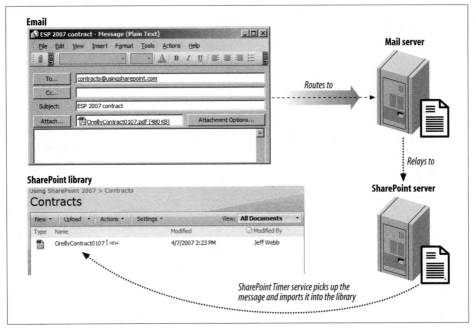

Figure 8-9. Emailing to a document library

The first three tasks above require special knowledge that is beyond the scope of this book. To find out more about those tasks, do the following:

- For WSS, search Microsoft.com for "Configure incoming email settings (Windows SharePoint Services)."
- For MOSS, search Microsoft.com for "Configure incoming email settings (Office SharePoint Server)."

These resources do a good job of describing the first three system-level tasks, but are less clear on the SharePoint topics, so I'll explain those in the following sections.

Allowing Incoming Email

Once the SharePoint server is set up to receive email relayed from your email server, and your security person has set up an OU that SharePoint can manage, you can turn on incoming email for libraries. There are several decisions you need to make before you do that, however:

- Should site owners be able to create new email aliases for libraries? If so, what approvals are required?
- Should libraries accept all email? If not, how should it be limited: by user or by source server?

Once you've made those decisions, you can configure SharePoint libraries to receive email. To allow incoming email:

1. Navigate to the SharePoint Central Administration web site, click the Operations tab, and then click "Incoming e-mail settings" under the Topology and Services heading. SharePoint displays the Configure Incoming E-Mail Settings page.

2. Complete the page as shown in Figure 8-10, and click OK when done.

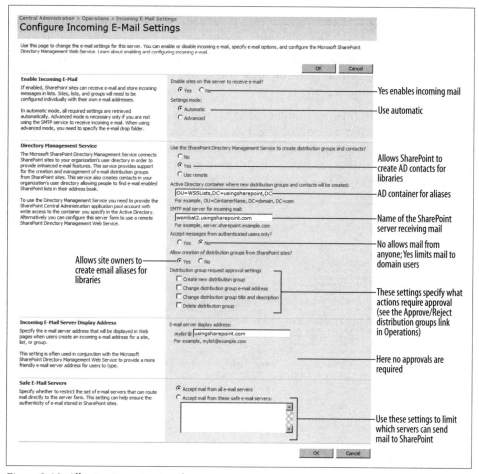

Figure 8-10. Allowing incoming email

The settings in Figure 8-10 allow site owners to create new email aliases for libraries, don't require approval, and accept all email. The AD container is set to:

```
OU=WSSLists,DC=usingsharepoint,DC=com
```

This means that the OU that I set up in Active Directory is named WSSLists, and it's in the *usingsharepoint.com* domain (my domain). SharePoint checks that string when you click OK, so you'll know if you get it wrong for your setup.

 Active Directory must be using the Exchange 2003 (or later) schema for these settings to work. If it is not, SharePoint can't create accounts or distribution groups.

I allow all site owners to create new aliases and don't require approvals because I have a small organization (me). You'll probably want to require approval for new distribution groups by selecting checkboxes in the Distribution group request approval settings. If you do that, you must check the Distribution Groups list periodically to approve or reject requests.

In Figure 8-10 the settings are configured to manage requests from the current server. If you have a server farm, you can select Remote under Directory Management Service to manage the requests from the central SharePoint server. In that case, the settings on that server determine how distribution groups are managed, and the local settings are not displayed (see Figure 8-11).

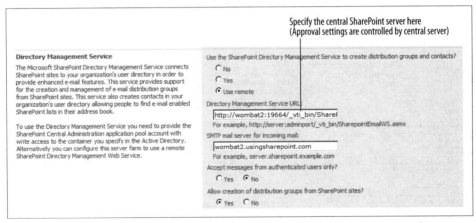

Figure 8-11. Managing distribution groups from a central SharePoint server in a server farm

Enabling Email for a Library

Once you've turned on email for libraries, SharePoint adds a link to the library settings pages so you can enable email for an individual library.

To enable a library to receive email:

1. Navigate to the library and click Settings → Library Settings, and then click "Incoming e-mail settings" under the Communications heading.

2. Complete the page as shown in Figure 8-12 and click OK.

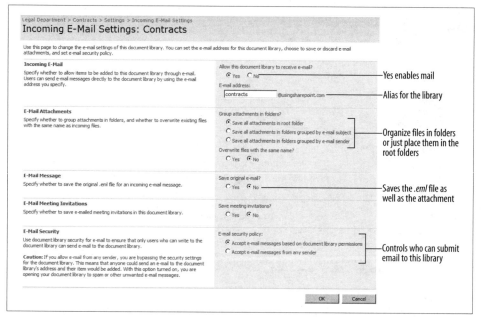

Figure 8-12. Enabling email for the Contracts library

Once you have enabled email access and security, you need to tell your users which email address to use to access the library. You might want to post this information in a "What's New" blog that's accessible to your team, or add the alias to the contacts list for your project.

Creating Workflows

The Problem Reports sample in Chapter 3 is a simple type of workflow based on an Issue Tracking list: the user submits a problem report, it's automatically assigned to the department manager, the manager reassigns the task to an employee; and the whole process is tracked through views of the list, as shown in Figure 8-13.

To handle more complex requirements, add a SharePoint workflow to the list or library. A *SharePoint workflow* is a set of steps that define a business process. For example, Figure 8-14 illustrates how a business processes employee expense reports.

The requirements for expense reporting are more complex than the Problem Reports sample because:

- You can't skip steps; expenses are always submitted, approved, and processed in that order.
- The approving manager varies based on who is submitting expenses.
- The final step is always handled by the Accounting department.
- Employees want to be able to track the progress of their expense report.

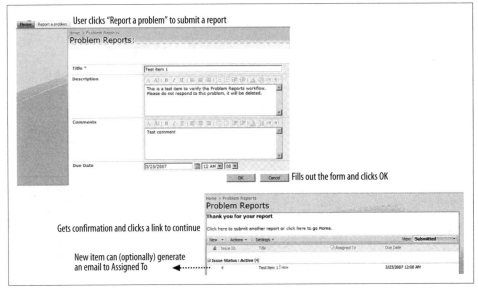

Figure 8-13. The Problem Reports sample as a simple workflow

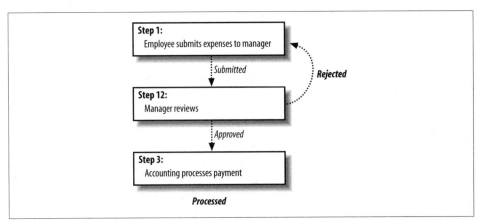

Figure 8-14. The employee expense-reporting process

The following sections describe how to create a workflow for the expense report process that meets all of those requirements. You can generalize this example for other approval processes in WSS. MOSS includes its own approval workflow that is easier to use than the three-state workflow. See "Creating Workflows in MOSS," later in this chapter, for details on that and other workflow templates included in MOSS.

Creating a Three-State Workflow

You create SharePoint workflows from a workflow template within a list or a library. WSS defines one built-in template called the three-state workflow. To use that template, you must first add columns to the list or library that track:

- The status of the item
- A due date for the workflow to complete
- The person or group responsible for each step of the process

The three-state workflow uses those columns to create tasks and record workflow history. For example, to use the three-state workflow to approve expense reports:

1. Create a document library named Expenses.
2. Add the following columns to the library.

Column name	Type	Settings	Default setting
Status	Choice	Choices: Submitted, Approved, Processed	Submitted
Manager	Person or group	Allow multiple selections: No	N/A
		Allow selection of: People only	
		Choose from: All Users	
		Show field: Name (with presence)	
Due Date	Date and Time	Date and Time format: Date only	=[Today] + 7

3. On the settings page, click "Workflow settings" under the Permissions and Management heading. SharePoint displays the Add a Workflow page.

4. Complete the Add a Workflow page as shown in Figure 8-15 and click Next. SharePoint displays the Customize page.

5. Complete the Customize page as shown in Figure 8-16 and click OK. SharePoint adds the workflow to the Expenses library.

6. You selected "New task list" and "New history list" in step 4, so SharePoint creates two new lists to handle the workflow: Expense Report Process Tasks and Expense Report Process History. Navigate to the Expense Report Process Tasks list and set that list to send alerts when ownership is assigned.

In the preceding sample, you created one library, and two lists are used as described in the following table.

Name	Used to	Show on Quick Launch?
Expenses Library	Create new expense reports	Yes
Expense Report Process Tasks	Approve and process expense reports	No
Expense Report Process History	Track the progress of the expense reports	No

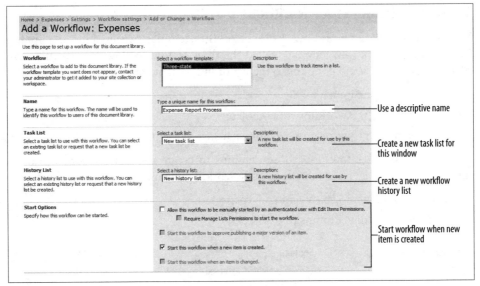

Figure 8-15. Adding a workflow to a library

The workflow links the Expenses library to these two lists, neither of which appears on Quick Launch. More than one workflow can use these lists; it's generally a good idea for related workflows to use the same history and task lists.

I turned off email from the workflow because that email only includes a link to the expense report. I turned on alerts in the Expense Report Process Tasks list because that email includes links to both the expense report and the task that needs to be completed (see Figures 8-17 and 8-18). It's important to include the actionable item (the task) in workflow alerts so the recipient knows what to do.

To test the Expense Report Process workflow:

1. Click New on the Expense Library toolbar to create a new expense report.

2. Save the file and set the Manager property as yourself. SharePoint adds the document to the library and starts the workflow.

3. In step 1 of the workflow, SharePoint adds an item to the Expense Report Process Tasks assigned to the manager (you, in this case) and the list sends an alert letting you know about the task, as shown in Figure 8-17.

4. Follow the instructions in the email: click "Edit this task" in the message body to edit the task and change the Status to Completed. SharePoint updates the workflow and moves to the next step, as shown in Figure 8-18.

5. In step 2, SharePoint adds a second item to the Expense Report Process Tasks assigned to Accounting and sends an alert. You won't get that alert since it's not your address, so refresh the task list to see the new item.

6. Edit the new item to change its Status to Completed. SharePoint completes the workflow.

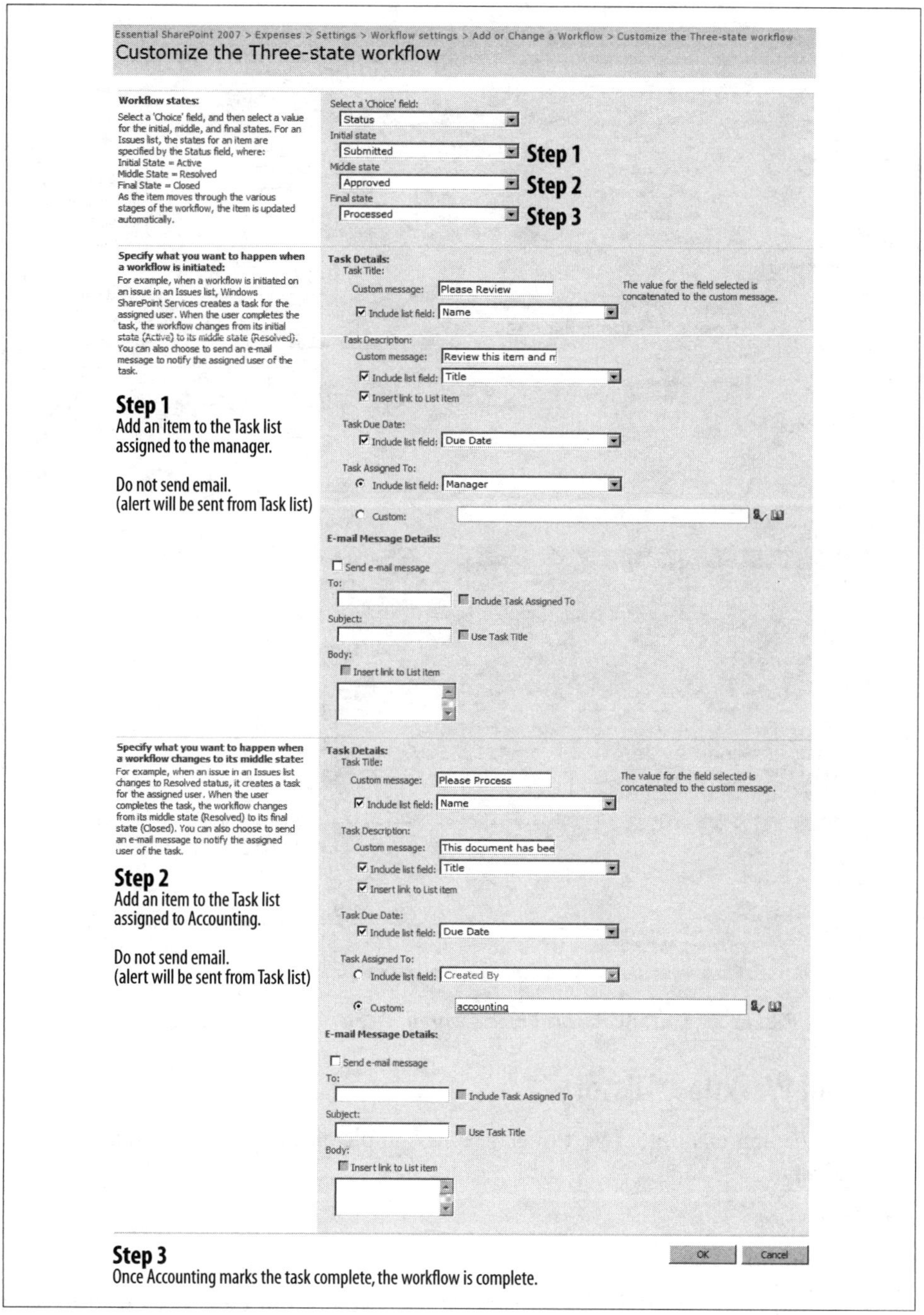

Customize the Three-state workflow

Workflow states:

Select a 'Choice' field, and then select a value for the initial, middle, and final states. For an Issues list, the states for an item are specified by the Status field, where:
Initial State = Active
Middle State = Resolved
Final State = Closed
As the item moves through the various stages of the workflow, the item is updated automatically.

Select a 'Choice' field:
Status

Initial state
Submitted — **Step 1**

Middle state
Approved — **Step 2**

Final state
Processed — **Step 3**

Specify what you want to happen when a workflow is initiated:

For example, when a workflow is initiated on an issue in an Issues list, Windows SharePoint Services creates a task for the assigned user. When the user completes the task, the workflow changes from its initial state (Active) to its middle state (Resolved). You can also choose to send an e-mail message to notify the assigned user of the task.

Step 1
Add an item to the Task list assigned to the manager.

Do not send email.
(alert will be sent from Task list)

Task Details:

Task Title:
Custom message: Please Review
☑ Include list field: Name

The value for the field selected is concatenated to the custom message.

Task Description:
Custom message: Review this item and m
☑ Include list field: Title
☑ Insert link to List item

Task Due Date:
☑ Include list field: Due Date

Task Assigned To:
◉ Include list field: Manager
○ Custom:

E-mail Message Details:

☐ Send e-mail message
To:
☐ Include Task Assigned To
Subject:
☐ Use Task Title
Body:
☐ Insert link to List item

Specify what you want to happen when a workflow changes to its middle state:

For example, when an issue in an Issues list changes to Resolved status, it creates a task for the assigned user. When the user completes the task, the workflow changes from its middle state (Resolved) to its final state (Closed). You can also choose to send an e-mail message to notify the assigned user of the task.

Step 2
Add an item to the Task list assigned to Accounting.

Do not send email.
(alert will be sent from Task list)

Task Details:

Task Title:
Custom message: Please Process
☑ Include list field: Name

The value for the field selected is concatenated to the custom message.

Task Description:
Custom message: This document has bee
☑ Include list field: Title
☑ Insert link to List item

Task Due Date:
☑ Include list field: Due Date

Task Assigned To:
○ Include list field: Created By
◉ Custom: accounting

E-mail Message Details:

☐ Send e-mail message
To:
☐ Include Task Assigned To
Subject:
☐ Use Task Title
Body:
☐ Insert link to List item

Step 3
Once Accounting marks the task complete, the workflow is complete.

OK   Cancel

Figure 8-16. Customizing the tasks and alerts sent by the workflow

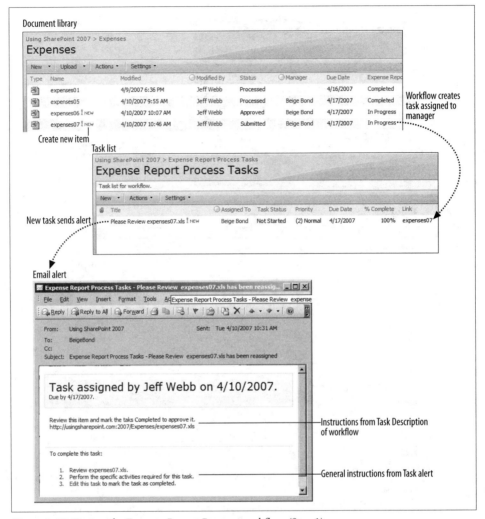

Figure 8-17. Testing the Expense Report Process workflow (Step 1)

Tracking Workflow History

In the preceding example, two things prevent employees from approving their own expense reports:

- Permissions
- Workflow history

Since the Expense Report Process Tasks list is separate from the Expenses library, it can have separate permissions that don't allow employees to change items. It's easiest to configure that at the site level by following these general steps:

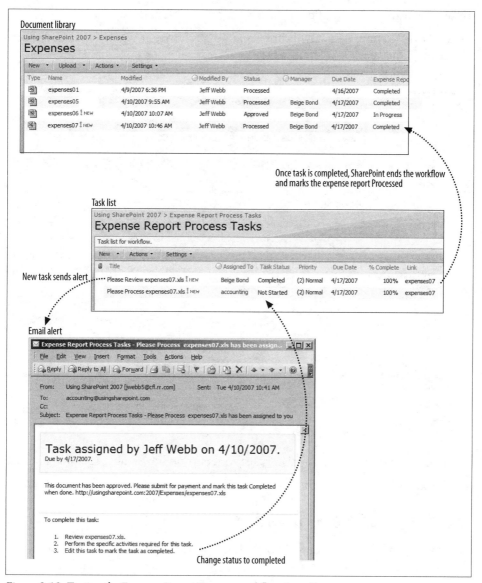

Document library

Using SharePoint 2007 > Expenses
Expenses

| New ▾ | Upload ▾ | Actions ▾ | Settings ▾ |

Type	Name	Modified	Modified By	Status	Manager	Due Date	Expense Repo
	expenses01	4/9/2007 6:36 PM	Jeff Webb	Processed		4/16/2007	Completed
	expenses05	4/10/2007 9:55 AM	Jeff Webb	Processed	Beige Bond	4/17/2007	Completed
	expenses06 ⁀ NEW	4/10/2007 10:07 AM	Jeff Webb	Approved	Beige Bond	4/17/2007	In Progress
	expenses07 ⁀ NEW	4/10/2007 10:46 AM	Jeff Webb	Processed	Beige Bond	4/17/2007	Completed

Once task is completed, SharePoint ends the workflow and marks the expense report Processed

Task list

Using SharePoint 2007 > Expense Report Process Tasks
Expense Report Process Tasks
Task list for workflow.

| New ▾ | Actions ▾ | Settings ▾ |

	Title	Assigned To	Task Status	Priority	Due Date	% Complete	Link
	Please Review expenses07.xls ⁀ NEW	Beige Bond	Completed	(2) Normal	4/17/2007	100%	expenses07
	Please Process expenses07.xls ⁀ NEW	accounting	Not Started	(2) Normal	4/17/2007	100%	expenses07

New task sends alert

Email alert

Expense Report Process Tasks - Please Process expenses07.xls has been assign...

| File | Edit | View | Insert | Format | Tools | Actions | Help |

Reply | Reply to All | Forward

From: Using SharePoint 2007 [jwebb5@cfl.rr.com]   Sent: Tue 4/10/2007 10:41 AM
To: accounting@usingsharepoint.com
Cc:
Subject: Expense Report Process Tasks - Please Process expenses07.xls has been assigned to you

Task assigned by Jeff Webb on 4/10/2007.
Due by 4/17/2007.

This document has been approved. Please submit for payment and mark this task Completed
when done. http://usingsharepoint.com:2007/Expenses/expenses07.xls

To complete this task:

1. Review expenses07.xls.
2. Perform the specific activities required for this task.
3. Edit this task to mark the task as completed.

Change status to completed

Figure 8-18. Testing the Expense Report Process workflow (step 2)

1. Add the Employee's AD account to the Visitors group for the site.

2. Add Accounting and Managers AD account to the Contributors group.

3. Change the permissions for the Expenses library to allow Visitors to add documents.

This approach still lets managers and Accounting approve their own items, but workflows track history so no one can really get away with that due to the built-in audit trail.

To see the history of a workflow:

- Click on the link in the workflow column as shown in Figure 8-19. SharePoint displays the Workflow Status page.

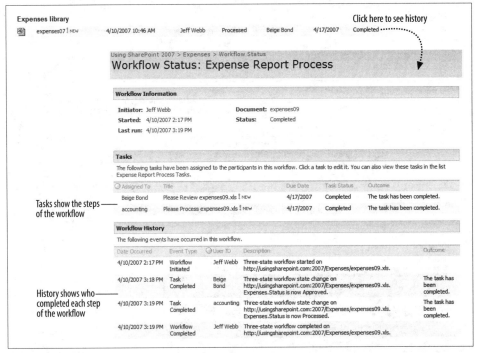

Figure 8-19. Viewing workflow history

You can also use the workflow history list to report on how long it took to complete tasks.

Creating Workflows in MOSS

In addition to the three-state workflow, MOSS provides the additional built-in work-flow templates listed in Table 8-1.

Table 8-1. Additional workflow templates available in MOSS

Workflow template	Use to
Approval	Route a document for approval. Approvers can approve or reject the document, reassign the approval task, or request changes to the document.
Collect feedback	Route a document for review. Reviewers can provide feedback, which is compiled and sent to the author when the workflow is complete.

Table 8-1. Additional workflow templates available in MOSS (continued)

Workflow template	Use to
Collect signatures	Gather signatures needed to complete a document. This workflow can be started only from Info-Path 2007.
Disposition approval	Allow workflow participants to decide whether to keep or delete expired documents.
Translation management	Route documents to translators. This workflow can only be used with the Translation Management library template.

These workflows are all variations of similar document management processes and offer these key advantages over the three-state workflow:

- Parallel or serial review
- Each review has due date with reminders
- Rejecting can cancel workflow

Adding Document Management Workflows to a Library

The MOSS workflow templates are designed specifically to work with document libraries. They handle the most common tasks associated with document management: feedback, review, and approval. You can add more than one workflow to a library, so it is possible to have workflows handle all of those processes for a single set of documents.

To add the MOSS document management workflows to a library:

1. Navigate to the document library, click Settings → Document Library Settings, and then click "Workflow settings" under the Permissions and Management heading. SharePoint displays the Change Workflow Settings page.

2. Click "Add a workflow." SharePoint displays the Add a Workflow page as shown earlier in Figure 8-15.

3. Select the Approval workflow, complete the page as described earlier, and click Next. SharePoint displays the Customize Workflow page for the Approval workflow.

4. Complete the page as shown in Figure 8-20 and click OK. SharePoint adds the workflow to the library.

5. Repeat steps 3 to 5 for the "Collect feedback" and "Disposition approval" workflows. Use the same task list and workflow history list for all three workflows. When done, the workflows are listed as shown in Figure 8-21.

Each of the document management workflows has very similar customization settings, so you'll probably want to use the same settings for each to maintain consistency. You can change the list of approvers when you start the workflow, so those settings should be the most commonly used ones.

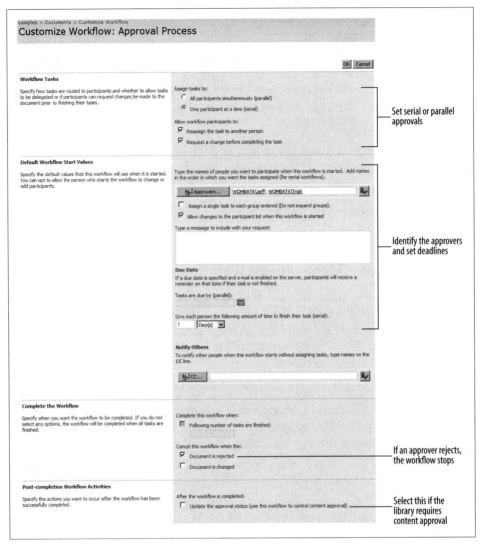

Customize Workflow: Approval Process

OK | Cancel

Workflow Tasks

Specify how tasks are routed to participants and whether to allow tasks to be delegated or if participants can request changes be made to the document prior to finishing their tasks.

Assign tasks to:

○ All participants simultaneously (parallel)

● One participant at a time (serial)

Allow workflow participants to:

☑ Reassign the task to another person

☑ Request a change before completing the task

> Set serial or parallel approvals

Default Workflow Start Values

Specify the default values that this workflow will use when it is started. You can opt to allow the person who starts the workflow to change or add participants.

Type the names of people you want to participate when this workflow is started. Add names in the order in which you want the tasks assigned (for serial workflows).

Approvers... | WOMBAT6\Jeff; WOMBAT6\Trish

☐ Assign a single task to each group entered (Do not expand groups).

☑ Allow changes to the participant list when this workflow is started

Type a message to include with your request:

> Identify the approvers and set deadlines

Due Date

If a due date is specified and e-mail is enabled on the server, participants will receive a reminder on that date if their task is not finished.

Tasks are due by (parallel):

Give each person the following amount of time to finish their task (serial):

1 | Day(s)

Notify Others

To notify other people when this workflow starts without assigning tasks, type names on the CC line.

CC...

Complete the Workflow

Specify when you want the workflow to be completed. If you do not select any options, the workflow will be completed when all tasks are finished.

Complete this workflow when:

☐ Following number of tasks are finished:

Cancel this workflow when the:

☑ Document is rejected

☐ Document is changed

> If an approver rejects, the workflow stops

Post-completion Workflow Activities

Specify the actions you want to occur after the workflow has been successfully completed.

After the workflow is completed:

☐ Update the approval status (use this workflow to control content approval)

> Select this if the library requires content approval

Figure 8-20. Customizing the approval workflow

In this case, all three workflows use the same task and workflow history lists because each workflow relates to a single library. If there are separate security requirements for the different workflows, you could create separate task lists instead.

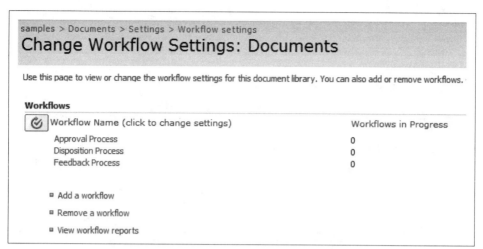

Figure 8-21. A single library with three document management workflows

Using the Document Management Workflows

To start a workflow:

1. Click Workflows on the document's Edit menu. SharePoint displays a page with the workflows that have been added to the library.

2. Click on the Workflow link under the Start a New Workflow heading. SharePoint displays the Start page for the workflow.

3. Complete the Start page as shown in Figure 8-22 and click Start to begin the workflow.

Once the workflow begins, you can view its progress through the workflow history, as shown earlier in Figure 8-19. Approvers can be changed from that page while the workflow is in progress.

Viewing Workflow Reports

The document management workflows provide activity and error reports that help you manage the workflows. To see the workflow reports:

1. Click "View workflow reports" on the Change Workflow Settings page. SharePoint displays the Workflow Reports page.

2. Click on the report to view. SharePoint opens the report as an Excel pivot table.

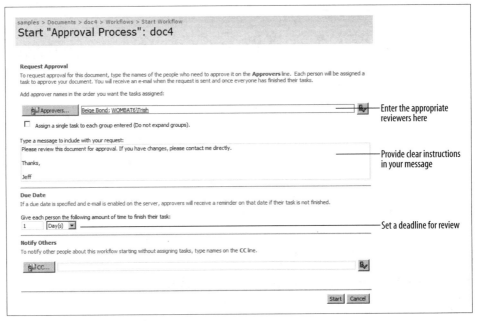

Figure 8-22. Starting a workflow

If you do not have Excel 2007, the report may open as an XML file. Save the file to your desktop as *Activity_Duration_Report.xml* or as *Cancellation_ Error_Report.xml* and open the file in Excel 2003.

Best Practices

- When creating alerts, choose daily summary over immediate alerts. Too much email is overwhelming.
- Make sure your antispam software does not block email from SharePoint.
- Use the Pentalogic SharePoint Reminder web part to create alerts for overdue tasks.
- Create workflows to implement a business process in SharePoint.
- Use the MOSS document management workflows to implement approval and review processes.

CHAPTER 9

RSS, Rollups, and Site Maps

This chapter is about ways to share information and to provide overviews of content across sites. The topics covered here allow you summarize and drill down into content, regardless of where it is stored, through:

- RSS feeds and readers such as the RSS Viewer web part
- Rollups such as the Site Aggregator web part
- Site maps, such as the sited directory and table of contents web part

Most of the web parts discussed in this chapter are only available in MOSS, but I provide alternatives for WSS-only installations where possible. The ability to share and summarize content across sites is one of the big advantages of MOSS over plain WSS.

I also expand on the technique of creating custom web pages and targeting IFrames that I touched on in Chapter 6. The Site Aggregator web part encapsulates that technique, and it's a good skill to know when working across sites.

RSS at a Glance

RSS is a way to publish information through feeds and readers. Every list and library in SharePoint provides an RSS feed indicated by an icon in the Action menu (Figure 9-1).

Figure 9-1. Every list and library provides an RSS feed

If you click on View RSS Feed, SharePoint displays the current content of the feed with a link to "Subscribe to the feed." Click that link, and SharePoint adds the feed to your browser's list of feeds. Figure 9-2 shows the Internet Explorer 7.0 feed list.

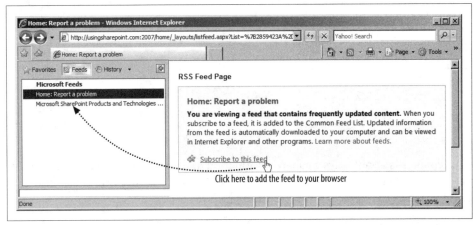

Figure 9-2. Subscribe to a feed to add it to your browser

Within Internet Explorer, you can view RSS feeds just as you would view your Favorites. In this case, the list is the feed and Internet Explorer is the reader. MOSS also includes an RSS Viewer web part to help build pages that combine one or more feeds as shown in Figure 9-3.

 If you don't have MOSS, there are several RSS reader web parts available on the web. Make sure they support authenticated RSS if you plan to use them to view SharePoint feeds.

The page in Figure 9-3 brings together content from an external site and from a SharePoint site on my intranet. Using RSS to display a list is similar to using a List View web part, but the RSS Viewer can cross-site boundaries so this page can appear in my top-level site even though the lists are stored in a subsite.

Using the MOSS RSS Viewer Web Part

RSS is the way SharePoint shares information across sites, a process called *aggregating content*. SharePoint RSS feeds are authenticated, meaning the RSS viewer must pass your credentials to the site before it will return any data. In other words, you need the same permissions to access an RSS feed as you do to access the list providing the feed.

The MOSS RSS Viewer web part supports authenticated RSS, so it only returns content you are authorized to see. If you don't have permission to view the list, the RSS Viewer is hidden on the page.

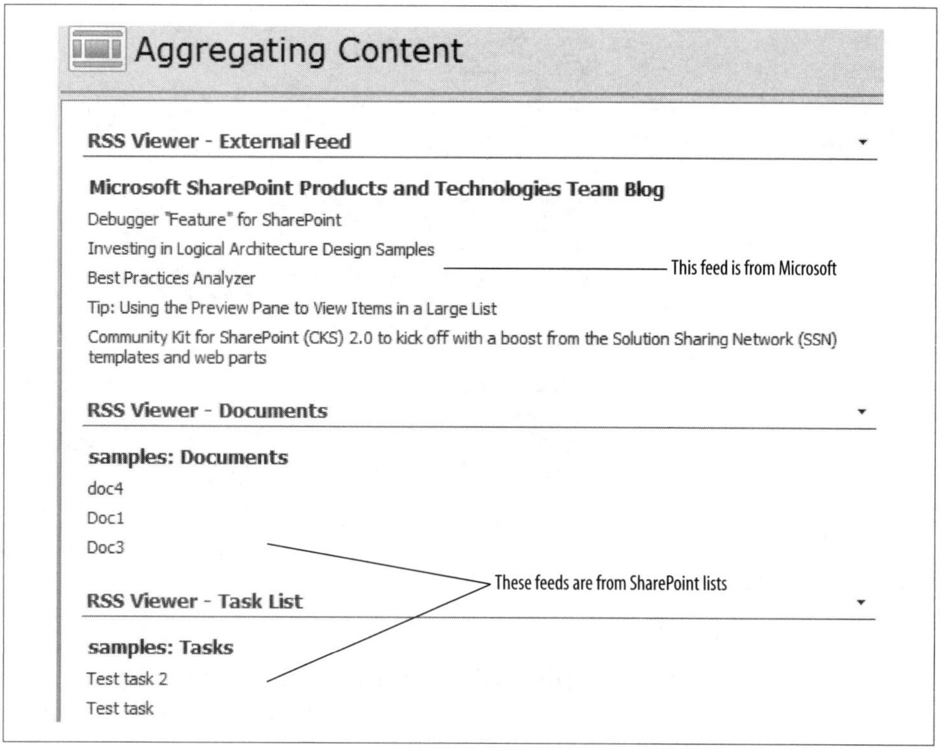

Figure 9-3. *Using the RSS Viewer web part to combine feeds on a page*

To use the RSS Viewer web part to aggregate content from a SharePoint list:

1. Navigate to the list that you want to get information from and click Actions → View RSS Feed. SharePoint displays the feed page for the list.

2. Copy the address of the RSS feed page.

3. Navigate to the page where you want to display the feed and add an RSS Viewer web part.

4. Click "Open the tool pane" on the web part, paste the address of the feed into the RSS Feed URL property as shown in Figure 9-4, and click OK. SharePoint displays the feed in the web part.

Modifying Feeds

RSS feeds are designed for time-sensitive information. By default, SharePoint feeds provide the 25 most recent items over the last seven days. The RSS Viewer web part may further narrow those results through the Feed Limit property shown in Figure 9-4. To display more results, change the RSS Viewer Feed Limit setting and modify the list feed to provide more results.

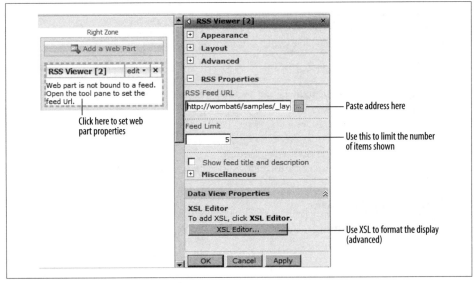

Figure 9-4. Using the RSS Viewer web part

To modify a SharePoint feed:

1. Navigate to the list providing the feed and click Settings → List Settings, and then click on "RSS settings" under the Communications heading. SharePoint displays the Modify List RSS Settings page.

2. Change the settings as shown in Figure 9-5 and click OK.

To turn off feeds from a list, select No in Figure 9-5. Turning off a feed does not stop existing viewers from getting the feed, it only prevents new ones from being added. You can also turn off feeds at the site or application levels.

To turn off feeds for a site:

1. Click Site Actions → Site Settings, and then click RSS under the Site Administration heading. SharePoint displays the RSS page.

2. Deselect "Allow RSS feeds in this site" and click OK.

To turn off feeds for an entire SharePoint application:

1. Navigate to the SharePoint Central Administration site and click Application Management → Web Application General Settings.

2. Scroll down, select No in the RSS Settings section, and click OK.

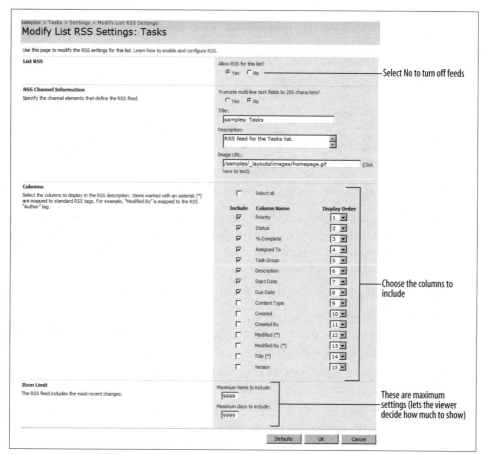

Modify List RSS Settings: Tasks

Use this page to modify the RSS settings for this list. Learn how to enable and configure RSS.

List RSS

Allow RSS for this list?
◉ Yes ○ No ———————————— Select No to turn off feeds

RSS Channel Information
Specify the channel elements that define the RSS feed.

Truncate multi-line text fields to 256 characters?
○ Yes ◉ No

Title:
samples: Tasks

Description:
RSS feed for the Tasks list.

Image URL:
/samples/_layouts/images/homepage.gif   (Click here to test)

Columns
Select the columns to display in the RSS description. Items marked with an asterisk (*) are mapped to standard RSS tags. For example, "Modified By" is mapped to the RSS "Author" tag.

☐ Select all

Include	Column Name	Display Order
☑	Priority	1
☑	Status	2
☑	% Complete	3
☑	Assigned To	4
☑	Task Group	5
☑	Description	6
☑	Start Date	7
☑	Due Date	8
☐	Content Type	9
☐	Created	10
☐	Created By	11
☐	Modified (*)	12
☐	Modified By (*)	13
☐	Title (*)	14
☐	Version	15

——— Choose the columns to include

Item Limit
The RSS feed includes the most recent changes.

Maximum items to include:
9999

Maximum days to include:
9999

——— These are maximum settings (lets the viewer decide how much to show)

[Defaults] [OK] [Cancel]

Figure 9-5. Modifying the RSS feed from a SharePoint list

Again, turning off feeds doesn't stop existing viewers from displaying the feed, it only prevents new viewers from being added for the feed. To stop a feed altogether, change the list's security settings, or delete and re-create the list with RSS feeds turned off.

Using Rollups

Rollups are another way of bringing together content from other sites. The MOSS Site Aggregator web part rolls up documents in other sites and displays them in a single pane with a tab bar across the top, as shown in Figure 9-6.

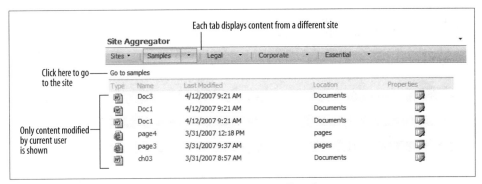

Figure 9-6. Using the MOSS Site Aggregator web part to roll up documents

Rollups give you a view of the content in other sites. The Site Aggregator web part displays the documents modified by and the tasks assigned to the current user within a particular site. My Sites include a Site Aggregator web part to help users manage their documents and tasks across projects.

To add a project site to the Site Aggregator web part on your My Site:

1. Navigate to your My Site.
2. On the SharePoint Sites web part, click Sites → New Site Tab. The web part displays the "Create a new site" tab pane.
3. Complete the pane, as shown in Figure 9-7, and click Create. SharePoint adds the tab to the web part.

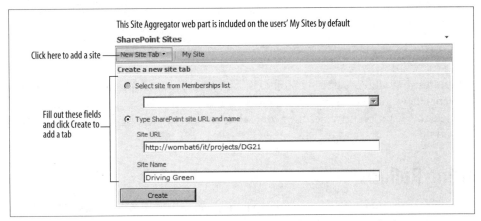

Figure 9-7. Use this web part on your My Site to keep track of projects you worked on

Modifying the Site Aggregator

The default Site Aggregator web part displays the *_layouts/MyInfo.aspx* page from each site. That page is global to all sites, and it's the part that determines what appears in the web part's display pane.

To change what appears in the display pane, complete these tasks:

- Create a new page to display.
- Change the web part's URL property to display that page.

For example, to only display your tasks in the Site Aggregator web part:

1. Go to the SharePoint server and open this folder:

   C:\Program Files\Common Files\Microsoft Shared\Web Server Extensions\12\ TEMPLATE\LAYOUTS

2. Make a copy of the *MyInfo.aspx* file and name it *MyTasks.aspx*.

3. Edit *MyTasks.aspx* to comment out the CrossListView web part for the documents (the code is shown later). Save the file when you are done.

4. In SharePoint, navigate to the page with the Site Aggregator web part and click Modify Shared Web Part on the web part's Edit menu.

5. Change the URL property to *_LAYOUTS\MyTasks.aspx* and click OK to close the property pane, as shown in Figure 9-8.

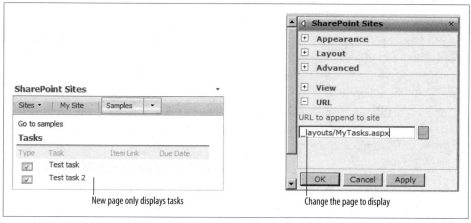

Figure 9-8. Changing the page that appears in the Site Aggregator

The following code shows the changes for the *MyTasks.aspx* page:

```
<!-- MyTasks.aspx, based on MyInfo.aspx -->
<%@ Page language="C#"    Inherits="Microsoft.SharePoint.Portal.
SiteAdminPage,Microsoft.SharePoint.Portal,Version=12.0.0.
0,Culture=neutral,PublicKeyToken=71e9bce111e9429c" %>
<%@ Register Tagprefix="SPSWC" Namespace="Microsoft.SharePoint.Portal.WebControls"
Assembly="Microsoft.SharePoint.Portal, Version=12.0.0.0, Culture=neutral,
PublicKeyToken=71e9bce111e9429c" %>
<%@ Register Tagprefix="SharePoint" Namespace="Microsoft.SharePoint.WebControls"
Assembly="Microsoft.SharePoint, Version=12.0.0.0, Culture=neutral,
PublicKeyToken=71e9bce111e9429c" %>
<script src="/_layouts/<%=System.Threading.Thread.CurrentThread.CurrentUICulture.
LCID%>/core.js"></script>
```

```
<script src="/_layouts/<%=System.Threading.Thread.CurrentThread.CurrentUICulture.
LCID%>/owsbrows.js"></script>
<HTML dir="<%$Resources:wss, multipages_direction_dir_value%>" runat="server">
<HEAD><TITLE><asp:Literal runat="server" Text="<%$Resources:sps, myinfo_
SiteDocuments%>" /></TITLE></HEAD>
<BODY>
    <SharePoint:CssLink runat="server"/>
    <table width="100%">
        <SPSWC:SiteLink runat="server" />
        <!-- JAW, 4/11/07: Hide My Docs list
        <SPSWC:CrossListView id="Docs" Title="<%$Resources:sps,
        myinfo_SiteDocuments%>" HideFileTypes="dwp;master;aspx;xsl;css"
        runat="server"/>
        -->
        <SPSWC:CrossListView id="Tasks" Title="<%$Resources:sps,
        myinfo_SiteTasks%>"  RenderTasks="true" runat="server"/>
    </table>
</BODY>
</HTML>
```

Displaying Custom Site Pages

The pages in the _layouts folder are available to all sites, so I saved *MyTasks.aspx* to that folder. The change is very simple, but it should be enough to get you started with those types of global pages. You can also use the Site Aggregator to display any page from a site—even the home page—but if you try that, you'll see the visual disaster shown in Figure 9-9.

All of the default site pages include the link bar, Quick Launch, and other navigational web parts that you don't want to display in the Site Aggregator pane. To solve that problem, complete these tasks:

- Create a library containing custom pages that omit the navigational elements.
- Add web parts to display the content you want to aggregate from the site.
- Display the pages from that library in the Site Aggregator.

You can use SharePoint Designer to create web pages that omit the link bar, Quick Launch, and other elements, but that's way too difficult to explain here (sorry). Instead:

1. Download the *NoNavPages10.stp* library template from this book's samples site.
2. Upload the template to your site collection's list templates gallery.
3. Create a new library named "Pages" using the template.

The Pages library includes 10 sample pages without the navigational elements. To add web parts to the page:

1. Display the page in the browser.
2. Click on Edit Shared Page → Design This Page. SharePoint displays the page in Edit mode.

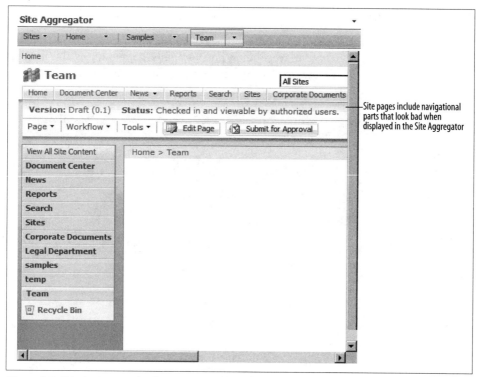

Figure 9-9. *Displaying standard site pages in the web part gets crowded*

3. Add web parts or modify the web parts as needed.

4. When you're done, click Edit Shared Page → Design This Page again to switch back to view mode.

Finally, set the Site Aggregator to display the custom page:

1. On the web part, click Sites → New Site Tab, and type the full address of the custom page in Site URL followed by #, as shown in Figure 9-10.

2. Click Create to create the tab.

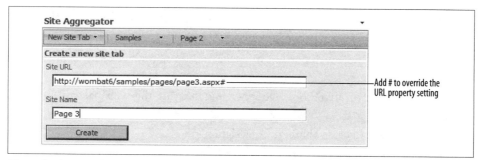

Figure 9-10. *Using custom pages to aggregate content*

Targeting Frames

When done, clicking the tab bar on the Site Aggregator web part displays the custom page in the web part's display pane. What's actually happening is the links in the tab bar target an IFrame created by the web part, as shown in Figure 9-11.

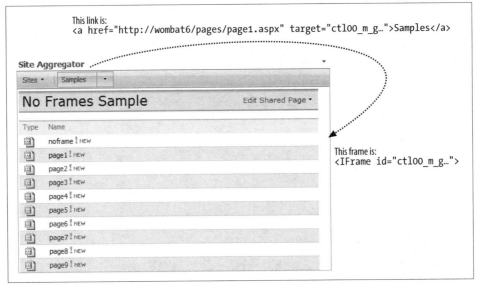

Figure 9-11. How the Site Aggregator works

Since the display pane is an IFrame, any links displayed there will open in the same frame. To open in the parent frame, you need to add a `target="_top"` attribute to the link. The *MyInfo.aspx* and *MyTasks.aspx* pages discussed earlier actually generate links with that attribute included. I include two samples in *NoNavPages10.stp*:

- *Example1.aspx* demonstrates targeting the current frame from a List View web part. That's the default target used throughout SharePoint.

- *Example2.aspx* demonstrates targeting the parent frame using a Data View web part.

To create a web part that targets the parent frame as demonstrated by *Example2.aspx*, follow these steps:

1. Create the List View web part on the page and format it as closely as possible to the final form.

2. Open the page in SharePoint Designer and convert the web part to an XSLT Data View.

3. Save the page and close SharePoint Designer.

4. Navigate to the page in the browser and switch to Edit mode.

5. Open the Data View web part's properties pane and click XSL Editor.

6. Modify the XSL to include a `target="_top"` attribute for each link. It's easiest to copy the XSL into Notepad, search and replace, and then paste back into the text window.

7. Click Save to save the XSL, and then click OK to close the property pane.

The following sample shows one of the changes to the XSL:

```
<xsl:choose>
    <xsl:when test="@IsCheckedoutToLocal=''"></xsl:when>
    <xsl:otherwise><A HREF="{ddwrt:URLLookup('', 'IsCheckedoutToLocal',
    string(@ID))}" target="_top"><xsl:value-of select="@IsCheckedoutToLocal"
    /></A></xsl:otherwise>
</xsl:choose>
```

Rollups Without MOSS

Several vendors offer rollup web parts and there are even some available for free download off the Web. Table 9-1 lists some of the vendors I am familiar with, but I encourage you to do your own research as well.

Table 9-1. Web part vendors

Company	Web site	Comments
CorasWorks	www.corasworks.com	Provides a large set of web parts and site templates. Sold as a server license.
BrightWork	www.brightwork.com	A smaller set of web parts than CorasWorks, but less expensive.
Bamboo Solutions	www.bamboosolutions.com	Web parts are sold à la carte with a free trial period.

Providing Site Maps

Site maps provide a table of contents for your site collections. Microsoft calls the site map in MOSS the *site directory*, and it appears on the Sites tab, as shown in Figure 9-12.

Each tab on the site directory provides a slightly different overview of the content included in your portal, as described in the following table.

Tab	Web part	Includes
Categories	Categories	Site listings included in the Sites list grouped by category.
Top Sites	Content Query	Site listings included in the Sites list where Top Site = True.
Site Map	Table of Contents	Site collections and subsites organized in alphabetical order.

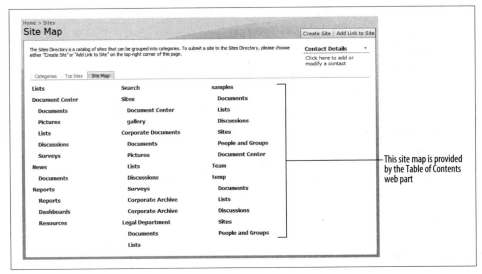

Figure 9-12. The MOSS site directory

The Table of Contents web part queries the actual site structure, so it is always up-to-date. The Categories and Content Query web parts get their data from the Sites list, which is built from site listings that are sometimes added when new sites are created. Figure 9-13 shows the settings on the Create Site page that determine whether or not a listing is created.

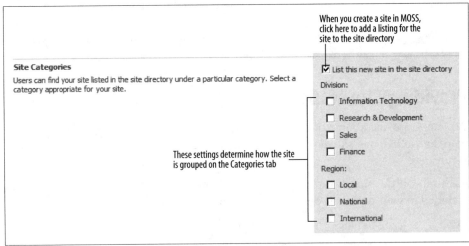

Figure 9-13. Adding a listing to the site directory when creating a site in MOSS

The divisions and regions shown in Figure 9-13 are determined by the Choice columns in the Sites list. To add or remove divisions and regions:

1. Navigate to the site directory and click View All Site Content, and then click Sites under the lists heading.

2. Click Settings → List Settings, and then click the Division link in the Columns list.

3. Edit the choices listed in the Additional Column Settings section and click OK. SharePoint changes the divisions listed on the Create Site page.

4. Repeat steps 2 and 3 for the Region column to add or remove regions.

Maintaining the Site Directory

New site listings created by nonadministrators must be approved before they appear in the site directory. The top-level site administrator should set an alert on the Sites list to receive notification when items are added so they can be approved or rejected. Someone should also periodically check which sites are flagged as Top Sites and adjust them as needed.

The Sites list can become out-of-date if sites are deleted, moved, or renamed. SharePoint can check for those problems by scanning the Sites list. To configure scanning:

1. Navigate to the SharePoint Central Administration site, click Operations, and then click "Site directory links scan" under the Global Configuration heading.

2. Complete the page as shown in Figure 9-14 and click OK.

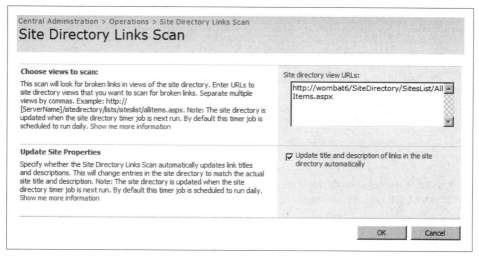

Figure 9-14. Checking for broken links in the site directory

Creating Site Maps in WSS

If you are using WSS, you won't have the Table of Contents, Categories, or Content Query web parts provided with MOSS. To create a simple site map in WSS:

1. Create a Sites list based on the Links list template.
2. Add a Categories column to the list.
3. Create a view that groups the links by Category.
4. Create a view that lists the links alphabetically.
5. Provide pages for each of the views.

To create a more sophisticated site map:

1. Add columns and create views with additional groupings.
2. Add the list as a web part to a page.
3. Convert the List View web part to a Data View web part.
4. Export the converted web part and use it to create new Site Map pages.

Figure 9-15 shows a site map page I created for my WSS site using those techniques. You can download the sample as a list template from my Samples site.

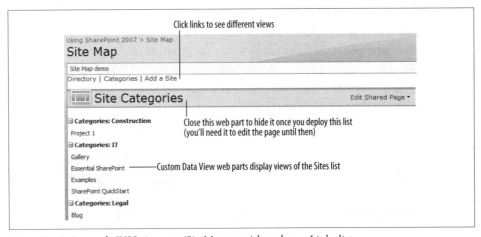

Figure 9-15. A sample WSS site map (SiteMap.aspx) based on a Links list

The sample page shown in Figure 9-15 is included in the sample list template *WSS_SiteMap10.stp*. It combines these techniques you learned earlier in:

- Converting List Views to Data Views (Chapter 6).
- Exporting and uploading Data Views (Chapter 6).
- Creating custom pages (Chapter 3).
- Targeting IFrames (Chapter 6 and this chapter).

Best Practices

- Add an alert to the site directory's Sites list so you can approve or reject site listings as they are added by others.

- Add # to the end of the Site URL in the Site Aggregator web part to show a specific page. Omit the # to use the default page for the web part.

- Leverage RSS and rollups on your My Site page to give you the best view of the SharePoint data you are personally interested in seeing.

- Build management-level dashboards using rollups, aggregators, and site maps to give managers with multiple responsibilities the best chance of quickly and easily finding information relevant to a specific project.

- Create company-level dashboards using RSS and rollups to provide high-level information about the whole company and broadcast company-wide announcements across departmental sites.

CHAPTER 10

Gathering Data with InfoPath

SharePoint can collect data using lists or InfoPath Form Libraries. Lists use the *NewForm.aspx* page to collect entries—I showed you how to customize that page in Chapter 4. You can do a lot with lists, but InfoPath is better suited for these tasks:

- Data validation
- Conditional formatting
- Submitting to database
- Submitting via email
- Collecting signatures
- Read-only views of data

In this chapter, I will show you how to use Microsoft InfoPath 2007 to leverage those advantages through SharePoint Form libraries and InfoPath Forms Services.

What Software Do You Need?

To fill out InfoPath forms, a user needs Microsoft InfoPath installed on her computer. InfoPath is included with the Microsoft Office 2007 Professional Plus, Enterprise, and Ultimate editions. It can also be bought separate from Office.

Others can edit or view completed forms without having InfoPath installed through InfoPath Forms Services, which are included with MOSS Enterprise Edition. Forms Services converts InfoPath forms to web-enabled forms that can be filled out using the standard web browser. However, web-enabled forms are more limited than full InfoPath forms, so you'll need to analyze the form requirements before you decide whether that will work for your application.

In addition, form developers may need Visual Studio Tools for Office (VSTO) or Visual Studio Tools for Applications (VSTA) to program InfoPath forms. InfoPath includes its own form designer, so the Visual Studio tools are only required if you are programming custom actions in .NET.

Table 10-1 lists the specific client software requirements for a typical installation based on user needs.

Table 10-1. InfoPath client software requirements by user role

User	Requirement	Software needs
Reader	View form data	Internet Explorer 6.0 or later
Data entry	Fill out and submit forms	InfoPath 2007
Form designer	Create new forms	InfoPath 2007, SharePoint Designer (for workflow)
Form developer	Program forms	InfoPath 2007, VSTA or VSTO, SharePoint Designer (optional)

Technically, InfoPath requires no server software. Forms can be deployed to a network share or via email. However, SharePoint offers a range of additional capabilities based on which edition you have. Table 10-2 lists the InfoPath features you get with the different SharePoint editions; the features are cumulative as you read down the table.

Table 10-2. InfoPath capabilities by SharePoint edition

SharePoint edition	Feature	Provides
WSS, MOSS Standard, MOSS/S	Form Library template	Ability to publish forms, create new forms from library
MOSS Enterprise (includes InfoPath Forms Services)	Document conversion	Convert XML form data to HTML
	Edit in Browser	Edit form data without InfoPath installed on client
	Manage Form Templates	Deploy and upgrade templates from Central Administration pages

Using Form Libraries

SharePoint form libraries are special document libraries for collecting data gathered through Microsoft InfoPath. InfoPath provides a platform for creating and displaying data-entry forms that may incorporate:

- Links to remote data sources such as SQL or Access databases
- Text fields that include simple formatting such as bold, italic, bulleted lists, etc.
- Office-like editing tools such as autocorrect and spellchecking
- Complex data validation
- Detail and summary views of data
- The ability to submit form data to a database or to an email recipient
- Property promotion so that form data automatically becomes part of the searchable SharePoint form library

InfoPath's form-creation tools are based on XML and its related standards. It is perhaps most useful for medium to large corporations that use XML schemas as part of their information architecture. If you're not familiar with XPath, XML, XSD, and XSLT, you may find designing InfoPath forms difficult. On the other hand, filling out an InfoPath form is very easy.

 The following sections assume you have InfoPath 2007 installed on your computer. For a trial copy of the product, search *www.microsoft.com* for "InfoPath 2007 trial."

Understanding Form Libraries

A *form library* is basically a document library that uses an InfoPath form template as a template rather than a Word, Excel, or PowerPoint file. To add a new item to the library:

- Click New on the library toolbar. SharePoint opens the template in InfoPath, as shown in Figure 10-1.

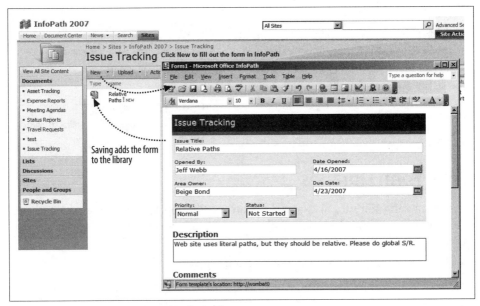

Figure 10-1. Creating a new item in a form library

SharePoint comes with several sample templates that you can try. To create a test form library using one of the sample templates:

1. Start InfoPath. InfoPath displays the Getting Started page.
2. Click Customize a Sample and double-click one of the built-in sample templates. InfoPath opens the template in Design mode.

3. Click File → Publish and save the template to your computer. InfoPath starts the Publishing Wizard.

4. Select the first option to publish to SharePoint and click Next.

5. Provide the address of a SharePoint site, click Next, and click Next again. Info-Path lists the other Form Libraries on the site.

6. Click Next, name the library, and click Next. InfoPath lists the form fields that will be mapped to columns in the library.

7. Click Next and then click Publish to create the form library.

InfoPath includes the built-in templates listed in Table 10-3 in the Getting Started page. The additional templates listed in Table 10-4 are installed with InfoPath at the following location:

    C:\Program Files\Microsoft Office12\Office12\INFFORMS\1033

Table 10-3. Built-in InfoPath form library templates

Form template	Use to
Absence Request	Request time away from work and to calculate remaining absence balances.
Asset Tracking	Keep a record of your company's equipment and property. You can track information such as primary user, location, and purchase date for each asset. The form can also be sorted, allowing you to quickly find the information you're looking for.
Expense Report	Create and submit an itemized list of expenses.
Meeting Agenda	Detail the agenda items, time allotments, guest speakers, attendees, and required materials for a meeting. This form can also be used to record meeting minutes, decisions, and action items.
Status Report	Provide an update on the status of various projects. These reports can then be combined into a single report.

Table 10-4. Additional built-in templates not shown on Getting Started

Form template	Use to
Applicant Rating	Rate job applicants, comment on applicants' strengths and weaknesses, and provide a hiring recommendation.
Change Order	Explain and specify changes to existing orders or projects, as well as track total cost and time adjustments.
Expense Report (International)	Create and submit an itemized list of expenses for international travel.
Invoice (Multiple Tax Rates)	Document sales and transactions, and bill customers for services rendered or equipment delivered.
Invoice (Single Tax Rate)	Same as above, one tax rate.
Invoice Request	Request the generation of an invoice for services rendered or equipment delivered.
Issue Tracking (Detailed)	Track an important issue, as well as provide details such as the due date, status, and owner for all action items that impact that issue.
Issue Tracking (Simple)	Provide and track the details of an important issue, including the progress, contributors, and date closed.

Form template	Use to
Project Plan	Provide the details for a project, such as a schedule, work items, materials, and a budget.
Purchase Order	List the total items, total amount due, and required delivery dates for an order, and authorize the delivery of the specified items.
Purchase Request	Create a request for items you want to purchase.
Sales Report	Record and track monthly sales of various items in different categories.
Service Request	Make requests for services or repairs.
Time Card (Detailed)	Track time worked, including times in/out per day, absences, and other payroll information.
Time Card (Simple)	Report the total hours worked during a specified time period.
Travel Itinerary	Create a schedule of events while traveling, which can include transportation arrangements, appointments, and various contacts.
Travel Request	Request the approval of a business trip and provide details such as travel dates, destinations, itinerary information, and preferences so that accommodations can be made.
Vendor Information	Specify the products and services provided by a particular vendor, and allow multiple individuals to rate the vendor according to cost, quality, and delivery.

When you save an InfoPath form to a form library, SharePoint saves the form data as an XML file in the library. SharePoint also maps elements from that XML file to columns in the SharePoint list. This process is similar to the way SharePoint promotes custom properties in Word and Excel document libraries. The advantage of this mapping is that you can use SharePoint to easily create different summary views of InfoPath data. These mapped fields are also included in searches of the site.

Designing a Form

InfoPath is both a form designer and a form viewer. To design a data-entry form in InfoPath:

- Start InfoPath, select one of the sample forms, and choose "Design this form." InfoPath opens the form in Design mode, as shown in Figure 10-2.

You can modify the form by selecting any of the options in the Task pane.

To preview the results of changes:

- Choose File → Preview → Form. InfoPath displays the form in Preview mode (see Figure 10-3).

 In Preview mode, you can view changes and test controls, but you can't save data entered on the form.

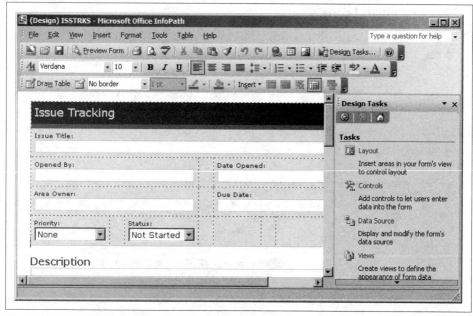

Figure 10-2. Modifying the Issue Tracking form using Design mode

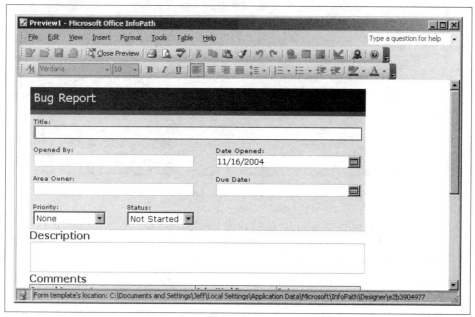

Figure 10-3. Viewing changes in Preview mode

Creating a Form Library

Once you are satisfied with a form, you have a choice: you can save the form for local use or testing, or publish the form to create a new form library in SharePoint. To publish a completed form:

1. Choose File → Publish. InfoPath starts the Publish wizard to walk you through the process.

2. Click Next to choose the type of location to publish the form to, as shown in Figure 10-4.

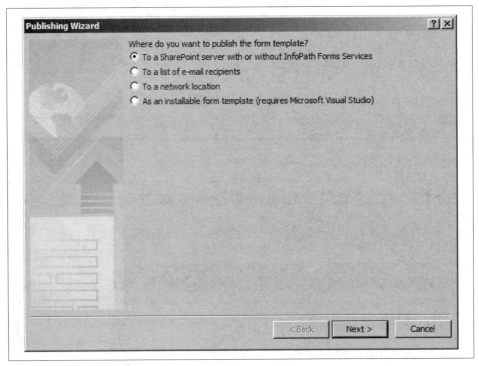

Figure 10-4. Use the Publishing Wizard to create a form library

3. If you chose to publish to a form library, the Wizard asks if you want to create a new form library or update the form in an existing library. Select "Create new form library" and choose Next.

4. Enter the SharePoint site in which to create the form library and choose Next. Info-Path logs on to the site, and it may prompt you for your user name and password.

5. Enter a name and description for the form library and choose Next. The Wizard displays the mapping step (see Figure 10-5). This step lets you map elements from the form's XML schema to columns in the form library.

6. Choose Add to create, Remove to delete, or Modify to change a mapping. Choose Finish to create the form library. InfoPath displays a success dialog box.

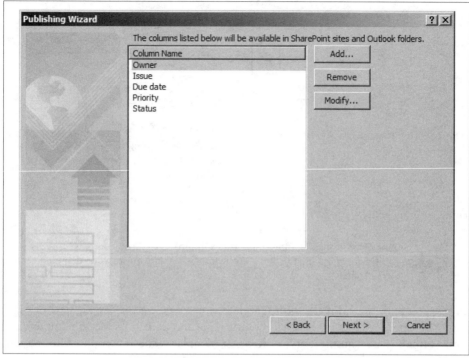

Figure 10-5. Use this step to change the mapping between form data and form library columns

Once you've published the form, members can open it for data entry by clicking New on the form library's toolbar. When users save the form, InfoPath creates a new item in the form library, as shown earlier in Figure 10-1.

Emailing Form Data

Form libraries are usually set up to collect data this way:

1. Choose New from the library toolbar.
2. Complete, save, and close the form to create a new item in the library.
3. Open the item from the library to view/edit/modify the form as needed.

InfoPath also provides a Submit action for use in place of Save. Submit sends the form's data in XML form to a database or to an email recipient. Since SharePoint is really a database frontend, it's a bit redundant to submit to a database from an InfoPath form library, unless you want to duplicate the data in another system for some reason.

However, submitting via email does make sense. Consider this scenario: a support person completes a visit to a customer, fills out a service request, and emails it to the service manager. The manager views the request in Outlook, and then saves it to a form library on SharePoint. Figure 10-6 illustrates this scenario.

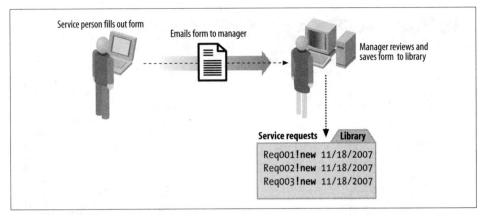

Figure 10-6. Submitting forms via email

 InfoPath's email features are tied to Outlook 2007. You can only submit a form via email if you are using Outlook 2007 as your default email client.

In this scenario, the InfoPath form template is installed on the service person's laptop or tablet as well as in the form library. That makes it possible to complete the form offline. The sample Service Request template doesn't come with Submit enabled. To add this feature:

1. Right-click on the Service Request template and click Design. The Service Request template is named *SVCREQ.XSN,* and it is installed at this location by default:

   C:\Program Files\Microsoft Office12\Office12\INFFORMS\1033

2. Choose Tools → Submit Options. InfoPath displays the Submit Options dialog box.

3. Select "Allow users to submit this form" and click Add. InfoPath starts the Data Connection Wizard (see Figure 10-7).

4. Enter the email address, subject, and message body you want to include when sending the form, click Next twice, and then click Finish to complete the task.

5. Click OK to close the Submit Options and save the template.

Once you've enabled Submit, you can publish the template to a form library as described in "Creating a Form Library." The first time the service person fills out the form online, the template is downloaded to his machine. Later, he can reuse the template even if he is offline by opening it from his list of Recently Used Forms on the InfoPath Getting Started page.

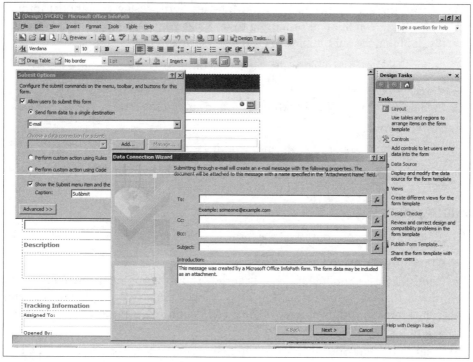

Figure 10-7. Enabling submit via email

Enabling Submit adds a Submit item to the File menu in InfoPath. Once the form is complete, the service person chooses File → Submit to send the form. You can also add a command button to submit the form. To do that:

1. Open the template in Design mode.
2. Choose Insert → More controls. InfoPath displays the controls task pane.
3. Drag the button control from the task pane onto the template.
4. Double-click the button. InfoPath displays the button's properties.
5. Select Action → Submit, and then click Options. InfoPath displays the submit options.
6. Click OK twice to close the dialog boxes.

Customizing Forms

To prevent members from opening a service request from the form library and accidentally submitting the request again, you might want to disable the Submit button whenever the form is opened from SharePoint.

You control the appearance of items on InfoPath forms using conditional formatting, but getting conditional formatting to do what you want can be tricky. Conditionally disabling the Submit button involves these major tasks:

1. Add a checkbox to enable or disable other controls.
2. Set conditional formatting on those controls based on the checkbox setting.
3. Create rules that set the checkbox value and submit the form.
4. Test the form.
5. Hide the checkbox once the form is working correctly.

The following sections demonstrate those tasks using the Service Request example.

Adding Controls

To add a new checkbox control on the form:

1. Open the template in Design mode.
2. Choose Tools → Submit Options, clear the "Show the Submit menu item and the Submit toolbar" button, and click OK. You can't enable or disable menu items from a form so you must remove the menu item if you want to control access to Submit.
3. Display the Data Source task pane and click "Add a Field or Group" at the bottom of the pane. InfoPath displays the Add Field or Group dialog box.
4. Add a Boolean field named DisableSubmit, as shown in Figure 10-8. Choose OK; InfoPath adds an element to the form's XML schema.
5. Drag my:DisableSubmit from the task pane onto the form. InfoPath creates a checkbox control on the form.

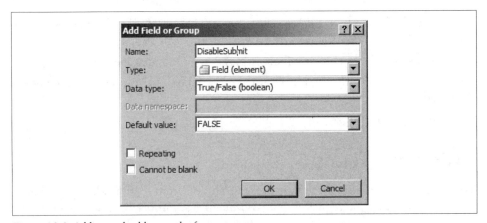

Figure 10-8. Adding a checkbox to the form

Setting Conditional Formatting

To enable/disable the Submit button based on the checkbox setting:

1. Double-click the Submit button and choose Display → Conditional Formatting → Add. InfoPath displays the Conditional Format dialog box.

2. Add the condition shown in Figure 10-9 to disable the control when the checkbox value is true. Click OK three times to close the dialog boxes.

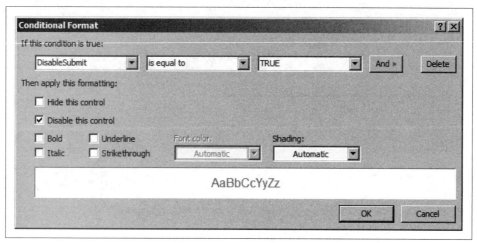

Figure 10-9. Disabling the Submit button when the checkbox is selected

Creating Rules

To create rules to control the checkbox value:

1. Double-click on the Submit button. InfoPath displays the button properties.

2. Click Submit Options and then click Rules. InfoPath displays the Rules for Submitting Forms as shown in Figure 10-10.

3. Click Add → Add Action, and then select "Set a field's value" and complete the dialog box as shown in Figure 10-11 to set the DisableSubmit checkbox to true( ). Click OK when you're done.

4. Click Add Action again and select "Submit using a data connection," then "Data connection: Main submit." Click OK when you're done.

5. Click OK four times to close the dialog boxes.

InfoPath uses Rules and Actions for common tasks that might otherwise require code.

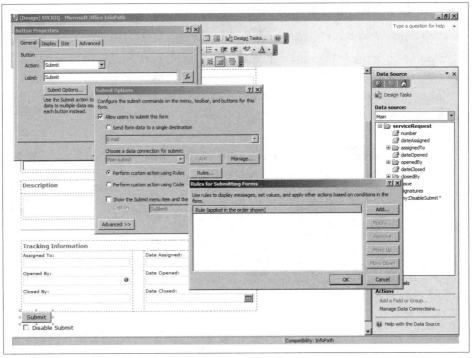

Figure 10-10. Adding a rule to submit a form

Testing a Form

To test the form:

1. Choose File → Preview → Form, and click Submit to check the rule. If an action causes an error, InfoPath displays a dialog box and you can click Show Details to get more information.

2. If the Preview is successful, select/clear the checkbox to make sure it enables/disables the Submit button.

3. Close the preview and choose File → Save to save the form.

Hiding Controls

You can't directly hide interactive controls in InfoPath. Instead, create a section to contain the controls to hide, and then hide that section:

1. From the InfoPath Controls task pane, drag a section control onto the form.

2. Drag the Disable Submit checkbox onto that section.

3. Double-click the section and choose Display → Conditional Formatting → Add.

4. Create the condition The expression 1 = 1 and select "Hide this control." Click OK three times to close the dialog boxes.

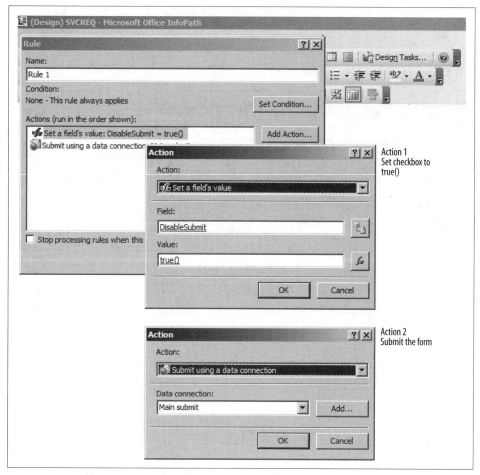

Figure 10-11. Adding actions to the rule

Making a Form Read-Only

The preceding section showed you how to disable the submit button after it is clicked once. That prevents the same form from being submitted multiple times. The same technique can be used to make all or part of a form read-only after it is first submitted.

For example, to prevent further changes to the Request Number field after the form is submitted:

1. Double-click on the Request Number field at the top of the form template. Info-Path displays the Text Box Properties dialog box.

2. Click Display → Conditional Formatting → Add. InfoPath displays the Conditional Format dialog box.

3. Complete the dialog box, as shown in Figure 10-12, to make the field read-only when DisableSubmit is selected.

4. Click OK three times to close the dialog boxes.

5. Preview the form to test the change.

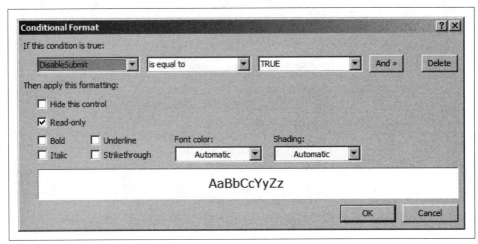

Figure 10-12. Making a field read-only after the form is submitted

You can't apply conditional formatting to more than one control at a time, so if you need to make an entire form read-only, you'll need to repeat this procedure for each control.

Populate a Control from a List

InfoPath forms can retrieve data from various types of data sources, including Share-Point lists. InfoPath's access to lists is read-only; it can't directly modify items in a list. InfoPath refers to this type of access as a *secondary data source*. In InfoPath, *primary data source* refers to where the form data is stored.

Secondary data sources can populate controls, such as drop-down lists, and they can be used to create reports (or *views*) of lists from SharePoint. The major steps to populating controls from a SharePoint list are:

1. Create a data connection to the list.

2. Add controls and bind their values to list fields.

3. Add filters to display the appropriate data.

The following sections demonstrate these steps using a list on my site that contains InfoPath programming samples categorized by language.

Creating a Data Connection

To create a data connection from an InfoPath form to a SharePoint list:

1. Design a new, blank form and choose Tools → Data Connections → Add. Info-Path starts the Data Connection Wizard.

2. Enter the settings in Table 10-5 and click Close when done.

Table 10-5. Data Connection Wizard settings

At Wizard step	Do this	And click...
1	Select Receive data	Next
2	Select SharePoint library or list	Next
3	Enter *http://www.essentialsharepoint.com/*	Next
4	Select the InfoPath Code Samples list	Next
5	Select ID, Title, Language, Example, and Description fields	Next
6	Deselect "Store a copy of the data in the form template"	Next
7	Select "Automatically retrieve data when form is opened"	Finish

Adding Bound Controls

To add controls that display items from the data connection:

1. Display the Controls task pane and create two drop-down lists by dragging and dropping the controls from the task pane onto the form.

2. Double-click on `field`; select "Enter values manually"; and add the values VBScript, VB.NET, C# .NET, Registry, and Other. Click OK to close the dialog box.

3. Double-click on `field2`, select "Look up values from an external data source," click Select XPath, select the InfoPath_Code_Samples group, and choose Filter Data as shown in Figure 10-13.

4. Specify the filter Language → is equal to → "Select a field or group" and select the `field1` element from the `Main` data source as shown in Figure 10-14. Click OK four times to return to the main dialog box.

5. Click "Set XPath for the Value field" and choose ID as shown in Figure 10-15, and then click OK to close the dialog box.

Step 4 filters the values in `field2` so that only the titles for the selected language are displayed. By binding `field` to InfoPath_Code_Samples, you can display Title, but use the unique ID to filter other fields in the next step.

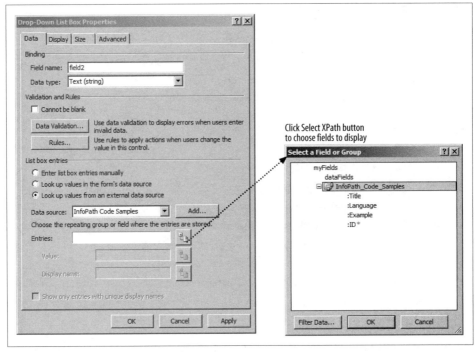

Click Select XPath button
to choose fields to display

Figure 10-13. Creating bound controls (Step 3)

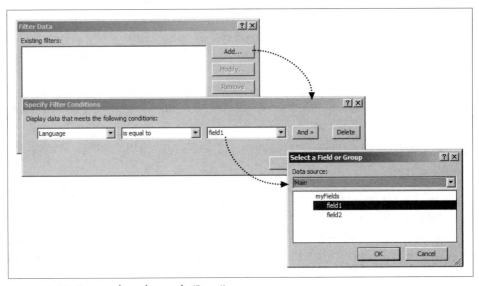

Figure 10-14. Creating bound controls (Step 4)

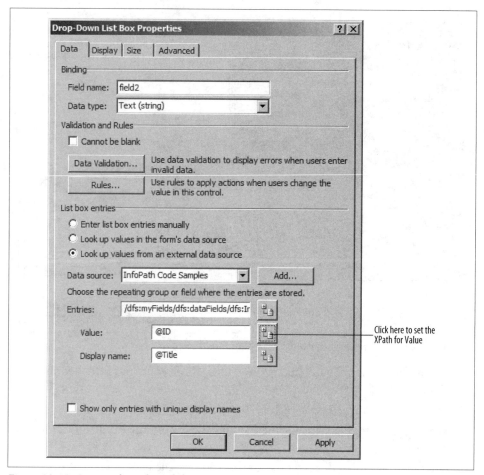

Figure 10-15. Creating bound controls (step 5)

Filtering Data

InfoPath list controls are built to receive arrays of values from data sources. Text box controls are a little different, however. To display a value from a list of repeating items, you must use a formula for the field's default value.

To see how that works:

1. Add a text box control to the form.

2. Double-click on the text box, click Display, select Multi-line, and select "Scrolling: Expand" to show all text.

3. Click Data, click the formula button after the Value field, click Insert Field or Group, and select the Description field from the InfoPath_Code_Samples group as shown in Figure 10-16.

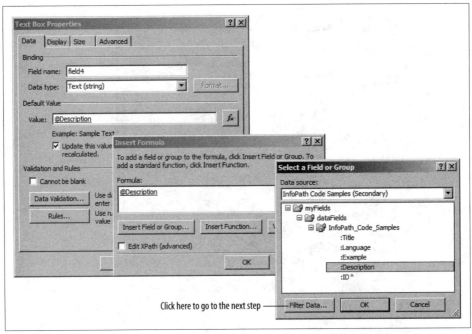

Click here to go to the next step

Figure 10-16. Displaying data from a secondary data source in a text box (step 3)

4. Choose Filter Data → Add, and add the filter "ID is equal to field2" as shown in Figure 10-17.

5. Click OK five times to close each of the open dialog boxes.

6. Repeat the preceding steps for the Example field from the InfoPath_Code_Samples group.

7. Add labels by typing directly on the form and save the template.

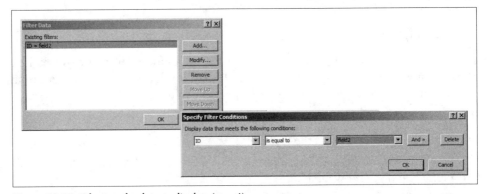

Figure 10-17. Filtering the data to display (step 4)

When complete, preview the form. It should look something like Figure 10-18.

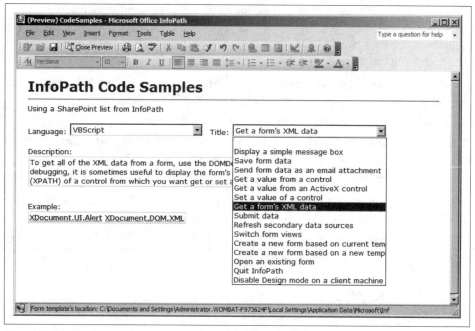

Figure 10-18. Previewing the form to test bound fields and filters

You may have noticed that InfoPath uses a very long series of dialog boxes to complete tasks. I've tried to keep it simple, but describing tasks in InfoPath is difficult. You may have better luck learning from the completed sample.

Validating Data

One advantage of using Submit rather than Save is that Submit enforces data validation. InfoPath allows you to save forms containing invalid data, but you can't submit the form until all fields are valid. InfoPath can validate fields using a variety of criteria. To add validation criteria to a control:

1. Display the control's properties and click Data Validation. InfoPath displays the Data Validation dialog box.

2. Click Add. InfoPath displays the dialog box for validation criteria. Enter a condition that results in a validation error.

3. Click OK and then preview the form and test the validation.

You can combine multiple criteria by choosing And >>, but you can only have one ScreenTip and Message per control.

Validation rules are checked as the user enters data on the form. If an invalid entry is made in a control, that entry is flagged as soon as the focus moves to another control.

Forms containing validation errors can't be submitted, but users only receive a warning if they save or email a form containing validation errors. There is no built-in way to prevent the user from saving, emailing, or printing a form containing validation errors, but you can avoid it by following these steps:

1. Choose Tools → Form Options → Open and Save. Disable the Save, Print, and Send to Mail Recipient options. Click OK to close the dialog box.
2. Add buttons to the form to save, print, or submit the form.
3. Add a checkbox to enable or disable the save/print/submit buttons as described in "Customizing Forms," earlier in this chapter.
4. Write code to control the setting of the checkbox based on validation.

Only the last step above is new, so I'll explain it further. InfoPath creates an Error object for each validation error on a form. Within script, you can use the XDocument object's Errors collection to check whether or not a form is valid. For example, the following script checks whether the form is valid each time the focus changes from one control to another:

```
' Do validation checking.
Sub XDocument_OnContextChange(eventObj)
    If eventObj.Type = "ContextNode" Then
        ' Get checkbox control
        Set x = XDocument.DOM.DocumentElement.SelectSingleNode("my:chkValid")
        If xdocument.errors.count = 0 Then
            ' Set value to True (valid).
            ' This enables Submit button through
            ' conditional formatting.
            x.text = "true"
        Else
            ' Not valid, set to False (disables Submit).
            x.text = "false"
        End If
        Exit Sub
    End If
End Sub
```

This code sets the checkbox to True if the form contains no validation errors.

Preventing Changes to Form Templates

InfoPath both designs and displays forms. Only members of the Web Designer or Administrative groups can create form libraries or change the InfoPath form template used by the library. However, templates deployed to clients can be changed. In most cases, you won't want members opening those templates in Design mode and tinkering with them. There are two approaches to solving this problem:

- Enable form protection. This approach discourages members from changing form templates, but does not prevent them from doing so.

- Disable Design mode on members' systems. This approach keeps users from changing existing form templates and prevents them from creating new ones.

To protect a template from changes:

1. Open the template in Design mode.

2. Choose Tools → Form Options → Advanced, select "Enable protection," and click OK.

Protected templates display a warning if the user opens them in Design mode. That's weak protection at best, but if you sign the protected template with a digital signature, you can both discourage changes and detect them if they are made (changes overwrite the digital signature, so the template will no longer be trusted).

A stronger solution prevents users from designing *any* templates. You can use the Custom Installation Wizard (CIW) to create a customized setup program for Office that omits the design features from InfoPath. In order to do that:

1. Run the CIW.

2. Open the InfoPath Windows Installer file (*INF12.msi*).

3. Configure Disable InfoPath Designer mode in step 10 of the wizard.

4. Finish creating the custom installation, and then use the generated Windows Installer to install InfoPath on the client machines.

Alternately, you can disable Design mode by changing a system registry setting like so:

```
HKEY_CURRENT_USER\Software\Microsoft\Office\12.0\InfoPath\Designer\
DisableDesigner=0x00000001
```

Editing the system registry requires special knowledge. This is an advanced technique. Disabling Design mode removes InfoPath's "Design this Form" button, "Design a Form" task pane, and the "File, Design a Form" menu option.

Using InfoPath Forms Services

MOSS Enterprise Edition includes InfoPath Forms Services. These server-side components integrate with SharePoint to provide the ability to:

- View and edit completed InfoPath forms using Internet Explorer 6.0 or later—InfoPath does not have to be installed on the client.

- Convert from InfoPath XML form data to ASPX web pages.

- Manage deployed InfoPath templates through SharePoint Central Administration.

The following sections explore those features in more detail. They assume that you are using MOSS Enterprise Edition.

Publishing Browser-Compatible Templates

When you publish a template to a web site that is running InfoPath Forms Services, the Publishing Wizard enables the option shown in Figure 10-19.

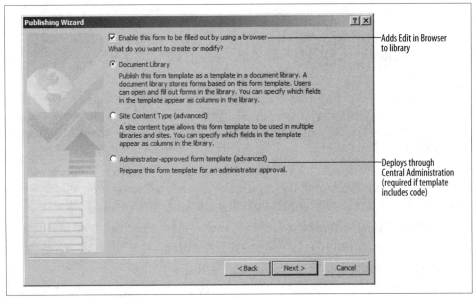

Figure 10-19. Publishing to an Enterprise server enables new features

To see how Edit in Browser works:

1. Publish the template and select "Enable this form to be filled out by using a browser," as shown in Figure 10-19. If that option does not appear, InfoPath Forms Services are not running on the SharePoint server.

2. Once the template is published, SharePoint adds the Edit in Browser option to the form's Edit menu.

3. Select Edit in Browser from the form's Edit menu. SharePoint displays the form in Edit mode as shown in Figure 10-20.

One thing you'll notice right away is that you can edit existing forms in the browser, but you can't create new ones unless you have InfoPath. To solve that problem:

1. Open the template in Design mode and add a Submit button to save the form to the library.

2. Add a Cancel button to close the form without saving.

3. Click Tools → Form Options, and remove the top and bottom toolbars to prevent users from overwriting the blank form you'll create in step 5.

4. Save and publish the template to the library.

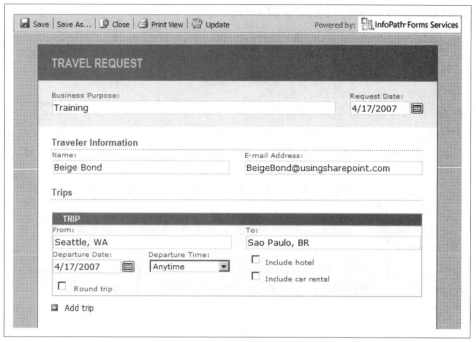

Figure 10-20. Editing an InfoPath form in the browser

5. Create a new, blank form named *New.xml* in the library using InfoPath.

6. Provide a link that opens *New.xml* in the browser to allow users to submit new forms without using InfoPath.

The Submit button that you created in step 1 uses a rule to submit the form via a data connection using a filename generated by this formula:

```
concat("Request: ", now())
```

That formula generates a unique file name for the request based on the current date and time. The Cancel button in step 2 uses a rule with an action to close the form without prompting for save.

You can get the link for step 6 by clicking Edit in Brower on *New.xml*'s Edit menu and then copying the URL from the browser's address bar. For example, the following link opens the form from the sample Travel Request library:

```
<a href="../_layouts/formserver.aspx?XmlLocation=/SiteDirectory/IP/Travel/New.
xml&OpenIn=Browser">Click here to submit a request using the Browser</a>
```

The Travel Request sample is available as a library template in this book's online samples. Download and install the template to examine the InfoPath submit rules more closely.

Checking for Browser Compatibility

Not all InfoPath controls can be rendered in the browser by InfoPath Forms Services, and JScript and VBScript code are not supported. To check a template for browser compatibility:

1. Open the template in Design mode.
2. Select Design Checker in the InfoPath task pane.
3. Click Change Compatibility Settings on the task pane and select "Design a form template that can be opened in a browser or InfoPath." Click OK to close the dialog box.
4. Click the Refresh button in the Design Checker task pane. InfoPath reports any compatibility errors in the task pane.

Converting Forms to Pages

Completed InfoPath form files can be published as ASPX pages for viewing in the browser. Once published, the page views are static, but can be updated by republishing the form to the same location.

To publish InfoPath for data as an ASPX page:

1. Create or open a site based on one of the publishing templates. The form library must exist in a publishing site for the conversion to work.
2. Publish an InfoPath template to the site that you opened or created in step 1. This step creates a form library in the site.
3. Fill out and save InfoPath forms in the new form library.
4. On the form file's Edit menu, click Convert Document → From InfoPath Form to Web Page. SharePoint displays the Create Page From Document page (see Figure 10-21).
5. Click Configure Converter Settings to select the InfoPath view to use for the conversion. Click OK when done.
6. Complete the page and click Create. InfoPath Forms Services converts the form to a web page and publishes it to the Pages library in the publishing site.

InfoPath Form Services do not seem to correctly read form views at the time of this writing. You may have better luck converting the page to XML and specifying a custom XSLT transformation to format the output.

Managing Templates from Central Administration

Templates that include code, require full trust, or use a data connection library can't be published directly by form designers. Instead, they must be prepared for publishing by the designer and then be approved and published by the SharePoint administrator.

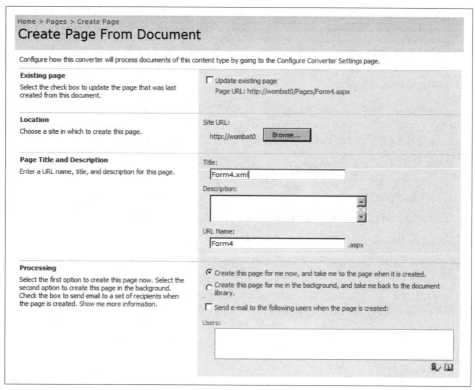

Figure 10-21. Publishing an InfoPath form as a web page

To prepare a form for publishing, the form designer must complete these steps:

1. Design the form, preview it, and debug any problems.

2. Save the completed template to a public network share.

3. Publish the template to the target form library. The designer must select the Administrator-approved option in the third step of the Publishing Wizard (see Figure 10-19).

4. Contact the SharePoint administrator to let her know the template is ready to be published.

Once prepared, the SharePoint administrator can publish the template through Central Administration. To do that:

1. Go to the Central Administration web site and click Application Management.

2. Click "Manage form templates" under the InfoPath Forms Services heading at the bottom of the page.

3. Click "Upload form template" on the toolbar.

4. Click Browse to select the template to upload, and then click Verify to check whether the form has been prepared for publishing by the form designer.

5. If the template passes verification, click Upload to deploy the template to the server. SharePoint uploads the template and adds it to the list on the Manage Form Templates page.

The Manage Form Templates page allows administrators to pause new forms from being created from a template. Microsoft calls that process *quiesce*, and it is used for upgrading deployed templates. For example, to upgrade a template on the server:

1. Navigate to the Manage Forms Templates page, and select Quiesce Form Template from the template's Edit menu. SharePoint displays the Quiesce Form Template page.

2. Enter the number of minutes to pause and click Start Quiescing.

3. Upload the new template to the server.

The period of time entered in Step 2 allows current sessions to submit their form data before the template is changed. Because new sessions are prevented from starting during the quiescence, the upgrade can occur smoothly. Once the quiescence period expires, users get the upgraded template.

Programming InfoPath

InfoPath implements a declarative programming model where you can define common tasks through rules and actions. You should try to use that approach as much as possible, but where it falls short, you can program InfoPath directly through COM or through .NET. Which approach you choose depends on a number of factors, described in Table 10-6.

Table 10-6. The InfoPath programming tools

Approach	Editor	Languages	Comments
COM	Microsoft Script Editor (MSE)	• JScript • VBScript	• Limited debugging • Legacy object model • No support for browser-enabled templates • Existing code base/examples
.NET	Visual Studio 2005 (VSTO/VSTA)	• C# • Visual Basic .NET	• Excellent debugging • New object model • Requires additional tool • Emerging code base/poor examples

In my opinion, if you are creating templates that require more than a little code, you should plan to program InfoPath in .NET. Visual Studio is a professional programming tool that gives you far more assistance than the script editor. Although the

Visual Studio .NET environment is complicated, the command completion, syntax checking, and debugging tools make it a great deal easier to program with InfoPath.

If you are working on templates that already contain JScript or VBScript code, you will probably want to continue in those languages for those templates. You'll also probably want to move to .NET for new templates, however.

Installing and Choosing the Language

The default Office setup does not install programming tools. To be able to program InfoPath templates, you must enable programming support.

To enable programming through .NET (C# or Visual Basic .NET):

1. From the Control Panel, click Add or Remove Programs, click Microsoft Office Enterprise 2007, and click Change. Windows starts the Office setup program.
2. Select Add or Remove Features and click Continue.
3. Expand Microsoft Office InfoPath → .NET Programmability Support → .NET Programmability Support for .NET Framework version 2.0 → Visual Studio Tools for Applications.
4. Select Run from My Computer, and click Continue.

To enable programming through COM (JScript or VBScript):

1. Repeat Steps 1 and 2 above.
2. Expand Office Tools → Microsoft Script Editor (HTML Source Editing) → Web Scripting → Web Debugging.
3. Select Run from My Computer, and click Continue.

Each template you create is associated with a programming language for its code. Once you set the language, you can't change it unless you first remove any code you've already written. In other words, you can't easily convert from one language to another.

InfoPath defaults to Visual Basic .NET as its programming language. To change that preference for the entire application:

1. Start InfoPath and click Tools → Options → Design.
2. Select the programming language to use from the drop-down lists and click OK.

To set the programming language for an individual template:

1. Open the template in Design mode.
2. Click Tools → Form Options → Programming, and select the language from the drop-down list and then click OK. If the template already includes code, you must click Remove Code before you can change the setting.

Adding Code to a Form in VSTA

To add code to a template in VSTA:

- Click Tools → Programming → Loading Event…

Or:

1. Add a button control to the temple.
2. Double-click the button and then click Edit Form Code.

InfoPath starts VSTA, as shown in Figure 10-22.

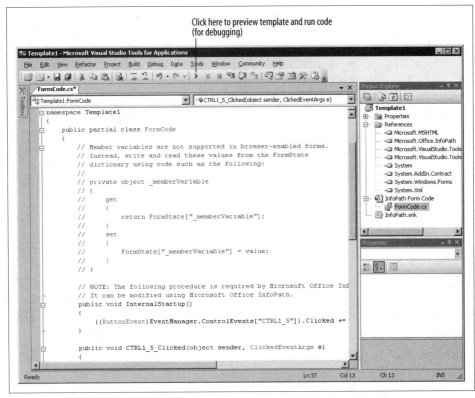

Figure 10-22. The Visual Studio Tools for Applications (VSTA) editor

Add your code to the procedure provided for the event. For example, the following code displays a hello message with the user's name:

```csharp
public void CTRL1_5_Clicked(object sender, ClickedEventArgs e)
{
    // Write your code here.
    System.Windows.Forms.MessageBox.Show("Hello " +
      this.Application.User.UserName);
}
```

Click the Run button in VSTA to compile the code and preview the form. You can set breakpoints, step through procedures, watch values, and use the Immediate window to debug your code.

Setting Trust

If you change the preceding code to this:

```
System.Windows.Forms.MessageBox.Show("Hello " +
    this.Application.User.LoginName);
```

and then try to run the code, you'll get a security exception. Accessing the user's login name requires full trust, but accessing the username only requires minimal trust. To work around this problem while you are developing a template:

1. Open the template in Design mode and click Tools → Form Options → Security and Trust.

2. Deselect "Automatically determine the security level," and select the Full Trust option, as shown in Figure 10-23.

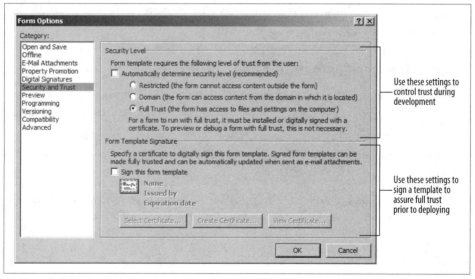

Figure 10-23. Setting trust for a form

Once you have finished developing the form, sign it with a digital certificate that will be trusted by your users. Most organizations control who has trusted certificates so that only forms that have passed testing are signed and deployed.

Templates require trust to access resources outside of the current form—for example, saving a form through code requires trust. You can avoid some of those issues by saving only through the built-in InfoPath controls.

Getting Values from Controls

Use the XPathNavigator class to get and set values from controls on the form. For example, the following code gets the value in a text box named field1 and copies it to a text box named field2:

```
public void CTRL6_5_Clicked(object sender, ClickedEventArgs e)
{
    // Get field 1
    XPathNavigator field1 =
      this.MainDataSource.CreateNavigator( ).SelectSingleNode(
      "/my:myFields/my:field1", NamespaceManager);
    // Get field 2
    XPathNavigator field2  =
      this.MainDataSource.CreateNavigator( ).SelectSingleNode(
      "/my:myFields/my:field2", NamespaceManager);
    // Copy value from one field to another.
    field2.SetValue(field1.Value);
}
```

To get the XPath for a control, display the Data Source task pane in InfoPath, right-click on the item, and click Copy Xpath, as shown in Figure 10-24.

Use the Programming menu in Figure 10-24 to add code for data change events and validation events for form data.

Writing Browser-Compatible Code

Only code written in C# or Visual Basic .NET is compatible with InfoPath Forms Service's edit-in-browser feature, and even then you need to observe these restrictions:

- Windows interface operations such as MessageBox are not supported.
- Other external libraries such as mshtml are not supported.
- Member variables must be stored in FormState.

Use the Design Checker task pane in InfoPath to verify that your code is browser-compatible (see the earlier section "Checking for Browser Compatibility").

Best Practices

- If you do not control your end-user environment, consider leveraging InfoPath Forms Services to publish your InfoPath forms as dynamic web pages.
- Try to keep your InfoPath forms as simple as possible. If you find you are working hard to make your InfoPath form do what you want, consider writing a custom web part in ASP.NET instead.

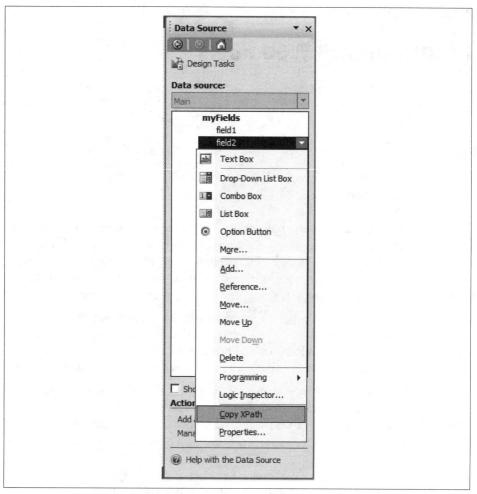

Figure 10-24. Finding the XPath of a control

- Use rules, actions, and conditional formatting before you turn to writing code. InfoPath is best suited to that declarative style of programming.
- If you do need to write code, use VSTA rather than JScript or VBScript. VSTA allows you to program in .NET, which is most complete and better supported than the scripting languages.

CHAPTER 11

Programming Web Parts

SharePoint delivers custom web applications without programming. To me, it is the evolution of the Visual Basic and ActiveX technologies that I worked on at Microsoft extended to the Web. Component-based development really took off with the introduction of Visual Basic custom controls, and today we are seeing something similar in the web space with web parts, widgets, and other prebuilt components.

You can do a lot with the web parts that come with SharePoint out of the box, but after a while you'll start getting requests for custom components that integrate some existing application into SharePoint or that present information about sites or lists in a way that the built-in parts can't. That's when you need to program a web part.

You have a lot of choices in how you begin. I try to start from the easiest approach and work to the more complex topics in this chapter. I also focus on how to use the new ASP.NET WebPart class, rather than the WSS 2.0 approach—you can still use the old approach but the new one is much simpler. There's a lot to cover, so let's get started!

 You must have Visual Studio 2005 and know a programming language such as Visual C# to complete the tasks in this chapter.

What to Build When...

You build web parts when your needs exceed what is available out of the box or from third parties. There are web parts available for free or at reasonable cost on the Web. It is often more economical to buy a web part than to create your own because:

- Buying a web part provides an immediate solution.
- Users adjust to what features are offered by commercial web parts, but will request changes to custom ones.
- Commercial web parts come with support, documentation, a user community, and regular enhancements.

Once you're sure it's best to build, buckle up your programming tool belt and we'll get started. Table 11-1 lists the different approaches to developing web parts in increasing level of complexity. You can often start with a simple approach as a prototype (or quick-and-dirty solution) and move to greater complexity as needs become clearer.

Table 11-1. Choosing a development approach

Type	Technique	Languages	Editor
Customized web part	Convert List View to Data View	XML/XSL	SharePoint Designer
Client-side web part	Content Editor, XML Viewer, Page Viewer	HTML, JavaScript, XML/XSL	Browser
Hosted	Build user controls and load them in SmartPart	Visual Basic. NET, C#	Visual Studio
Rendered	Write code based on the WebPart class	Visual Basic .NET, C# (preferred)	Visual Studio
Global page	Build ASP.NET web page and deploy to _layouts	Visual Basic .NET, C#	Visual Studio

The first two techniques in Table 11-1 were covered in Chapter 6. They require minimal code and are simple to deploy, but they are mostly limited to client-side tasks. If you need access to database, SharePoint, Active Directory, or other objects on the server, you'll need to use the hosted, rendered, or global page approach.

Hosted web parts

Are based on SmartPart, which loads ASP.NET user controls (*.ascx*) into SharePoint. User controls are developed visually out of ASP.NET built-in controls. It's easy to migrate existing ASP.NET applications to SharePoint using this approach.

Rendered web parts

Are written entirely in code—there is no visual designer. They are based on the new ASP.NET WebPart class, which renders the component controls. They are harder to write than hosted web parts, but are easier to deploy to multiple servers. This is the technique that commercial web parts use.

Global pages

Are ASP.NET pages deployed to the *_layouts* folder on the SharePoint server. Pages in that folder are available to all sites, such as the *MyInfo.aspx* page used by the Site Aggregator web part (see Chapter 9).

The following sections explore how to develop, debug, and deploy web parts using the hosted and rendered approaches.

What to Download

Before you start developing web parts, download the following components:

- Return of SmartPart from *http://www.codeplex.com/smartpart*.
- SharePoint Server 2007 SDK from *http://www.microsoft.com/downloads*. The filename is *OfficeServerSDK.exe*.
- Visual Studio 2005 Extensions Web Part Templates at *http://www.microsoft.com/downloads*. The filename is *VSeWSS.exe*.
- The web part sample code from this book's online samples (see Preface).

This chapter makes use of those components, and the following sections cover how to install and use those components in greater detail.

Creating Hosted Web Parts

SmartPart is actually a series of web parts created by Jan Teilens (*http://weblogs.asp.net/jan*). The version for WSS 3.0 is called Return of the SmartPart. To start using it:

1. Download the SmartPart from *http://www.codeplex.com/smartpart*.
2. Follow the instructions provided with the download to install the web part on the server.
3. Create a *UserControls* folder in the physical folder for your SharePoint web site. For example:

   C:\Inetpub\wwwroot\wss\VirtualDirectories\2007\UserControls

4. Deploy your user controls to this *UserControls* folder.
5. Add the SmartPart web part to a page, select the user control, and click Apply as shown in Figure 11-1. SmartPart loads the control and displays it on the page.

The user control shown in Figure 11-1 uses ASP.NET 2.0 compile-on-the-fly, so I put both the page markup (*.acsx*) and code (*.cs*) in the UserControls folder. The *HelloSmartPart.ascx* sample included with SmartPart packages the code and description in a single file using <script> blocks.

Code that is shared among user controls should be stored in a separate project, compiled, and deployed to the BIN folder in the web site root.

Developing Under Windows XP

One of the tricks in programming web parts is setting up your development environment: the SharePoint DLLs run only under Windows 2003, but most development machines run Windows XP Professional. You can develop, compile, and even run hosted web parts on a Windows XP machine if you follow these steps:

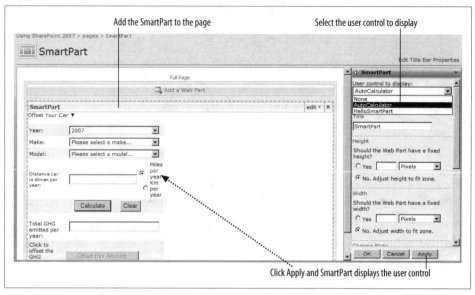

Figure 11-1. *Using the SmartPart to host user controls*

1. Create a web project in Visual Studio.

2. Create a DLLs folder in the web project and copy the *ReturnOfSmartPart.dll* and the *Microsoft.SharePoint.dll* files to it.

3. Add a reference to the two DLLs.

4. Create a test page (*.aspx*) in the project and add the user control to it.

5. Run the project and verify that the user control displays correctly.

The *ReturnOfSmartPart.dll* is included with the SmartPart installation files. To get the SharePoint DLL, copy it from this location on the server:

C:\Program Files\Common Files\Microsoft Shared\web server extensions\12\ISAPI

The SharePoint DLL won't run under Windows XP, but it is required to compile correctly. Using this technique, you can design the user control visually, verify how it looks at runtime, and use most functionality. You *won't* be able to debug any features that rely on the SharePoint object model.

That last limitation isn't as bad as it sounds: hosted web parts often deal with existing business logic, access to databases, and other things that are independent of SharePoint. All those things work fine under Windows XP.

 Windows Vista requires Visual Studio 2005 SP1 or later. In addition, you can't develop code using .NET 1.1 under Vista; only .NET 2.0 and later development is supported. See the Microsoft web site for details on developing under Vista.

Writing User Controls for SmartPart

There are a couple of things you hit right away when developing with SmartPart:

- The displayed name for the user control in SmartPart isn't user-friendly.
- Your user control doesn't have access to web part properties.

To change the name of the user control displayed by SmartPart:

- Add a `ClassName` attribute to the Control declaration as shown here:

```
<%@ Control Language="C#" AutoEventWireup="true" CodeFile="AutoCalc.ascx.cs"
Inherits="AutoCalc" ClassName="AutoCalculator" %>
```

SmartPart provides an interface for accessing web part properties from SharePoint. To provide access to those properties from your user control:

1. Add the `SmartPart.IAdvancedUserControl` interface to your user control class.
2. If you select Implement Interface from the smart tag, Visual Studio adds a template for the interface. Make the changes shown here:

```
// JAW, 04/21/07: Implemented interface to enable web part properties.
#region IAdvancedUserControl Members

// Member variable to use for property access.
private SmartPart.SmartPart _wp;

public Microsoft.SharePoint.WebPartPages.ToolPart[] GetCustomToolParts()
{
    //throw new Exception("The method or operation is not implemented.");
    return null;
}

public void SetContext(SmartPart.SmartPart webpart)
{
    //throw new Exception("The method or operation is not implemented.");
    _wp = webpart;
}

#endregion
```

Use the `_wp` variable to access the web part properties. For example, the following code changes the title of the web part:

```
private void cmdSetTitle_Click(object sender, System.EventArgs e)
{
    _wp.Title = ("New web part title");
    _wp.SaveWebPartProperties = true;
}
```

To add browsable properties to a user control:

1. Create a property; add `Personalizable`, `Browsable`, and `WebDisplayName` attributes.
2. Use the `SetCustomProperty` and `GetCustomProperty` methods to store and retrieve the property settings.

For example, the following code creates a `Target` property for the user control:

```
private string _default = "http://www.drivinggreen.com/shoppingcartsp.asp";

[Personalizable(PersonalizationScope.Shared, false),
Browsable(true),
WebDisplayName("Target")]
public string Target
{
    get
    {
        string res = (string)_wp.GetCustomProperty("Target");
        if (res == null) res = _default;
        return res;
    }
    set
    {
        _wp.SetCustomProperty("Target", value);
        _wp.SaveWebPartProperties = true;
    }
}
```

The attribute settings in the preceding code control how the property is saved and how it appears in the web part properties page. In this case, the property setting is shared by all users and the value will be exported with the web part. Figure 11-2 shows how the property is displayed.

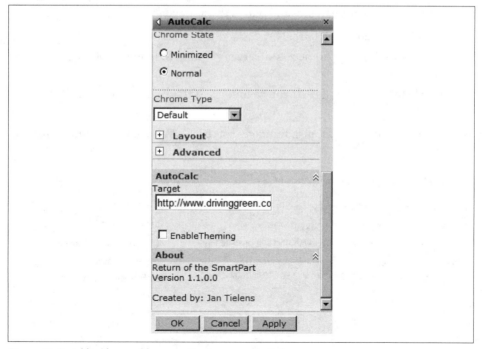

Figure 11-2. Adding browsable properties to a user control

Deploying User Controls As Web Parts

To deploy a user control as a web part:

1. Add the user control files to the *UserControls* folder on the server.
2. Create a test page with a SmartPart containing the control to deploy.
3. Set the Title of the web part to match the name of the user control.
4. Click Edit → Export on the web part title bar, and save the web part file (*.dwp*) to your computer.
5. Upload the exported web part file to the web part gallery of your site collection. Others can now reuse the web part through the Add Web Parts page.

Preparing to Develop Rendered Web Parts

In the previous version of SharePoint, web parts were hard to develop. That's the main reason why so many people are grateful to Jan Teilens for SmartPart. With this release, Microsoft has made things somewhat easier, and you can now create, deploy, and debug SharePoint web parts from within Visual Studio. However, for everything to work correctly you must be running Windows 2003 SP1 on your development machine.

As mentioned earlier, most developers use Windows XP Professional, so doing web part development means you must do one of the following:

- Upgrade to Windows 2003.
- Use Remote Desktop to access a server running Windows 2003 and do your development there.
- Use Microsoft Virtual PC to run Windows 2003 within Windows XP on your desktop.

The main advantages and disadvantages of each approach are summarized in Table 11-2.

Table 11-2. Possible web part development approaches

Approach	Advantage	Disadvantage
Upgrade	Best performance for development	Changing your desktop OS is disruptive
Remote Desktop	Server can be shared with other developers/testers	Requires an additional physical server
Virtual PC	Contained on single desktop, you can create/change server configurations without affecting others	Reduced performance Usually requires a memory upgrade

Don't develop on a production server. Doing development resets Internet Information Explorer (IIS) periodically, which is disruptive for users.

 You *can* create and compile web parts under Windows XP if you copy and reference the SharePoint DLL as mentioned in the preceding section. However, you can't deploy or debug web parts under XP.

Configuring the Server for Development

Regardless of how you run Windows 2003, you must install the development tools on that Windows 2003 server and change some settings before you can develop and debug web parts.

To install the development tools and configure the server for development:

1. Verify that the Windows 2003 server has the current service packs and that SharePoint is installed correctly. Use a basic single-server WSS installation for development.

2. Install Visual Studio .NET 2005. You can create web parts using Visual Basic .NET or Visual C#, but the web part templates are only provided in C# at this time.

3. Install Visual Studio 2005 Extensions Web Part Templates, available from *http://www.microsoft.com/downloads*. The download filename is *VSeWSS.exe*.

4. Install SharePoint Server 2007 SDK from *http://www.microsoft.com/downloads*. The filename is *OfficeServerSDK.exe*.

5. Create a root folder for your web part projects, such as *C:\WebParts*. Creating this folder makes it easier to use required command-line tools.

6. Open the *Web.config* file from SharePoint root web site and change the trust level and debug settings, as shown in this snippet:

```
<configuration>
    ...
  <system.web>
    ...
    <compilation batch="false" debug="true" />
    <trust level="WSS_Medium" originUrl="" />
  </system.web>
</configuration>
```

Changing the debug attribute enables Visual Studio to attach to the *w3wp.exe* process to step into web part code. Setting the trust level to WSS_Medium allows your web part to access the SharePoint object model, which allows you to retrieve information about lists, libraries, web sites, and other SharePoint components.

Using the Visual Studio Web Part Extensions

To use the web part extensions from within Visual Studio:

1. Click File → New Project and select Visual C# → SharePoint → Web Part, as shown in Figure 11-3. Click OK to create the project.

2. Modify the Render method to output some text (just uncomment the supplied line).

3. Click Project → Properties → Debug, and enter the address of the SharePoint 2007 site collection where the web part should be deployed, as shown in Figure 11-4.

4. Click Run. Visual Studio compiles the project, creates a solution file, deploys the solution to the server, and restarts IIS. It takes a while.

5. Open the browser and navigate to a test page on the SharePoint site.

6. Click Site Actions → Edit Page, and click on Add a Web Part. Select the new web part and add it to the page.

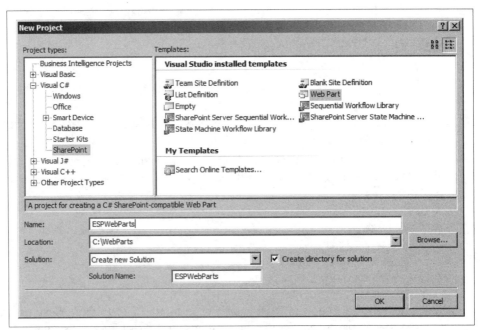

Figure 11-3. Creating a new web part project in Visual Studio

If you expand the project types for Visual Basic in Figure 11-3, you'll notice that the web part project type is missing. I'm not sure why that is, but if you prefer Visual Basic, check with Microsoft—it may add that language in the future.

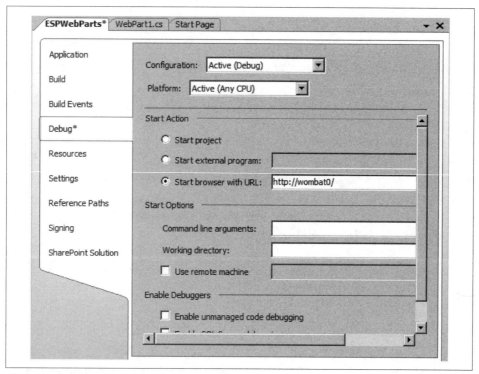

Figure 11-4. Setting the web site for deployment

The Start Action setting in Figure 11-4 determines what site is used for deployment—that might seem a bit strange, but if you omit it you'll get a deployment error when you build. The URL must be on the local machine in order to deploy.

If you don't want to automatically deploy, choose Build → Build Solution instead of Run. That will compile the project without all the time-consuming deployment steps.

Debugging Web Parts

Web part projects are class libraries, so they don't have a start object to automatically attach to for debugging. To debug a web part:

1. Set a breakpoint in the code you want to debug.
2. Click Debug → Attach to Process. Visual Studio displays a list of the current processes.
3. Select "Show processes in all sessions" and then click the *w3wp.exe* process and click Attach. Visual Studio attaches to the process and starts debugging.

4. In the browser, add the web part being debugged to a test web part page and take some action that calls the code with the breakpoint. Visual Studio stops at the breakpoint.

5. Step through the code as needed.

If more than one *w3wp.exe* process is shown, you can select them both. I use the User Name column to determine which I want to attach to; that identity maps to the IIS application pool user account that the web application is using.

If Visual Studio doesn't stop at the breakpoint as expected, check to make sure the web part you are using in the browser is the correct version—you can "orphan" web parts in the web part gallery during development. Delete the web part from the web part gallery and redeploy.

Converting Existing Projects

Web parts developed for the previous version of SharePoint need to be rebuilt if they:

- Access the SharePoint object model
- Require enhancements that use the .NET 2.0 Framework
- Need to be deployed as solutions rather than as DWP files

In other words: you'll probably want to rebuild existing web part projects. Because the web part project template has changed as well, it's best to start fresh and move your existing web part classes over to a new project, rather than trying to upgrade the original project.

To convert an existing WSS 2.0 web part project to use the new Visual Studio web part extensions template:

1. Create a new web part project using Visual Studio 2005 web part extensions.

2. Copy the class files (*.cs* or *.vb*) and any supporting files (*.htm*, *.dwp*, etc.) from the existing project to the new project's code folder.

3. Add the files to the new project.

4. Change the namespace for the classes to the current project's namespace.

5. Build the project and resolve any errors or warnings.

Much of the existing code will compile successfully using the new SharePoint and ASP.NET references. However, there is some overlap between the ASP.NET and SharePoint WebPart classes, so you may get errors like the following:

```
'MenuItem' is an ambiguous reference between 'System.Web.UI.WebControls.MenuItem' and
'Microsoft.SharePoint.WebPartPages.MenuItem'
```

You can fix those errors by fully qualifying the class, as shown here:

```
_mnuSave = new Microsoft.SharePoint.WebPartPages.MenuItem("Save Settings",
    "mnuSave", new EventHandler(this._mnuSave_Click));
```

In addition to errors, you'll see a list of warnings about methods that are now obsolete in the SharePoint namespace. Those warning aren't critical, but they are usually fairly easy to resolve. For example, Page.IsClientScriptBlockRegistered is replaced by Page.ClientScript.IsClientScriptBlockRegistered.

If you deploy the web part project after resolving these errors, you'll notice that only the web part created by the Visual Studio extensions shows up from the assembly—none of your existing classes are included! In order for the Visual Studio extensions to deploy a web part, a class must:

- Inherit directly from System.Web.UI.WebControls.WebParts.WebPart.
- Have a Guid attribute.

The web part project template uses the Guid attribute of the WebPart class to identify the features in the web part solution. The Visual Studio extensions add those features to the solution so they are installed when you deploy. The extensions also create an installation script for the solution so you can deploy to other servers once development is complete.

To see a list of the features the project will deploy:

- Click Project → Properties → SharePoint Solution. Visual Studio displays the web parts as elements of the solution, as shown in Figure 11-5.

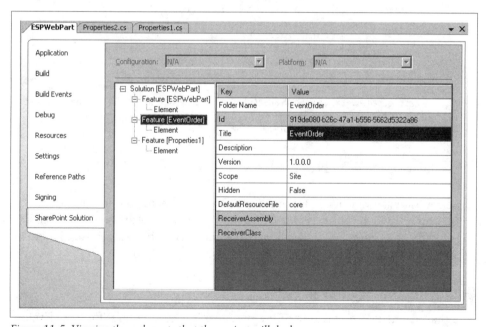

Figure 11-5. Viewing the web parts that the project will deploy

Converting from SharePoint to ASP.NET Web Parts

ASP.NET 2.0 added the `System.Web.UI.WebControls.WebParts.WebPart` class, which is now inherited by the SharePoint `WebPart` class. You can use the base class to create web parts that work in both SharePoint and ASP.NET web part pages, but converting a web part from the SharePoint `WebPart` class to the ASP.NET `WebPart` class requires some work.

To see how much work the conversion would require for a web part:

1. Change the class type from `Microsoft.SharePoint.WebPart` to `System.Web.UI.WebControls.WebParts.WebPart`.

2. Add a `Guid` attribute to each web part class definition.

3. Change the `RenderWebPart` method to `Render`.

4. Add a `base.CreateChildControls();` line to the `CreateChildControls` method.

5. Compile the project and check for errors.

The following code shows the changes in place:

```
[Guid("6D9B7DBA-C365-4d18-A453-86102CCEA61A")]  // Added Guid
public class Properties1 : System.Web.UI.WebControls.WebParts.WebPart
                    //^ was: Microsoft.SharePoint.WebPartPages.WebPart
{
        protected override void CreateChildControls( )
        {
            // implementation omitted...
            this.ChildControlsCreated = true;
            base.CreateChildControls( );  // <-- added.
        }

        protected override void Render(HtmlTextWriter output) // was: RenderWebPart
        {
            RenderChildren (output);
        }

// implementation omitted here...
}
```

The error list will give you an idea of whether it is practical to convert the class or not. If not, simply undo the changes to revert to the SharePoint `WebPart` class. The web part will work in SharePoint and it is still included in the assembly—it just isn't automatically registered in SharePoint.

Deploying Old-Style Web Parts

As a practical matter, it may best to use the ASP.NET `WebPart` class for new development and leave existing web parts to rely on the SharePoint `WebPart` class. The only thing you really gain with the new class is built-in deployment from Visual Studio, and that is fairly easy to work around by registering the web part.

To register a web part based on the SharePoint WebPart class during development:

1. Edit the web part's DWP file from the previous version of the project.
2. Edit the *web.config* file to mark all types from the web part assembly as safe.
3. Run *iisreset.exe* to load the changes to *web.config*.
4. Upload the DWP file to the web part gallery or install it using the stsadm command-line utility.

The Visual Studio extensions only mark web part types as safe explicitly. To allow SharePoint to trust all types from the assembly, change the TypeName attribute in *web.config* to *, as shown here:

```
<SafeControl Assembly="ESPWebPart, Version=1.0.0.0, Culture=neutral,
PublicKeyToken=9f4da00116c38ec5" Namespace="ESPWebPart" TypeName="*" Safe="True" />
```

This example shows a DWP file for a web part that was too hard to fully convert:

```
<?xml version="1.0" encoding="utf-8"?>
<WebPart xmlns:xsi="http://www.w3.org/2001/XMLSchema-instance"
  xmlns:xsd="http://www.w3.org/2001/XMLSchema"
  xmlns="http://schemas.microsoft.com/WebPart/v2">
    <Title>ConnectConsumer</Title>
    <Description></Description>
    <Assembly>ESPWebPart</Assembly>
    <TypeName>ESPWebPart.ConnectConsumer</TypeName>
</WebPart>
```

You only need to do this procedure once for your existing web parts, although you will need to upload changes to the DWP if you change the type name or namespace of the web part in code.

Programming Rendered Web Parts

Web parts are made up of ASP.NET and HTML controls that are then sent to a web part page for display. The code for a web part is simply a class based on the WebPart class as shown here (my comments identify key parts):

```
using System;                            // Standard namespaces...
using System.Runtime.InteropServices;
using System.Web.UI;
using System.Web.UI.WebControls.WebParts;// The WebPart class lives here.
using System.Xml.Serialization;

using Microsoft.SharePoint;              // The old-style WebPart class lives here.
using Microsoft.SharePoint.WebControls;
using Microsoft.SharePoint.WebPartPages;

namespace WebPart1
{
    [Guid("93909b28-3853-4510-b76e-a14878dcbdae")]  //Guid identifies the feature.
    public class WebPart1 : System.Web.UI.WebControls.WebParts.WebPart
```

```
    {                   // ^ This is a new style (ASP.NET) web part!
        protected override void Render(HtmlTextWriter writer)
        {   // This method draws the web part.
            // TODO: add custom rendering code here.
            // writer.Write("Output HTML");
        }
    }
}
```

Table 11-3 summarizes the major programming tasks you need to perform to turn this basic code template into a useful web part. I also list the key members, clauses, attributes, and interfaces used to complete each task.

Table 11-3. Web part programming tasks

Task	Summary	Key members

Create user interface	Add controls to the `Controls` collection, then render those controls and additional HTML.	`Controls`
		`CreateChildControls`
		`RenderControls`
		`RenderControl`
		`Render`

Add JavaScript and HTML	Write code to import and modify HTML control IDs to use the SharePoint-generated names.	`ClassResourcePath`
		`IsClientScriptBlockRegistered`
		`RegisterClientScriptBlock`
		`UniqueID`

Handle child control events	Hook up server-side event handling for ASP.NET controls in the `Controls` collection.	`+=new EventHandler`

Create properties	Add property procedures to a web part and specify attributes that tell SharePoint how to display them in the property task pane and whether or not to save their values.	`WebBrowsable` (attribute)
		`WebDisplayName` (attribute)
		`WebDescription` (attribute)
		`Category` (attribute)
		`Personalization` (attribute)
		`SetPersonalizationDirty`
		`ExportMode`

Add menus	Add items to the web part drop-down menu that respond to server or client events.	`Verbs`
		`WebPartVerb`
		`WebPartVerbCollection`

Customize property task pane	Change the display of a web part's properties in the property task pane and control how the web part is updated from those settings.	`CreateEditorParts`
		`EditorPart`
		`EditorPartCollection`
		`SyncChanges`
		`ApplyChanges`

Make web parts connectable	Implement interfaces in the web part class to provide data to other web parts or consume data from other web parts.	`interface` `ConnectionProvider` (attribute) `ConnectionConsumer` (attribute)

You can find reference information for these keywords in the Visual Studio Help or in the SharePoint SDK *WSS3sdk.chm* Help file. The SharePoint SDK mainly documents web parts using the SharePoint WebPart class—not the ASP.NET class that Microsoft recommends you use for new development.

Creating Web Part Appearance

The core of the web part template code is the Render method. This method is called just before the control is disposed, and it determines the appearance of the part on the page.

To create this appearance, you write HTML to the writer object. For example, the following code displays a simple table containing information about the current user's identity:

```
// Requires this line at class level
// using System.Security.Principal
protected override void Render (HtmlTextWriter writer)
{                      // ^ in SharePoint WebPart class this is RenderWebPart
    // Get the User identity.
    IPrincipal user = this.Context.User;
    // Write table to writer
    writer.Write("<TABLE id='tblUser'>");
    writer.Write("<TR><TD>Authenticated</TD><TD>");
    writer.Write(user.Identity.IsAuthenticated.ToString());
    writer.Write("</TD></TR><TR><TD>User name</TD><TD>");
    writer.Write(user.Identity.Name);
    writer.Write("</TD></TR><TR><TD>Authentication type</TD><TD>");
    writer.Write(user.Identity.AuthenticationType);
    writer.Write("</TD></TR><TR><TD>Code is impersonating</TD><TD>");
    writer.Write(WindowsIdentity.GetCurrent().Name);
    writer.Write("</TD></TR><TR><TD>Request language: </TD><TD>");
    writer.Write(this.Context.Request.UserLanguages[0]);
    writer.Write("</TD></TR><TR><TD>Request host: </TD><TD>");
    writer.Write(this.Context.Request.UserHostName);
    writer.Write("</TD></TR><TR><TD>Request IP: </TD><TD>");
    writer.Write(this.Context.Request.UserHostAddress);
    writer.Write("</TD></TR></TABLE>");
}
```

 This example uses the ASP.NET WebPart base class. In the SharePoint WebPart class, the web part is rendered by the RenderWebPart method.

At runtime, the preceding web part displays user information in a two-column table (Figure 11-6).

HTML tables are useful for controlling the layout of web parts, but embedding all those table, row, and item tags results in code that is hard to debug, update, and localize.

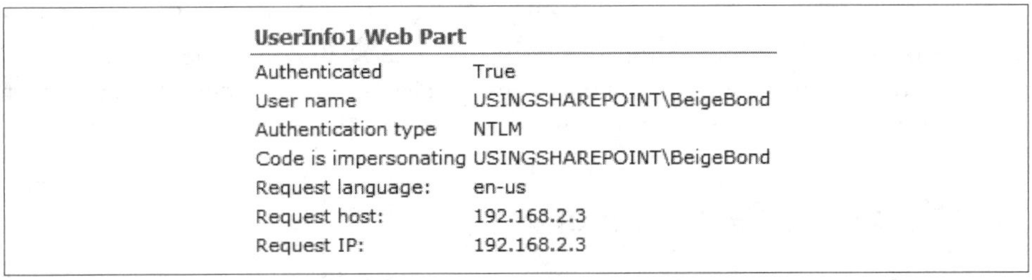

UserInfo1 Web Part

Authenticated	True
User name	USINGSHAREPOINT\BeigeBond
Authentication type	NTLM
Code is impersonating	USINGSHAREPOINT\BeigeBond
Request language:	en-us
Request host:	192.168.2.3
Request IP:	192.168.2.3

Figure 11-6. Rendering UserInfo web part at runtime

The only way to see the result of your HTML is to run the project, and it's easy to make errors in those string literals.

Fortunately, there's a better way. Instead of embedding HTML literals in code, create your tables as HTM files stored as resources, and then load those and modify those files at runtime. This approach uses .NET's powerful `string` functions to substitute values from code into the table. To see how this works:

1. Create a new *.HTM* file in your web part project.

2. Set the file's `Build Action` property to `Embedded Resource`.

3. Edit the HTM page with Visual Studio's design tools to create the table; add headings, scripts, or controls as needed. Use literal placeholders (example: {0}) for items you will fill in from code.

4. Create a procedure to load the resource by filename.

5. Create a procedure to fill in the table variables using the `string` object's `Format` or `Write` methods.

6. Write the result to the `output` object in the `RenderWebPart` event.

Figure 11-7 shows a user information table created in Visual Studio's Design mode that has seven placeholders for values to be filled in from code.

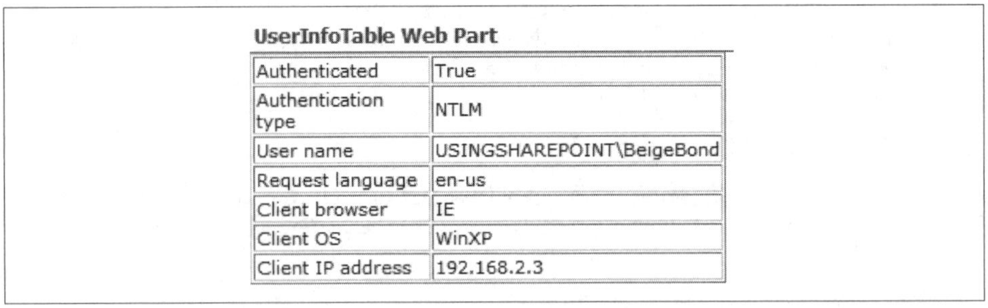

UserInfoTable Web Part

Authenticated	True
Authentication type	NTLM
User name	USINGSHAREPOINT\BeigeBond
Request language	en-us
Client browser	IE
Client OS	WinXP
Client IP address	192.168.2.3

Figure 11-7. Creating a web part table in Visual Studio's Design mode

The following utility procedure loads the resource from the assembly and returns its HTML as a string. Resource names are case-sensitive, so be sure to correctly capitalize the filename when calling this procedure.

```
// Requires this line at class level:
// using System.Reflection
internal string GetHtml(string fName)
{
    // Get the web part assembly.
    Assembly asm = Assembly.GetExecutingAssembly();
    // Build the full name of the resource (case-sensitive).
    string resName = asm.GetName().Name + "." + fName;
    // Declare a stream for the resource.
    System.IO.Stream stream;
    stream = asm.GetManifestResourceStream(resName);
    // Create a reader for the stream.
    System.IO.StreamReader reader = new System.IO.StreamReader(stream);
    // Read the stream and return it as a string.
    return reader.ReadToEnd();
}
```

Next, the BuildTable procedure creates an array of values to plug into the table's literal placeholders, gets the table from the assembly, and performs the substitution. I put this task in a dedicated procedure, rather than in Render, to make it easier to extend Render later—it's a good idea to keep that event uncluttered.

```
// Builds the UserInfo Table
string BuildTable()
{
    // Create an array for table variables
    string[] arr = new string[7];
    // Populate the array with info from the current context.
    arr[0] = this.Context.User.Identity.IsAuthenticated.ToString();
    arr[1] = this.Context.User.Identity.AuthenticationType;
    arr[2] = this.Context.User.Identity.Name;
    arr[3] = this.Context.Request.UserLanguages[0];
    arr[4] = this.Context.Request.Browser.Browser;
    arr[5] = this.Context.Request.Browser.Platform;
    arr[6] = this.Context.Request.UserHostAddress;
    // Read the table resource.
    string sTable = GetHtml("userInfoTable.htm");
    // Substitute the user info values into the table and return.
    return String.Format(sTable, arr);
}

protected override void Render(HtmlTextWriter writer)
{
    // Write table to output
    writer.Write(BuildTable());
}
```

At runtime, the web part loads the table from the assembly, fills in the placeholders, and displays the result. This approach isn't limited to tables. You can add client-side scripts, controls, styles, formatting, or any other type of valid HTML. Since the output is stored in an HTM file, you can preview the output in the browser, test the scripts, and edit and localize versions much easier than if the output was embedded in code.

Adding Child Controls

The UserInfoTable web part isn't interactive—the information flows only from the server to the browser. To make a web part that can interact with users:

1. Declare the web controls to display in the web part.

2. Override the CreateChildControls event to set control properties.

3. Add each control to the controls collection.

4. Set the ChildControlsCreated property to render to controls,

   or

   Render the child controls in the RenderWebPart method.

The following code demonstrates these steps to create a Sum web part containing a text box to input a series of numbers, a command button to perform the calculation, and a label to display the result:

```
[Guid("6D9B7DBA-C365-4d18-A453-86102CCEA61A")]
public class Sum : System.Web.UI.WebControls.WebParts.WebPart
{
        // 1) Declare child controls.
        TextBox _txt = new TextBox();
        Literal _br = new Literal();
        Button _btn = new Button();
        Label _lbl = new Label();

        protected override void CreateChildControls()
        {
            // 2) Set child control properties.
            _txt.Width = Unit.Pixel(300);
            _txt.Height = Unit.Pixel(150);
            _txt.TextMode = TextBoxMode.MultiLine;
            _txt.ToolTip = "Enter a series of numbers to add.";
            _br.Text = "<br>";
            _btn.Width = Unit.Pixel(50);
            _btn.Height = Unit.Pixel(25);
            _btn.Text = "Sum";
            _btn.ToolTip = "Click here to get total.";
            _lbl.Width = Unit.Pixel(100);
            _lbl.Height = Unit.Pixel(30);
            _lbl.Text = "Total: ";
            // 3) Add the controls in the order to display them
            Controls.Add(_txt);
            Controls.Add(_br);
            Controls.Add(_btn);
            Controls.Add(_lbl);
            // Register the event handler.
            _btn.Click += new EventHandler(_btn_Click);
            // 4) Set property to render web part.
            ChildControlsCreated = true;
            // Required: Call the base class.
            base.CreateChildControls();
```

```
    }

    /* 5) Or render the child controls here (comment out ChildControlsCreated)
    protected override void Render (HtmlTextWriter writer)
    {
        RenderChildren(writer);
    } */
}
```

The ChildControls property in step 4 flags the controls to be rendered in the order they were added to the Controls collection. If you comment out that line, you can use the Render method to render the controls instead. That allows you to change the order in which they are placed on the page, or add HTML elements. The following code shows how to write the controls one at a time in a different order:

```
protected override void Render(HtmlTextWriter writer)
{
    // Alternate approach, use different order.
    _lbl.RenderControl(writer);
    _br.RenderControl(writer);
    _txt.RenderControl(writer);
    _br.RenderControl(writer);
    _btn.RenderControl(writer);
}
```

Using RenderControl makes it a little easier to intersperse HTML literal strings with the controls, but I try to avoid that. Instead, I tend to use literal controls such as _br in the preceding example. That's my attempt to keep control definitions organized.

The command button control (_btn) registers an event handler so that user actions raise events that can be handled in the web part's code. To respond to an event from a child control, create a procedure using the event handler signature:

```
// this line registers event handler:
// _btn.Click += new EventHandler(_btn_Click);
string _total = "";

private void _btn_Click(object sender, EventArgs e)
{
    //Calculate the total.
    _total = GetSum().ToString();
    // Display the total.
    _lbl.Text = "Total: " + _total;
}

double GetSum( )
{
    double total = 0;
    // Make sure there are numbers to add.
    if (_txt.Text.Length > 0)
    {
        string[] arr ;
        arr = _txt.Text.Split( "\n\r".ToCharArray( ));
        foreach (string itm in arr)
        {
```

```
                    try
                    {
                        total += Convert.ToDouble(itm);
                    }
                    catch {}
                    finally {}
                }
            }
            else
            {
                total = 0;
            }
            return total;
    }
```

At runtime, the Sum web part adds the series of numbers entered in the text box and displays the result when the user clicks Sum (see Figure 11-8).

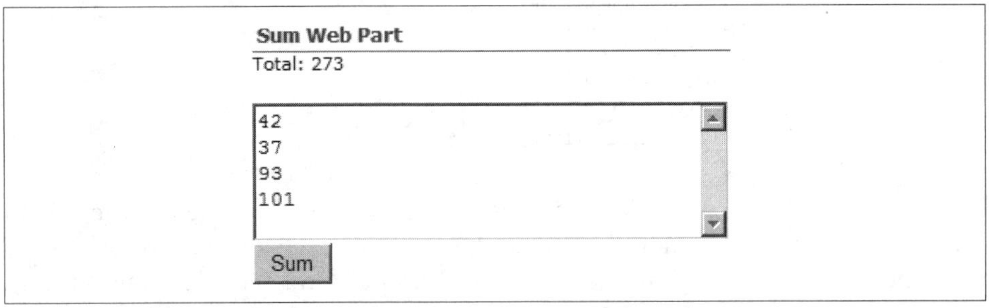

Sum Web Part
Total: 273

```
42
37
93
101
```

[Sum]

Figure 11-8. Responding to events from child controls

Working on the Client Side

The Sum web part performs its calculations on the server, but that's not really necessary or efficient. For high-volume applications, it's a good idea to do as much work on the client side as possible. For example, the following HTML creates an equivalent client-side web part that doesn't require a round-trip to the server to perform the calculations:

```
<html>
    <head>
        <script id="clientEventHandlersJS" language="javascript">
function _btn_onclick( ) {
    var arr = new Array("");
    // Use getElementById, direct control refs don't work
    var _txt = document.getElementById("_txt");
    var _div = document.getElementById("_div");
    var total = 0, s = _txt.value;
    arr = s.split("\n");
    for (var i in arr)
    {
        total += parseFloat(arr[i]);
```

```
    }
    _div.innerText = "Total: " + total;
    return;
}
        </script>
    </head>
    <body>
        <form id="_frm">
            <div id="_div">Total:
            </div>
            <TEXTAREA id="_txt" name="_txt" rows="10" cols="35">
            </TEXTAREA>
            <br>
            <INPUT id="_btn" type="button" value="Sum"
                onclick="return _btn_onclick()">
        </form>
    </body>
</html>
```

This code is stored as an HTM file in a resource, and then loaded and rendered by the following line:

```
protected override void RenderWebPart(HtmlTextWriter writer)
{
    output.Write(GetHtml("clientSum.htm"));
}
```

At runtime, this web part is visually identical to the server-side web part in Figure 11-8, but the calculation is done on the client computer via JavaScript. The result is much better performance and less network traffic, because the page isn't sent back to the server every time the member clicks the Sum button.

Using Scripts with Web Controls

The ClientSum web part is efficient, but you can't easily get values from the contained HTML controls once the page returns to the server. To see this limitation, enter some values in ClientSum and refresh (F5)—the values you entered are cleared. That happens because the HTML controls don't automatically preserve their state the way that ASP.NET web controls do.

To solve this problem, use ASP.NET web controls rather than HTML controls. In other words, create a hybrid web part that uses both server-side controls and client-side scripts. Using client-side scripts with web controls requires a couple of special steps:

1. Choose your web control type carefully—not all web controls are easy to access from client-side code. For example, I had to change label control to a read-only text box in order to get its value both on the client side and the server side.

2. Add an ID property for each web control. This property allows you to get a reference to the control from client-side scripts through the getElementsByName method.

3. Add the web controls to the Controls collection. This step ensures that the controls preserve their state.

4. Write code to get the web part's `UniqueID` and pass that value to scripts.

5. Write client-side scripts that combine the passed-in `UniqueID` with the element IDs created in step 2.

When SharePoint renders a web part, it includes a lot of special code to preserve the state of web controls in the Controls collection. To make sure that code gets the right values, SharePoint prepends a unique identifier to each `name` and `id` element in the generated HTML, as shown here:

```
<textarea name="FullPage:g_03d3b969_e9c0_4846_9cf5_b14b5e7f6aa7:_txt"
id="FullPage_g_03d3b969_e9c0_4846_9cf5_b14b5e7f6aa7__txt"
title="Enter a series of numbers to add." style="height:150px;width:300px;">
</textarea>
```

If you don't add an ID property to the control (step 2), SharePoint generates a `name` attribute and omits `id`. If you don't add the web controls to the Controls collection (step 3), SharePoint doesn't preserve the state of the control and consequently doesn't prepend `UniqueID`.

The following code shows these steps implemented for the Sum control:

```
// Declare child controls.
TextBox _txt = new TextBox();
Literal _br1 = new Literal();
Literal _br2 = new Literal(); // Added second _br
TextBox _lbl = new TextBox(); // 1) Changed to TextBox
// Deleted _btn

protected override void CreateChildControls()
{
    // Set child control properties.
    _txt.ID = "_txt"; // 2) Added ID for scripts
    _txt.Width = Unit.Pixel(300);
    _txt.Height = Unit.Pixel(150);
    _txt.TextMode = TextBoxMode.MultiLine;
    _txt.ToolTip = "Enter a series of numbers to add.";
    _br1.Text = "<br>";
    _br2.Text = "<br>";
    _lbl.ID = "_lbl"; // 2) Added ID for scripts
    _lbl.Width = Unit.Pixel(100);
    _lbl.Height = Unit.Pixel(30);
    _lbl.Text = "Total: ";
    // 3) Add the controls in the order to display them
    Controls.Add(_lbl);
    Controls.Add(_br1);
    Controls.Add(_txt);
    Controls.Add(_br2);
    // Removed _btn
    // Required: Call the base class.
    base.CreateChildControls();
}
```

```
protected override void Render (HtmlTextWriter writer)
{
    // Load client-side script
    writer.Write(GetHtml("sumFinal.js"));
    // Write controls to output stream.
    RenderChildren(writer);
    // 4) Add button to run script.
    writer.Write("<INPUT id='_btn' type='button' value='Sum'
        onclick='return _btn_onclick(\"" +
        this.UniqueID + "\")' name='_btn'>");
    writer.Write("<INPUT id='Submit1' type='submit' value='Postback'
        name='Submit1'>");
}
```

Step 4 above is a little tricky. I embedded the HTML button control in my code (despite telling you to avoid this), because it's only one control and it makes it easier to include this.UniqueID as an argument to _btn_onclick. SharePoint provides a ReplaceTokens method to replace embedded tokens with SharePoint values. For example, it replaces _WPID_ with the web part's unique ID:

```
// Alternate approach -- use ReplaceTokens (requires SharePoint WebPart class).
writer.Write(ReplaceTokens("<INPUT id='_btn' type='button' value='Sum'
    onclick='return _btn_onclick('''FullPage:_WPID_''')' name='_btn'>"));
```

ReplaceTokens can replace the following literals. See the SharePoint SDK for additional details.

Token	Replacement value
WPR	ClassResourcePath property
WPQ	Qualifier property
LogonUser	Request.ServerVariables("LOGON_USER")
WPID	ID property (Control.ID)
WebLocaleId	The LCID of the web site
WPSRR	The ServerRelativeClassResourcePath property

The client-side script uses the passed-in UniqueID to get references to web controls through getElementsByName, as shown here:

```
// Javascript running on the client (sumFinal.js).
<script id="clientEventHandlersJS" language="javascript">
// Pass in unique page ID generated by SharePoint.
function _btn_onclick(uID) {
    var arr = new Array("");
    // Get elements using passed-in unique ID.
    var _txt = document.getElementsByName(uID + ":_txt")[0];
    var _lbl = document.getElementsByName(uID + ":_lbl")[0];
    var total = 0, s = _txt.value;
    arr = s.split("\n");
    for (var i in arr)
        total += parseFloat(arr[i]);
```

```
        _lbl.innerText = "Total: " + total;
        return;
    }
</script>
```

This completed control will now perform its calculation on the client side and pre-serve its settings. Also, the values of the _lbl and _txt web controls are now available to the server. To see how that works, add this code, set a breakpoint, and click the Postback button to see the values displayed in the Visual Studio Debug window:

```
private void _btn_Click(object sender, EventArgs e)
{
    // Display values from controls
    System.Diagnostics.Debug.WriteLine(_txt.Text);
    System.Diagnostics.Debug.WriteLine(_lbl.Text);
}
```

Figure 11-9 shows the completed control at runtime in Debug mode.

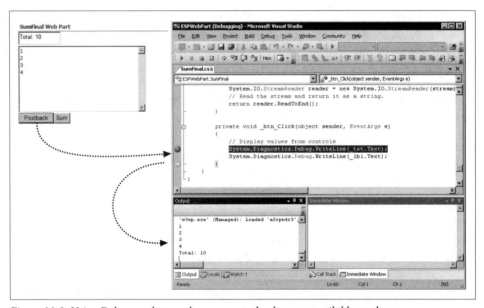

Figure 11-9. Using Debug mode to make sure control values are available on the server

Importing Script Blocks

I showed you how to store HTML as a resource as a better way to build tables and other display elements of a web part, and I just used that same technique to insert a client-side script into a web part. That's OK for small scripts, but it means you have to rebuild the assembly each time you change the script.

You can import externally stored scripts directly into a web part using the RegisterClientScriptBlock method. That method imports scripts from a server folder at runtime so you can modify and debug scripts without rebuilding the assembly. Instead, you can simply refresh the page (F5) to get the changes.

To import script blocks into a web part:

1. Create a subfolder in the server's wpresources or _wpresources virtual folder for the scripts.
2. Copy the script to the new folder.
3. Add code to the web part's PreRender event to load the script from the new location.

 The physical locations shown here are the defaults used when IIS and SharePoint are installed. Your locations may be different. Check the *wpresources* or *_wpresources* virtual folders in IIS for your actual paths.

Where you store the scripts depends on how the web part is installed. For web parts installed in a *bin* folder, create a subfolder named after the web part assembly in the *wpresources* folder. For example:

C:\Inetpub\wwwroot\wss\VirtualDirectories\2007\wpresources\ESPWebParts

For web parts installed in the global assembly cache (GAC), create the assembly folder in *_wpresources*; then create a subfolder in the new folder using the Version, Culture, and PublicKeyToken attributes from the web part's SafeControl element in *Web.config*. The name has the following form:

    version_culture_token

Omit *culture* if the assembly culture is neutral. For example:

C:\Program Files\Common Files\Microsoft Shared\Web Server Extensions\ wpresources\ESPWebParts\1.0.0.0__fb6919fe58e4ba63

When you copy the script files to the new folder, remember to remove surrounding <script> tags from the file, or you will get syntax errors when you import the script. Scripts should only be loaded once per page, so you need to create a unique key for each script file and check whether the file has already been imported by checking IsClientScriptBlockRegistered before calling RegisterClientScriptBlock:

```
private void ImportScripts_PreRender(object sender, EventArgs e)
{
    const string sKey = "sumFinal.js";
    string sFile  = this.ClassResourcePath + "/sumFinal.js";
    string sBlock = "<script language='javascript' src='" + sFile + "'/>";
    // Load client-side script once.
    if (!this.Page.ClientScript.IsClientScriptBlockRegistered(sKey))
    this.Page.ClientScript.RegisterClientScriptBlock(this.GetType(),
      sKey, sBlock);
}
```

ASP.NET 2.0 added the ClientScriptManager object; previous direct access to these methods is obsolete.

In the preceding code, ClassResourcePath returns the location of the folder you created for script storage. The RegisterClientScriptBlock method inserts the script tag sBlock on the page and registers the script as sKey so it won't be loaded again. At runtime, SharePoint renders this output:

```
<script language='javascript' src='http://<server>/wpresources/ESPWebPart/sumFinal.js'/>
```

Understanding Event Order

From event perspective, web part programming is very different from Windows Forms programming. In Windows Forms applications, code runs as long as the form is displayed, and code as events occur. Web part code runs only in short bursts—beginning when the request is received by the server and ending shortly after the response is returned to the client browser.

The performance difference between the server and client Sum controls illustrates a basic principle of web part design: *avoid unnecessary postbacks*. The button web control and Submit button trigger postback events by default, but you can also set the AutoPostback property on text box, list, and checkbox controls to cause postbacks. When a postback event occurs, the browser sends the current state of the page back to the server, which then processes web part events and overridden methods in the order shown in Table 11-4.

Table 11-4. Order of major server events/methods in a web part

Event/method	Use to
OnInit event	Create the web part.
LoadViewState method	Override the web part's base class behavior when reading control properties from the web part's ViewState object.
CreateChildControls method	Add web controls to the Controls collection.
OnLoad event	Initialize resources used by the web part.
Cached child control events	Process cached events from child controls, such as TextChanged or SelectedIndexChanged.
Postback child control event	Process the event that caused the postback—for example, the button Click event.
OnPreRender event	Set child control properties and complete any processing before rendering the part.
SaveViewState method	Override the web part's base class behavior when saving control properties to the web part's ViewState object.
RenderWebPart method	Draw the web part as HTML.
Dispose method	Release resources used by the web part.
OnUnload event	Finalize the release of resources.

Web parts have many more events and methods than those listed in Table 11-4, but the ones there are critical to understanding how to code web parts and avoid unexpected results. That's also why I combined events and methods in the same table—it's important to know that the CreateChildControls method is called before the OnPreRender event occurs, for example.

The other thing that's important about Table 11-4 is that cached events occur before the event that caused the postback. *Cached events* are server-side events that occur on a child control that don't cause a postback. SharePoint determines what cached events occurred by checking the web part's ViewState, then SharePoint raises those events after the web part loads.

See the EventOrder sample to test the sequence of events on a web part. That sample records the order of events and displays the results after a postback, as shown in Figure 11-10.

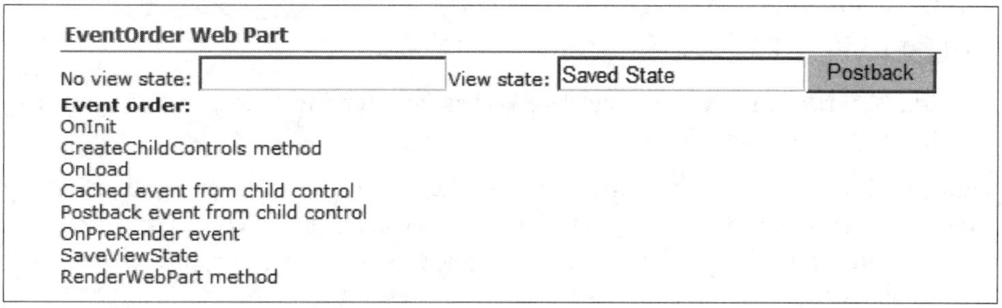

EventOrder Web Part

No view state: [   ]   View state: [Saved State   ]   [Postback]

Event order:
OnInit
CreateChildControls method
OnLoad
Cached event from child control
Postback event from child control
OnPreRender event
SaveViewState
RenderWebPart method

Figure 11-10. Testing the order of events and method calls

The code for the EventOrder simply appends a string to display, as shown here:

```
protected override void OnInit(EventArgs e)
{
  _msg += "OnInit<br>";
  base.OnInit (e);
}

protected override void OnLoad(EventArgs e)
{
  _msg += "OnLoad<br>";
  base.OnLoad (e);
}

protected override void LoadViewState(object savedState)
{
  _msg += "LoadViewState<br>";
  base.LoadViewState (savedState);
}

...
```

Adding Properties

Any property you add to your web part class is a web part property. The trick is getting those properties to interact with SharePoint. The most common tasks you need to perform with web part properties are:

- Store them between visits (SharePoint calls this *personalization*).
- Display them in the property pane (make them browsable).
- Get and set their values from web part controls.

To store a property:

- Add a `Personalization` attribute to the property definition.

Properties can be stored for individual users or shared among all users. This is referred to as *personalization scope* (user or shared). Properties can also be marked as sensitive to prevent them from being exported.

To display a property in the web part property pane:

- Add `WebBrowsable`, `WebDisplayName`, `WebDescription`, and `Category` attributes to the property definition.

Those attributes control the appearance of the property in the web part property pane. For example, the following set of attributes creates a property that is displayed as shown in Figure 11-11. The property has a shared scope, meaning changes are seen by all users.

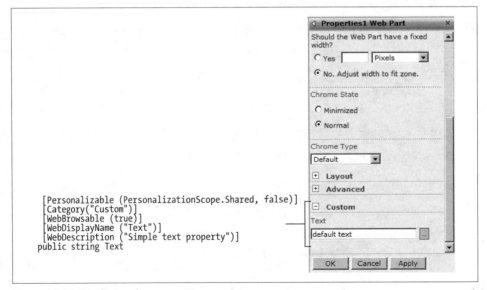

Figure 11-11. Displaying the custom Text property

```
// Text property definition
private const string defaultText = "default text";
private string _text = defaultText;

[Personalizable(PersonalizationScope.Shared, false)] // Storage.
[Category("Custom")]      // Section in properties pane.
[WebBrowsable(true)]      // Show in properties pane.
[WebDisplayName("Text")]    // Name to show.
[WebDescription("Simple text property")] //Tooltip
public string Text
{
  get
  {
    return _text;
  }

  set
  {
    _text = value;
  }
}
```

The Text property can now get values from the property pane, but it doesn't interact with users. To implement that:

1. Add TextBox and Button controls to the web part.

2. Display the value of the Text property in the text box.

3. Write a button Click event procedure to set the Text property from the text box.

The following code shows those steps:

```
// Child control declarations.
TextBox _txt = new TextBox( );
Button _btnSave = new Button( );

 // Constructor (hooks up event procedures)
public Properties1( )
{
  _btnSave.Click +=new EventHandler(_btnSave_Click);
}

// 1) Add to controls collection
protected override void CreateChildControls( )
{
  // Set control properties
  _txt.ID = "_txt1";
  _btnSave.Text = "Save Settings";
  // 2) Display the Text property in the text box.
  _txt.Text = this.Text;
  Controls.Add(_txt);
  Controls.Add(_btnSave);
```

```
  // Create the child controls.
  this.ChildControlsCreated = true;
  base.CreateChildControls( );
}

// 3) Save all the property settings to the content database.
private void _btnSave_Click(object sender, EventArgs e)
{
  this.Text = _txt.Text;          // 3a) Set the Text property.
  this.SetPersonalizationDirty( ); // 3b) Save the control setting.
}
```

The SetPersonalizationDirty method flags the web part to save the Text property setting before exiting. Now, a user can change the Text property from the web part, and all users will see the change when they view the page, as shown in Figure 11-12.

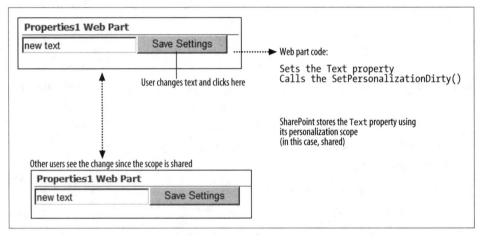

Figure 11-12. Saving a property with shared personalization scope

Table 11-5 explains the most common attribute settings used with web part properties.

Table 11-5. Web part property attribute settings

Namespace	Attribute	Setting
System.ComponentModel	Category	The section on the task pane to include the property in. This defaults to Miscellaneous if omitted or if you specify one of the built-in categories, like Appearance.
	DefaultValue	The default value of the property. This affects serialization only: if the property setting is the default, it will not be serialized.
	ReadOnly	true prevents change in the task pane. false allows changes. Only affects settings from the task pane.

Table 11-5. Web part property attribute settings (continued)

Namespace	Attribute	Setting
System.Web.UI.WebControls.WebParts	Personalizable	Sets how the property is stored.
	WebBrowsable	true displays the custom property in the property task pane. false hides the property.
	WebDisplayName	The caption to display for the property in the task pane.
	WebDescription	The tool tip to display for the property in the task pane.

Specifying a default value reduces the web part's storage requirements because the property's value is only stored if it is different from the default. Because of this, it's important to ensure that the DefaultValue attribute matches the setting used in code.

Personalization properties must have both get and set methods. To prevent changes, add a ReadOnly attribute, as shown here:

```
[Personalizable(PersonalizationScope.Shared)]
[Category("Custom")]
[WebBrowsable(true)]
[WebDisplayName("Version")]
[WebDescription("WebPart Version")]
[ReadOnly(true)]
public string Version
{
    get
    {
        string ver;
        ver = string.Format("{0}, Version {1}",
        this.GetType().ToString(), "2.0");
        return ver;
    }
    set
    {
        // to show in property pane this has to be here
        // Personalization property must be read/write, but
        // they can be marked ReadOnly above.
    }
}
```

The Version property above displays information about the web part in the property task pane, but the user can't edit it.

Exporting Web Parts

Users sometimes want to customize a web part and then reuse those changes on other pages. To do that from the browser, they make their changes, export the web part, and then import it on a new page.

To make a web part exportable, set the web part's `ExportMode` property as shown here:

```
// Constructor (hooks up event procedures)
public Properties4()
{
    // Allow non-sensitive properties to be exported.
    this.ExportMode = WebPartExportMode.NonSensitiveData;
}
```

The preceding code exports all properties not marked as sensitive in the Personalization attribute. Once the web part is marked as exportable, SharePoint adds an Export item to the web part's Edit menu, as shown in Figure 11-13.

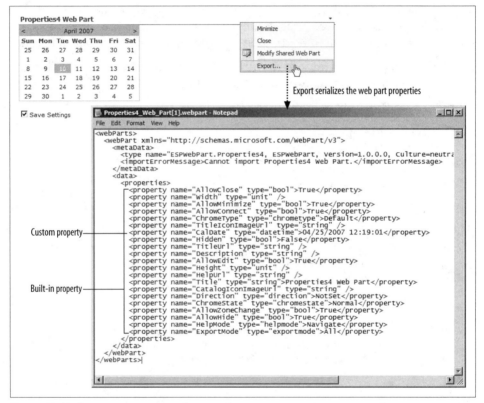

Figure 11-13. Exporting a custom web part

Within the web part page, the properties are serialized, as shown here:

```
<WpNs0:Properties4 runat="server" ID="g_ca01d903_5f15_49b9_8553_3942dadb87d5"
ExportMode="NonSensitiveData" Title="Properties4 Web Part" CalDate="04/25/2007 12:19:
01" ImportErrorMessage="Cannot import Properties4 Web Part." __
MarkupType="vsattributemarkup" __WebPartId="{CA01D903-5F15-49B9-8553-3942DADB87D5}"
WebPart="true" __designer:IsClosed="false" partorder="2"></WpNs0:Properties4>
```

The `ExportMode` property sets the default mode used for the web part. You can override that setting by changing it in the web part tag above. The tag prefix used on the web part page is generated automatically.

You can store any type that can be serialized, including enumerations. The Framework picks up the serialization type automatically from the property type as shown here by a web part that includes numeric, enumeration, string, date, and Boolean properties:

```
<webParts>
  <webPart xmlns="http://schemas.microsoft.com/WebPart/v3">
    <metaData>
      <type name="ESPWebPart.Properties2, ESPWebPart, Version=1.0.0.0,
        Culture=neutral, PublicKeyToken=9f4da00116c38ec5" />
      <importErrorMessage>Cannot import Properties2 Web Part.</importErrorMessage>
    </metaData>
    <data>
      <properties>
        <property name="Number" type="double">3.14</property>
        <property name="Color" type="ESPWebPart.Properties2+enumColor, ESPWebPart,
          Version=1.0.0.0, Culture=neutral,
          PublicKeyToken=9f4da00116c38ec5">Gray</property>
        <property name="Text" type="string" />
        <property name="Date" type="datetime">04/25/2007 13:13:41</property>
        <property name="Boolean" type="bool">True</property>
        ...
      </properties>
    </data>
  </webPart>
```

 In the SharePoint `WebPart` class, a `ShouldSerialize`*`PropName`* method is required for serialization. The ASP.NET `WebPart` class handles that with the `ExportMode` property instead.

Adding Menus

To add a menu to a web part, override the `Verbs` property to add `WebPartVerb` objects to the web part's `WebPartVerbCollection`. Web part menus can respond to events with server-side code, client-side code, or both. The following example adds two menu items to a web part:

- The Save Settings item runs server-side code to save the web part properties.
- The Help item runs JavaScript to display a help page in a new window.

```
public override WebPartVerbCollection Verbs
{
  get
  {
```

```
// Create a list to hold the verbs.
ArrayList verbSet = new ArrayList();
// Add the built-in verbs to the list.
verbSet.AddRange(base.Verbs);
// Create a custom server-side verb.
WebPartVerb vSave = new WebPartVerb("vSave",
    new WebPartEventHandler(vSave_Click));
vSave.Description = "Saves web part properties.";
vSave.Text = "Save Settings";
// Add it to the list of verbs.
verbSet.Add(vSave);
// Create a custom client-side verb.
WebPartVerb vHelp = new WebPartVerb("vHelp",
    "javascript:window.open('page1.aspx','_help',
    'height=200,width=200');");
vHelp.Description = "Show Help in new window.";
vHelp.Text = "Help";
// Add it to the list of verbs.
verbSet.Add(vHelp);

// Return the new list.
return new WebPartVerbCollection(verbSet);
    }
}

protected void vSave_Click(object sender, WebPartEventArgs e)
{
    this.SetPersonalizationDirty();
}
```

Figure 11-14 shows the web part menu in action.

Figure 11-14. Adding a menu item to a web part

Customizing the Property Task Pane

SharePoint generates the controls displayed in the web part properties pane based on the data type of the property and whether or not it is marked as WebBrowsable in the property attributes. Table 11-6 lists the controls generated for various data types.

Table 11-6. Default property pane control types

Type	Generated control
String	Text box
Numeric	Text box
Date	Text box
Boolean	Checkbox
Array	Drop-down box
Enumeration	Drop-down list box

You can override that behavior by creating custom editor parts that render one or more controls in the properties pane.

To display a custom editor part in the web part properties task pane:

1. Create an `EditorPart` class that renders the editor to display.
2. Override the web part's `CreateEditorParts` method to add the new `EditorPart` to the `EditorPartCollection`.

For example, the following class creates an editor part that displays a calendar in the properties pane:

```
// Create a custom EditorPart to edit the WebPart.
class CalendarEditorPart : EditorPart
{
  Calendar _cal;
  DateTime _date;

  // Get settings from web part.
  public override void SyncChanges()
  {
    Properties4 part =
      (Properties4)this.WebPartToEdit;
    _date = part.CalDate;
  }

  // Apply new settings to web part.
  public override bool ApplyChanges()
  {
    Properties4 part =
      (Properties4)this.WebPartToEdit;
    // Update the web part with the selected date.
    part.CalDate = this._cal.SelectedDate;
    return true;
  }

  // Render the control.
  protected override void CreateChildControls()
  {
```

```
       // Set the title to display in the properties pane
       this.Title = "Calendar";
       // Add a calendar control.
       _cal = new Calendar();
       _cal.SelectedDate = _date;
       Controls.Add(_cal);
       this.ChildControlsCreated = true;
       // Required
       base.CreateChildControls();
   }
}
```

The SyncChanges method gets the initial setting for the editor from the web part. The ApplyChanges method sends the date selected in the editor back to the web part when the user clicks Apply or OK in the properties pane. You can render the editor part with CreateChildControls or by using the Render method—both of which are identical to the WebPart equivalents.

The following code adds the editor to the properties pane for the web part. I included the class declaration for clarity; you are overriding the CreateEditor method of the web part:

```
[Guid("4D8EE9A0-2772-47fa-85F7-C4DD62857B00")]
public class Properties4 : WebPart
{

    // Display a custom editor in the tool pane.
    public override EditorPartCollection  CreateEditorParts()
    {
      // Create an array to hold the editor parts.
      ArrayList arEditor = new ArrayList();
      // Create a new editor part.
      CalendarEditorPart edPart = new CalendarEditorPart();
      // Set its ID.
      edPart.ID = this.ID + "_editor1";
      // Add it to the array.
      arEditor.Add(edPart);
      // Return the editors.
      return new EditorPartCollection(arEditor);
    }

    // code omitted here ...
}
```

At runtime, the editor appears in the properties pane, as shown in Figure 11-15.

Connecting Parts

A web part that can exchange data with another web part is *connectable*. You create a connectable web part by completing these major tasks:

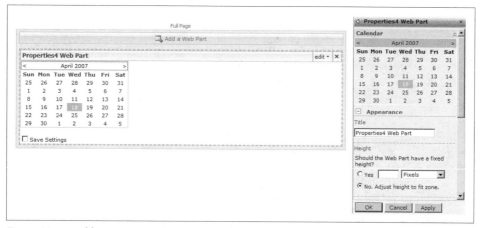

Figure 11-15. Adding a custom editor for a property

1. Define an interface for the connection.

2. Implement the interface in the connection provider web part.

3. Add a connection point to the provider web part.

4. Add a connection point to the consumer web part.

The interface defines the type of data used by both the provider and consumer web parts. The following code shows a very simple interface for exchanging text data between web parts:

```
// 1) Interface used for text connections.
public interface ITextProvider
{
    string TextConnection { get; }
}
```

The web part providing the connection must implement this interface and supply a method that returns the connection point. The following code shows a very simple web part that provides a text connection:

```
[Guid("C4288D94-D8F0-4f8f-8443-3A40F05E6B92")]
public class ConnectProvider : WebPart, ITextProvider // 2) Implement interface
{
    // 2) Implement interface.
    #region ITextProvider Members

    public string TextConnection
    {
        // Return Text property.
        get { return this.Text; }
    }
```

```csharp
#endregion

// 3) Add provider connection point.
[ConnectionProvider("TextConnection")]
public ITextProvider ConnectionProvider()
{
    // Return this web part.
    return this;
}

// Web part UI.
#region WebPart properties and controls

const string defaulttext = "";
private string text = defaulttext;

[Personalizable(PersonalizationScope.Shared)]
[Category("Custom")]
[WebBrowsable(true)]
[WebDisplayName("Text")]
[WebDescription("Text property")]
public string Text
{
    get
    { return text; }

    set
    { text = value;
        _txt.Text = value;}
}

// Child controls.
TextBox _txt = new TextBox();
Button _btn = new Button();

protected override void CreateChildControls()
{
    _btn.Text = "Save";
    _btn.Click +=new EventHandler(_btn_Click);
    Controls.Add(_txt);
    Controls.Add(_btn);
    this.ChildControlsCreated = true;
    base.CreateChildControls();
}

private void _btn_Click(object sender, EventArgs e)
{
    this.Text = _txt.Text;
    this.SetPersonalizationDirty();
}
#endregion
}
```

The ConnectionProvider attribute identifies the method as a connection point. Web parts that consume connections use that method as a callback. The type (ITextProvider) identifies the interface that the provider supports and allows the callback to be type-safe. A provider that supports multiple interfaces would have multiple connection points.

The web part consuming the connection simply includes a connection point that uses the matching interface. In this case, the web part consumes the text connection created earlier:

```
[Guid("686CB525-7218-44b8-8C64-28AF61D09B42")]
public class ConnectConsumer : System.Web.UI.WebControls.WebParts.WebPart
{
    // 4) Add consumer connection point.
    private ITextProvider _txtProvider;

    [ConnectionConsumer("TextConnection")]
    public void GetProvider(ITextProvider txtProvider)
    {
        _txtProvider = txtProvider;
    }

    // Web part UI.
    #region Web Part properties and controls
    protected override void Render(HtmlTextWriter writer)
    {
        string text = "";
        if (_txtProvider != null) text = _txtProvider.TextConnection;
        writer.Write(text);
    }
    #endregion
}
```

The consumer web part calls GetProvider when the web part is connected to a provider. If the web part is not connected, _txtProvider is null so you need to test for that before trying to access the provider. Figure 11-16 illustrates the two web parts in action.

Deploying Web Parts

The Visual Studio web part extensions automatically create an installation script in the project's *bin\Debug* folder when you deploy your web part project during development. To build a release version:

1. Click Build → Configuration Manager, select "Release from the Active solution configuration" drop-down list, and then click Close.

2. Click Project → Properties → Debug, and enter the address of your development SharePoint site in Start Action (as shown earlier in Figure 11-4).

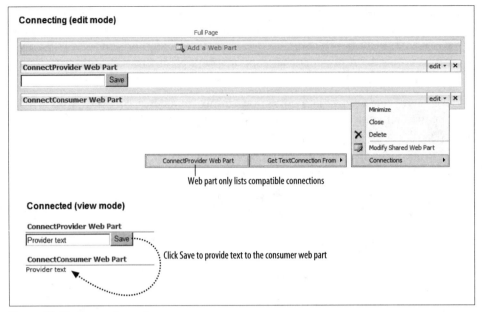

Figure 11-16. Connecting web parts

3. Click Debug → Deploy. Visual Studio rebuilds the project in Release mode, creates the setup script, and deploys the web parts to your development machine.

4. Edit the *setup.bat* script created in the *bin\Release* folder to change the TargetUrl.

To deploy the web parts on a production server:

1. Copy the *Release* folder to a public share.

2. Log on to the target server.

3. Run *setup.bat* from the *Release* folder copied in step 1.

Best Practices

- Create hosted web parts to quickly create web parts that only need to be deployed on one or two servers.
- Create rendered web parts when deploying on multiple servers or when creating web parts that will be used by others.
- Use the ASP.NET WebPart class for new development.
- Use the SharePoint WebPart class for web parts originally developed for WSS 2.0.
- Use the Visual Studio web part extensions to simplify deployment of rendered web parts.

CHAPTER 12

Consuming SharePoint Services

Web parts use the SharePoint object model from the server side. Remote programming allows client-side applications to get and change content, create and delete lists, and perform other tasks on the SharePoint server without installing or running new components on the server. There are several different means for remote programming:

- The Office 2003/2007 object models provide SharePoint objects for workspaces, libraries, and members.

- SharePoint web services provide access to a more complete set of SharePoint tasks.

- URL commands provide a quick way to read SharePoint content in XML format using HTTP GET requests.

- Remote Procedure Call (RPC) methods allow you to get and change SharePoint content in XML format using HTTP POST requests.

In this chapter, we'll look at each of these approaches for writing remote programs that can leverage the SharePoint server. Using these techniques, you can add or change content, create and delete lists, set up sites, and perform other tasks on the SharePoint server all without opening a web browser.

 You must have access to VBA or .NET programming tools and knowledge of a programming language to complete the tasks in this chapter.

Choosing an Approach

The approach you choose depends mainly on the type of client you want to create. Table 12-1 shows a set of recommendations for programming different types of applications.

Table 12-1. Choosing an approach based on the type of client

Type of client	Use this approach
Office application or an application that integrates with Office	Office object model
Windows application	Web services
Non-Windows application	Web services
ASP.NET application	Web services, URL commands, or RPC methods
SharePoint web part page	URL commands or RPC methods

The last item in the table doesn't look like a remote client since the page exists on the SharePoint server. However, URL commands and RPC methods are sent from the client browser via HTTP GET or POST. The commands and methods reside on the client browser and therefore can be considered remote programming. You'll learn more about that later.

There is some overlap in each of the remote programming approaches, but only web services and RPC methods offer complete sets of features. To explain the recommendations a bit more, Table 12-2 summarizes the advantages and disadvantages of each approach.

Table 12-2. Comparing remote programming approaches

Approach	Advantage	Disadvantage
Office object model	Built into Office	Limited to Office-related objects
	Available from VBA or .NET	Requires Office 2003 or 2007
	Easy to use	
Web services	Provides complete set of objects	More complicated than Office object model
	Available on many platforms	Adds overhead
	Built-in authentication	
URL commands	Easiest to use	Limited to getting data
	Can run from a SharePoint page	Data returned in XML (sometimes an advantage)
		Uses GUIDs to identify lists
RPC methods	Provides access to most SharePoint tasks (similar to web services)	Difficult to learn
	Lower overhead than web services	Data returned in XML (sometimes an advantage)
	Can run from a SharePoint page	Uses GUIDs to identify lists
		Requires FormDigest control for authentication

For most programmers, the decision is simple: use the programming technique you are most familiar with and look at the other approaches when you hit a wall. For instance, Office programmers can do a lot with the Office object model, but will need to add web services in order to add attachments to a list.

Using the Office Object Model

The Office object library includes a set of objects for working with documents stored in document workspace sites and document libraries. You can use those objects from VBA, Visual Basic .NET, or C#.

The SharePoint objects are connected to the top-level Office document in each application. For example, the following lines get a reference to the document workspace in Excel, Word, and PowerPoint, respectively, from within VBA:

- `Set wsXL = ActiveWorkbook.SharedWorkspace`
- `Set wsWord = ActiveDocument.SharedWorkspace`
- `Set wsPPT = ActivePresentation.SharedWorkspace`

From the document object, the SharePoint objects are organized as seen in Figure 12-1.

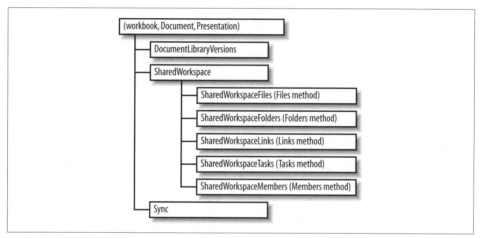

Figure 12-1. Office objects for SharePoint Services

From VBA

Use the `SharedWorkspace` object to create, get, or delete a SharePoint document workspace site. The technique is the same for any of the supported document types. For example, to create a new workspace:

1. Save the document.
2. Call the `SharedWorkspace` object's `CreateNew` method to create the document workspace.
3. Use the document's `SharedWorkspace` object to add members, tasks, links, files, or folders.

Table 12-3 lists frequently asked questions as a quick reference for VBA programming.

Table 12-3. SharePoint VBA quick reference

How do I?	Do this
Open a document library file?	Use the `Open` method and specify the document's web address.
Add a file to a document library?	Use the `SaveAs` method and save to the document library's web address.
Display the document's site?	Use the `FollowHyperLink` method to open *document*.`SharedWorkspace.Url`.
Include multiple documents in a shared workspace?	Open a document from the workspace and use *document*.`SharedWorkspace.Files.Add` to add the files.
Send mail to site members?	Use the `Member` object's `Email` property to get the address; then use `FollowHyperLink("`*mailto:*`" &`*address*`)`.
Delete a workspace?	Notify workspace members; then use *document*.`SharedWorkspace.Delete`.
Remove a file?	Get the file from the `Files` collection; then use *file*.`Delete`.
Respond to update events?	Write code for the document class's `Sync` event.

From .NET

The Office Professional edition provides primary interop assemblies (PIAs) to allow you to use the Office object libraries from Visual Basic .NET and C#. These assemblies are installed in your global assembly cache (GAC) when you install Office Professional with .NET Programmability selected (which is the default).

To use the PIAs from Visual Studio .NET:

1. Add references to the Microsoft Office Object Library, Microsoft Excel Object Library, and so on. The libraries are found on the COM tab of the References dialog box.

2. Include Imports/using declarations for the `Microsoft.Office.Interop` and `Microsoft.Office.Core` namespaces.

3. Use the object model to get a reference to a document object.

The following .NET console application demonstrates using the Office object model to create a document workspace, add members and tasks, send mail to members, and delete the workspace:

```
Imports Microsoft.Office.Interop
Imports Microsoft.Office.Core

Imports System.Reflection

' Simple demo of using Office SharePoint objects from .NET.
Module Module1
    ' Address of SharePoint site.
    Const SPSite As String = "http://wombat1/"

    ' From Microsoft.Interop namespace.
    Dim WithEvents _wb As Excel.Workbook
    ' From Microsoft.Office.Core namespace.
    Dim _sp As SharedWorkspace
```

```
Sub Main()
    OpenWorkbook()
    GetWorkspace()
    AddMember()
    AddTask()
    SendMail()
    DeleteWorkspace()
End Sub

Sub OpenWorkbook()
    ' Start  Excel
    Dim xl As Excel.Application = GetObject(, "Excel.Application")
    xl.Visible = True
    ' Get the workbook object.
    ChDir("..")
    _wb = xl.Workbooks.Open(CurDir() & "\xlSPDemo1.xls")
End Sub

Sub GetWorkspace()
    ' Check whether workspace exists; if it doesn't,
    ' create it.
    Try
        Debug.Write(_wb.SharedWorkspace.URL)
    Catch ex As Exception
        _wb.SharedWorkspace.CreateNew(SPSite, "xlSPDemo")
    End Try
    ' Get the workspace object.
    _sp = _wb.SharedWorkspace
End Sub

Sub AddMember()
    ' Note: 'wombat1\ExcelDemo' must be a valid account.
    _sp.Members.Add("ExcelDemo@hotmail.com", "wombat1\ExcelDemo", _
        "Excel Demo", "Contributor")
End Sub

Sub AddTask()
    ' Note: 'wombat1\ExcelDemo' must be a valid account.
    _sp.Tasks.Add("Task1", _
        MsoSharedWorkspaceTaskStatus.msoSharedWorkspaceTaskStatusInProgress, _
        MsoSharedWorkspaceTaskPriority.msoSharedWorkspaceTaskPriorityHigh, _
        "wombat1\ExcelDemo", _
        "Some task", _
        Today)
End Sub

Sub SendMail()
    Dim toAddress As String
    ' Build address string.
    For Each mem As SharedWorkspaceMember In _sp.Members
        toAddress = toAddress & mem.Email & ";"
    Next
    ' Send mail from client.
    _wb.FollowHyperlink("mailto:" & toAddress & _
        "?Subject=Deleting " & _sp.URL)
```

```
    End Sub

    Sub DeleteWorkspace()
        ' Delete the workspace.
        _sp.Delete()
    End Sub

  End Module
```

There are a couple of tricks in the preceding code that merit some explanation:

- I use GetObject to connect to a running instance of Excel if it is already loaded. If Excel is not running, GetObject starts Excel. Using CreateObject or Dim As New always starts a new instance of Excel, which uses a lot of memory.

- I use a Try/Catch block to see whether the workbook is already shared. The way the PIAs work, you can't use IsNothing to test whether the object exists.

You can't get help on Office objects from within Visual Studio. It's a good idea to create a shortcut to the Office VBA help files and open those files manually when you need reference information on Office objects.

For help on...	Open this file
SharePoint and other core Office objects	C:\Program Files\Microsoft Office\OFFICE11\1033\VBAOF11.CHM
Excel objects	C:\Program Files\Microsoft Office\OFFICE11\1033\VBAXL10.CHM
Word objects	C:\Program Files\Microsoft Office\OFFICE11\1033\VBAWD10.CHM
PowerPoint objects	C:\Program Files\Microsoft Office\OFFICE11\1033\VBAPP10.CHM

Microsoft sells a programming toolkit for working with Office from .NET called Visual Studio Tools for the Microsoft Office System (VSTO for short). VSTO provides project templates for creating document-based applications in .NET.

VSTO applications offer two key advantages over VBA-based applications:

- The application assemblies can be deployed to a trusted network address, so they can be maintained from a single location. Users automatically get the latest release without having to install the assembly locally.

- Using .NET assemblies rather than VBA allows you to lock down macro security in Office, prohibiting users from running macros while still allowing automation.

However, there are some disadvantages to using VSTO over VBA:

- VSTO only supports Office 2003 and 2007 applications.

- Performance is generally slower since object access is through the .NET PIAs rather than a more direct path through COM.

 What about VSTA? In Chapter 10, I showed you how to use Visual Studio Tools for Application (VSTA) with InfoPath. VSTA only works with InfoPath at this time.

Using Web Services

SharePoint web services allow remote applications to get and modify SharePoint sites and content. These services are more complete than the VBA object model and can be used from any web-service-aware programming language such as Visual Basic .NET, C#, C++, VBA, Java, and so on.

Table 12-4 lists the web services SharePoint provides, and Table 12-5 lists additional services provided by MOSS. All services except *Admin.asmx* are installed in the *_vti_bin* virtual folder, which maps to *C:\Program Files\Common Files\Microsoft Shared\Web Server Extensions\12\ISAPI* under the default SharePoint installation.

Table 12-4. SharePoint web services

Service	Use to
Administration (*Admin.asmx*)	Manage SharePoint sites (for example, create or delete sites). This service is only installed for the SharePoint Central Administration site in the *_vti_adm* folder.
Alerts (*Alerts.asmx*)	Get or delete alerts on a site.
Authentication (*Authentication.asmx*)	Log in to a SharePoint site with a username and password.
Copy (*Copy.asmx*)	Copy items between lists and libraries.
Data Adapter (*DwsSts.asmx*)	Performs queries against sites and lists.
Document Workspace (*Dws.asmx*)	Manage document workspace sites and the data they contain.
Forms (*Forms.asmx*)	Get forms used in the user interface when working with the contents of a list.
Imaging (*Imaging.asmx*)	Create and manage picture libraries.
Lists (*Lists.asmx*)	Work with list libraries.
List Data Retrieval *(DspSts.asmx)*	Perform a query on a list to retrieve data.
Meetings (*Meetings.asmx*)	Create and manage meeting workspace sites.
Permissions (*Permissions.asmx*)	Work with the permissions for a site or list.
People (*People.asmx*)	Work with security groups.
Search (*SPSearch.asmx*)	Perform a search on a single site.
Site Data (*SiteData.asmx*)	Get metadata or list data from sites or lists.
SharePoint Email (*SharePointemailws.asmx*)	Work with distribution groups.
Sites (*Sites.asmx*)	Get information about the site templates for a site collection.
Users and Groups (*UserGroup.asmx*)	Work with users, site groups, and cross-site groups.
Versions (*Versions.asmx*)	Work with versions within a document library.
Views (*Views.asmx*)	Work with views of lists.
Web Part Pages (*WebPartPages.asmx*)	Get web part pages; get, add, delete, or change web parts.
Webs (*Webs.asmx*)	Work with sites and subsites.

Table 12-5. *Additional web services provided by MOSS*

Service	Use to
Area Service (*areaservice.asmx*)	Add or delete topic areas and site directory listings.
Business Data Catalog Field Resolver (*bdcfieldsresolver.asmx*)	Retrieve a list of fields from the Business Data Catalog.
Business Data Catalog (*businessdatacatalog.asmx*)	Access data in the Business Data Catalog.
Area Toolbox (*contentAreaToolboxService.asmx*)	Used internally.
Excel Services (*ExcelService.asmx*)	Interact with Excel Services.
Official File (*officialfile.asmx*)	Send files to a records repository.
Published Links (*publishedlinksservice.asmx*)	Retrieve links targeted at the current user.
Search (*search.asmx*)	Search across SharePoint sites.
SharePoint Crawl (*spscrawl.asmx*)	Used internally.
User Profile Change (*userprofilechangeservice.asmx*)	Change information in a user profile.
User Profiles (*userprofileservice.asmx*)	Get information from a user profile.
Workflow (*workflow.asmx*)	Retrieve, change, or start a workflow.

Detailed reference information about these web services and their methods is available in the SharePoint SDK.

From VBA

The Office object library provides objects for working with SharePoint document workspaces and document libraries. In general, you'll use those objects when programming SharePoint from VBA. However, there are some cases where you may need to use the SharePoint web services to access lower-level tasks not available through the object library.

To use a web service from VBA:

1. Install the Web Services Toolkit from *http://www.microsoft.com/downloads*.

2. Close and restart any running Office applications.

3. Open the Visual Basic Editor and select Web References from the Tools menu. Visual Basic displays the Microsoft Office Web Services Toolkit references dialog box (see Figure 12-2).

4. Select the Web Service URL option button and type the address of the web service using this form: *http://sharepointURL/_vti_bin/service.asmx*. For example: *http://wombat1/xlSPDemo/_vti_bin/Lists.asmx*.

5. Click Search. The Toolkit should find the web service and display it in the Search Results list.

6. Select the checkbox beside the service in Search Results and click Add.

7. The Toolkit generates a proxy class named `clsws_Service` and adds it to the current project.

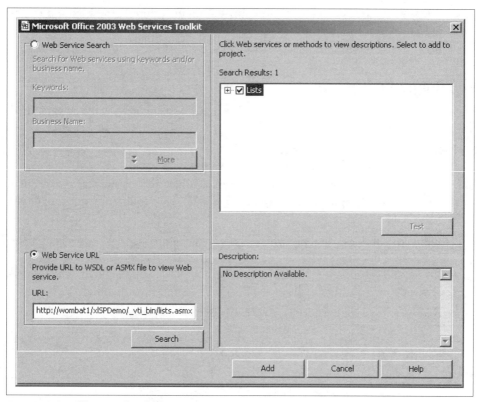

Figure 12-2. Adding a web reference in VBA

 If you install the web services toolkit for Office 2003, it will work in Office 2007. However, you must have Office 2003 installed first before you can install the toolkit (kind of a chicken–egg problem!).

The SharePoint server must authenticate the user before you can call any of the web service methods. If the user has not been authenticated, a Maximum retry on connection exceeded error occurs. In Visual Basic .NET or C# .NET, you authenticate the user from code by creating a Credentials object for him. For example, the following .NET code passes the user's default credentials to a web service:

```
wsAdapter.Credentials = System.Net.CredentialCache.DefaultCredentials
```

Unfortunately, you can't do that directly in VBA. Instead, you must use one of the following techniques to connect to the SharePoint server through the Office application:

- Update or refresh a document that is shared on the server.
- Insert an existing SharePoint list on an Excel worksheet. This can even be a dummy list placed on the server solely for the purpose of establishing connections.
- Navigate to the SharePoint site in code.

Any of these techniques displays SharePoint's authentication dialog box and establishes a user session for the Office application. Afterward, you can call web service methods, and they will be authorized using the current session.

VBA Programming Tips

The generated proxy classes hardcode the site address as a constant in the generated proxy class modules:

```
Private Const c_WSDL_URL As String = _
    "http://wombat1/xlSPDemo/_vti_bin/lists.asmx?wsdl"
```

You can change the c_WSDL_URL constant to target other sites or subsites. SharePoint creates a _vti_bin virtual folder for any new web site. That folder mirrors _vti_bin at the top-level site.

One thing you will notice quickly when using the generated proxy classes is that the error reporting is minimal. When a method fails on the server side, you receive only a general error. To get more detail, change the proxy class's error handler. The following code shows how to add details to the Lists web service error handler:

```
Private Sub ListsErrorHandler(str_Function As String)
    If sc_Lists.FaultCode <> "" Then
        Err.Raise vbObjectError, str_Function, sc_Lists.FaultString & _
            vbCrLf & sc_Lists.Detail ' Add detail
    'Non SOAP Error
    Else
        Err.Raise Err.Number, str_Function, Err.Description
    End If
End Sub
```

Working with Lists

One of the most useful scenarios for using web services in VBA is calling the Lists web service from Excel. The Lists web service lets you perform tasks on the server that you cannot otherwise perform through Excel objects. Specifically, you can use the List web service to:

- Add an attachment to a row in a list.
- Retrieve an attachment from a row in a list.
- Delete an attachment.
- Delete a list from a SharePoint server.
- Perform queries.

The following sections demonstrate how to perform those tasks in VBA using the Lists web service.

Adding attachments

Use the Lists web service `AddAttachment` method to add a file attachment to a row in a list; then, use `GetAttachmentCollection` to retrieve attachments from within Excel. For example, the following code attaches the image file *joey.jpg* to the second row of a shared list:

```
' Requires Web reference to SharePoint Lists.asmx
Dim lws As New clsws_Lists, src As String
src = ThisWorkbook.Path & "\joey.jpg"
dest = lws.wsm_AddAttachment("Excel Objects", "2", "joey.jpg", FileToByte(src))
```

The `AddAttachment` method's last argument is an array of bytes containing the data to attach. To convert the image file to an array of bytes, the preceding code uses the following helper function:

```
Function FileToByte(fname As String) As Byte()
    Dim fnum As Integer
    fnum = FreeFile
    On Error GoTo FileErr
    Open fname For Binary Access Read As fnum
    On Error GoTo 0
    Dim byt() As Byte
    ReDim byt(LOF(fnum) - 1)
    byt = InputB(LOF(fnum), 1)
    Close fnum
    FileToByte = byt
    Exit Function
FileErr:
    MsgBox "File error: " & Err.Description
End Function
```

Retrieving attachments

Use the Lists web service `GetAttachmentCollection` method to retrieve an attachment from a list. The `GetAttachmentCollection` method returns an XML node list that contains information about each attachment for the row. The following code retrieves the location of the file attached in the previous section:

```
Dim lws As New clsws_Lists ' Requires Web reference to SharePoint Lists.asmx
Dim xn As IXMLDOMNodeList  ' Requires reference to Microsoft XML
Set xn = lws.wsm_GetAttachmentCollection("Excel Objects", "2")
ThisWorkbook.FollowHyperlink (xn.Item(0).Text)
```

Notice that the returned XML node list is a collection since rows can have multiple attachments. Since the preceding example only attached one file, this sample simply retrieves the first item from the node list. The `Text` property of this item is the address of the attachment on the SharePoint server.

Deleting attachments

Finally, it is very simple to delete an attachment using the `DeleteAttachment` method:

```
Dim lws As New clsws_Lists   ' Requires Web reference to SharePoint Lists.asmx
lws.wsm_DeleteAttachment "Excel Objects", "2", _
SPSITE & "/Lists/Excel Objects/Attachments/2/joey.jpg"
```

Since `DeleteAttachment` requires the fully qualified address of the attachment, it is useful to save the address of each attachment somewhere on the worksheet or to create a helper function to retrieve the address from the SharePoint server as shown here:

```
Function GetAttachment(ListName As String, ID As String) As String
    Dim lws As New clsws_Lists ' Requires Web reference to SharePoint Lists.asmx
    Dim xn As IXMLDOMNodeList  ' Requires reference to Microsoft XML
    Set xn = lws.wsm_GetAttachmentCollection(ListName, ID)
    GetAttachment = xn.Item(0).Text
End Function
```

Performing queries

You don't commonly need to perform queries through the Lists web service. Most of the operations you want to perform on the list data are handled through the Excel interface or through the Excel list objects.

However, advanced applications—or especially ambitious programmers—may use the Lists web service to exchange XML data directly with SharePoint. For instance, you may want to retrieve a limited number of rows from a very large shared list. In this case, you can perform a query directly on the SharePoint list using the `GetListItems` method. For example, the following code gets the first 100 rows from a shared list:

```
Dim lws As New clsws_Lists ' Requires Web reference to SharePoint Lists.asmx
Dim xn As IXMLDOMNodeList  ' Requires reference to Microsoft XML
Dim query As IXMLDOMNodeList
Dim viewFields As IXMLDOMNodeList
Dim rowLimit As String
Dim queryOptions As IXMLDOMNodeList
rowLimit = "100"
Dim xdoc As New DOMDocument
xdoc.LoadXml ("<Document><Query /><ViewFields />" & _
    "<QueryOptions /></Document>")
Set query = xdoc.getElementsByTagName("Query")
Set viewFields = xdoc.getElementsByTagName("Fields")
Set queryOptions = xdoc.getElementsByTagName("QueryOptions")
Set xn = lws.wsm_GetListItems("Shared Documents", "", query, _
    viewFields, rowLimit, queryOptions)
```

The results are returned as XML. To see them, you can simply display the root node of the returned object as shown here:

```
Debug.Print xn.Item(0).xml
```

The key to the preceding query is the XML supplied to the LoadXml method. You create conditional queries using the Query element and determine the columns included in the results using the ViewFields element. Perhaps the simplest way to create these queries is to write them as a text file in an XML editor (or Notepad), and then load them from that file using the Load method shown here:

```
xdoc.Load ("query.xml")
```

The query file takes this form:

```
<Document>
<Query>
  <OrderBy>
      <FieldRef Name="Column 1" Ascending="FALSE"/>
    </OrderBy>
  <Where>
    <Gt>
        <FieldRef Name="_x0031_" />
        <Value Type="Value">6</Value>
      </Gt>
    </Where>
  </Query>
<ViewFields>
      <FieldRef Name="ID" />
      <FieldRef Name="_x0031_" />
      <FieldRef Name="_x0032_" />
      <FieldRef Name="_x0033_" />
</ViewFields>
<QueryOptions>
  <DateInUtc>FALSE</DateInUtc>
  <Folder />
  <Paging />
  <IncludeMandatoryColumns>FALSE</IncludeMandatoryColumns>
  <MeetingInstanceId />
  <ViewAttributes Scope="Recursive" />
  <RecurrenceOrderBy />
  <RowLimit />
  <ViewAttributes />
  <ViewXml />
</QueryOptions>
</Document>
```

Notice that the FieldRef elements sometimes use the internal SharePoint names to identify columns—lists don't always use the titles displayed in the columns as column names. You can get the internal column names by examining the list's XML. To see the list's XML, use the GetList method as shown here:

```
Dim lws As New clsws_Lists
Dim xn As IXMLDOMNodeList ' Requires reference to Microsoft XML
Set xn = lws.wsm_GetList ("Shared Documents")
Debug.Print xn(0).xml
```

From .NET

Working with SharePoint web services from Visual Studio .NET is much the same as working from VBA, except you are using a somewhat different language (VB.NET or C#), and you use the .NET Framework objects rather than the Microsoft Soap and XML type libraries.

To use a web service from Visual Studio .NET:

1. Choose Project → "Add web reference," enter the URL of the web service, and click Go. Visual Studio displays Figure 12-3.

2. Click Add Reference to add the reference. Visual Studio adds a namespace containing the class provided by the web service. The format is *server.class*; for example: wombat1.Webs.

3. Create a new object from the class.

4. Set the object's Credentials property to the user's default credentials.

5. Call the web service methods from the object.

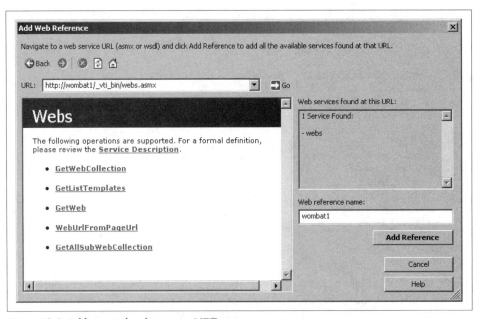

Figure 12-3. Adding a web reference in .NET

For example, here is a very simple console application that gets all of the web sites on the SharePoint server and displays their description:

```
Module Module1
    Sub Main( )
        ' Create a new object from the web service.
        Dim webs As New wombat1.Webs
```

```
        ' Pass the service the default credentials.
        webs.Credentials = System.Net.CredentialCache.DefaultCredentials
        Dim xdoc As New Xml.XmlDocument
        ' Load the results in an XML document.
        xdoc.LoadXml(webs.GetWebCollection.OuterXml)
        ' Save the results
        xdoc.Save("..\temp.xml")
        ' Display results in the default XML editor.
        Process.Start("..\temp.xml")
    End Sub
End Module
```

The last line displays the resulting file using whatever editor is registered on your system for displaying XML. On my system, that is Internet Explorer, which displays the result as shown in Figure 12-4.

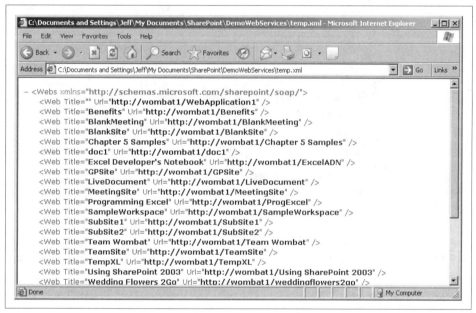

Figure 12-4. Displaying the result of the web service

 Process.Start is the .NET equivalent of Shell; using it to open documents in their default editor is a handy trick to know.

.NET Programming Tips

You can change the site that the web service acts on by changing the Web Reference URL property for the web service. You can also rename the namespace so it is more descriptive.

To set the web reference properties:

1. Select the item under Web References in the Solution Explorer.
2. Set the properties in the Properties window, as shown in Figure 12-5.

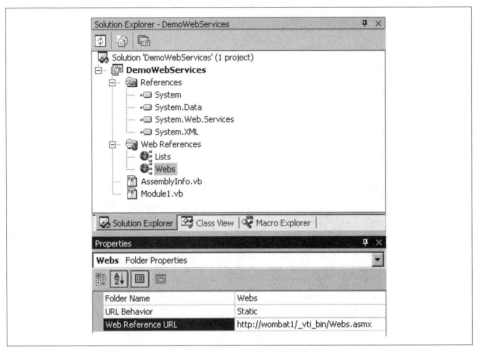

Figure 12-5. Changing web reference properties

The .NET Framework contains many useful classes for working with XML and integrates its database support with XML. For instance, you can load XML directly into a DataSet, and then use that object to easily iterate over elements or load the items into a data grid. The following code shows how to display the results from a web service in a data grid on a Windows form:

```
Private Sub Form1_Load(ByVal sender As System.Object, _
  ByVal e As System.EventArgs) Handles MyBase.Load
    ' Create a new object from the web service.
    Dim webs As New wombat1.Webs
    Dim ds As New DataSet, str As String
    ' Pass the service the default credentials.
    webs.Credentials = System.Net.CredentialCache.DefaultCredentials
    ' Get the list of sites.
    str = webs.GetWebCollection.OuterXml()
    ' Read the string into a stream.
    Dim sr As New IO.StringReader(str)
    ds.ReadXml(sr)
```

```
      ' Display results.
      dGrid.DataSource = ds.Tables(0)
      sr.Close( )
  End Sub

  Private Sub Form1_Resize(ByVal sender As Object, _
    ByVal e As System.EventArgs) Handles MyBase.Resize
      dGrid.PreferredColumnWidth = Me.Width / 2
      dGrid.Width = Me.Width
      dGrid.Height = Me.Height
  End Sub
```

Figure 12-6 illustrates the results from this very simple program.

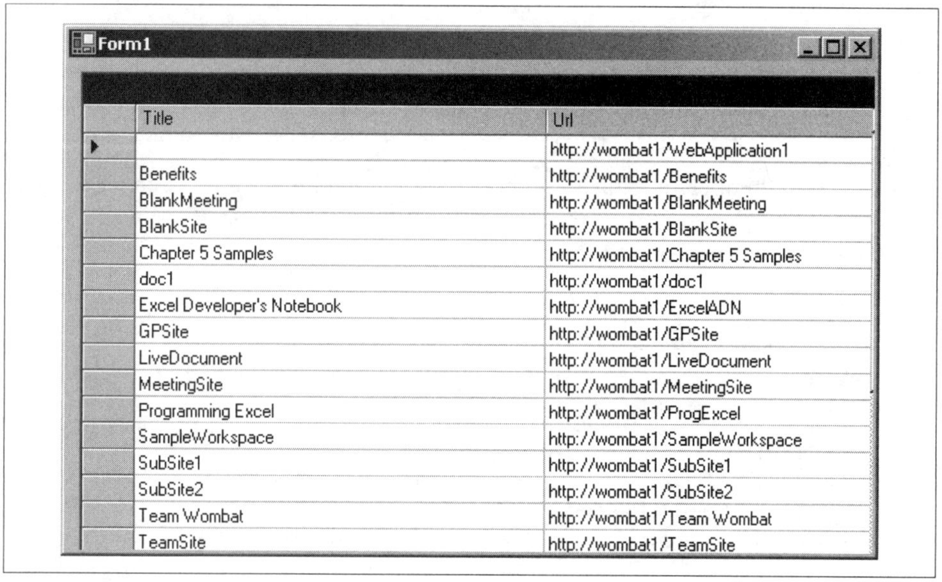

Figure 12-6. Quick results from using data sets with XML

Often in .NET you can assemble a few very powerful classes to create quick results with a few lines of code. In fact, Form1_Load in the previous code example is verbose in order to separate the steps. Here's how the code would typically be written:

```
  Private Sub Form1_Load(ByVal sender As System.Object, _
    ByVal e As System.EventArgs) Handles MyBase.Load
      ' Create a new object from the web service.
      Dim webs As New wombat1.Webs, ds As New DataSet
      ' Pass the service the default credentials.
      webs.Credentials = System.Net.CredentialCache.DefaultCredentials
      ' Shortened form of load/read.
      ds.ReadXml(New IO.StringReader(webs.GetWebCollection.OuterXml( )))
      ' Display results.
      dGrid.DataSource = ds.Tables(0)
  End Sub
```

From ASP.NET

When using SharePoint web services from ASP.NET applications on other servers, you must still provide valid credentials of authorized users. In most cases, you'll want to do that by impersonating the current user and passing his credentials to the service. To impersonate the current user in an ASP.NET web application, change the *Web.config* of the application as shown here:

```
<authentication mode="Windows" />
<authorization>
    <deny users="?" /> <!-- Deny unauthenticated users -->
</authorization>
<identity impersonate="true" />
```

These settings enforce Windows authentication and then run the ASP.NET code under the current user's identity. You can use other authentication and authorization techniques, but the concept is the same—the code invoking the web service must impersonate a user authorized to make the request on the SharePoint server.

Once the code is impersonating an authorized user, invoking the web service is basically the same as shown previously, with the addition that the DataGrid web control requires a DataBind method to load data:

```
Dim ds as DataSet

Private Sub Page_Load(ByVal sender As System.Object, _
  ByVal e As System.EventArgs) Handles MyBase.Load
    ' Create a new object from the web service.
    Dim webs As New wombat1.Webs
    ' Pass the service the default credentials.
    webs.Credentials = System.Net.CredentialCache.DefaultCredentials
    ' Shortened form of load/read.
    ds.ReadXml(New IO.StringReader(webs.GetWebCollection.OuterXml()))
    ' Display results.
    dGrid.DataSource = ds.Tables(0)
    ' Bind data (required for DataGrid web control).
    dGrid.DataBind()
End Sub
```

Using the Admin Service

The *Admin.asmx* web service is not installed on the root SharePoint site, but rather is provided as part of the Central Administration site, which SharePoint installs on a separate port number. To create a web reference for this service:

1. Find the port number for the Central Administration site. To do that, open the site in the browser and record the port number used in the Address bar.

2. Specify the port number and the *_vti_adm* folder in the URL of the web reference. For example:

    http://wombat1:2933/_vti_adm/Admin.asmx

The Admin service provides two main methods: CreateSite and DeleteSite. These methods require administrative privileges to use, but are otherwise straightforward. For example, the following code adds a "Delete site" feature to the previous ASP.NET data grid example:

```
Private Sub dGrid_DeleteCommand(ByVal source As Object, _
  ByVal e As System.Web.UI.WebControls.DataGridCommandEventArgs) _
  Handles dGrid.DeleteCommand
    ' Display the delete panel.
    pnl.Visible = True
    ' Show the site to delete.
    lbl.Text = ds.Tables(0).Rows(e.Item.ItemIndex).Item(1)
End Sub

Private Sub cmdDelete_Click(ByVal sender As System.Object, _
  ByVal e As System.EventArgs)
    ' Create admin object.
    Dim adm As New wombat1Adm.Admin
    ' If an item is selected
    If lbl.Text <> "" Then
        Try
            ' Delete the site.
            adm.DeleteSite(lbl.Text)
            ' Display success.
            status.text = lbl.Text & " deleted."
        Catch ex As Exception
            ' Otherwise, note the error.
            status.text = "Error: " & ex.Message
        End Try
    End If
    ' Hide panel.
    pnl.Visible = False
End Sub

Private Sub cmdNo_Click(ByVal sender As Object, _
  ByVal e As System.EventArgs) Handles cmdNo.Click
    ' Clear the site and hide the panel.
    lbl.Text = ""
    pnl.Visible = False
End Sub
```

In addition to the data grid, the preceding code uses some controls defined in the following ASP.NET web form:

```
<form id="Form1" method="post" runat="server">
    <asp:Panel id="pnl" runat="server" Visible="False">
    Are you sure you want to delete
    <asp:Label id="lbl" runat="server"></asp:Label>?
    <asp:Button id="cmdYes" runat="server" Text="Yes"></asp:Button>
    <asp:Button id="cmdNo" runat="server" Text="No"></asp:Button></asp:Panel>
    <asp:Label id="status" runat="server"></asp:Label><br>
    <asp:DataGrid id="dGrid" runat="server" Width="432px" AllowSorting="True">
        <Columns>
            <asp:ButtonColumn Text="Delete"
```

```
                CommandName="Delete"></asp:ButtonColumn>
          </Columns>
      </asp:DataGrid>
  </form>
```

At runtime, the user can select a site from the grid and delete it as shown in Figure 12-7.

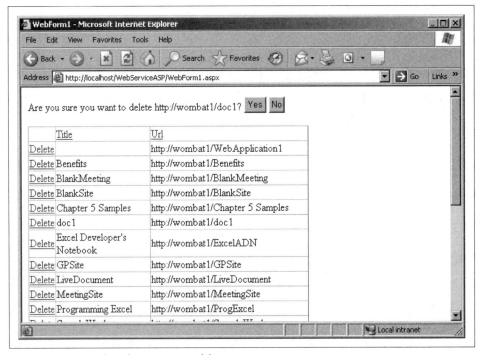

Figure 12-7. Using the Admin service to delete a site

Using URL Commands

URL commands get XML results from a SharePoint server through HTTP GET requests. You invoke the commands by specifying them as query strings in an address that has this form:

```
http://server/subsite/_vti_bin/owssvr.dll?Cmd=cmdname&param=value&param=value ...
```

URL commands don't alter the content database, so they don't require authentication. The RPC protocol provides a similar approach, but uses HTTP POST instead of GET, and so can include authentication information and thus change content. Table 12-6 lists the commands that can be invoked through HTTP GET.

Table 12-6. SharePoint URL commands

Command	Parameters	Use to
dialogview	dialogview, location, FileDialogFilterValue	Open the view used in a dialog box for opening or saving files to a document library; or open the custom property form that is used when saving a file to a document library.
Display	List, XMLDATA	Run a database query against the list and return XML or HTML.
DisplayPost	PostBody, URLBase	Render the Collaborative Application Markup Language (CAML) assigned to the PostBody parameter.
ExportList	List	Export in CAML format the schema of the list.
GetProjSchema		Request the XML Schema for a web site.
GetUsageBlob	BlobType	Get information about web site usage.
HitCounter	Page, Image, Custom, Digits	Render a hit counter in an img element on a page.
RenderView	List, View, URLBase	Request the contents of a view for the list.

The URL commands also accept the set of optional parameters in Table 12-7 to modify the returned results.

Table 12-7. URL optional parameters

Parameter	Use to
FileDialogFilterValue	Set filters for a view, and return the list of all files of a specified type from a document library according to filename extension (for example, *.doc, *.ppt, or *.xls).
FilterField*n*	Specify the name of a field in the database, where *n* is an integer that is limited only by the number of fields allowed in the database table or by the length allowed for the URL field.
FilterValue*n*	Specify the string value on which to filter a field, where *n* is an integer that is limited only by the length allowed for the URL field.
SortField	Specify the name of the field on which to sort.
SortDir	Indicate an ascending (asc) or descending (desc) sort order.
Using	Specify a particular file containing CAML for the server to evaluate and render.

Getting GUIDs

The List and View parameters of the URL commands are the unique identifiers (GUIDs) that SharePoint uses internally. There's no URL command to get a GUID from a name, so you have to use the SharePoint object model or a web service to get the values.

The following sections demonstrate how to get the list and view GUIDs in three different scenarios:

- Server .NET code in a web part using the SharePoint object model.
- Remote .NET code using web services.
- Remote VBA code using web services.

The return values of all the procedures are the same, but as you can see from the code, the way you get the result varies.

Using SharePoint objects

If you're working within SharePoint, you can get GUIDs through the SharePoint object model. The following procedures get a reference to the current web using the GetContextWeb shared method, and then use that object to get the list or view by name from the Lists or Views collections. The ID property is a GUID, which must be converted to a string in order to be used from the URL command:

```
' Requires: Imports Microsoft.SharePoint.Webcontrols
Function GetListGuid(ByVal lName As String) As String
    Try
        ' Get the web from the current context.
        Dim web As SPWeb = SPControl.GetContextWeb(context)
        ' Get the list by name.
        Dim lst As SPList = web.Lists(lName)
        ' Get the GUID of the list.
        Dim guid As System.Guid = lst.ID
        ' Format the GUID as a string.
        Return ("{" & guid.ToString & "}")
    Catch ex As Exception
        Debug.Write(ex.Message)
        Return ""
    End Try
End Function

Function GetViewGuid(ByVal lName As String, _
  ByVal vName As String) As String
    Try
        ' Get the web from the current context.
        Dim web As SPWeb = SPControl.GetContextWeb(context)
        ' Get the view by name.
        Dim view As SPView = web.Lists(lName).Views(vName)
        ' Get the GUID of the list.
        Dim guid As System.Guid = view.ID
        ' Format the GUID as a string.
        Return ("{" & guid.ToString & "}")
    Catch ex As Exception
        Debug.Write(ex.Message)
        Return ""
    End Try
End Function
```

The error handling in these and subsequent procedures is very basic and simply returns "" if the list or view was not found. You may want to change that in your own code.

Using web services (.NET)

The Lists web service GetList method returns an XML description of the list that contains an ID attribute with the list's GUID. You can use SelectSingleNode to extract the ID attribute from the XML as shown here:

```
' Requires a web reference to the Lists.asmx.
Function GetListGUID(ByVal lName As String) As String
    Dim xn As Xml.XmlNode, lws As New Lists.Lists
    Try
        ' Get the XML result from the web service.
        xn = lws.GetList(lName)
        ' Get the GUID (it's the ID attribute of the root element).
        Return xn.SelectSingleNode("//@ID").InnerText
    Catch ex As Exception
        Return ""
    End Try
End Function
```

The Views web service GetViewCollection returns an XML description listing the views available for a list. Each view has a Name attribute containing the GUID of the view. To extract that information, you need to find the view by its DisplayName attribute using an XPath expression in SelectSingleNode as follows:

```
' Requires a web reference to the Views.asmx.
Function GetViewGUID(ByVal lName As String, ByVal vName As String) As String
    Dim xn As Xml.XmlNode, vws As New Views.Views
    Try
        ' Get the XML result from the web service.
        xn = vws.GetViewCollection(lName)
        ' Get the GUID (it's the Name attribute)
        ' where @DisplayName matches the view name.
        Return xn.SelectSingleNode("//*[@DisplayName='" & _
            vName & "']/@Name").InnerText
    Catch ex As Exception
        Return ""
    End Try
End Function
```

Using web services (VBA)

Getting the GUIDs from VBA is similar to using the web services from .NET, however the XML objects and error handling are different than those available in .NET:

```
' Requires web reference to Lists.asmx.
Function GetListGUID(lName As String) As String
    On Error Resume Next
    Dim lws As New clsws_Lists
    Dim xn As IXMLDOMNodeList, guid As String
```

```
    ' Get the list.
    Set xn = lws.wsm_GetList(lName)
    ' Extract the GUID (it's the ID attribute).
    guid = xn(0).selectSingleNode("//@ID").Text
    ' Return "" if not found.
    If Err Then guid = ""
    ' Return the GUID.
    GetListGUID = guid
End Function


' Requires web reference to Views.asmx.
Function GetViewGUID(lName As String, vName As String) As String
    On Error Resume Next
    Dim vws As New clsws_Views
    Dim xn As IXMLDOMNodeList, guid As String
    ' Get the list's views.
    Set xn = vws.wsm_GetViewCollection(lName)
    ' Extract the GUID (it's the Name attribute).
    guid = xn(0).selectSingleNode("//*[@DisplayName='" & _
        vName & "']/@Name").Text
    ' Return "" if not found.
    If Err Then guid = ""
    ' Return the GUID.
    GetViewGUID = guid
End Function
```

Executing URL Commands

You can use the URL commands as part of a link rendered on a page. For example, the following link displays the schema of a list:

```
<a href="http://wombat1/_vti_bin/owssvr.dll?Cmd=ExportList&List={70F9FF01-15E5-4129-
A370-9A31090204E9}">Show list schema</a>
```

Or, you can get the resulting XML in code using the .NET XML objects, as shown here:

```
' .NET: Use URL protocol to get a list's XML.
Function GetListSchema(ByVal lName As String) As String
    Dim xdoc As New Xml.XmlDocument
    Dim guid As String = GetListGUID(lName)
    ' Create a reader for the URL.
    Dim xr As New Xml.XmlTextReader("http://wombat1/_vti_bin/owssvr.dll" & _
        "?Cmd=ExportList&List=" & guid)
    ' Load the response.
    xdoc.Load(xr)
    ' Return the XML as a string.
    Return xdoc.OuterXml
End Function
```

Here's the same code in VBA:

```
' VBA: Use URL protocol to get a list's XML.
Function GetListSchema(ByVal lName As String) As String
    Dim guid As String, xdoc As New DOMDocument
    guid = GetListGUID(lName)
```

```
' Load the response.
xdoc.Load ("http://wombat1/_vti_bin/owssvr.dll" & _
  "?Cmd=ExportList&List=" & guid)
' Return the XML as a string.
GetListXML xdoc.Text
End Function
```

You can experiment with the URL commands to get the right combination of parameters. It is often easier to compose the command in the browser's address bar or as an HTML link before using it in code. For example, the first link below displays the visible list items in XML, whereas the second includes all of the hidden fields because it includes the parameter Query=*:

```
<a href="http://wombat1/_vti_bin/owssvr.dll?Cmd=Display&List={70F9FF01-15E5-4129-
A370-9A31090204E9}&XMLDATA=TRUE">Display list XML (minimal)</a><br>

<a href="http://wombat1/_vti_bin/owssvr.dll?Cmd=Display&List={70F9FF01-15E5-4129-
A370-9A31090204E9}&XMLDATA=TRUE&Query=*">Display list XML (full)</a>
```

For complex queries, it is often easier to use web services or RPC.

Using RPC

The SharePoint Remote Procedure Call (RPC) methods provide yet another way to change SharePoint sites and get content remotely. The RPC methods are similar to the URL commands discussed earlier, except RPC uses HTTP POST rather than GET to send requests.

Use RPC methods when you want to compose your changes or queries in Collaborative Application Markup Language (CAML) rather than through web service methods. CAML is a declarative approach to programming SharePoint using XML rather than a procedural programming language such as Visual Basic .NET. There are several advantages to this approach:

- RPC methods can be included on a web page as content rather than as server-side code.
- Users can compose and run their own queries in CAML without installing web parts or other code on the server.
- SharePoint templates and descriptions are in CAML, so understanding it helps you create custom site definitions.
- RPC incurs less overhead than web services.

That said, CAML is another skill to learn—and a fairly advanced one at that. RPC is the logical choice for customizing a SharePoint site without using web parts.

Table 12-8 lists the methods available through RPC. The URL commands are also available through RPC but aren't included in the table since they are already listed in Table 12-6.

Table 12-8. *SharePoint RPC methods*

Method	Parameters	Use to
Cltreq	UL, STRMVER, ACT, URL	Perform web discussion operations such as adding, editing, or deleting a discussion associated with a web page or with a document stored in a document library.
Delete	ID, List, NextUsing, owsfileref	Delete an item in a list.
DeleteField	List, Field, owshiddenversion	Delete a field from the list.
DeleteList	List, NextUsing	Delete a list.
DeleteView	List, View	Delete the view.
ImportList	Title, RootFolder, ListSchema	Create a list based upon a specified XML schema.
ModListSettings	List, OldListTitle, NewListTitle, Description, ReadSecurity, WriteSecurity, SchemaSecurity	Change the properties of the list.
NewField	List, FieldXML, AddToDefaultView, owshiddenversion	Add a new field to the list specified.
NewList	ListTemplate, Description, displayOnLeft, VersioningEnabled, GlobalMtgDataList, AllowMultiVote, showUsernames	Create a list of a specified type, such as Contacts, Discussions, or Survey.
NewViewPage	List, PageURL, DisplayName, HiddenView	Add a new view page to the list.
NewWebPage		Create a new web part page or a new basic page in the document library.
ReorderFields	List, ReorderedFields	Change the order in which fields in the list are displayed on the data entry form.
Save	ID, List, NextUsing	Save a new list or save modifications to an existing list.
SiteProvision	CreateLists	Add the default set of lists to an existing SharePoint site.
UpdateField	List, FieldXML, owshiddenversion	Modify the schema of an existing field in the list.

Preparing a Page for RPC

Because RPC methods can change content, the post must include user information so SharePoint can authenticate and authorize the method. That means you must take a couple of special steps to execute RPC commands on a web page:

1. Add a FormDigest control to the page.

2. Create a form element that includes the method to execute and that posts its contents to *http://server/site/_vti_bin/owssvr.dll*.

3. Create a client-side script to insert the value from the `FormDigest` control into the form before it is posted.

4. Add a Submit button to post the form.

When creating a page that includes RPC commands, it's easiest if you start with a web part page generated by SharePoint since those pages include the @ Register directive for the SharePoint web controls.

For example, I created *RPCDemo.aspx* in the TestPages document library, and then edited it using FrontPage to create a platform for testing RPC commands. I added the following script to the HEAD element at the beginning of the page:

```
<!-- This directive registers the FormDigest WebControl -->
<%@ Register Tagprefix="SharePoint" Namespace="Microsoft.SharePoint.WebControls"
Assembly="Microsoft.SharePoint, Version=11.0.0.0, Culture=neutral,
PublicKeyToken=71e9bce111e9429c" %>
<html dir="ltr">
<HEAD>
<!-- Add this script to include user info in the CAML -->
<script type="text/javascript" language="JavaScript">
function InsertSecurityValidation(oForm)
{
    var sFormDigest = '<SetVar Name="__REQUESTDIGEST">' +
      oForm.elements["__REQUESTDIGEST"].value + "</SetVar>\n";
    var oPostBody = oForm.elements["PostBody"];
    var rePattern = /<\/Method>/g;
    oPostBody.value = oPostBody.value.replace(rePattern, sFormDigest + "</Method>");
}
</script>
</HEAD>
```

Then I added the following form after the closing form tag generated by SharePoint:

```
<!-- SharePoint web part zones omitted here -->
<\form>
<!-- Form used to post RPC commands to SharePoint -->
<form class="ms-formbody" method="post"
  action="http://wombat1/_vti_bin/owssvr.dll"
  onsubmit="InsertSecurityValidation(this);"
  target="result" >
  <!-- This control provides user information -->
  <SharePoint:FormDigest runat="server"/>
  Enter CAML containing RPC methods and click Run to see the result:
  <input type="hidden" name="Cmd" value="DisplayPost" />
  <!-- Source for CAML -->
  <textarea name="PostBody" style="width=100%;height=200">
  </textarea>
  <br>
  <input type="submit" value="Run" />
  <input type="reset" value="Clear" />
  <br>
  Result:
  <!-- Target for results -->
  <IFRAME name="result" src="::blank.htm" style="width=100%;height=200"/>
</form>
```

Figure 12-8 shows the resulting web part page. You can enter CAML in the text box, click Run, and see the results in the IFRAME, as shown in the figure.

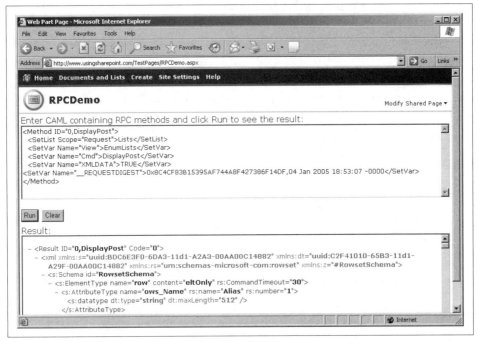

Figure 12-8. Using RPCDemo.aspx to test RPC methods

I created *RPCDemo.aspx* as a test bed for composing RPC method calls. If the CAML is incorrect, an error displays in the result. You can cut and paste samples from the SharePoint SDK into the text box, modify the parameters, and run the commands to see how they work.

Once you're satisfied with the results, you can hardcode the CAML onto a new web page using a hidden input control, as shown here:

```
<!-- Embedded RPC -->
<form class="ms-formbody" method="post"
  action="http://wombat1/_vti_bin/owssvr.dll"
  onsubmit="InsertSecurityValidation(this);"
  target="_blank" >
  <!-- This control provides user information -->
  <SharePoint:FormDigest runat="server"/>
  Click Run to see the result in a pop-up window.
  <input type="hidden" name="Cmd" value="DisplayPost" />
  <!-- Source for CAML -->
  <input type="hidden" name="PostBody" value="
    <Method ID='0,DisplayPost'>
        <SetList Scope='Request'>Lists</SetList>
        <SetVar Name='View'>EnumLists</SetVar>
        <SetVar Name='Cmd'>DisplayPost</SetVar>
        <SetVar Name='XMLDATA'>TRUE</SetVar>
```

```
      </Method>" />
    <br>
    <input type="submit" value="Run" />
  </form>
```

Don't forget to add the InsertSecurityValidation script to the new page's header. This sample displays the results in a new pop-up window (target="_blank") rather than on the page in an inline frame.

Common RPC Tasks

The following sections make up a quick tour of some common tasks you might want to perform using RPC. In each of these samples, you'll need to replace the GUIDs provided for lists and views with values from your own sites.

Identifying lists

RPC methods identify the list they act on by the list's GUID. You can get the GUIDs of all the lists in a site through RPC by calling the DisplayPost method with the View parameter set to EnumLists, as shown here:

```
<Method ID="0,DisplayPost">
  <SetList Scope="Request">Lists</SetList>
  <SetVar Name="View">EnumLists</SetVar>
  <SetVar Name="Cmd">DisplayPost</SetVar>
  <SetVar Name="XMLDATA">TRUE</SetVar>
</Method>
```

Once you find the GUID of the list you want, you specify that value in the SetList element. For example, the following method exports the Announcements list:

```
<Method ID="0,ExportList">
  <SetList Scope="Request">{41D7D046-1E0A-4FB2-A096-C063D210D552}</SetList>
  <SetVar Name="Cmd">ExportList</SetVar>
</Method>
```

Combining multiple methods

Use the Batch element to combine two or more RPC methods in a single post. For example, the following CAML adds two items to the Announcements list:

```
<ows:Batch Version="6.0.2.5608" OnError="Return">
  <Method ID="Anouncement1">
    <SetList>{41D7D046-1E0A-4FB2-A096-C063D210D552}</SetList>
    <SetVar Name="ID">New</SetVar>
    <SetVar Name="Cmd">Save</SetVar>
    <SetVar Name="urn:schemas-microsoft-com:office:office#Title">Announcement
Title1</SetVar>
    <SetVar Name="urn:schemas-microsoft-com:office:office#Body">Announcement text
</SetVar>
    <SetVar Name="urn:schemas-microsoft-com:office:office#Expires">2005-09-14T00:00:
00Z</SetVar>
  </Method>
```

```
<Method ID="Announcement2">
  <SetList>{41D7D046-1E0A-4FB2-A096-C063D210D552}</SetList>
  <SetVar Name="ID">New</SetVar>
  <SetVar Name="Cmd">Save</SetVar>
  <SetVar Name="urn:schemas-microsoft-com:office:office#Title">Announcement Title2
</SetVar>
  <SetVar Name="urn:schemas-microsoft-com:office:office#Body">Announcement text
</SetVar>
  <SetVar Name="urn:schemas-microsoft-com:office:office#Expires">2005-12-18T00:00:
00Z</SetVar>
  </Method>
</ows:Batch>
```

The Batch element's OnError attribute determines what happens if one of the methods fails. The Return setting causes the methods to stop as soon as an error occurs; Continue causes SharePoint to skip to the methods with errors and continue with the next method.

Querying lists

Use the Display method to perform a query on a list and return only a specific set of fields. For example, the following query returns three fields from a list using the filter criteria introduced=2000 (note that field names are case-sensitive):

```
<Method ID="0,Display">
  <SetList Scope="Request">{5E6561D4-7048-45AB-BFA1-2D1991BAF3B1}</SetList>
  <SetVar Name="Cmd">Display</SetVar>
  <SetVar Name="XMLDATA">False</SetVar>
  <SetVar Name="Query">name Title introduced</SetVar>
 <SetVar Name="FilterField1">introduced</SetVar>
 <SetVar Name="FilterValue1">2000</SetVar>
</Method>
```

For queries that require filtering or sorting, you can also specify a view that defines those criteria. For example, the following query returns items from the list specified by one of the list views:

```
<Method ID="0,Display">
  <SetList Scope="Request">{5E6561D4-7048-45AB-BFA1-2D1991BAF3B1}</SetList>
  <SetVar Name="Cmd">Display</SetVar>
  <SetVar Name="XMLDATA">False</SetVar>
  <SetVar Name="View">{21E03766-D0CF-4942-B2C0-DF4E3706DD50}</SetVar>
</Method>
```

Creating lists

Use the NewList method to create a new list or document library on a site. The ListTemplate parameter determines what type of list is created (see Table 12-9).

Table 12-9. ListTemplate settings

Setting	List type	Setting	List type
100	Generic	101	Document library
102	Survey	103	Links
104	Announcements	105	Contacts
106	Events list	107	Tasks
108	Discussion board	109	Picture library
110	Data sources	111	Site template gallery
113	Web Part gallery	114	List template gallery
115	Form library	120	Custom grid for a list
200	Meeting Series	201	Meeting Agenda
202	Meeting Attendees	204	Meeting Decisions
207	Meeting Objectives	210	Meeting text box
211	Meeting Things To Bring	212	Meeting Workspace Pages
1100	Issue tracking		

For example, the following method creates a new document library:

```
<Method ID="0,NewList">
  <SetVar Name="Cmd">NewList</SetVar>
  <SetVar Name="ListTemplate">101</SetVar>
  <SetVar Name="Title">New Document Library</SetVar>
</Method>
```

Creating pages

To add a new web page to the document library created in the preceding section, get the library's GUID, and then use the NewWebPage method:

```
<Method ID="0,NewWebPage">
  <SetList Scope="Request">{28F54F4C-BA98-43E9-A60F-8C81E5365560}</SetList>
  <SetVar Name="Cmd">NewWebPage</SetVar>
  <SetVar Name="ID">New</SetVar>
  <SetVar Name="Type">WebPartPage</SetVar>
  <SetVar Name="WebPartPageTemplate">3</SetVar>
  <SetVar Name="Overwrite">true</SetVar>
  <SetVar Name="Title">TempPage</SetVar>
</Method>
```

The WebPartPageTemplate parameter determines the layout of the new page (see Table 12-10).

Table 12-10. WebPartPageTemplate settings

Setting	Page layout
1	Full Page, Vertical
2	Header, Footer, 3 Columns
3	Header, Left Column, Body
4	Header, Right Column, Body
5	Header, Footer, 2 Columns, 4 Rows
6	Header, Footer, 4 Columns, Top Row
7	Left Column, Header, Footer, Top Row, 3 Columns
8	Right Column, Header, Footer, Top Row, 3 Columns

Deleting items

The following code deletes the web page created in the preceding section:

```
<Method ID="0,Delete">
  <SetList Scope="Request">28F54F4C-BA98-43E9-A60F-8C81E5365560</SetList>
  <SetVar Name="Cmd">Delete</SetVar>
  <SetVar Name="ID">1</SetVar>
  <SetVar Name="owsfileref">http://wombat1/New Document Library/TempPage.aspx</
SetVar>
</Method>
```

Deleting lists

The following code deletes the document library created earlier:

```
<Method ID="0,DeleteList">
  <SetList Scope="Request">28F54F4C-BA98-43E9-A60F-8C81E5365560</SetList>
  <SetVar Name="Cmd">DeleteList</SetVar>
</Method>
```

Best Practices

- Use the Office object model to access SharePoint document workspaces.
- Use SharePoint web services to access sites, lists, and libraries from within Office applications.
- When working with web services from Office 2007, install Office 2003 and the Office 2003 web services toolkit to enable that feature in Office 2007.

CHAPTER 13

Administering SharePoint

In Chapter 1, I showed you how to get started with SharePoint with a basic installation. I didn't go into detail there because I wanted to focus on what you can do with SharePoint rather than on the specifics of installing and administering a server. In this chapter, I expand on your installation options and show you how to configure SharePoint in a production environment. After installation, I show you how to enable:

- Access via the Internet
- Anonymous access
- Forms-based authentication for external users (extranet)
- Self-service site creation
- Backups and restores
- Activity auditing to help maintain security
- Search and icons for PDFs and other file types

These tasks will help you get your server up and running smoothly. Information on administering other aspects of SharePoint is included with the task-specific chapters earlier in this book. Information on upgrading from earlier versions of SharePoint is found in Appendix A, and a guide to the *stsadm.exe* utility command is found in Appendix B.

Installing SharePoint

You can install SharePoint in different configurations that range from simple to complex. The main configuration options are listed in Table 13-1.

Table 13-1. *Overview of SharePoint installation options*

Installation option	Server type	Advantages	Disadvantages
Basic	N/A	Dead-simple installation	Database runs on same server (WID)
			Can't add SharePoint servers to this configuration
Advanced	Standalone	Simple installation	Database runs on same server (WID)
		Can change the location of the database to store the file on a different drive	Can't add servers to this configuration
	Web frontend	Database runs on separate server	Requires additional steps for install
		You can add servers	
	Complete (MOSS only)	Database runs on separate server	Requires additional steps for install
		You can add servers	
		All services run on current server	

The basic and standalone installations use the Windows Internal Database (WID) which runs on the same server as SharePoint, and so competes for resources. You can't connect to a WID database from another server and so you can't extend those installations with additional web servers that share the same configuration database.

The web frontend and complete installations allow you to connect to a SQL Server on your network. That is usually a more efficient configuration because SQL Server and SharePoint both use a lot of memory. Having a dedicated server for SharePoint and a dedicated server for SQL Server ensures that they don't compete for memory. If you already have an SQL Server, this configuration makes best use of your resources.

Here are some recommendations based on my experience:

Basic install
    Use this option for staging and development servers only.

Advanced, standalone
    Use for small businesses that aren't running Microsoft SQL Server 2000 or 2005. Be sure to put the database file on a separate drive (see "Installing WSS," later in this chapter).

Advanced, web frontend
    Use for Windows SharePoint Services (WSS) installations where a SQL Server is available.

Advanced, complete
    Use for initial install of Microsoft Office SharePoint Server (MOSS) to start a server farm.

As I mentioned in earlier chapters, it's a good idea to create a staging server that can be used by the development and testing teams. You can do a test installation on that server to work out the exact configuration you want to use before deploying on the production server. That's a very good idea if you are deploying to a "live" server that already hosts other applications.

Before You Begin

You should verify that hardware, software, and security requirements are met before you begin installation. Tables 13-2 to 13-5 describe those requirements.

Table 13-2. Server hardware requirements

Component	Minimum (staging)[a]	Recommended (production)
Processor	1 GHz	Dual 3 GHz
RAM	512 KB	2 GB
Storage	NTFS with 3 GB free	NTFS with 3 GB of free space plus adequate space for web sites
Drive	N/A	DVD
Display	N/A	1,024 × 768 or higher resolution monitor
Network	Any network connection	56 Kbps to clients
		1 Gbps between servers

[a] Microsoft cites different minimums, but these will work for staging or development; please use the recommended settings for production.

NTFS drives must not be compressed. Setup will fail on compressed drives.

The future storage needs of a SharePoint installation depend on many factors, but often you can get a general idea based on your current requirements for shared drive space. For example, if your company is using 200 GB of space on shared drives, your first-year requirements will probably be less than 200 GB because:

- Many files stored on shared drives are redundant or obsolete.
- My Site quotas force users to trim their needs.
- Larger files are blocked by the default maximum upload size (50 MB).

Those factors cause users to evaluate what to keep and what to delete in ways that network storage often does not. It's a good idea to provide a facility for long-term archiving when making the transition from shared drives to SharePoint.

Another way to figure storage requirements is to base your estimates on a combination of site quotas and best-guess estimates. For example:

Number of employees with My Sites × 100 MB
Plus number of top-level department sites × 10 GB
Plus records center × 10 GB

So, a company with 300 employees, eight top-level department sites, and a records center would require:

$$300 \times 100 \text{ MB}$$
$$+ 8 \times 10 \text{ GB}$$
$$+ 1 \times 10 \text{ GB}$$
$$\text{Total} = 120 \text{ GB}$$

Beyond the first year, it's best to project forward based on historical growth. Estimates are only intended to avoid capacity problems after the initial rollout.

Table 13-3 lists the software that must be installed on the server before you can install SharePoint. You will be able to use Windows Server 2008 instead of Windows Server 2003 once it is available.

Table 13-3. Server software requirements

Component	Requirement	Details
Operating System	Windows Server 2003 SP1	Install ASP.NET application server role *without* FrontPage server extensions; optionally install SMTP service.
Framework	.NET 2.0	Install from *dotnetfx.exe* download from Microsoft.
	.NET 3.0	Install from *dotnetfx3setup.exe* download from Microsoft.
Database	Windows Internal Database (WID)	Included with SharePoint for basic installation.
	SQL Server 2005 (preferred) or SQL Server 2000 SP4	Required for server farm installation installed. A dedicated SQL server is preferred.
Other services for MOSS	Active Directory	Required for MOSS server farm deployment.

The client software requirements are very simple (see Table 13-4), but to get the most out of SharePoint, most users will need Microsoft Office 2007 Professional edition or higher. SharePoint Designer is *not* required by most users in a typical installation.

Table 13-4. Client software requirements

Component	Required	Recommended
Operating System	Any	Windows XP Professional or Windows Vista Business Edition
Browser	Any	Internet Explorer 6.0 or higher; Internet Explorer 7.0 preferred
Office suite	None	Office 2003 Professional Edition or higher; Office 2007 Professional preferred
Forms client	None	Microsoft InfoPath 2007
Online presence	None	Windows Live Communicator

Security should also be considered a requirement. Security includes the identities used by the IIS application pool and the other services that are running on the server.

You can use built-in accounts (such as Network Service) for those services, but that makes it hard to identify which are being used by SharePoint and which are used by other applications. It is best to create new accounts that are not associated with a specific person since people come and go, but SharePoint goes on forever....

Table 13-5. Security requirements

Component	Item	Comments
Domain accounts	Application identity	Used to run the IIS application pool used for SharePoint web sites. Requires User rights on the server and Public rights on the SQL database.
	Administration identity	Used to run the IIS application pool for the Central Administration site. Requires local administration rights on the server and Create rights on the SQL database.
	Search identity (MOSS)	Used to perform cross-site searches.
Firewall	Various	Servers that are exposed to external access via the Internet should be protected.
Virus scan (optional)	Microsoft Forefront Security for SharePoint	Scans uploaded documents for viruses and monitor's content for objectionable material.

If your server is connected to the Internet, you will need some type of firewall to protect it. Most routers provide some level of firewall protection, and there are more sophisticated firewalls that provide monitoring and protection against denial of service (DOS) attacks if needed. Alternately, remote access can be provided through a virtual private network (VPN) for users with domain accounts.

Preinstall Checklist

Before you proceed, verify that your server meets the following hardware requirements as described in the preceding section:

- Processor speed
- RAM
- Disk space
- Network

Verify that the following software is installed on the server:

- Windows 2003 SP1 with latest updates
- Configured as ASP.NET application server, SMTP service enabled
- .NET 2.0
- .NET 3.0
- SQL Native Client (farm configuration)

Verify that you have the following information, which you will need during the install:

- Product key for SharePoint installation
- SQL Server name and instance to use for databases (farm install)
- Server administrator username and password for installing software; this user must have rights to create a database on the SQL server
- Domain username and password for accessing database on the SQL server

Finally, make sure you can access the SharePoint installation DVD or download the installation software from *http://www.microsoft.com/downloads*:

- To install WSS, download *SharePoint.exe*.
- To install MOSS, download *OfficeServer.exe*.

If using the MOSS download, record the product installation keys from the download page once the download is complete.

Installing WSS

WSS provides the basic SharePoint functionality without the cross-site searching, aggregation web parts, document management workflows, and enterprise templates provided by MOSS.

To install WSS:

1. Log on to the target server using a domain account that has local administration rights and create database permission on the SQL server where data will be stored.
2. Run *SharePoint.exe*. Because WSS is a component of Windows 2003, you do not need to enter a product key.
3. Choose Basic or Advanced setup. Basic installs a single, standalone server using the Windows Internal Database (WID). Advanced allows you to specify a database and other options. If you choose Basic, setup will complete without additional choices. The remaining steps assume the Advanced option.
4. Choose the server type as shown in Figure 13-1. Table 13-6 explains the WSS server type choices.
5. Once installation is complete, click Close, and the SharePoint Configuration Wizard guides you through the rest of the setup process.

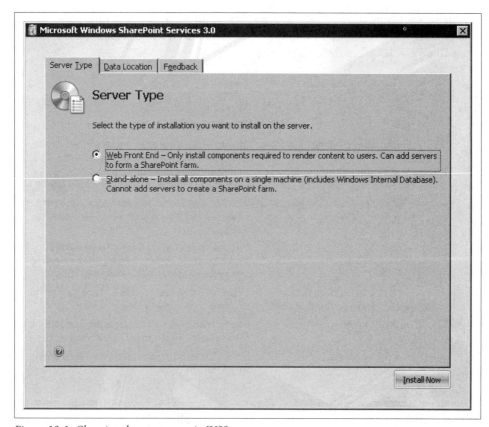

Figure 13-1. Choosing the server type in WSS

Table 13-6. Choosing a WSS server type

Server type	Use to
Web Front End	Create a SharePoint server that uses a SQL database on another server. This is the most common choice for production installations.
Stand-alone	Install SharePoint and its databases on the current server. This option is a single-server configuration and you *can't* add other SharePoint servers to the configuration database after installation.

If you are installing a standalone server, click the Data Location tab shown in Figure 13-1 and set the location of the database file. SharePoint installs the database on the primary partition by default, and you should change that to a different disk drive to help manage storage in the future.

The SharePoint Configuration Wizard walks you through the remaining setup steps, which create the configuration database and install the Central Administration web site. Table 13-7 describes these steps.

Table 13-7. WSS SharePoint Configuration Wizard steps

Step	Title	Explanation
1	None	Introduction to wizard.
2	Specify Configuration Database Settings	This is the SQL Server and database name where information about SharePoint users and web applications is stored. The database access account is used to read from and write to the database. The database is created using your current account.
3	Configure SharePoint Central Administration Web Application	The Central Administration site uses a randomly generated port number by default. You can override that default to use a trusted port.
		You can also choose between NTLM and Kerberos authentication: use Kerberos if your Active Directory service is already set up to use Kerberos authentication, otherwise use NTLM.
4	Completing the SharePoint Products and Technologies Configuration Wizard	Confirms the settings you have chosen. To enable account creation mode, click Advanced Settings at this point.
4 (advanced)	Advanced Settings	Enter the Active Directory domain and organizational unit where SharePoint will automatically create new accounts.
5	Configuration Successful	Confirms that the wizard has completed setup and displays the settings that were used.

Account creation mode allows SharePoint to create new AD accounts that are then sent by email to the users. This configuration is only allowed in WSS, and it's generally used by commercial hosting services. For most business installations, you will want to administer AD accounts directly.

If you choose account creation mode, you need to create an AD organizational unit (OU) and delegate control of that OU to the domain account used by SharePoint (entered in step 2). SharePoint can then add users to that OU as needed.

You can't turn account creation mode on after you install SharePoint. You can only enable it during installation.

Installing MOSS

MOSS includes WSS, so you don't need to install WSS before installing MOSS.

To install MOSS:

1. Log on to the target server using a domain account that has local administration rights and create database permission on the SQL server where data will be stored.

2. Run *OfficeServer.exe*.

3. Enter the product key. If you are installing the trial software, the product key is provided at the end of the download process.

4. Choose Basic or Advanced setup. Basic installs a standalone server using WID. The remaining steps assume Advanced.

5. Select the server type as shown in Figure 13-2. Once the installation is complete, setup starts the Configuration Wizard.

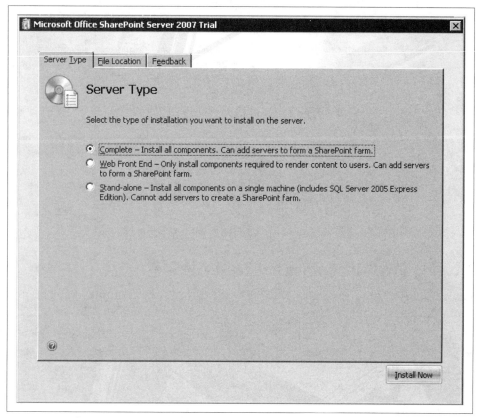

Figure 13-2. Choosing the server type in MOSS

Table 13-8 explains the MOSS server type choices.

Table 13-8. Choosing a MOSS server type

Server type	Use to
Complete	Start a server farm or install a standalone server that uses a separate SQL database. This is the most likely choice for new MOSS installations.
Web Front End	Add a server to an existing server farm. Use this installation to add servers after an initial Complete installation.
Stand-alone	Install SharePoint and its databases on the current server. This option is a single-server configuration and you *can't* add other SharePoint servers to the configuration database after installation. Use this installation for setting up a development environment or virtual PC image.

The SharePoint Configuration Wizard walks you through the remaining setup steps, which create the configuration database and install the Central Administration web site. Table 13-9 describes the steps.

Table 13-9. MOSS SharePoint Configuration Wizard steps

Step	Title	Explanation
1	None	Introduction to wizard.
2	Connect to a server farm	If this is a new install, click No. If you are adding this server to an existing installation, click Yes.
3	Specify Configuration Database Settings	This is the SQL Server and database name where information about SharePoint users and web applications is stored. The database access account is used to read from and write to the database. The database is created using your current account.
4	Configure SharePoint Central Administration Web Application	The Central Administration site uses a randomly generated port number by default. You can override that default to use a trusted port.
		You can also choose between NTLM and Kerberos authentication: use Kerberos if your Active Directory service is already set up to use Kerberos authentication, otherwise use NTLM.
5	Completing the SharePoint Products and Technologies Configuration Wizard	Confirms the settings you have chosen. To enable account creation mode, click Advanced Settings at this point.
6	Configuration Successful	Confirms that the wizard has completed setup and displays the settings that were used.

Creating a Web Application and Top-Level Site

Once the installation is complete, the Wizard displays the Central Administration site, which lists the remaining administrative tasks as shown in Figure 13-3.

Figure 13-3 is your confirmation that installation succeeded and that everything is working as expected. The task lists in Figure 13-3 walk you through the next steps on the server. If you chose the Web Front End or Complete installation options, you will also need to complete these major tasks:

- Configure MOSS services.
- Create a web application and top-level site.
- Enable MOSS shared services.

Setup automatically performs those tasks for basic and standalone installations. Skip the two MOSS tasks if you are only installing WSS.

To configure the MOSS services:

1. Click Operations → "Services on server" under the Topology and Services heading. SharePoint displays a list of the services that must be started before you can create sites as shown in Figure 13-4.

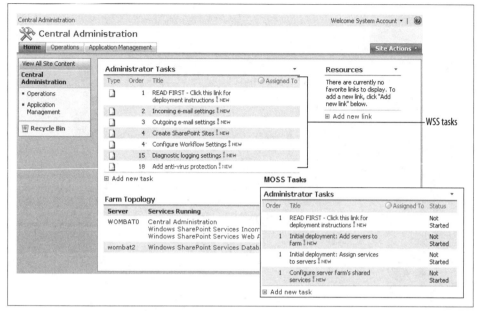

Figure 13-3. Remaining tasks after install

2. Select the server type and click Start on each of the required services. SharePoint displays a page for the database and user information used by each service. Complete each page and click OK to start the service.

3. Once the services are started, proceed to creating the web application and top-level web site.

Each MOSS service can run under a separate identity, and some services, such as Search, run on a specific schedule. You configure those settings to optimize security and performance, and you can change them later through the Operations tab as needed.

To create a new web application and top-level content site:

1. Click Application Management, and then click "Create or extend a Web application" under the SharePoint Web Application Management heading.

2. Click "Create a new Web application." SharePoint displays the Create New Web Application page.

3. Complete the page as shown in Figure 13-5 and click OK. SharePoint creates the new web application and displays an Application Created page when done.

4. Click Create Site Collection on the Application Create page to create a top-level site.

The template you choose for the top-level site is important since it is the entry point for all other web sites. The standard WSS configuration uses a Team Site template. The standard MOSS configuration uses the Collaboration Portal publishing template.

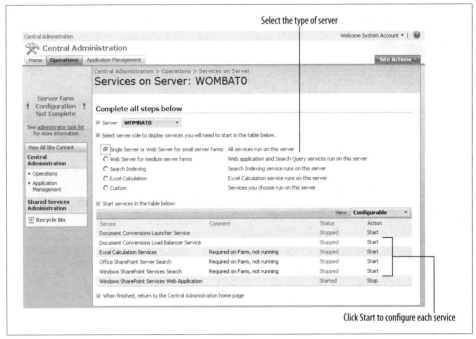

Figure 13-4. Configuring the MOSS Services before creating sites

After you create the top-level site, you should enable the shared services used by MOSS to provide My Sites and other services across the web farm. Creating the top-level site before this task lets you place the My Sites in the correct top-level site.

To enable the MOSS shared services:

1. Once the top-level site is created, click Shared Services Administration on the left side of the page, and then click New SSP on the toolbar. SharePoint displays the New Shared Services Provider page.

2. Complete the page as shown in Figure 13-6 and click OK. SharePoint creates a SSP site for the server farm. The default install uses MySite for the My Site redirect URL, and it is a good idea to use that same setting to avoid confusion later.

Once you create the SSP site, SharePoint removes the warning that configuration is not complete, and the MOSS services such as Business Data Catalog, cross-site search, Excel Services, and My Sites are enabled.

Removing SharePoint

Most SharePoint settings can be changed from the Central Administration site, but a few things, such as account creation mode in WSS, can only be enabled during installation. If you want to change those settings after installing, you need to uninstall, and then reinstall SharePoint.

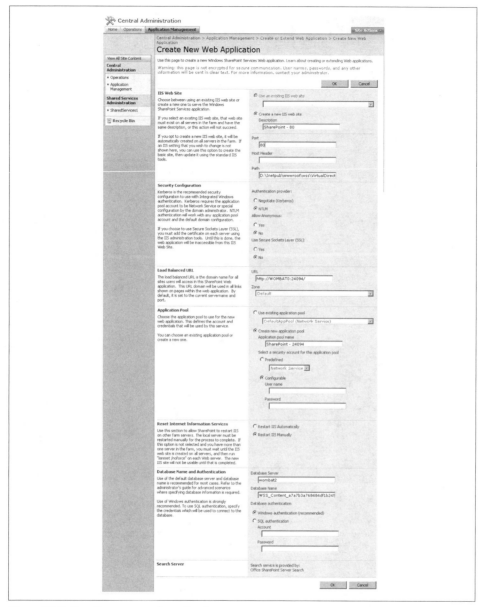

Figure 13-5. Creating a new web application

If you need to remove either WSS or MOSS at any point:

1. Rerun the setup program (*SharePoint.exe* or *OfficeServer.exe*).

2. Choose Remove, and click Continue. Setup uninstalls SharePoint.

3. Optionally, delete the configuration and content databases created on the server.

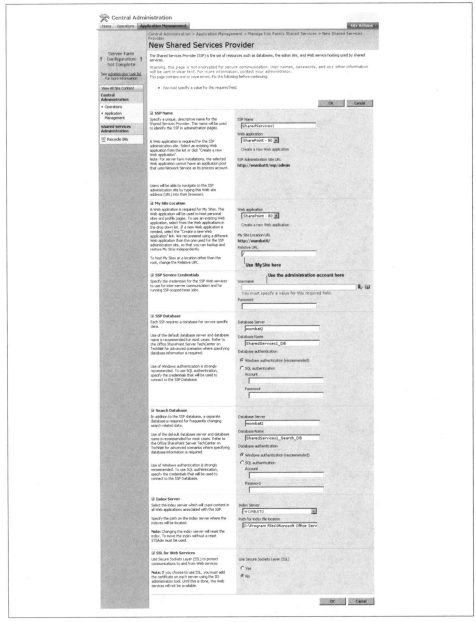

Figure 13-6. Creating the Shared Services Provider (SSP) site in MOSS

If you leave the databases in place, you can reinstall and reconnect to them later using a different server or a different configuration.

Enabling Internet Access

SharePoint is primarily used as an internal network for sharing information and collaborating on projects within an organization, but SharePoint sites can also be used across the Internet to access the same information from home or while traveling for work.

Before choosing to enable Internet access to your SharePoint sites, you should consider the security requirements of sharing documents across a public network. Not all documents are sensitive, but those that are may require encryption or IRM, or may be accessible only through HTTPS. Compare your current email controls to planned web access—are users allowed to send all documents as email attachments?

Your company probably has policies regulating how servers are connected to the outside world and how they are secured. You'll need to review that information and probably get approval before connecting a SharePoint server to the Internet. The following procedure outlines the process once you get that approval.

To connect a SharePoint server for access over the Internet:

1. Obtain a domain name from a domain name registrar such as GoDaddy.com or No-IP.com.

2. Add a DNS Host A record at the domain name registrar for each SharePoint web application you expose to Internet access. Web application use host headers to create subdomains, so you may have entries such as *www.somecompany.com, intranet.somecompany.com, extranet.somecompany.com,* as well as a top-level domain entry for *somcompany.com.*

3. Configure your network to assign the server a permanent IP address and to direct HTTP traffic (port 80) from your public IP address to the server. Make sure your firewall has port 80 open for the server.

4. Configure your SharePoint web application to use port 80 (the default) and the host header with the Host A record entered in step 2.

5. Create aliases for the server on your internal network so that *www, intranet,* and *extranet* all resolve to the server's IP address. That will direct internal traffic to the server where the host header will then resolve the web site to display.

6. Wait for the Host A record changes to propagate, and then verify external access to your web site.

7. Monitor access using the IIS logfiles (see "Auditing Activity," later in this chapter).

To host multiple web applications on a single server, use IIS host headers to provide friendly addresses. For example, a single server might host the web applications shown in Table 13-10.

Table 13-10. *Typical web applications and host headers on a single SharePoint server*

Address	Description	Authentication
http://www.somecompany.com	Public web site (may be SharePoint or conventional *.htm* files).	Anonymous; users don't have accounts.
http://extranet.somecompany.com	External SharePoint site for partners and others who need to upload or download documents in a secure way.	Forms-based; user accounts are stored in a database.
http://intranet.somecompany.com	Internal SharePoint site for employees.	Windows; users have AD accounts.
http://svr-web:12345	Central Administration site for SharePoint. This site doesn't have a friendly address because it is not widely available—instead it is hidden under an obscure port number.	Windows; users have AD accounts with Administrator privileges.

To add a host header to a SharePoint web application:

- Specify the host header when you create the web application (see Figure 13-5).

Or:

- Re-extend an existing web application to create an alternate access mapping.

An *alternate access mapping* defines a different URL (and namespace) for an existing SharePoint web application. In the previous version of SharePoint, you did that by adding host headers in the IIS manager. With SharePoint 2007, you must create an alternate access mapping through Central Administration to update the links throughout the site. You create alternate access mappings to:

- Add a host header to a web application that was originally created without one.

- Enable a different authentication mode, such as forms-based authentication, for a web application.

- Create zones to help manage the security policy for the web application.

To create an alternate access mapping for an existing web application:

1. Navigate to the Central Administration site, click Application Management, and then click "Create or extend a Web application" under the SharePoint Web Application Management heading.

2. Click "Extend an existing Web application." SharePoint displays the Extend Web Application to Another IIS Web Site page.

3. Select a web application, complete the page as shown in Figure 13-7, and click OK. SharePoint creates a new IIS web application and associates it with the existing SharePoint web application.

4. Copy the *web.config* file from the existing web application to the new web application so that the SafeControls and other settings are used by both web sites.

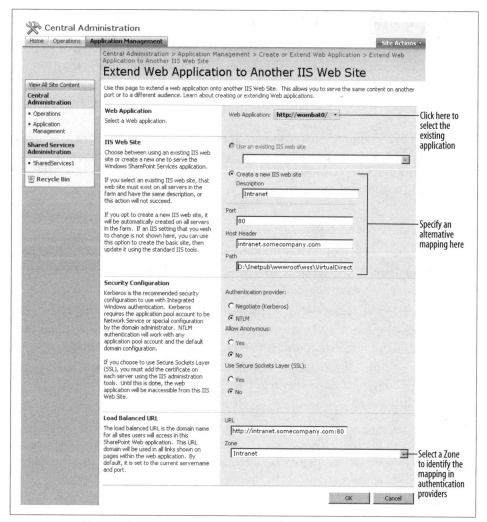

Figure 13-7. Adding an alternate access mapping

The IIS Web Site path in Figure 13-7 determines where the *web.config* file is stored. You can use the same path as the existing web application to avoid having to copy the file from the existing application to the new mapping; however, that file determines the authentication method used, so you'll want to have separate folders if you want to enable forms-based authentication later. You can change the path setting through the IIS manager later if you like—that setting is managed through IIS, not SharePoint.

Enabling Anonymous Access

In SharePoint, all users are authenticated. Internal users are authenticated by the network, and their credentials are used by SharePoint to determine what they can see and do. External users are prompted for their usernames and passwords when they first visit a SharePoint site. You can turn off that prompt by enabling anonymous access.

Anonymous access allows SharePoint to impersonate a built-in account administered by IIS. That account provides limited access to content within SharePoint. You enable anonymous access when you want to share the content in a site or library with the entire company or, if the server is connected to the Internet, the entire world.

To enable anonymous access:

1. Navigate to the Central Administration site.
2. Click Application Management, and then click "Authentication providers" under the Application Security heading.
3. Click the Default link, and then select "Enable anonymous access" and click Save.
4. Navigate to the top-level site and click Site Actions → Site Settings, and then click Advanced Permissions under the Users and Permissions heading.
5. On the toolbar, click Settings → Anonymous Access. SharePoint displays the Change Anonymous Access Settings page.
6. Select the level of access to allow and click OK.

Allowing anonymous access to the entire web site lets everyone view the home page and all lists and libraries that are not specifically restricted by unique permissions; allowing anonymous access to lists and libraries grants access to lists that are specifically enabled for anonymous access by unique permissions.

Allowing anonymous access to a top-level site causes all subsites that inherit permissions to also allow anonymous access. To prevent that:

1. Navigate to the subsite and click Site Actions → Site Settings, and then click Advanced Permissions under the Users and Permissions heading.
2. On the toolbar, click Settings → Edit Permissions, and click OK to stop inheriting permissions from the parent site.
3. On the toolbar, click Settings → Anonymous Access. SharePoint displays the Change Anonymous Access Settings page.
4. Select the level of access to allow and click OK.

Since each site collection has its own top-level site, anonymous access is not inherited across those boundaries. So, if you allow anonymous access to the top-level site in your web application, department sites—which reside in their own site collections—do not automatically allow anonymous access.

Enabling Forms-Based Authentication

By default, SharePoint web applications use Windows authentication. User credentials can be passed automatically from their network logon to SharePoint so employees aren't constantly prompted for their usernames and passwords. That's great if you have a domain account, but if you are an external partner working for another company, it can be tough.

SharePoint solves that problem by allowing web applications to use forms based authentication in addition to Windows authentication. With forms-based authentication, the usernames and passwords for external users are stored in a database rather than Active Directory.

To enable forms-based authentication, complete these tasks:

- Create an alternate access mapping for the web application.
- Create a database to store usernames, roles, and passwords.
- Edit the web application's *web.config* file to enable forms authentication.
- Edit the Central Administration site's *web.config* file to allow users to be found in the forms authentication database.
- Add users and roles to the database.
- Enable forms-based authentication for a zone within the web application.
- Grant the external users access to the web application zone.

See "Enabling Internet Access," earlier in this chapter, for instructions on creating an alternate access mapping. That task creates a zone for the web application that is accessed through a unique URL for external users. A web application can only have one authentication mode per zone, and each zone must have its own URL. For example, you might create an alternate access mapping for *extranet.somecompany.com* in the extranet zone.

To create the database to store usernames, roles, and passwords:

1. Log on to the SharePoint server as an Administrator.
2. Run the following commands (replace *dbserver* with the database server used by SharePoint):

   ```
   Path=%path%; C:\WINDOWS\Microsoft.NET\Framework\v2.0.50727
   aspnet_regsql -S dbserver -A all -E
   ```
3. The `aspnet_regsql` utility creates a database named `aspnetdb` to store user accounts for forms-based authentication.

To enable forms-based authentication in the extranet site:

1. Locate the web site's *web.config* file. By default it is stored in a subfolder of *C:\ Inetpub\wwwroot\wss\VirtualDirectories*.
2. Make a backup copy of the *web.config* file so you can restore the original settings if needed.

3. Open the *web.config* file and add connectionStrings, membership, and roleManager elements (shown later).

4. Save the file and display a page from the extranet site to verify that there are no errors in the *web.config* file. Even a minor typo will cause the web site to break!

The following abridged *web.config* file shows the changes to make to the extranet site. These changes are also available in the online samples:

```
<!-- Extranet web.config  -->
<configuration>
  <SharePoint>
    <!-- details omitted -->
  </SharePoint>
  <!-- JAW, 05/02/2007: Added for forms-based authentication. -->
  <connectionStrings>
    <add name="AspNetSqlProvider" connectionString="server=wombat2;
database=aspnetdb;
    Trusted_Connection=True" /> <!-- change wombat2 to your SQL server name -->
  </connectionStrings>
  <system.web>
    <!-- details omitted -->
    <!--JAW, 05/02/2007: Added for forms-based authentication -->
    <membership defaultProvider="AspNetSqlMembershipProvider">
      <providers>
        <remove name="AspNetSqlMembershipProvider" />
          <add connectionStringName="AspNetSqlProvider" passwordAttemptWindow="10"
          enablePasswordRetrieval="false" enablePasswordReset="true"
          requiresQuestionAndAnswer="true" applicationName="/"
requiresUniqueEmail="false"
          passwordFormat="Hashed" description="Stores and retrieves membership data
from the
          Microsoft SQL Server database" name="AspNetSqlMembershipProvider"
          type="System.Web.Security.SqlMembershipProvider, System.Web, Version=2.0.
3600.0,
          Culture=neutral, PublicKeyToken=b03f5f7f11d50a3a" />
      </providers>
    </membership>
    <roleManager enabled="true" defaultProvider="AspNetSqlRoleProvider">
      <providers>
        <remove name="AspNetSqlRoleProvider" />
        <add connectionStringName="AspNetSqlProvider" applicationName="/"
        description="Stores and retrieves roles data from the local Microsoft SQL
Server database"
        name="AspNetSqlRoleProvider" type="System.Web.Security.SqlRoleProvider,
System.Web,
        Version=2.0.3600.0, Culture=neutral, PublicKeyToken=b03f5f7f11d50a3a" />
      </providers>
    </roleManager>
    <!-- End change -->
  </system.web>
</configuration>
```

To enable forms-based authentication in the Central Administration site:

1. Repeat the preceding procedure for the Central Administration site, but change the `roleManager` element's `defaultProvider` to `AspNetWindowsTokenRoleProvider`.

2. Save the *web.config* file and display a Central Administration site page to verify the change.

The following shows the change to the `roleManager` element for the Central Administration site:

```
<!-- Central Administration web.config, note the difference from extranet web.config -->
<roleManager enabled="true" defaultProvider="AspNetWindowsTokenRoleProvider">
```

To add users to the database:

1. Create a new web application in Visual Studio.

2. Make the same changes to the new application's *web.config* file as you did for the SharePoint web application.

3. Change the authentication element in *web.config* to `Forms` as shown here:

```
<authentication mode="Forms" />
```

4. Click Website → ASP.NET Configuration, and then click Security. Visual Studio displays the ASP.NET Web Site Administration Tool as shown in Figure 13-8.

5. Click "Create user" to add users.

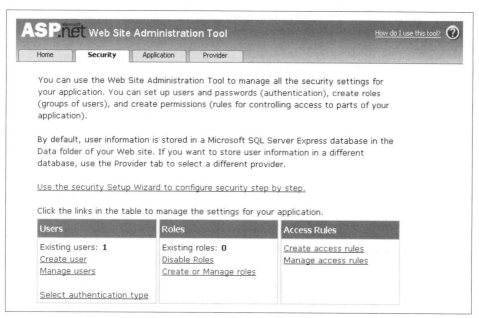

Figure 13-8. Use the Visual Studio Web Site Administration Tool to quickly add users

To enable forms-based authentication for the web application:

1. Navigate to the Central Administration site and click Application Management → Authentication providers. The alternate access mappings you created in the first task should appear as shown in Figure 13-9. If not, make sure the correct web application is selected.

2. Click on the zone name of the alternate mapping on which to enable forms-based authentication. SharePoint displays the Edit Authentication page.

3. Complete the page as shown in Figure 13-10 and click Save.

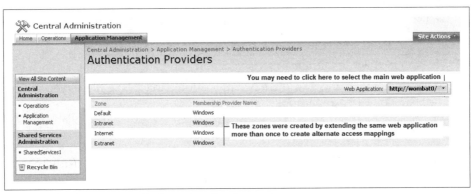

Figure 13-9. Selecting a zone for forms-based authentication

To grant external users access to this zone through forms-based authentication:

1. Click Application Management, and then click "Policy for Web application" under the Application Security heading.

2. Click Add Users on the toolbar. SharePoint displays the first step of the Add Users page.

3. Select the zone to add users to (Extranet, in this case), and click Next.

4. Type the names of the users you added to the *aspnetdb* database previously, select a Permission level, and click Finish (see Figure 13-11). SharePoint verifies that the users exist in the database and grants them access.

Once all of the tasks are complete, external users will see the SharePoint forms login screen when they access the extranet URL, as shown in Figure 13-12.

Using Zones

It's common to have both public and private information on SharePoint sites. To avoid confusing users, I usually create separate web applications for sites shared to the world (www), partners (extranet), and internal to the company (intranet).

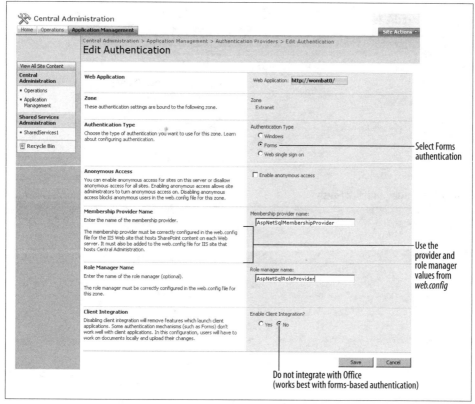

Figure 13-10. Enabling forms-based authentication for the extranet zone

All three may be available over the Internet; the separation is there to let users know that when they upload something to www or extranet, folks outside the company can see it; and when they upload to the intranet, it is shared only within the company.

In that scenario, I create separate web applications with their own content databases and unique permissions. That separation is easy to understand, but it sometimes requires that files be copied from one web site to another.

You can avoid that by using zones to create different views of a single web application. Figure 13-9 shows a single web application (*wombat0*) with zones for Intranet, Internet, and Extranet. Each zone has its own URL used to access it, but the zones all map to the same web application and content.

Each zone can have its own set of members, security policy, and even authentication mode, which effectively lets you create a different experience for each entry point. Table 13-11 summarizes how that works for the zones shown in Figure 13-9.

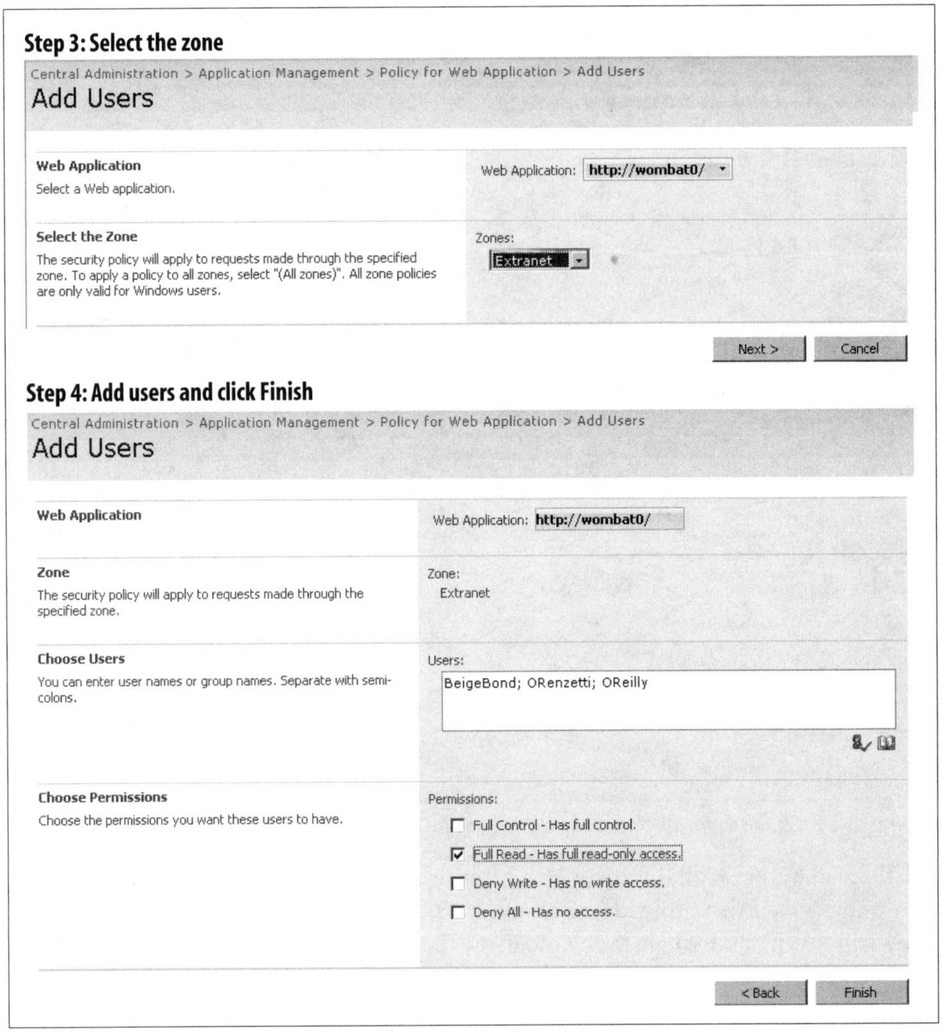

Step 3: Select the zone

Central Administration > Application Management > Policy for Web Application > Add Users

Add Users

| **Web Application** | Web Application: **http://wombat0/** ▾ |
| Select a Web application. | |

| **Select the Zone** | Zones: |
| The security policy will apply to requests made through the specified zone. To apply a policy to all zones, select "(All zones)". All zone policies are only valid for Windows users. | Extranet ▾ |

`Next >`   `Cancel`

Step 4: Add users and click Finish

Central Administration > Application Management > Policy for Web Application > Add Users

Add Users

| **Web Application** | Web Application: **http://wombat0/** |

| **Zone** | Zone: |
| The security policy will apply to requests made through the specified zone. | Extranet |

| **Choose Users** | Users: |
| You can enter user names or group names. Separate with semi-colons. | BeigeBond; ORenzetti; OReilly |

Choose Permissions	Permissions:
Choose the permissions you want these users to have.	☐ Full Control - Has full control.
	☑ Full Read - Has full read-only access.
	☐ Deny Write - Has no write access.
	☐ Deny All - Has no access.

`< Back`   `Finish`

Figure 13-11. Granting users access to the forms-based zone

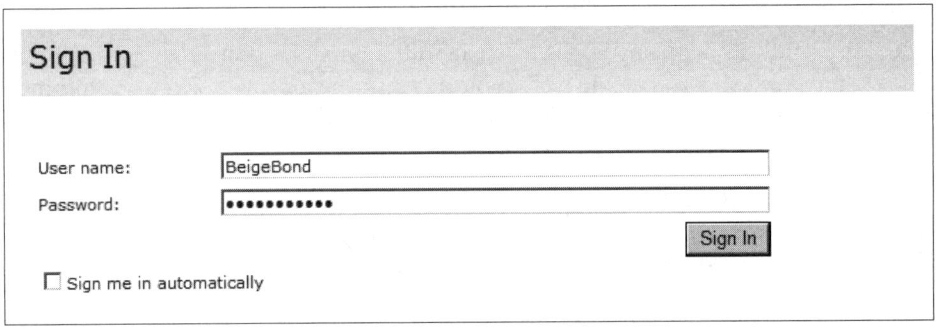

Sign In

| User name: | BeigeBond |
| Password: | •••••••••• |

`Sign In`

☐ Sign me in automatically

Figure 13-12. Logging in using forms-based authentication

Table 13-11. Using zones to create different experiences for a single web application

Zone	URL (entry point)	Login	Experience
Internet	*http://www.essentialsharepoint.com*	None; Windows authentication with anonymous access enabled	Everyone can view sites, but no one can add or change information or settings (deny write policy).
Extranet	*http://extranet.essentialsharepoint.com*	Forms-based	External partners can view information and contribute in a limited way.
Intranet	*http://intranet.essentialsharepoint.com*	Windows integrated; log on is automatic within LAN	Employees can view and contribute as permitted.

Zones let you expose the same content to different sets of users who are authenticated using different mechanisms. To create a zone, follow the steps for creating an alternate access mapping in "Enabling Internet Access," earlier in this chapter. Zones, alternate access mappings, authentication methods, and security policies are interrelated, so the "Enabling Internet Access, "Enabling Anonymous Access," and "Enabling Forms-Based Authentication" sections all apply to zones.

 Zones are a new concept with SharePoint 2007, so I encourage you to do a proof-of-concept web application on a staging server before you decide to implement them.

Enabling Self-Service Site Creation

By default, only SharePoint Administrators with access to the Central Administration web site can create new site collections. To allow others to create new site collections, enable self-service site creation. To do that:

1. Navigate to the Central Administration site, click Application Management, and then click "Self-service site management" under the Application Security heading.

2. Complete the page, as shown in Figure 13-13, and click OK.

Enabling self-service site creation adds an announcement with a link to the *scsignup.aspx* page in WSS, but not in MOSS. To help users find the page in MOSS:

1. Navigate to the top-level site in MOSS.

2. Click Site Actions → Site Settings → Modify All Site Settings, and then click "Site directory settings" under the Site Collection Administration heading.

3. Complete the page, as shown in Figure 13-14, and click OK.

Enabling site collections in the MOSS site directory changes the Create Site link on the MOSS Sites tab from "Creating a new subsite" to "Creating a new site collection." Subsites inherit their permissions from the parent site and so are a little easier to use.

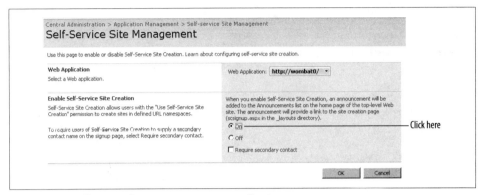

Figure 13-13. Allowing others to create new site collections

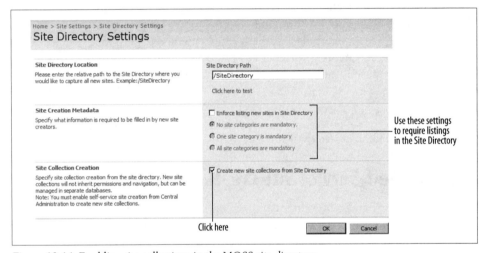

Figure 13-14. Enabling site collections in the MOSS site directory

Site collections have unique permissions, can be stored in separate databases, and are administered independently from other sites, so they offer more control.

Scheduling Backups

Use the Central Administration site to back up SharePoint databases manually. SharePoint stores content and configuration data in separate databases, so you must use the SharePoint tools rather than the tools provided with SQL Server.

To perform a manual backup:

1. Navigate to the Central Administration site, click Operations, and then click "Perform a backup" under the Backup and Restore heading.

2. Select the item to back up and click Continue to Backup Options on the toolbar.

3. Select Full or Differential backup, specify a location for the backup, and click OK. SharePoint displays the Backup and Restore Status page.

4. SharePoint updates the status page as the backup is performed and shows the Phase as Completed when the backup is finished.

The WSS Administration and Timer services must be running in order to perform the backup. If the backup doesn't start after a few minutes, open the Microsoft Management Console (MMC) to make sure those services are running.

There is no built-in way schedule the backup process using the SharePoint timer job, so to create a backup process that runs automatically you must:

1. Create a command script that uses the `stsadm` utility.

2. Schedule the script to run using Windows Scheduled Tasks.

For example, the following command script performs a full backup on the current server, saves the files on the *\\wombat0\spbackups* share, and logs the progress of the backup in a logfile:

```
REM sts_backup.cmd
path = %path%;C:\Program Files\Common Files\Microsoft Shared\web server extensions\
12\BIN
stsadm -o backup -directory \\wombat0\spbackups -backupmethod full
```

To schedule the preceding script to run nightly:

1. Log on to the SharePoint server as an Administrator.

2. Click Start → All Programs → Accessories → System Tools → Scheduled Tasks. Windows opens the Scheduled Tasks window.

3. Click Add Scheduled Task. Windows starts the Scheduled Task Wizard.

4. Click Next → Browse and select the backup script. Specify a schedule for the task, when to run it, an identity to run under, and click Finish, as shown in Figure 13-15.

The backup script writes folders to the backup location. Each folder contains the backup files, a log of the backup, and an XML description of the backup. You'll need to periodically archive and delete old backups to avoid running out of storage space.

You can also use `stsadm` to back up individual site collections. For example, the following command line backs up the top-level site collection:

```
stsadm -o backup -url http://wombat0 -filename wombat0root.bak —overwrite
```

You can use site collection backups to protect against errors when performing global tasks or to archive the state of a site before deleting subsites or reorganizing the site.

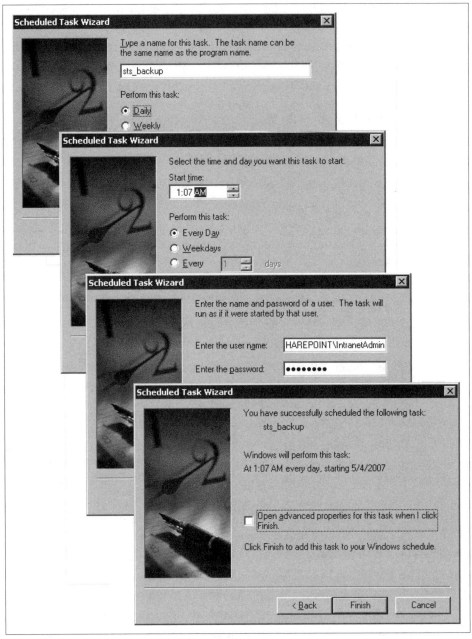

Figure 13-15. Scheduling the backup script to run nightly

Restoring

Use the Central Administration site to restore from backups made manually. Use the `stsadm` utility to restore from scheduled backups. You can't use the Central Administration site to restore from a `stsadm` backup.

If restoring after a catastrophic failure, you will need to perform these tasks before restoring:

- Restore the configuration database from SQL Server. Backup saves the configuration database, but it must be restored from SQL Server.
- Reinstall custom solutions.
- Rebuild alternate access mappings (if any).
- Recreate the IIS metabase.

To restore from the Central Administration site:

1. Click Operations and then click "Restore from backup" under the Backup and Restore heading.
2. Select the location where the manual backups were stored and click OK. This should be the folder containing the *spbrtoc.xml* file.
3. Select the backup to restore and click Continue Restore Process on the toolbar. SharePoint displays a list of the items that you can restore from the backup.
4. Select the items to restore and click Continue Restore Process. SharePoint displays a set of restore options.
5. Select "New configuration" to create a new database or "Same configuration" to overwrite the existing database. Click OK to begin restoring.

To restore from a scheduled backup, use the `stsadm` command. For example, the following command line performs a full restore from a folder in backups:

```
stsadm -o restore -directory \\wombat0\spbackups\spbr0003 -restoremethod overwrite
```

To restore a single site collection, use a command line similar to this:

```
stsadm -o restore -url http://wombat0 -filename wombat0root.bak –overwrite
```

Auditing Activity

SharePoint and IIS keep logs of user activity and server events. You can use those logs to get reports on site usage, find out who made changes at specific times, and diagnose problems on the server.

To enable reporting on general site usage:

1. Navigate to the Central Administration site.

2. Click Operations and then click "Usage analysis processing" under the Logging and Reporting heading.

3. Select "Enable logging" and specify an easy-to-find folder. By default, Share-Point stores logfiles in the application folder, but it is more convenient to put all of the logfiles together in a single folder for each web application.

4. Click "Enable usage analysis processing," select a time to process the information, and click OK.

If you are using MOSS, you should also enable advanced usage logging. To do that:

1. Click the Shared Services site link in the Central Administration site.

2. Click "Usage reporting" under the Office SharePoint Usage Reporting heading.

3. Select "Enable advanced usage analysis processing" and click OK.

The usage analysis reports are not available until after they are processed. Once they are complete, you can view usage data for the 30 days of history. To view usage reports in WSS:

- Click Site Action → Site Settings, and then click "Site usage report" under the Site Administration heading.

To view usage reports in MOSS:

1. Click Site Action → Site Settings → Modify All Site Settings, and then click "Site usage report" under the Site Administration heading.

2. For more detailed information, click Back, and then click "Audit log reports" under the Site Collection Administration heading.

The MOSS Audit log reports provide detailed analysis of different types of activity within the site collection. The standard usage reports simply show which pages were viewed by day, month, or user. Both reports are historical; you can get a list of current activity by looking directly at the IIS logs.

IIS stores its logs in the system *LogFiles* folder. I like to change that to a more obvious location so I can find all of a web application's logfiles easily. To change the location of the IIS logs:

1. Log on to the server as an Administrator.

2. Create a folder for the IIS logs for each web application on your server. For example: *D:\MOSS\Logs\Wombat0*.

3. Open the IIS Manager, right-click on the web application and select Properties.

4. On the Web Site tab, click Properties and change the logfile directory to the folder created in step 2.

5. Click OK twice to close the dialog boxes.

6. Repeat steps 4 and 5 for each of the web applications on the server.

Writing IIS logfiles to a well-named folder helps you identify them—otherwise, they are assigned a cryptic title that means little. IIS creates detailed activity logs, and you can see who requested what and how long it took the server to respond.

The IIS logs aren't easy to read, but they can really help you track down actions by specific users. For example, to find out who deleted a site, open the logfile and search for *deleteweb.aspx*. You can see who visited that page (GET) and whether they deleted the site (POST).

To diagnose problems on the server, use the Application event logs to watch for errors. To see the Application event log:

1. Log on to the server as an Administrator.

2. Click Start → Administrative Tools → Computer Management. Window runs the MMC.

3. Expand the Event Viewer and click Application to see the application events, as shown in Figure 13-16.

4. Double-click on an event to see its details.

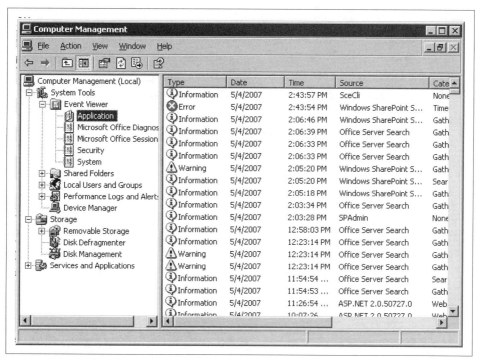

Figure 13-16. Looking for errors on the server

The Application Event log in Figure 13-16 shows activity by the services running on the server. Services are written to be somewhat fault-tolerant, so they may report an error and then soldier on with other tasks. Don't be alarmed by a few errors in the Application Event log—that's often normal. Do be concerned if you see the same error reported over and over in quick succession; that's definitely a symptom of something gone wrong.

Enabling PDFs and Other File Types

SharePoint does not include built-in support for file types invented by other companies such as Adobe PDF files. That means that by default, Search does not look inside PDF files, and when you upload a PDF file it doesn't appear with the correct icon.

To enable search within PDF files:

1. Download the PDF text filter (*ifilter60.exe*) from *http://www.adobe.com/support/downloads/detail.jsp?ftpID=2611*.
2. Run *ifilter60.exe* to install the filter on the server.

To add the PDF icon to SharePoint:

1. Download the PDF icon file from *http://www.adobe.com/images/pdficon.gif*.
2. Save the file to this folder on the server:

    C:\Program Files\Common Files\Microsoft Shared\web server extensions\12\TEMPLATE\IMAGES

3. Edit the *DOCICON.XML* file found in this folder on the server:

    C:\Program Files\Common Files\Microsoft Shared\web server extensions\12\TEMPLATE\XML

4. Add the following line to the <ByExtension> element:

    ```
    <Mapping Key="pdf" Value="pdficon.gif" OpenControl=""/>
    ```

5. Save and close *DOCICON.XML*.
6. Run *iisreset.exe* to load the changes.

You can use the same technique to enable Search and add icons for other file types. In each case, the filter and icon comes from the originator of the file type, however, since it owns the file format.

Best Practices

- If you are using WID in WSS or MOSS installation, click the Location tab during setup (refer to Figures 13-1 or 13-2) to set the location of the database file. Install the database on a drive with plenty of room. This is hard (or impossible) to change after installation.
- Use the Team Site template for the top-level site in a custom WSS installation.
- Use the Collaboration Site template for the top-level site in a custom MOSS installation.
- For optimal performance, use a single application pool for all SharePoint web applications.

Upgrading

There are three different approaches to upgrading an existing WSS 2.0 or SharePoint Portal Server 2003 installation to WSS 3.0 or MOSS 2007, which can be summarized as follows:

For this type of installation	Use this recommended approach
Small deployment with few customizations	In-place upgrade
Large deployment with customizations	Side-by-side (gradual) upgrade
Farm deployment with hardware upgrade	Database migration

Table A-1 lists the differences between each approach.

Table A-1. Approaches to upgrading

Approach	Description	Advantages	Disadvantages
In-place	Sites are replaced with new version.	• Simple • Site URLs don't change	• Can't be undone • Sites are offline during upgrade
Side-by-side	Both versions of SharePoint run on the server and site collections are moved one at a time.	• Can revert if needed • Reduces time sites are offline	• Site URLs may be different during upgrade
Database migration	Content databases are copied and then upgraded in place.	• Can revert if needed • Minimizes time offline • Allows deployment to new hardware	• Complex • Site URLs may be different during upgrade

Before You Upgrade

Before you upgrade, complete these tasks:

- Review your hardware to verify that there is enough disk space for the type of upgrade you are planning.
- Review your existing SharePoint installation to verify that it is up-to-date.

- Run the pre-upgrade scan tool (*PRESCAN.EXE*) to find custom site definitions and customized (unghosted) pages.
- Perform a trial upgrade of one or more site collections.
- Review upgrade issues and plan corrective actions based on the trial upgrade.
- Communicate upgrade plans with users, explaining downtime and other issues.

The following sections discuss each of these tasks in more detail.

Reviewing Hardware

Your hardware must meet the requirements listed in Chapter 13 in order to install and run SharePoint. In general, hardware running the previous version of SharePoint works fine with the new version.

If you are performing a side-by-side upgrade, you'll need sufficient disk space on the SQL server to accommodate duplicate content databases for the site collections as they are upgraded. Microsoft recommends having free disk space greater than or equal to three times the size of the largest content database.

If you cannot free enough space, reduce the size of the content databases by performing one or more of these tasks:

- Clean up existing sites: delete unused sites, unneeded lists and libraries, and unneeded documents.
- Remove document library version history if possible: archive document libraries with version history and then remove versioning from those libraries.
- Break up content databases: move site collections into separate content databases. Search *www.microsoft.com* for "SharePoint Utility Suite" to get the tools needed to move site collections to new databases.

Microsoft also cites some thresholds that might cause problems with upgrading:

- Document libraries with over 250,000 files in the root folder might take a very long time to upgrade. Microsoft recommends moving files into folders with no more than 2,000 documents per folder.
- Content databases over 100 GB might take a very long time to upgrade. Microsoft recommends breaking databases that large into several smaller ones. If the content database is a single site collection, you'll need to divide it into several site collections.

Reviewing Your Existing Installation

The server you are planning to upgrade should be running the latest service pack and hotfixes. At minimum, SP2 and the June 1, 2006 hotfix should be installed since that hotfix includes that `stsadm databaserepair` command used later in the upgrade process.

The application pool used by the existing SharePoint web applications should use an identity with access to the SQL database server. By default, WSS 2.0 used the Network Service built-in account for application pools. It is better to use a domain account created specifically for the SharePoint services because that helps you identify the processes used by SharePoint.

Finally, existing installations that use localhost as the database server are very difficult to upgrade. You should make sure the database name used by the SharePoint content and configuration databases is the explicit server name—even if it is the same as the current server. You may need to detach and reattach the database in WSS 2.0 in order to change this.

Running Prescan

The *PRESCAN.EXE* utility is installed with WSS 3.0 in the following folder:

```
C:\Program Files\Common Files\Microsoft Shared\web server extensions\12\BIN
```

If you installed SharePoint to a staging server as I recommended in earlier chapters, you can copy *PRESCAN.EXE* and *preupradescanconfig.xml* to the production server and run it. You don't need to install the new SharePoint version on the production server at this point.

Prescan checks for errors, orphaned lists and libraries, and customizations that may need additional work after the upgrade. All prescan errors must be resolved before you can upgrade a web application.

To scan a WSS 2.0 web application:

1. Run *PRESCAN.EXE* from the command line. For example:

    ```
    prescan /v http://www.somecompany.com
    ```

2. Review the logfiles created by prescan. The files are written to the user profile *Temp* folder.

3. If prescan reports errors, run the `stsadm databaserepair` command. For example:

    ```
    stsadm -o databaserepair -url http://www.somecompany.com -databasename WSS_
    Content01 -deletecorruption
    ```

4. Run prescan to verify that the database errors are resolved.

5. Repeat steps 3 and 4 until prescan completes without errors.

To scan a SharePoint Portal Server 2003 web application:

1. Run *PRESCAN.EXE* and include the *preupradescanconfig.xml* configuration file in the command line. For example:

    ```
    prescan /c preupradescanconfig.xml /v http://www.somecompany.com
    ```

2. Review the logfiles created by prescan. The files are written to the user profile *Temp* folder.

3. If prescan reports errors, run the `stsadm databaserepair` command. For example:

```
stsadm -o databaserepair -url http://www.somecompany.com -databasename WSS_
Content01 -deletecorruption
```

4. If prescan reports errors in the configuration database, run the `spsadm repairorphans` command. For example:

```
spsadm repairorphans http://www.somecompany.com
```

5. Run prescan to verify that the errors are resolved.

6. Repeat steps 3 through 5 until prescan completes without errors.

The configuration file helps prescan identify the built-in portal server site definitions. Otherwise, they are all flagged as custom site definitions.

Save the final prescan report file. It includes the addresses of customized (unghosted) pages that you should review once the upgrade is complete.

Performing a Trial Upgrade

It's a good idea to do a trial upgrade of a typical site collection or web application if possible. This will give you an idea of how long the process takes and help shake out any problems before you upgrade the production server. Plus, it gives you confidence that you know what you're doing before you have impatient users waiting to get back online.

If you have a staging server configured, you can perform the trial upgrade there to avoid any disruption with the production environment. In fact, you might consider using the staging server as a way to upgrade sites offline and then move them to production from staging.

To configure your staging server for a trial upgrade:

1. Uninstall the 2007 version of SharePoint.

2. Install WSS 2.0 (*stsv2.exe*) and service pack 2 (*WSS2003SP2-KB887624-FullFile-ENU.exe*).

3. Create a web application in IIS and extend it using the WSS 2.0 Central Administration site. Do not create a top-level web site at this time.

4. On the production server, use the WSS 2.0 *smigrate.exe* utility to make a backup copy of the web application to upgrade. For example:

```
smigrate -w http://www.somecompany.com -f somecompany.fwp -e -u user -pw password
```

5. Copy the *.fwp* files to the staging server and use the *smigrate.exe* utility to install the web site at the web application you created in step 3. For example:

```
smigrate -r -w http://www.somecompany.com -f somecompany.fwp
```

6. Verify that the new web site works under WSS 2.0.

To perform the trial upgrade on the staging server:

1. Install WSS 3.0 (*SharePoint.exe*). You must install WSS 3.0 with WSS 2.0 already installed to get the upgrade options during installation. Choose the Gradual upgrade option as shown in Figure A-1 during setup.

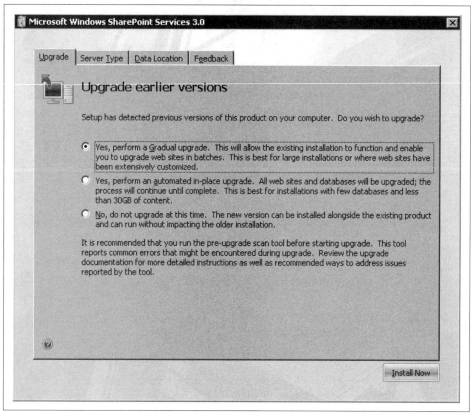

Figure A-1. Choose the Gradual upgrade option when reinstalling WSS 3.0 on the staging server

2. Configure the WSS 3.0 installation to use the database server used by the production SharePoint server if possible.

3. Navigate to the WSS 3.0 Central Administration site and click Operations → "Site content upgrade status" under the Upgrade and Migration heading. SharePoint displays the Site Content Upgrade Status page with the site you created in the preceding procedure. If the site does not appear, verify that prescan succeeded, run *iisreset.exe*, and refresh the page.

4. Click the link next to the site to upgrade. SharePoint displays the Set Target Web Application page.

5. Complete the page, as shown in Figure A-2. Be sure to use an application pool that is separate from the application pool used by the WSS 2.0 version.

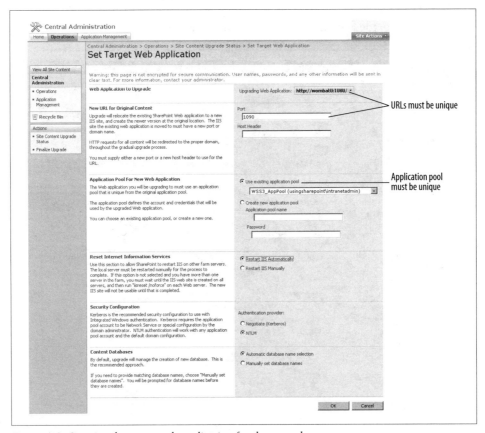

Figure A-2. Creating the target web application for the upgrade

6. Click OK when done. SharePoint displays the Sites Selected for Upgrade page.
7. Click Upgrade Sites. SharePoint creates a timer job to perform the upgrade and displays the Upgrade Running page, as shown in Figure A-3.

SharePoint updates the page shown in Figure A-3 as the job progresses and displays a job failed message if there is a problem with the upgrade. If the job fails, review the *Update.log* file in the following folder:

C:\Program Files\Common Files\Microsoft Shared\web server extensions\12\LOGS

Fix the problem and resume the update from the Content Upgrade Status page (step 3).

If you used the production database server in step 2, you can deploy the upgraded web site simply by creating a new web application on the production SharePoint server and attaching it to the upgraded content database. You'll want to verify that the site is working correctly before you do that, but I mention it here as a deployment option.

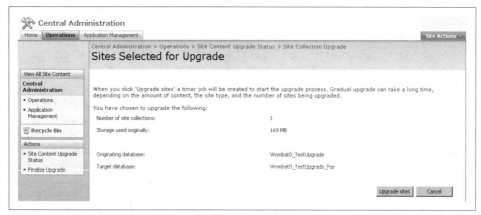

Figure A-3. Viewing the upgrade status

Reviewing Upgrade Issues

Once the trial upgrade is complete, open the upgraded web site in the browser and verify that the pages display correctly. Table A-2 lists the common problems you are likely to encounter along with their corrective actions.

If you are working from a trial upgrade, record the steps that you take at this point so you can repeat them smoothly once you upgrade the production server. Most of these issues relate to customizations. The more deeply you customize your sites, the more issues you will encounter.

Table A-2. Upgrade issues and corrective actions

Issue	Corrective action
Administrators get Access Denied errors browsing sites	Grant Administrators Full Control by adding them through the policy settings. In Central Administration, click Application Management → Policy for Web application → Add Users.
Site branding is lost	Reapply branding using Master Pages and/or an alternate cascading style sheet (CSS). See Chapter 6.
Themes are lost	Apply a new theme. Click Site Settings → Site theme.
Pages modified in FrontPage 2003 don't work correctly	Reset the pages and then recreate the changes using SharePoint Designer 2007. To reset a page, click Site Settings → "Reset to site definition" and enter the URL of the page to revert. See Chapters 4, 6, and 9 for information on working with SharePoint Designer.
Resetting the custom page fails	New pages created by FrontPage 2003 aren't associated with the site template and so can't be reset.
Hardcoded URLs no longer work	The URL's portal areas (C2, for example) are changed during the upgrade process; search for these types of hard-coded links and correct them. Links created by SharePoint are automatically updated; this only applies to hardcoded links.
Sites based on customize site definitions don't work	Create a new site definition for WSS 3.0, and then create an upgrade definition file so the upgrade process can map your old site definition elements to the new site definition. For instructions, search *www.microsoft.com* for the article titled "Develop new custom site definitions and create upgrade definition files."

Table A-2. Upgrade issues and corrective actions (continued)

Issue	Corrective action
Customized InfoPath form libraries don't work	Support for InfoPath form libraries has changed to document libraries. Rebuild your InfoPath form libraries using that approach.
Custom Alert messages are lost	The custom messages are preserved, but you must manually transfer the message file to the new path. See the `stsadm updatealerttemplates` command in Appendix B.
Custom web parts don't appear	Web parts deployed to */bin* have to be redeployed on the new web application. Web parts installed in the GAC should still work.
Rendered web parts developed for WSS 2.0 no longer work	Most web parts should still work, however they may need to be recompiled if they are heavily obfuscated.
Rendered web parts still don't work	Some web parts may rely on resources that have changed or moved in the new version. You will need to debug the web part. See Chapter 11.
Some files no longer appear	The file extensions *.asmx*, *.rem*, *.resx*, *.soap*, and *.ashx* were added to the blocked files list. To allow those file extensions, open Central Administration and click Operations → Blocked file types.

Preparing Users

Upgrading SharePoint sites will take the sites offline at least briefly even with the most careful planning. That usually isn't an issue if users have forewarning and if the upgrade is performed during a quiet time.

More importantly, the user interface and Office integration features of SharePoint changed from 2003 to 2007. There are new features and site templates available, so it is best to provide some training when rolling out the upgraded web sites. If users are already familiar with SharePoint, they will pick up the new system quickly—it's just best to be ahead of the curve.

Performing an In-Place Upgrade

The in-place upgrade is best for site collections smaller than 30 GB with few customizations. It is simple, but less flexible than the other approaches. It also takes the web applications offline during the upgrade process, which may or may not be OK.

To perform an in-place upgrade:

1. Perform a full backup of the content and configuration database, as well as the IIS metabase, and the web application folders. This assures that you can recover your system if there is a catastrophic failure.

2. Run *PRESCAN.EXE /all*. Prescan must succeed without errors for the upgrade process to work.

3. Install SharePoint (*SharePoint.exe*) on the server and select the "Automated in-place upgrade" (refer to Figure A-1).

4. SharePoint begins the upgrade process.

5. Once the upgrade is complete, review the web sites to verify that they work correctly.

6. Optionally uninstall the previous version of SharePoint from the server.

Performing a Side-by-Side Upgrade

The side-by-side upgrade is best for site collections larger than 30 GB, and may be required in situations where the upgrade might fail because of disk space issues on the database server.

If you host multiple web applications, as most of us do, the side-by-side upgrade process lets you upgrade web applications one at a time to provide training and ease the transition. You can also upgrade individual site collections within a web application, but since the top-level site must be upgraded first, that scenario seems somewhat rare.

To perform a side-by-side upgrade:

1. Perform a full backup of the content and configuration databases.

2. Run *PRESCAN.EXE /all*. Prescan must succeed without errors for the source web applications to appear in the Site Content Upgrade Status page in Central Administration.

3. Install WSS 3.0 (*SharePoint.exe*) on the production server. Choose the Gradual upgrade option during setup (see Figure A-1).

4. Configure the SharePoint installation to use production database server and email settings.

5. If using MOSS, install it at this point by running *OfficeServer.exe*. You must install WSS before installing MOSS when performing an upgrade.

6. Navigate to the WSS 3.0 Central Administration site and click Operations → "Site content upgrade status" under the Upgrade and Migration heading.

7. Click the link next to the site to upgrade. SharePoint displays the Set Target Web Application page. Complete the page discussed earlier in "Performing a Trial Upgrade" (refer to Figure A-2).

8. Click OK when you're done. SharePoint displays the Sites Selected for Upgrade page.

9. Click Upgrade Sites. SharePoint creates a job and begins the upgrade.

While the upgrade is in process, requests for the original site are automatically redirected to a temporary address that hosts the pre-upgrade site. Once the upgrade is complete, the redirect is removed and the upgraded site is displayed.

Review the upgraded web sites for issues you uncovered when performing your trial upgrade. If you skipped that step, see "Reviewing Upgrade Issues," earlier in this appendix.

Performing a Database Migration

The database migration upgrade is best when you are changing hardware as well as upgrading SharePoint. For example, if both SharePoint and SQL Server are hosted on the same server, you can use this approach to move the content database to a dedicated SQL Server for better performance. (SharePoint and SQL Server compete for memory, so using a dedicated SQL Server usually results in better performance.)

Database migration is also the way to go if you want to leave the existing web application in place after upgrade process. Using this process, you can host both the pre- and post-upgrade web applications on the same server. To switch from one to the other, you simply stop one web application in IIS and start the other. You can even use the same URL for both web applications as long as only one is running at a time.

To perform a database migration:

1. Run *PRESCAN.EXE* on the web application to upgrade. Prescan must succeed without errors in order to be able to upgrade the web application.
2. Set the web application's content database to read-only to prevent changes during the upgrade process.
3. Copy the existing content database to a new database.
4. Create a new WSS 2.0 web application and attach the copied content databases to that web application. You can do this on your staging server if you have one.
5. Verify that the new web application works as expected.
6. Upgrade the new WSS 2.0 web application to WSS 3.0. You can use the in-place or side-by-side upgrade procedure.
7. Create a new WSS 3.0 web application and attach it to the upgraded database created by step 7. If you performed the upgrade on a staging server, you'll want to create this new web application on the production server. To use the same URL as the original web application, stop the existing web application in IIS before creating the WSS 3.0 web application in Central Administration.
8. Re-establish the security settings for the upgraded web application.

Completing the Upgrade Process

Once all upgrades are complete, you can remove the upgrade options by clicking Operations → "Finalize upgrade" in Central Administration. That prevents you from upgrading additional sites in the future, so only do it when you are absolutely sure you are done.

Upgrading 2007 Editions

Upgrading between SharePoint 2007 editions is straightforward. There are only a couple of issues worth mentioning, included here in the interest of completeness.

To upgrade from WSS 3.0 to MOSS:

- Run *OfficeServer.exe*. The setup process installs the additional web parts, templates, and services. See Chapter 13 for information about installation options.

Once MOSS is installed, you may want to replace your top-level web site with a new site based on the Collaboration Portal site template, which is the default template for most MOSS installations. To do that:

1. Copy the existing top-level site collection to a new location.
2. Navigate to the Central Administration site and click Application Management → Delete Site Collection to delete the existing top-level site collection.
3. Click "Create site collection" and create a new top-level site collection using the Collaboration Portal template found on the Publishing tab of the site template list.
4. Create the new top-level site collection from Central Administration.

To upgrade from MOSS Standard Edition to Enterprise Edition:

1. Navigate to the Central Administration site and click Operations → Enable Enterprise Features under the Upgrade and Migration heading.
2. Select Enterprise and click OK.

Setup installs the full version MOSS no matter which edition you initially choose. The features are simply enabled or disabled based on your license key.

If you need to uninstall SharePoint from a server that has both WSS 3.0 and MOSS installed, you must uninstall MOSS first, then WSS 3.0. If the server was upgraded from WSS 2.0, you will need to uninstall WSS 2.0 *before* uninstalling MOSS.

APPENDIX B

Reference Tables

Office Versions

SharePoint works with Office versions 2000 to 2007. However, the feature sets vary a great deal among these versions. Basically, all versions allow you to save and open files from SharePoint sites through the browser; 2002 supports some integration (export list to spreadsheet); and 2003 provides full integration through the Shared Documents task pane. Table B-1 further details Microsoft Office version compatibility.

Table B-1. Microsoft Office version compatibility

Product	Feature	Office version			
		2000	2002	2003	2007
All	Save and open files from SharePoint sites	X	X	X	X
	Shared Workspace task pane			X	X
	Document updates for shared attachments			X	X
	View and edit a shared attachment	X	X	X	X
	Create new documents in web browser		X	X	X
	Collect metadata automatically			X	X
	Promote and demote file properties and metadata automatically	Limited	X	X	X
	Track document versions			X	X
	Check out and check in documents			X	X
	Manage Microsoft Project documents, risks, and issues			X	X
	Upload multiple documents			X	X
	Inline discussions	X	X	X	X
	Microsoft Office Components for SharePoint			X	X
	Person Names Smart Tag			X	X
	Integration with Microsoft Business Solutions			X	X

Table B-1. Microsoft Office version compatibility (continued)

Product	Feature	Office version			
		2000	2002	2003	2007
	Shared attachments			X	X
	Create Document Workspace sites			X	X
Outlook	Create Meeting Workspace sites automatically			X	X
	Synchronize calendar and contact list sites			X	X
	Receive alerts	X	X	X	X
	Alert integration with Outlook			X	X
Excel	Two-way synchronization with SharePoint lists			X	X
	Export list data to Excel spreadsheet		X	X	X
	Create custom list from Excel spreadsheet			X	X
Access	Link table to SharePoint list			X	X
	Export list data to Access database table			X	X
	Create custom list from Access database table			X	X
FrontPage	Edit and customize Windows SharePoint Services Web sites			X	
	Create and customize data-driven Web Part Pages			X	
	Solution packages			X	
	Browse and search Web Part galleries			X	
	Manage list views			X	
	Design templates			X	
	Web Part connections			X	
	Backup and restore site			X	
SharePoint Designer	Edit and customize Windows SharePoint Services Web sites				X
	Create and customize data-driven Web Part Pages				X
	Solution packages				X
	Browse and search Web Part galleries				X
	Manage list views				X
	Design templates				X
	Web Part connections				X
	Backup and restore site				X
InfoPath	Business Document Library	N/A	N/A	X	X
	Edit documents in InfoPath	N/A	N/A	X	X
	Aggregate business reports	N/A	N/A	X	X

StsAdm Commands

The *StsAdm.exe* utility allows Administrators to maintain and modify SharePoint sites through a command-line interface. The *StsAdm.exe* command-line has the general form:

```
stsadm.exe -o command -url siteAddress commandParameters
```

This utility is installed in the *C:\Program Files\Common Files\Microsoft Shared\Web Server Extensions\12\BIN* folder. If a command parameter includes a space or other special character, enclose the command parameter in quotation marks. Table B-2 lists the stsadm commands with their uses and parameters.

Table B-2. Stsadm commands

Command	Use to	Parameters
activatefeature	Activate a feature after it has been deployed.	-filename or -name or -id
		-url
		-force
addalternatedomain	Create an alternate access mapping.	-url
		-incomingurl
		-urlzone
		-resourcename
addcontentdb	Create a new content database.	-url
		-databasename
		-databaseserver
		-databaseuser
		-databasepassword
		-sitewarning
		-sitemax
addpath	Add a defined path to a virtual server.	-url
		-type (explicitinclusion or wildcardinclusion)
addpermissionpolicy	Create a new permission policy.	-url
		-userlogin
		-permissionlevel
		-zone
		-username
addsolution	Add a SharePoint solution package (WSP) to the server's solution store.	-filename
		-lcid
addtemplate	Add a site template to the template gallery.	-filename
		-title
		-description

Command	Use to	Parameters

`adduser`	Add a user account to the specified site and assign it to the specified site group.	`-url`
		`-userlogin`
		`-useremail`
		`-role`
		`-username`
		`-siteadmin`

`addwppack`	Add a Web Part package to your server Web Part gallery.	`-filename` or `-name`
		`-url`
		`-globalinstall`
		`-force`
		`-lcid`

`addzoneurl`	Create an alternate access mapping for a resource outside of SharePoint.	`-url`
		`-urlzone`
		`-zonemappedurl`
		`-resourcename`

`authentication`	Set the authentication method and authentication properties for a web application.	`-url`
		`-type` (`windows`, `forms`, or `websso`)
		`-usebasic`
		`-usewindowsintegrated`
		`-exclusivelyusentlm`
		`-membershipprovider`
		`-rolemanager`
		`-enableclientintegration`
		`-allowanonymous`

`backup (site collection)`	Create a backup of the site collection at the specified URL.	`-url`
		`-filename`
		`-overwrite`

`backup (catastrophic)`	Create a backup of all the server's web applications. The directory parameter is the location to store the backup.	`-directory`
		`-backupmethod` (`full` or `differential`)
		`-item`
		`-percentage`
		`-backupthreads`
		`-showtree`
		`-quiet`

Table B-2. Stsadm commands (continued)

Command	Use to	Parameters
backuphistory	Display the history of catastrophic backup and/or recovery.	-directory -backup or -restore
binddrservice	Register a data retrieval service.	-servicename -setting
blockedfilelist	Add or remove a file extension to the blocked file list.	-extension -add or -delete -url
canceldeployment	Cancel the deployment of a feature.	-id
changepermissionpolicy	Add or remove a permission level for a user permission policy.	-url -userlogin -zone -username -add or -delete -permissionlevel
copyappbincontent	Copy web application-specific files from the 12\CONFIG folder to each web application on the server.	None
createadminvs	Create the administration virtual server for Microsoft Windows SharePoint Services.	-admapcreatenew -admapidname -admapidtype -admapidlogin -admapidpwd
creategroup	Create a new SharePoint security group.	-url -name -description -ownerlogin -type member, visitor, or owner
createsite	Create a site at the specified URL.	-url -ownerlogin -owneremail -ownername -lcid -sitetemplate -title -description -quota

Command	Use to	Parameters
createsiteinnewdb	Create a site at the specified URL and create a new content database.	-url -ownerlogin -owneremail -ownername -databaseuser -databasepassword -databaseserver -databasename -lcid -sitetemplate -title -description -secondarylogin -secondaryemail -secondaryname
createweb	Create a subsite at the specified URL.	-url -lcid -sitetemplate -title -description -unique
databaserepair	Delete orphaned items and repair corruption in a content database.	-url -databasename -deletecorruption
deactivatefeature	Deactivate a feature.	-filename, -name, or -id -url -force
deleteadminvs	Delete the administration virtual server.	None
deletealternatedomain	Remove an alternate access mapping.	-url (ignored) -incomingurl
deleteconfigdb	Delete the configuration database.	None
deletecontentdb	Remove a content database.	-url -databasename -databaseserver
deletegroup	Remove a SharePoint security group.	-url -name

Table B-2. Stsadm commands (continued)

Command	Use to	Parameters
deletepath	Remove an included or excluded path from the list of paths.	-url
deletepermissionpolicy	Remove a permission policy.	-url -userlogin -zone
deletesite	Delete the specified site.	-url -deletedaccounts
deletesolution	Remove a SharePoint solution package (WSP) after it was retracted.	-name -override -lcid
deletetemplate	Delete the specified site template.	-title -lcid
deleteuser	Delete the specified user.	-url -userlogin
deleteweb	Delete the specified subsite.	-url
deletewppack	Remove the Web Parts in a Web Part package from a virtual server.	-name -url -lcid
deletezoneurl	Remove an alternate access mapping for resources outside of Share-Point.	-url -urlzone -resourcename
deploysolution	Deploy a SharePoint solution package (WSP).	-name -url -allcontenturls -time -immediate -local -allowgacdeployment -allowcaspolicies -lcid -force
deploywppack	Deploy a web part package (MSI).	-name -url -time -immediate -local -lcid -globalinstall -force

Command	Use to	Parameters
disablessc	Disable Self-Service Site Creation for the specified virtual server.	-url
displaysolution	Displays the status of a SharePoint solution package (WSP).	-name
email	Set the email configuration settings for your server or for a specific virtual server.	-outsmtpserver -fromaddress -replytoaddress -codepage -url
enablessc	Enable Self-Service Site Creation for the specified virtual server.	-url -requiresecondarycontact
enumalternatedomains	List alternate access mapping for resources outside of SharePoint.	-url -resourcename
enumcontentdbs	List the content databases for a web application.	-url
enumdeployments	List all active and pending deployments.	None
enumgroups	List the site groups that are available for use in a particular site or subsite.	-url
enumroles	List the SharePoint security groups for a web application.	-url
enumservices	List the status and type information for all SharePoint services.	None
enumsites	List all of the site collections that have been created under a particular virtual server.	-url
enumsolutions	List the SharePoint solution packages (WSP) in the server's solution store.	None
enumsubwebs	List the subsites that have been created under a particular site collection.	-url
enumtemplates	Lists the site templates that are available.	-lcid
enumusers	List the users of a particular site or subsite.	-url
enumwppacks	List the Web Part Packages currently in your server Web Part gallery.	-name -url
enumzoneurls	List the alternate access mappings for resources outside of SharePoint.	-url -resourcename

Table B-2. Stsadm commands (continued)

Command	Use to	Parameters
execadmsvcjobs	Execute pending administrative service jobs.	None
export	Export a web site and its subsites as CAB files (*.cmp*) to archive or move the sites to another location. The versions parameter is an integer from 1 to 4 with these meanings: 1 Last major version (default) 2 The current version 3 Last major and last minor version 4 All versions	-url -filename -overwrite -includeusersecurity -haltonwarning -haltonfatalerror -nologfile -versions -cabsize -nofilecompression -quiet
extendvs	Extend an existing IIS web application with SharePoint and create a new content database.	-url -ownerlogin -owneremail -exclusivelyusentlm -ownername -databaseuser -databaseserver -databasename -databasepassword -lcid -sitetemplate -donotcreatesite -description -sethostheader -apidname -apidtype -apidlogin -apidpwd -allowanonymous

Table B-2. Stsadm commands (continued)

Command	Use to	Parameters

`extendvsinwebfarm`	Extend an existing IIS web application with SharePoint for use in a server farm.	`-url`
		`-vsname`
		`-exclusivelyusentlm`
		`-apidname`
		`-apidtype`
		`-apidlogin`
		`-apidpwd`
		`-allowanonymous`

`forcedeletelist`	Delete a list.	`-url`
`getadminport`	Return the administration port for Windows SharePoint Services.	None
`getproperty`	Return the property value for the specified property name. See Table B-3 for a list of valid property names.	`-propertyname` `-url`
`getsitelock`	Return the lock status of a site.	`-url`
`geturlzone`	Return the zone of a site.	`-url`

`import`	Import sites and subsites from a .*cmp* file created by the `export` command. The `updateversions` parameter takes one of the following settings:
	
	1 Add new versions (default)
	
	2 Overwrite the file and all versions
	
	3 Ignore the file if it exists on the destination
		`-url`
		`-filename`
		`-includeusersecurity`
		`-haltonwarning`
		`-haltonfatalerror`
		`-nologfile`
		`-updateversions`
		`-nofilecompression`
		`-quiet`

`installfeature`	Install a feature from a SharePoint solution package (WSP).	`-filename` or `-name` `-force`
`listlogginglevels`	List the diagnostic logging levels.	`-showhidden`
`localupgradestatus`	Display the upgrade status of the server.	None

Table B-2. Stsadm commands (continued)

Command	Use to	Parameters
managepermissionpolicylevel	Add or delete a policy level.	-url
		-name
		-add or -delete
		-description
		-siteadmin (true or false)
		-siteauditor (true or false)
		-grantpermissions
		-denypermissions
migrateuser	Change a user name.	-oldlogin
		-newlogin
		-ignoresidhistory
provisionservice	Start or stop a service.	-action (start or stop)
		-servicetype
		-servicename
refreshdms	Update the directory management service.	-url
refreshsitedms	Update the directory management service for a specific site collection.	-url
registerwsswriter	Register the Volume Shadow Copy Service (VSS) for use with third-party backup and restore software.	None
removedrservice	Remove a data retrieval service.	-servicename
		-setting
removesolutiondeploymentlock	Remove locking that prevents solution deployment.	-server
		-allservers
renameserver	Change the name of a server.	-oldservername
		-newservername
renameweb	Rename a subsite.	-url
		-newname
restore (site collection)	Restore a site collection from a backup file.	-url
		-filename
		-hostheaderwebapplicationurl
		-overwrite

Table B-2. Stsadm commands (continued)

Command	Use to	Parameters
restore (catastrophic)	Restore an entire web application from a backup file.	-directory
		-restoremethod (overwrite or new)
		-backupid
		-item
		-percentage
		-showtree
		-suppressprompt
		-username
		-password
		-newdatabaseserver
		-quiet
retractsolution	Remove a deployed SharePoint solution package (WSP). Use retractsolution before calling deletesolution.	-name
		-url
		-allcontenturls
		-time
		-immediate
		-local
		-lcid
retractwppack	Remove a deployed web part package (MSI).	-name
		-url
		-time
		-immediate
		-local
		-lcid
scanforfeatures	Scan deployed solutions for new features and install them if found.	-solutionid
		-displayonly
setadminport	Set the port number for the administration virtual server.	-port
		-ssl
		-admapcreatenew
		-admapidname
		-admapidtype
		-admapidlogin
		-admapidpwd

Table B-2. Stsadm commands (continued)

Command	Use to	Parameters
setapppassword	Establish a key used to encrypt/decrypt passwords used by the people picker to search for users across domain boundaries.	-password
setconfigdb	Create the configuration database or specify the connection to an existing configuration database.	-databaseserver -connect -databaseuser -databasepassword -databasename -hh -adcreation -addomain -adou
setlogginglevel	Set the diagnostic logging level.	-category (CategoryName or Manager:CategoryName) -default or -tracelevel (None or Unexpected or Monitorable or High or Medium or Verbose) -windowslogginglevel (None or ErrorServiceUnavailable or ErrorSecurityBreach or ErrorCritical or Error or Warning or FailureAudit or SuccessAudit or Information or Success)
setproperty	Set a property by name. See Table B-3 for a list of valid property names.	-propertyname -propertyvalue -url
setsitelock	Lock a site.	-url -lock (none or noadditions or readonly or noaccess)
setworkflowconfig	Change the workflow configuration settings.	-url -emailtonopermission-participants (enable or disable) -externalparticipants (enable or disable) -userdefinedworkflows (enable or disable)
siteowner	Set the owner or secondary owner of a site collection.	-url -ownerlogin or -secondownerlogin

Table B-2. Stsadm commands (continued)

Command	Use to	Parameters
spsearch	Start, stop, or change the Share-Point search settings.	-action (list or start or stop or attachcontentdatabase or detachcontentdatabase or fullcrawlstart or fullcrawlstop)
		-f (suppress prompts)
		-farmperformancelevel (Reduced or PartlyReduced or Maximum)
		-farmserviceaccount
		-farmservicepassword
		-farmcontentaccessaccount
		-farmcontentaccesspassword
		-indexlocation
		-databaseserver
		-databasename
		-sqlauthlogin
		-sqlauthpassword
spsearchdiacriticsensitive	Enable or disable diacritic sensitivity in search. When disabled, characters like *ñ* and *n* are treated as the same.	-setstatus (True or False)
		-noreset
		-force
syncsolution	Update a deployed solution with changes from a new version in the solution store.	-allsolutions or -name
		-lcid
		-alllcids
unextendvs	Removes SharePoint from a virtual server.	-url
		-deletecontent
uninstallfeature	Remove a feature from the list of available features.	-filename or -name
		-id
		-force
unregisterwsswriter	Remove the registry for the Volume Shadow Copy Service (VSS) used with third-party backup and restore software.	None
updateaccountpassword	Change the password for a user account.	-userlogin
		-password
		-noadmin
updatealerttemplates	Change the name of the template file used by SharePoint alerts. By default, SharePoint uses *alerttemplates.xml*.	-url
		-filename
		-lcid

Command	Use to	Parameters
updatefarmcredentials	Change the passwords for the Central Administration application pool account.	-identitytype -userlogin -password -local (-keyonly)
upgrade	Upgrade a site collection from WSS 2.0 to WSS 3.0. Run the upgradetargetwebapplication command before running upgrade.	-inplace or -sidebyside -url -forceupgrade -quiet -farmuser -farmpassword -reghost -sitelistpath
upgradesolution	Upgrade an existing solution in the solution store.	-name -filename -time -immediate -local -allowgacdeployment -allowcaspolicies -lcid
upgradetargetwebapplication	Create a new web application to host site upgraded from WSS 2.0 to WSS 3.0.	-url -relocationurl -apidname -apidtype -apidlogin -apidpwd -exclusivelyusentlm
userrole	Add or remove a user to a SharePoint security group within a site.	-url -userlogin -role -add or -delete

The setpropery and getproperty commands accept the propertyname parameter values listed in Table B-3.

Table B-3. Property names used by getproperty and setproperty

Server farm properties	
avallowdownload	delete-web-send-email
avcleaningenabled	irmaddinsenabled
avdownloadscanenabled	irmrmscertserver
avnumberofthreads	irmrmsenabled
avtimeout	irmrmsusead
avuploadscanenabled	job-ceip-datacollection
command-line-upgrade-running	job-config-refresh
database-command-timeout	job-database-statistics
database-connection-timeout	job-dead-site-delete
data-retrieval-services-enabled	job-usage-analysis
data-retrieval-services-oledb-providers	job-watson-trigger
data-retrieval-services-response-size	large-file-chunk-size
data-retrieval-services-timeout	token-timeout
data-retrieval-services-update	workflow-cpu-throttle
data-source-controls-enabled	workflow-eventdelivery-batchsize
dead-site-auto-delete	workflow-eventdelivery-throttle
dead-site-notify-after	workflow-eventdelivery-timeout
dead-site-num-notifications	workflow-timerjob-cpu-throttle
defaultcontentdb-password	workitem-eventdelivery-batchsize
defaultcontentdb-server	workitem-eventdelivery-throttle
defaultcontentdb-user	

Web application properties	
alerts-enabled	job-diskquota-warning
alerts-limited	job-immediate-alerts
alerts-maximum	job-recycle-bin-cleanup
change-log-expiration-enabled	job-usage-analysis
change-log-retention-period	job-workflow
data-retrieval-services-enabled	job-workflow-autoclean
data-retrieval-services-inherit	job-workflow-failover
data-retrieval-services-oledb-providers	max-file-post-size
data-retrieval-services-response-size	peoplepicker-activedirectorysearchtimeout
data-retrieval-services-timeout	peoplepicker-distributionlistsearchdomains
data-retrieval-services-update	peoplepicker-nowindowsaccountsfornonwindows-authenticationmode

Table B-3. Property names used by getproperty and setproperty (continued)

Web application properties	
`data-source-controls-enabled`	`peoplepicker-onlysearchwithinsitecollection`
`days-to-show-new-icon`	`peoplepicker-searchadcustomquery`
`dead-site-auto-delete`	`peoplepicker-searchadforests`
`dead-site-notify-after`	`presenceenabled`
`dead-site-num-notifications`	`recycle-bin-cleanup-enabled`
`defaultquotatemplate`	`recycle-bin-enabled`
`defaulttimezone`	`recycle-bin-retention-period`
`delete-web-send-email`	`second-stage-recycle-bin-quota`
`job-change-log-expiration`	`send-ad-email`
`job-dead-site-delete`	

PSConfig Commands

The *PSConfig.exe* utility allows Administrators to set up and repair installations of SharePoint. It is the command-line equivalent of *PSConfigUi.exe*, which displays the repair and uninstall options for SharePoint interactively. The *PSConfig.exe* command-line has the general form:

```
psconfig.exe -cmd command commandParameters
```

This utility is installed in the *C:\Program Files\Common Files\Microsoft Shared\Web Server Extensions\12\BIN* folder. Table B-4 lists the PSConfig commands.

Table B-4. PSConfig commands

Command	Use to	Parameters
`adminvs`	Add or remove the Central Administration site on the current server. Provision adds the site; unprovision removes it.	`-provision` `-unprovision` `-port` `-windowsauthprovider` (enablekerberos or onlyusentlm)
`applicationcontent`	Copy shared application content to existing web application virtual directories.	`-install`

Table B-4. PSConfig commands (continued)

Command	Use to	Parameters
configdb	Create, connect, or disconnect the current server from a SharePoint server farm.	-create -disconnect -connect -server -database -dbuser -dbpassword -user -password -addomain -adorgunit -admincontentdatabase
evalprovision	Install SharePoint in standalone mode.	-provision -port -overwrite
helpcollections	Install the SharePoint Help collections.	-installall
installfeatures	Install and register the built-in SharePoint features.	None
quiet	Write status messages to a *PSCONFIG* logfile rather than to the console.	None
secureresources	Enforce security on SharePoint files, folders, and registry keys.	None
services	Install and register services provided by SharePoint.	-install -provision
setup	Install SharePoint on the current server.	-lcid
standaloneconfig	Configure SharePoint for standalone use (single server, local database).	-lcid
upgrade	Upgrade a server from WSS 2.0 to WSS 3.0.	-wait -force -reghostonupgrade -finalize -inplace (v2v or b2b) -sidebyside

PreScan Commands

The *PRESCAN.EXE* utility allows Administrators to view errors in existing WSS 2.0 sites before upgrading them to WSS 3.0. The *PRESCAN.EXE* command-line has the general form:

```
prescan.exe [/C file] /ALL | [/V] urls
```

This utility is installed in the *C:\Program Files\Common Files\Microsoft Shared\Web Server Extensions\12\BIN* folder. Table B-5 lists the PreScan commands.

Table B-5. PreScan commands

Command	Use to	Parameters
/C	Specify a configuration file for custom templates.	file
/All	Scan the entire farm.	None
/V	Scan one or more specific web applications or site collections.	urls

Running *PRESCAN.EXE* generates a logfile and pre-upgrade report that you should review before performing an upgrade. The files are written to the current user's *Local Settings\Temp* folder.

Server Files and Locations

Table B-6 lists the folders that are found under the install path of SharePoint Services. Typically, that is *C:\Program Files\Common Files\Microsoft Shared\Web Server Extensions\12*.

Table B-6. Folders used by SharePoint

Folder	Description	Files and purpose
\ADMISAPI	The physical directory addressed by the SharePoint Central Administration _vti_adm virtual directory.	admin.asmx Web service for administration
\BIN	Contains the core binary files for Windows SharePoint Services.	*.DLL Core binary files OWSTIMER.EXE Microsoft SharePoint Timer service PRESCAN.EXE Scans WSS 2.0 sites prior to upgrading them STSADM.EXE Stsadm utility PSCONFIG.EXE Configuration Wizard (command-line tool) PSCONFIGUI.EXE Configuration Wizard (interactive tool)

Folder	Description	Files and purpose

\BIN\LCID\	Contains the core binary files used by specific languages.	FPEXT.MSG
		  Error messages and text strings
		Microsoft.SharePoint.Msg.dll
		  Core international binary file

\CONFIG	Contains configuration files and default values for the server.	*.xml
		  XML files used to map default values for time zones, blocked files, and file types
		appwpresweb.config
		  Configuration file
		adminweb.config
		  Configuration file for the administrative virtual server
		web.config
		  Default configuration file settings for new virtual servers
		wss_mediumtrust.config
		  Security policy that allows access to SharePoint object model
		wss_minimaltrust.config
		  Default security policy for web applications

\HCCab\LCID\	Contains Help files and support files used in the Help system.	*.CAB Compressed XML, HTML, and GIF files used by the Help system

\ISAPI	The physical directory addressed by the /_vti/_bin virtual directory.	*.asmx
		  SOAP protocol receptors
		*.aspx
		  Form pages
		Global.asax
		  ASP.NET namespace definition
		*.xml
		  XML file for managed code
		*.DLL
		  Core binary files for managed code
		web.config
		  Configuration file

\ISAPI\HELP\LCID\STS\IMAGES	Contains images used in the Help system.	*.gif
\ISAPI_VTI_ADM	Contains Microsoft Office FrontPage 2003 legacy binary files.	ADMIN.DLL Binary file used for administration from Office FrontPage 2003
\ISAPI_VTI_AUT	Contains Office FrontPage 2003 legacy binary files.	AUTHOR.DLL Binary file used for authoring from Office FrontPage 2003

Folder	Description	Files and purpose
\TEMPLATE	Contains all site templates and core web site files.	
\TEMPLATE\Site Templates\Blog	Contains files that are copied to the root of the web site upon instantiation with a Blog template (for example, *default.aspx*).	**.aspx* Form pages
\TEMPLATE\Site Templates\Blog\Lists	Contains the actual lists used in the Blog templates, along with schema definition and default views.	**.aspx* Form pages
\TEMPLATE\Site Templates\Blog\XML	Contains the available lists in the Blog templates, base types for fields (*onet.xml*), and the standard view template for new views.	*ONET.XML* XML file for site schema and views
\TEMPLATE\Site Templates\MPS	Contains files that are copied to the root of the web site upon instantiation with a Meeting Workspace template (for example, *default.aspx*).	**.aspx* Form pages
\TEMPLATE\Site Templates\MPS \ DOCTEMP\SMARTPGS\	Contains files used for Web Part Pages in Meeting Workspaces.	*spstd1.aspx* Form page
\TEMPLATE\Site Templates\MPS\LISTS	Contains the actual lists used in the Meeting Workspace templates, along with schema definition and default views.	
\TEMPLATE\Site Templates\MPS\LISTS\ AGENDA	Contains files used for the Agenda list.	**.aspx* Form pages *SCHEMA.XML* Schema file
\TEMPLATE\Site Templates\MPS\LISTS\ DECISION	Contains files used for the Decisions list.	**.aspx* Form pages *SCHEMA.XML* Schema file
\TEMPLATE\Site Templates\MPS\LISTS\ DOCLIB	Contains files used for document libraries in the Meeting Workspace templates.	**.aspx* Form pages **.HTM* Dialog boxes *SCHEMA.XML* Schema file
\TEMPLATE\Site Templates\MPS\LISTS\ MEETINGS	Contains files used for the Meeting Workspace templates.	*MoveToDt.ASPX* Form page *SCHEMA.XML* Schema file

Table B-6. Folders used by SharePoint (continued)

Folder	Description	Files and purpose
\TEMPLATE\Site Templates\MPS\LISTS\ OBJECTIV	Contains files used for the Objectives list.	*.aspx Form pages SCHEMA.XML Schema file
\TEMPLATE\Site Templates\MPS\LISTS\ PEOPLE	Contains files used for the Attendees list.	*.aspx Form pages SCHEMA.XML Schema file
\TEMPLATE\Site Templates\MPS\LISTS\ TEXTBOX	Contains files used for the Text Box list.	*.aspx Form pages SCHEMA.XML Schema file
\TEMPLATE\Site Templates\MPS\LISTS\ THGBRING	Contains files used for the Things to Bring list.	*.aspx Form pages SCHEMA.XML Schema file
\\TEMPLATE\Site Templates\MPS\LISTS\ WKSPGLIB	Contains files used for lists in the Meeting Workspace templates.	SCHEMA.XML Schema file
\TEMPLATE\Site Templates\MPS\XML	Contains the available lists in the Meeting Workspace templates, base types for fields (onet.xml), and the standard view template for new views.	ONET.XML XML file for site schema and views
\TEMPLATE\SiteTemplates\STS	Contains files that are copied to the root of the web site upon instantiation with the Team Site template (for example, default.aspx).	default.aspx Default home page for sites based on Team Site templates
\TEMPLATE\SiteTemplates\STS\XML	Contains the available lists in the Document Workspace templates, base types for fields (onet.xml), and the standard view template for new views.	ONET.XML XML file for site schema and views
\TEMPLATE\Site Templates\Wiki	Contains files that are copied to the root of the web site upon instantiation with a Wiki template (for example, default.aspx).	
\TEMPLATE\Site Templates\Wiki\XML	Contains the available lists in the Wiki templates, base types for fields (onet. xml), and the standard view template for new views.	ONET.XML XML file for site schema and views
\TEMPLATE\LCID\STS\DOCTEMP\ BLANKPGS	Contains the default document templates.	bpstd.aspx _blankpage.htm
\TEMPLATE\LCID\STS\DOCTEMP\FP	Contains document templates for Office FrontPage.	FPTMPL.HTM Default document templates for FrontPage documents

Table B-6. Folders used by SharePoint (continued)

Folder	Description	Files and purpose
\TEMPLATE\LCID\STS\DOCTEMP\PPT	Contains document templates for Microsoft Office PowerPoint.	FILELIST.XML MASTER03.CSS MASTER03.HTM MASTER03.XML PPTMPL.HTM PPTMPL.POT PPTMPL.PPTX PRES.XML PREVIEW.WMF SLIDE001.HTM
\TEMPLATE\LCID\STS\DOCTEMP\SMARTPGS	Contains document templates for Web Part Pages.	spstd*.aspx _webpartpage.htm
\TEMPLATE\LCID\STS\DOCTEMP\WORD	Contains document templates for Microsoft Office Word.	WDTMPL.DOC WDTMPL.DOCX WDTMPL.HTM
\TEMPLATE\LCID\STS\DOCTEMP\XL	Contains document templates for Microsoft Office Excel.	FILELIST.XML SHEET001.HTM SHEET002.HTM SHEET003.HTM STYLE.CSS TABSTRIP.HTM XLTMPL.HTM XLTMPL.XLS XLTMPL.XLSX
\TEMPLATE\LCID\STS\DOCTEMP\XMLFORMS\BLANK	Contains document templates for Microsoft Office InfoPath.	TEMPLATE.XML Default document templates for XML documents
\TEMPLATE\FEATURES	Contains folders for each of the installed features. Features include web parts, lists, and workflows.	
\TEMPLATE\FEATURES\ADMINLINKS	Contains the links for the Operations and Application Management pages of the Central Administration site.	Applications.xml Application Management page links Feature.xml Feature description Operations.xml Operations page links
\TEMPLATE\FEATURES\ANNOUNCEMENTSLIST	Contains files used for the Announcements list.	Feature.xml Feature description

Folder	Description	Files and purpose
\TEMPLATE\FEATURES\ ANNOUNCEMENTSLIST\Announce	Contains template content.	*schema.xml* Field descriptions and views of the list
\TEMPLATE\FEATURES\ ANNOUNCEMENTSLIST\ListTemplates	Contains template description.	*Announcements.xml* Name and default settings to use when creating new lists from this template
\TEMPLATE\FEATURES\LIST	Other list templates follow the same pattern as the Announcements list above.	See Announcements list above
\TEMPLATE\FEATURE\BasicWebParts	Contains the feature description and web part description files for the built-in WSS web parts.	*Feature.xml* Feature description *elements.xml* Element manifest **.dwp and *.webpart* Web part descriptions
\TEMPLATE\FEATURE\WEBPART	Custom web parts follow the same pattern as the BasicWebParts feature above.	See BasicWebParts above
\TEMPLATE\LCID\XML	Contains the XML files with base list and field types defined for all site templates.	*DEADWEB.XML* Email sent to notify site owner when a site is no longer actively being visited *RGNLSTNG.XML* Region settings *WEBTEMP.XML* Available site templates (from site definitions)
\TEMPLATE\ADMIN	Contains files used for the site administration pages.	**.aspx, *.ascx. *.master* Administration pages, controls, and support files
\TEMPLATE\IMAGES	Contains images shared by all pages on the server, addressed by the virtual directory /_layouts/images.	**.gif, *.jpg, *.png*
\TEMPLATE\LAYOUTS	Addressed by the virtual directory /_layouts, this directory contains language subdirectories that hold the forms for creating lists, site administration pages, and so on. These directories are shared by all sites.	*Global.asax* ASP.NET namespace definition **.aspx* Form pages *web.config* Configuration file

Table B-6. Folders used by SharePoint (continued)

Folder	Description	Files and purpose
\TEMPLATE\LAYOUTS\LCID	Contains forms for creating lists, site administration pages, and so on, for a specific language.	**.aspx* Form pages **.css* Style sheets **.htm* Dialog boxes **.htc* Menu control **.js* JavaScript files **.xml* XML templates **.xsd* XML definitions
\TEMPLATE\LAYOUTS\LCID\IMAGES	Contains images used in the default site pages for a specific language.	**.gif, *.jpg*
\TEMPLATE\LAYOUTS\LCID\STYLES	Contains style sheets shared by all site templates for a particular language. Addressable by the virtual directory /_layouts/styles.	**.CSS* Style sheets
\TEMPLATE\LAYOUTS\BIN	Contains core binary files.	*Microsoft.SharePoint.ApplicationPages.dll* Core binary
\TEMPLATE\LAYOUTS\GLOBAL	Contains master page definitions.	*default.master* Main master page *mwsdefault.master* Meeting Workspace master page
\TEMPLATE\LAYOUTS\MOBILE	Contains mobile-device views of standard pages.	**.aspx* Page files *Web.config* Configuration file
\TEMPLATE\LAYOUTS\STYLES	Contains core styles.	*corefixup.css* Cascading style sheet
\TEMPLATE\SQL	Contains stored procedures for Microsoft SQL Server.	**.SQL* Stored procedures for SQL Server
\TEMPLATE\THEMES	Contains the list of themes.	*THEMES.INF* Themes list
\TEMPLATE\THEMES\Theme	Contains files used by a specific theme.	**.gif* Images **.css* Style sheets *theme.INF* Theme definition file

Table B-6. Folders used by SharePoint (continued)

Folder	Description	Files and purpose
\TEMPLATE\XML	Contains XML files used by all site templates in all languages.	*alerttemplate.xml* Email message sent for user alerts *BASE.XML* Templates used across all languages and site types *DOCICON.XML* Mapping that determines the icons displayed for document types *FLDTYPES.XML* Standard field types used in lists
\TEMPLATE\XML\HELP	Contains XML files used by the Help system.	*STS.XML* Context-sensitive Help mapping file *WSSADMIN.XML* Context-sensitive Help mapping file for the Central Administration site

Content Not Stored in Database

In addition to SharePoint content files listed in the preceding section, the web application files listed in Table B-7 are stored in the following folder on the server:

> *C:\Inetpub\wwwroot\wss\VirtualDirectories\folder*

The *folder* placeholder is generated by SharePoint based on the web application name and port number.

Table B-7. Content files not stored in the database

Folder	Description	Files
\ *(root)*	Configuration file	*web.config*
	ASP.NET application file	*global.asax*
._app_bin	Site map	*layouts.sitemap*
._vti_pvt	SpeedDial shortcuts	*service*
		services
.\App_Browsers	Compatible browsers and features list (primarily for mobile devices)	*compat.browser*
.\App_GlobalResources	Resource files used by SharePoint	**.resx*
.\aspnet_client	.NET client-side scripts	**.js*
.\wpresources	Configuration file for Web Parts and other resources	*web.config*

CSS Styles

The main CSS files are stored in this folder on the server:

*C:\Program Files\Common Files\Microsoft Shared\web server extensions\12\
TEMPLATE\LAYOUTS\LCID\STYLES*

These files are listed in Table B-8.

Table B-8. The main CSS files

File	Description
CALENDAR.CSS	Controls calendar list view appearance
CORE.CSS	Main style sheet used throughout SharePoint
DATEPICKER.CSS	Controls the date picker control appearance
HELP.CSS	Main style sheet used by Help pages
MENU.CSS	Controls menu control appearance
OWS.CSS	Legacy styles from WSS 2.0
OWSMAC.CSS	Legacy styles from WSS 2.0
OWSNOCR.CSS	Legacy styles from WSS 2.0

To view the style applied to an object in SharePoint:

1. Download the Style Viewer web part from this book's online samples.

2. Upload the Style Viewer web part to a page.

3. Mouse over the element to view. The Style Viewer displays the style of the element, as shown in Figure B-1.

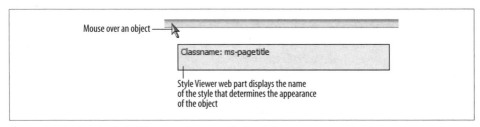

Figure B-1. Using the Style Viewer web part to find a style

Working with CSS in SharePoint (or anywhere) can be tricky because you can't easily trace where the styles are overridden. For that reason, it is easiest to develop new CSS styles by working directly on the page through a Content Editor web part. To develop your styles:

1. Add a Content Editor web part to the page.

2. Add style elements to the Content Editor to override the built-in styles.

3. Apply the changes from the Content Editor to preview their effect.

For example, the following style element changes the title bar to black (it's ugly, but you notice it!):

```
<style>
TD.ms-titleareaframe,Div.ms-titleareaframe,.ms-pagetitleareaframe,.ms-
mwspagetitleareaframe,.ms-consoletitleareaframe{
background-image:url("/_layouts/images/pageTitleBKGD.gif");
background-repeat:repeat-x;
background-position:left top;
background-color:#000000;
text-align:center;
}
</style>
```

Once you work out the alternate styles, deploy them by doing one of the following:

- Copy the style element to the *default.master* page on the server. That makes the change to all content pages throughout the server.
- Save the style element as an alternate CSS file and link it through the Master Page settings in MOSS.
- Export the Content Editor web part, and then upload it to the specific pages you want to restyle. That deploys the change selectively.

Glossary

Account creation mode

An option set during the installation of WSS that allows WSS to create new AD accounts that are then sent by email to the users. This option is only allowed in WSS, and it's generally used by commercial hosting services.

Aggregating content

The process of collecting related lists and libraries from various web sites onto a single page. MOSS uses RSS feeds from lists, the RSS Viewer web part, and the Site Aggregator web part to aggregate content.

Alerts

Send email when an item in a list or library changes. Users create alerts to receive notification when these types of events occur.

Alternate access mapping

Defines a different URL (and namespace) for an existing SharePoint web application. This allows a single web application to have multiple entry points, each of which uses a different security policy and/or authentication method.

Blogs

Personal journals with comments from the audience. Entries are organized chronologically. Blogs are a good way for subject-area experts to share their knowledge.

Cached events

Server-side events that occur on a child control within a web part that don't cause a postback.

Client-side web parts

Custom web parts built from the Content Editor or XML Viewer web parts, which run code on the client, not on the server.

Connectable web parts

Web parts that provide values to other web parts or consume values from other web parts.

Cross-site groups (see SharePoint Groups)

Current Navigation

The MOSS name for the Quick Launch web part that appears on the left side of most pages.

Dashboards

A type of management application where related tasks and reports are centralized for easy access.

Document control

Manages version and change control for standard forms such as NDAs, vacation requests, and so forth. This category also includes repositories for executed agreements, which can be scanned in as PDFs.

Edit menu

The drop-down list that appears when you click the triangle to the right of the filename in a document library.

Excel lists

Ranges of cells that can easily be sorted, filtered, or shared. Excel lists can be linked to SharePoint lists.

Extranet portals

Provide a contact point among your business, customers, and partners. You can use these to provide external access to your corporate information in a limited and secure way.

Global Navigation

The MOSS name for the top link bar web part that appears at the top of most pages.

Global pages

Custom ASP.NET pages deployed to the _layouts folder on the SharePoint server. Pages in that folder are available to all sites, such as the *MyInfo.aspx* page used by the Site Aggregator web part.

Groups

Control access based on the user's role. If you add a user to a group, then she will have permissions that are appropriate for that role. SharePoint groups may map to Active Directory security groups in your company. It is a good idea to use security groups wherever possible in SharePoint, rather than adding users individually. Then when employees are hired or fired, those changes are automatically reflected in SharePoint.

Hosted web parts

Custom web parts based on SmartPart, which loads ASP.NET user controls (*.ascx*) into SharePoint. User controls are developed visually out of ASP.NET built-in controls, and it's easy to migrate existing ASP.NET applications to SharePoint using this approach.

Internet Information Services (IIS)

The Microsoft Windows component that handles web requests on the server.

Libraries

Organize content within a site. Technically, libraries are a special type of list that provides special features related to the creation, storage, revision, and versioning of files.

List columns

Define the types of data that a list contains. For example, the Links list contains columns for a URL, Title, and Notes as well as a set of predefined columns that SharePoint uses such as ID, Created, Created By, and so on. Those predefined columns are usually not displayed. Columns are also called fields in the Microsoft documentation.

List items

The rows of data in a list. Users add new list items or change existing ones.

List View

A special type of web part created automatically for each list or library in a site. You display lists and libraries on web part pages using the list view web part.

List views

Control what columns are displayed, how they appear, and what filters or grouping are applied to the rows. Views are similar to reports.

Logical navigation

The term Microsoft uses to describe navigating through the Quick Launch web part, which allows new links to be added by site administrators. Use logical navigation for content-oriented sites such as Document Centers where you want to feature some libraries and hide others.

Master pages

How SharePoint defines the layout, web zones, navigational web parts, and styles used on pages through the site. Master pages are used to rebrand a portal for a specific company.

Meeting series

A meeting workspace created for recurring meetings.

Meeting workspace

A SharePoint site that can be created from meeting requests sent from Outlook. Meeting workspaces are meant to prepare attendees by publishing the objectives and agenda before a meeting is held, and they help record decisions and related documents after the meeting takes place.

Metadata

Describes the properties of a document in a document library. Metadata forms the basis for organizing documents logically through views.

Microsoft Office SharePoint Server (MOSS)

The server product that provides advanced collaboration features. MOSS includes additional services, templates, web parts, and workflows that extend WSS (see also Windows SharePoint Services).

MOSS (see Microsoft Office SharePoint Server).

My Sites

Personal web sites that define a user's identity on the intranet. They are used to store and share information that doesn't fit neatly into a project or department site.

Personalization features

SharePoint features such as My Sites and blogs, which are tied to the user's identity and help maintain his presence on the Web.

Personalization

The process of editing the saved properties of a web part in a shared or personal view of a page. The view of the page determines the scope of the personalization: changes to the shared view are visible to all users; changes to the personal view are only visible to the current user.

Physical navigation

The term Microsoft uses to describe navigating through the Tree View web part, which displays lists and subsites hierarchically. Use physical navigation for dashboard-type or top-level sites where the subsites are already organized logically (such as by project) and where there are many subsites.

Primary data source

A read/write source of data in InfoPath. The primary data source is the target of the InfoPath form.

Publishing sites

Present corporate communications (newsletters, press releases, events, holidays, announcements, etc.) through one or more web pages. This category also includes communication managed by employees through blogs and Wikis, which may or may not fit in your corporate culture.

Quiescence

The process of waiting for a quiet time to make changes to an InfoPath template. Changes to templates lose the state of forms that are currently being edited, so it is important to wait for editing sessions to end before deploying changed templates.

Rebranding

The process of customizing the appearance of a portal by editing the master pages and Cascading Style Sheets (CSS) used by SharePoint.

Rendered web parts

Custom web parts written entirely in code—there is no visual designer. They are based on the new ASP.NET WebPart class, which renders the component controls. They are harder to write than hosted web parts, but are easier to deploy to multiple servers. This is the technique that commercial web parts use.

Rollups

A way of summarizing content from other sites. For example, the MOSS Site Aggregator web part rolls up documents in other sites and displays them in a single pane with a tab bar across the top.

RSS feeds

Streams of data provided by a SharePoint list for display in an RSS reader.

RSS

A standard for sharing frequently changing information across web sites.

RSS Viewer

A MOSS web part used to display an RSS feed from a list that resides in another site.

Secondary data source

A read-only source of data in InfoPath. Secondary data sources can populate controls, such as drop-down lists, and they can be used to create reports.

Self-service site creation

A feature that enables users to create new site collections from a link to the *scsignup.aspx* page. A link to that page is automatically added to the Site Directory (MOSS) or to the Announcement list (WSS) when the feature is enabled through Central Administration.

Shared workspaces

Special sites that allow team members to work together privately on revisions, and then publish those revisions once they are approved. SharePoint can also track version history and control access to documents through a check out/check in procedure.

SharePoint Administrator

The person who organizes, customizes, maintains, and supports a SharePoint portal.

SharePoint calendar

A special type of list that displays events in a calendar view. SharePoint calendars can be viewed from Outlook much like Exchange shared calendars. Also, you can export individual events from a SharePoint calendar into your personal Outlook calendar so you can get reminders and plan your time while offline.

SharePoint Groups

The security groups that determine permissions across one or more site collections. Use SharePoint groups when users have a specific role across sites, such as approving documents or designing web pages. Previous versions of SharePoint called these *cross-site groups*.

Site collection owners

Users that have full control over all the sites in the site collection. They may also receive email from the site collection when someone requests access to the site, or when a site exceeds its size limit or is no longer actively used.

Site definitions

Core site templates made up of XML and ASPX files stored in physical folders on the server. These come with SharePoint and are sometimes provided by add-on vendors. Custom site templates are based on these site definitions.

Site directory

The table of contents for a portal provided by MOSS.

Site Master Page

The master page that controls the appearance of the publishing pages in MOSS. (See also *master pages*.)

Site owner

The person who creates and maintains parts of the portal—usually there is one site owner for each department, and that person organizes the content and appearance of her department's site.

Site templates

Determine what lists and libraries are included automatically in the new site.

Sites

Group-related lists and libraries. Use sites to control access.

System Master Page

The master page that controls the appearance of list and library pages in MOSS. (See also *master pages*.)

Wikis

Web sites that allow multiple authors to easily contribute and edit web pages. Wikis are well suited for creating online Help systems, glossaries, and other topic-oriented sites with multiple authors.

Windows SharePoint Services (WSS)

The set of technologies included with Microsoft Windows Server 2003 that form the foundation of SharePoint. WSS includes core services that run in the background on the server, templates, web parts, Central Administration site, and Help pages.

Workflow applications

Encompass any multistep task that follows a defined process. A common workflow example is Issue Tracking, where a problem is reported, assigned to a team member, resolved, the resolution approved, and then published to a knowledge base for future reference.

Workflows

A set of tasks that must be completed in a particular order within a specified time frame.

WSS (see Windows SharePoint Services)

Index

We'd like to hear your suggestions for improving our indexes. Send email to *index@oreilly.com*.

I

I need to... web part, 136
icon for site, 74
IFrame
    displaying page as, 136, 148, 151–153
    targeting, from rollups, 218
IIS (Internet Information Services), 404
    logs, 358
iisreset.exe utility, 81, 160
Image web part, 136
images, displaying as web part, 136, 150
Imaging web service, 303
import command, StsAdm.exe utility, 383
Import Spreadsheet list template, 84
ImportList method, 322
Inbox, Outlook, displaying as web part, 137
.inf files, 75
InfoPath, 224
    best practices for, 254
    disabling design features of, 245
    features by Office version, 375
    installing trial version of, 226
    programming with
        browser-compatible code, 254
        enabling, 251
        getting values from controls, 254
        language for, setting, 251
        setting trust for, 253
        tools for, 250
    software requirements for, 224
    version requirements for, 7
    (see also form libraries; forms, InfoPath)
InfoPath Forms Services, 224, 245
    best practices for, 254
    checking templates for browser
        compatibility, 248
    managing templates, 248
    publishing browser-compatible
        templates, 246–247
    publishing forms as pages, 248
in-place upgrade
    performing, 370
    when to use, 363
installation
    basic installation, 330
    best practices for, 361
    complete installation, 330, 337, 338–340
    downloading installation software, 334
    hardware requirements for, 331
    MOSS, 8, 336
    operating system requirements, 332

    options for, 329–331
    post-install configuration, 338–340
    pre-install checklist, 333
    security requirements for, 332
    software requirements for, 332
    standalone installation, 330, 335, 337
    storage requirements for, 331
    top-level site, creating, 339
    uninstalling SharePoint, 340
    web frontend installation, 330, 335, 337,
        338–340
    WSS, 334–336
        account creation mode option, 403
        for evaluation, 8
installfeature command, StsAdm.exe
        utility, 383
installfeatures command, PSConfig.exe
        utility, 391
instructions in sites, 29
International Expense Report form library
        template, 227
Internet access, enabling, 343–345
Internet Explorer, version requirements
        for, 7
Internet Information Services (IIS), 404
Internet zone, 353
Intranet zone, 353
Invoice form library templates, 227
Invoice Request form library template, 227
Israel, Shel (Naked Conversations: How
        Blogs are Changing the Way
        Business Talk with
        Customers), 174
Issue Status site column, 92
Issue Tracking example, 96–99
Issue Tracking form library templates, 227
Issue Tracking list template, 84, 96
Issue Tracking lists, assignment notification
        for, 188
items in list, 85
IView web part, 137

J

JavaScript
    for rendered web parts, 270, 276–282
    importing script blocks into web
        parts, 280–282
    including on page, 136, 148
.js files, 399
JScript, programming InfoPath using, 250,
    251

K

Key Performance Indicators web part, 137
KPI Details web part, 137
KPI List list template, 84

L

Language site column, 92
Languages and Translators list template, 84
_layouts folder, global pages in, 216, 257, 404
layouts.sitemap file, 399
LDAP, importing user profiles from, 174
libraries, 10, 113, 404
    adding documents to, 13
    application to use for new documents in, 120
    best practices for, 133
    content types for, adding, 121–123
    creating, example of, 24
    displaying as web part, 68, 135
    document template for, changing, 119–121
    email from, 192
    email to, 193–197
    folders in, 124, 126
    for Wikis, 182
    included in each template, 61–62
    incoming mail, enabling, 194–197
    location of, 123, 133
    mixed-type, 121
    number of, 123
    number of documents in, 123
    of pages for development, 142
    organization of, 123–126, 133
    replacing network drives with, 24
    saving as template, 127
    uploading files to, example of, 25
    versioning for, 134
    viewing from home page, 13
    viewing in Windows Explorer, 14
    views in, 124, 125–126
    workflows for, 205–206
    (see also Shared Documents library)
library applications
    Archive library application, 132
    Document control library application, 131
    Project library application, 128
    Task library application, 129–130
    types of, 128

library templates
    deploying to another site collection, 127
    list of, 113
    removing document templates in, 114–116
    saving libraries as, 127
    selecting, 114
Limited Access permission, 72
Link Bar web part, 136
link bar web part (see top link bar, WSS)
links
    from libraries, emailing, 192
    publishing in News Site template, 62
Links button, Document Management task pane, 36
Links list template, 84, 222
Links list, adding links to, 13
List Data Retrieval web service, 303
List parameter, URL commands, 317–319
list templates
    deploying, 112
    gallery of, 84, 112
    list of, 4, 84
    saving lists as, 110
List View web part, 135, 138, 404
    best practices for, 165
    connecting summary and detail views, 139–140
    converting to Data View web part, 140–142, 145
    converting to drop-down list, 143–145
    deploying, 146
    exporting, 145
    importing, 146
    moving to other pages, 143
list views (see views)
list-based applications, 83
listlogginglevels command, StsAdm.exe utility, 383
lists, 10, 83
    access control for, 51, 103–105, 112
    access control for individual items in, 104
    adding items to
        feedback after, 108, 112
        form for, 106
        from home page, 108
    attachments to, with Lists web service, 307
    best practices for, 112
    columns in (see columns in list)
    connecting to InfoPath forms, 239

WSS (*continued*)
    upgrading to version 3.0 (see upgrading to WSS 3.0 or MOSS 2007)
    when to use, 6
WSS3sdk.chm Help file, 271

X

XLSX document format, 32
XML Web Part, 136, 148, 153–155
XPathNavigator class, 254

XSL transformations
    displaying as web part, 153–155
    rendering XML using, 136, 148
XSL, editing for Data View web part, 146

Y

Yes/No columns in list, 88

Z

zones, 350

About the Author

Jeff Webb is a SharePoint consultant and trainer who has written about computers and technology for 20 years. Among his published O'Reilly titles are *Essential Share-Point*, *SharePoint Office Pocket Guide*, *Programming Excel with VBA and .NET*, and *Excel 2003 Programming: A Developer's Notebook*. Jeff was an original member of Microsoft's Visual Basic team.

Colophon

The animal on the cover of *Essential SharePoint 2007* is a wombat (*Vombatus ursinus*). Averaging about 40 inches in length and weighing about 55 pounds, this Australian marsupial is the largest of the burrowing animals; as such, it is compared to the badger, but it is most closely related to the koala. Because wombats walk with an awkward waddle, they appear to be docile and slow, but are actually quite alert and agile—when necessary, they can move over short distances with the speed of an Olympic sprinter. Although wombats are not particularly territorial, they do prefer solitude. They are known to mark their often-overlapping feeding grounds by rubbing trees, sometimes to a polished appearance, and to leave their distinctive cube-shaped dung atop elevated items such as rocks, mushrooms, and even upright sticks.

The cover image is an original illustration from *Animate Creation*. The cover font is Adobe ITC Garamond. The text font is Linotype Birka; the heading font is Adobe Myriad Condensed; and the code font is LucasFont's TheSans Mono Condensed.

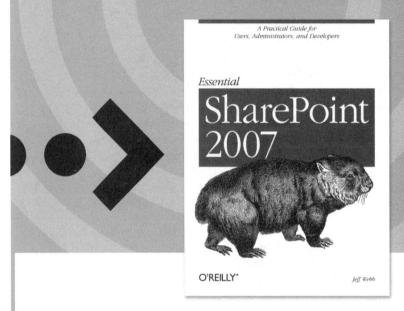

Related Titles from O'Reilly

Windows Users

Access Cookbook,
  2nd Edition

Access 2003 Personal Trainer

Access 2003 for Starters:
  The Missing Manual

Access 2007: The Missing Manual

Access 2007 for Starters:
  The Missing Manual

Access Database Design &
  Programming, *3rd Edition*

Analyzing Business Data
  with Excel

Excel Annoyances

Excel Hacks

Excel Pocket Guide

Excel 2003 Personal Trainer

Excel 2007: The Missing Manual

Excel 2007 for Starters: The
  Missing Manual

Excel Scientific and Engineering
  Cookbook

Fixing Access Annoyances

Fixing PowerPoint Annoyances

Fixing Windows XP Annoyances

FrontPage 2003:
  The Missing Manual

Outlook 2000 in a Nutshell

Outlook Pocket Guide

PC Annoyances, *2nd Edition*

PCs: The Missing Manual

Photoshop Elements 4:
  The Missing Manual

PowerPoint 2003 Personal Trainer

PowerPoint 2007: The Missing
  Manual

QuickBooks 2006:
  The Missing Manual

Quicken 2006 for Starters:
  The Missing Manual

Windows Vista Annoyances

Windows Vista for Starters: The
  Missing Manual

Windows Vista Pocket Reference

Windows Vista: The Missing
  Manual

Windows XP Annoyances
  For Geeks, *2nd Edition*

Windows XP Cookbook

Windows XP Hacks,
  2nd Edition

Windows XP Home Edition: The
  Missing Manual, *2nd Edition*

Windows XP in a Nutshell,
  2nd Edition

Windows XP Personal Trainer

Windows XP Pocket Reference

Windows XP Power Hound

Windows XP Pro: The Missing
  Manual, *2nd Edition*

Windows XP for Starters:
  The Missing Manual

Windows XP Unwired

Word Annoyances

Word Hacks

Word Pocket Guide, *2nd Edition*

Word 2003 Personal Trainer

Word 2007 for Starters: The
  Missing Manual

Word 2007: The Missing Manual